RIPE FOR RESOLUTION

RIPE FOR RESOLUTION

Conflict and Intervention in Africa

UPDATED EDITION

I. William Zartman

A COUNCIL ON FOREIGN RELATIONS BOOK

New York   Oxford
OXFORD UNIVERSITY PRESS
1989

Oxford University Press

Oxford   New York   Toronto
Delhi   Bombay   Calcutta   Madras   Karachi
Petaling Jaya   Singapore   Hong Kong   Tokyo
Nairobi   Dar es Salaam   Cape Town
Melbourne   Auckland

and associated companies in
Berlin   Ibadan

Copyright © 1985, 1989 by The Council on Foreign Relations

First published in 1985 by Oxford University Press, Inc.,
200 Madison Avenue, New York, New York 10016

First issued as an Oxford University Press paperback, 1989

Oxford is a registered trademark of Oxford University Press

Library of Congress Cataloging-in-Publication Data
Zartman, I. William.
Ripe for resolution.
"A Council on Foreign Relations book."
Includes bibliographies and index.
1. Africa—Politics and government—1960-
2. Africa—Foreign relations—1960-
3. Africa—Foreign relations—United States.
4. United States—Foreign relations—Africa.
5. Pacific settlement of international disputes.
I. Council on Foreign Relations. II. Title.
DT30.5.Z37   1989   327′.096   89-2965
ISBN 0-19-505931-X (pbk.)

9 8 7 6 5 4 3 2 1

Printed in the United States of America
on acid-free paper

To Alexander and Danièle
for 15, 30, and everything

Foreword

The Africa Project of the Council on Foreign Relations was designed to focus both on Africa and on its significance for the United States. Undertaken in response to a perceived need for greater knowledge about African realities on the part of the American foreign policy community, the project aimed to produce and disseminate original research on Africa's changing role in the international community and to stimulate discussion and debate within the Western, and particularly American, policymaking communities.

The project proceeded in two ways, each calculated to reinforce the other's impact: through a marked expansion of attention to Africa in the council's regular activities and through a series of studies and publications. The process aimed at bringing together regional specialists with people in government, business, the professions, and the public media whose views are likely to have an effect on Africa policy. The Africa Project books were designed to fill what the council saw as a serious gap in information and public understanding, bringing a detailed knowledge of African issues to bear on the larger questions that confront U.S. citizens and policymakers. Their authors have sought to use their expert knowledge to interpret African developments in a way that addresses the concerns of an informed but largely nonspecialist audience.

This study by I. William Zartman follows Crawford Young's book *Ideology and Development in Africa*. William Foltz and Henry Bienen's *Arms and the African* was published at the same time. Dr. Zartman is the Jacob Blaustein Professor of International Organization and Conflict Resolution and Director of African Studies at the Johns Hopkins University School of Advanced International Studies.

The Africa Project was made possible by generous grants from the Ford and Rockefeller foundations. Their advice and assistance along the way has proved invaluable.

William J. Foltz
Africa Project Director

Jennifer Seymour Whitaker
Editor, Africa Project Book Series

Preface

This study is concerned with local sources of conflict in the Third World, notably Africa. It seeks to show that such conflicts, which pose a threat to international stability, find their origins in the politics and relations of the countries involved and not in the machinations of external powers, whether past colonizers or present cold war antagonists. It is also concerned with external powers' responses to these conflicts, and particularly with the possibility of positive intervention for the resolution of conflict, rather than military intervention or participation in the conflict. In the process, it seeks to develop some guidelines for positive intervention, including a notion of the ripe moment which is considered to be central to its success, and to spell out a policy toward Africa involving preemptive treatment of conflict.

In dealing with American policy toward Africa in the Carter and Reagan administrations, I attempt to evaluate particular positions, but not from any partisan point of view. However, I make the basic assumption that there is such a thing as a national interest, broadly based on objective elements of geography, position, role, and fundamental values. Proper policy cannot be read directly out of these elements, but the debate over correct policy in any situation should be grounded on them. Ideological considerations enter into the debate as fundamental values but they contain common concerns and are tempered by the other, more constant elements of national interest. The result is not wide swings of interpretation from one administration to another (despite some politically necessary rhetoric to the contrary), but a broad base of common referents and criteria within which differences in approach can be argued. This view of national interest may not be shared by all. But it is likely that proponents of a different notion of interest will have a hard time maintaining a logical debate if the basic notion of national interest itself is subject to ideological relativity.

In dealing with African policies, the same point of view applies. This study is not an advocacy of any particular African country's policy but an attempt to understand the views of the countries that make up the conflict. Here, too, national interest comes into play, although one of the characteristics of developing countries is the yet unsettled nature of their notions of national interest. Nonetheless, it is significant that despite some wide ideological shifts by some of the countries studied, their notions of national interest and their positions in the conflicts with their neighbors have remained rather constant throughout.

In addition to considerations of national interest, the discussions of African positions in the conflicts studied have included some mention of anthropological material on national cultural attitudes toward conflict resolution. Although such cultural attitudes are not presented as determinant, they do suggest that there are some general predispositions toward the process that can be useful in explaining problems and approaches.

This study is based on many types of sources, including as much of the available written material on the cases as was possible to find, extensive interviews with officials and observers from participant countries and movements, as well as interviews from the United States, interested European countries, and the Soviet Union. Specific contributions are not cited in every instance, for this would often be misleading: Factual and even motivational statements in the analysis are not based merely on one source, oral or written, but on a weighing of claims and evidence from many sources.

In conducting this study, I am grateful for support from a number of sources. This project was undertaken as part of the Africa Project of the Council on Foreign Relations. Jennifer Whitaker of the Council was of particular help and support throughout the project, and I am happy to acknowledge my warm personal gratitude for her having returned my interest to Africa after a long absence. Additional assistance relating to travel and research in Africa in connection with the individual sections of the book was made possible through personal travel grants from the Office of External Research of the Department of State and the United States Information Agency. In addition, much of the original draft was completed under a grant from the National Endowment for the Humanities awarded through the American Research Center in Egypt. Travel to South Africa was provided by the United States South Africa Leadership Exchange Program (USSALEP). I am grateful to many students at New York University, the American University in Cairo, and the Johns Hopkins School of Advanced International Studies, who helped me wrestle with some of my ideas and test them in particular cases. I am also grateful to Theresa Simmons, my assistant, who has typed the manuscript often enough and well enough to know it by heart. Finally, I deeply appreciate the help, support, and understanding of Danièle and Alexander, who kept the faith.

Washington, D.C.   I.W.Z.
November 1984/February 1989

Contents

RIPE FOR RESOLUTION

1
Conflict in Africa

War is a mere continuation of policy by other means.

Clausewitz

Every war has a political solution.

Hassan II

In a world precariously poised on the edge of destruction, crisis management is an art of survival. Conflicts of interest and policy escalate into crises whose runaway dynamics dominate parties and bystanders alike. To protect their interests, policymakers must weigh measures for capitalizing on crises against measures for dampening them. The problems are compounded when the crises originate with third parties in which great powers have an interest. This study deals with the ability of the big powers to deal with crises among the small.

Since the early 1960s, the world has been compelled to focus its attention on the way in which the superpowers have managed their bilateral crises and specifically on the question of how peace has been preserved since World War II. This concern was aroused by an event and an anniversary. The event was the Cuban missile crisis of 1962, when war and peace stood eye to eye. The anniversary marked the passage in 1965 of the same number of years that separated World War II from World War I, but this time without the culminating catastrophe. In search for an answer to the question, some studies[1] looked at bilateral crises in the intervening years—Cuba, the Berlins, Quemoy and Matsu, Laos. Others[2] made their comparisons with an earlier period when efforts to stave off crisis proved unsuccessful— usually 1914 because the errors of the years 1936-39 were too recent and too egregious.

The answers have been found in a scrutiny of system and of process.[3] As a system, the balance of terror, first in the hands of the status quo power and then jointly held by both superpowers, has thus far imposed limits on crisis that have enabled the two parties gradually to become accustomed enough to the situation to develop conventions for crisis management. Over the last decade and more, they have even begun to work out rules for the limitation of the balance of terror itself. As a process, a manner of responsive communication has been developed by the two superpowers in order to diminish the chances of misinterpretation—a remarkable feat, considering the major ideological differences that create noise in the communications channels. From either angle the situation has given rise to strategies and tactics of crisis management that paradoxically allow crises both to be pursued seriously for one-sided advantage and to be kept under control to avoid bilateral catastrophe.

Until recently, little concern about conflict management has been manifest apart from issues directly affecting the great powers.[4] The weak, poor, unstable countries of the Third World, newly emergent from colonial rule, usually still remained in some great power's sphere of influence; or else they were considered to be in a regional ghetto, where they could tiff and squabble with their neighbors without disturbing the global balance. In the few cases that mattered, conflict arose either between Third World states acting as great power proxies (as in Korea or Vietnam) or in areas where great powers acted to preserve their spheres of influence or the ghetto (as in Guatemala or the Congo [Zaire]). Until the 1970s, only the Middle East seemed capable of producing an indigenous conflict of its own, with enough pits and plums to induce the great powers to think of conflict management and resolution.[5]

In Africa, the prolonged Congo [Zaire] crisis of the early 1960s produced an early set of rules for East-West relations. It served notice that the Western powers could mobilize the United Nations to prevent the continent's newly independent states from falling into Communist hands (whether or not the country would, in fact, have fallen into Communist hands).[6] Africa was consigned to be a combination of ghetto and sphere of influence. The mixture could be ambiguous because the lessons of the Congo crisis were well learned, especially by the Soviet Union. Russia was content to develop good relations with some friendly African countries but did not feel a need or have the ability to press these relations to the point of "taking over" their government or of turning their conflicts with their neighbors into cold war disputes. Even the West gave up its expectations of seeing African governments turn into parliamentary democracies and settled for close economic relations instead. Africa became a nonaligned segment of the Free World, economically part of the West but unattached to East or West in political and security terms.

Now all this is changing. Two decades later, the lessons of the Congo crisis have been challenged. Less important conflicts are becoming more significant in the global context. As the battle line across southern Africa surged forward with Portugal's withdrawal, Western countries feared Soviet entrance into the continent through the Namibian, Zimbabwean, and South African national liberation movements. The Soviet Union, using military advisers, arms, and Cuban troops, challenged Western influence in Angola and Ethiopia and won. After subduing the opposition against which it had been called, the Soviet Union stayed on at the behest of its African clients. By the beginning of the 1980s, four African countries—Ethiopia, Angola, Mozambique, and Congo—had friendship treaties with the Soviet Union. Each of the first two had on its soil more than twice as many Soviet and Cuban troops as there were Western soldiers (essentially French) on the entire continent, and both had become official observers at Comecon (the Soviet economic community).

Looked at from the African standpoint, the states on the continent are developing greater military power, thereby raising their conflicts to higher levels of unilateral effectiveness but also to higher levels of bilateral stalemate. (Much of this power is made available by external sources in the form of heavy conventional armament, but it is paid for by African economies and used by African armies.) Except in a few cases, such as Algeria, Zimbabwe, and the Portuguese colonies, the metropole's resistance to African demands for independence in the earlier period was relatively weak, and the need for power was limited. The struggle for independence could be primarily political. Similarly, the resistance of African states to the demands of others in inter-African conflict was weak, and the conflicts could usually be waged at relatively unsophisticated levels of weapons. Now the colonialist resistance has been forced back to its core redoubt in South Africa and is fighting for its life. African conflicts, which formerly erupted only briefly, lasting at worst until the exhaustion of current military stocks, now continue for prolonged periods while military stocks are renewed, as in the Ogaden war of 1977-78 and the Chadian round after 1982. African conflicts, if left to run their course, can thus become serious enough to attract outside help and to draw in the great powers.

From the position of the great powers, the very measures that permitted an attenuation of the balance of terror at the center also induced greater possibilities for conflict at the periphery. The development of conventions about bilateral superpower conflict reduces its risk, but the stabilization of Cold War relations at the point of direct contact in Western Europe moves the conflict to other areas. Ironically, instead of capitalist saturation of the home market pushing the West to colonization as Lenin postulated, one finds cold war saturation of the core area of conflict pushing the protagonists—but above all the Soviet Union—into conflict situations in the Third World.

Soviet policy then changed under the new challenge. The diplomatic instruments of foreign policy that were available to the Soviet Union in Africa in the earlier period proved to be of limited effectiveness just when new capabilities came to hand. In the 1960s, after the Congo affairs of 1960-61 and 1964, Russia relied principally on diplomatic means; not only were close political or military relations excluded, but the Soviet capability to intervene was also limited. Transport, logistics, overflight rights, strike forces, and legitimate allies were all lacking in the first decade of African independence. By the 1970s, however, the Soviets had developed an impressive intervention capability. The shipment of Soviet troops to Angola and, even more rapidly, to Ethiopia, and of Cuban troops in much larger numbers to both locations, was possible only because of enhanced Soviet logistic and transport capabilities and the acquisition of crucial refueling and overflight rights in Brazzaville and Aden, which were unavailable fifteen years before. The willingness of Cuban troops to join in the adventure was crucial because a leading "nonaligned" presence softened Soviet intervention. Sovietologists may debate whether this capability was developed with specific targets in mind or whether it evolved through a general development in military technology that then made possible a new strategy to exploit the technology. But however this chicken-and-egg argument is resolved, capabilities and strategies both were different by the mid-1970s.

Similarly, just at the moment when foreign policy opportunities available to the Soviet Union in an earlier period had shown themselves to be of limited attractiveness, new opportunities came into view. In the 1960, Soviet ideologists argued whether Egypt, Guinea, Ghana, and Mali could be considered as truly socialist;[7] the Russians generally decided that the African socialists were not yet successful but were headed in the right direction, a conclusion that fitted the type of friendly but not dominant relations that the post-Congolese era permitted. When Nkrumah fell in 1966, the Soviets were truly surprised, and when the socialism of other African states seemed no more rigorous than it was effective, the policy of friendly but not close relations seemed only appropriate.

But after the fall of the Portuguese colonial regime in 1974-75, Marxist-Leninist parties closer to the orthodoxy of the founding fathers of communism than any other parties in Africa came to power in Angola and Mozambique. Although their ideology was less clear, the national liberations movements of Zimbabwe were willing to turn to the Soviet Union (and China) for the military wherewithal to enable them to fight for independence. As the liberation struggle moved toward South Africa, which held the first African population that could be called a proletariat, the ideological lure of the "action area" of the continent again increased. Perhaps the most important event, however, was the Ethiopian revolution in 1974, which, if not proletarian, so much resembled the Russian revolution against feudal autocrats that it was hailed as a major event in Marxist terms. In a relatively short time, the revolutionary opportunities in the continent seemed more promising than those warranting simply friendly relations. They were worth major efforts at intervention when the openings appeared. When a United States Congress, emboldened by a post-Vietnamese backlash, tied the hands of the American administration to prevent intervention against the Russians in Angola in 1975, the opening was there.

In such a situation, even when the specific attractions of an Ethiopian revolution or an Angolan liberation are not present, African conflicts risk entangling great powers in areas where their only interest is in keeping the other party out. Indeed, despite the attractiveness of the new opportunities for the Russians, the African situation resembles the classic prisoners' dilemma: a unilaterally selfish policy challenged leaves everyone worse off whereas a cooperative agreement is better for both parties (and here for the third parties as well) than every other alternative except the unilaterally selfish policy if it can go unchallenged.

It is, therefore, important for the United States to devise a policy that avoids this dilemma, where small state conflicts can pull great powers toward unwanted outcomes. Limiting superpower involvement will almost invariably best serve U.S. interests. Thus, it is important not only to identify the need for such a policy but also to study the ways in which the policy works best and the ways in which it has been used—successfully or unsuccessfully. It is also important to recognize the times when conflicts are best left untouched and to distinguish them from those occasions when a great power can take a more active and positive role. The result can be not only a more effective implementation of unilateral policy initiatives but also the development of conventions to avoid conflict and regulate bilateral competition in the Third World. An appropriate policy can also work to preserve the friendly neutrality of the African continent that has obtained for the past two decades, utilizing the access available to Western powers to help African states resolve or at least manage their conflicts. Such attention is no less important than the management of conflict on the direct bipolar level, and it is long overdue. The Carter administration was not unmindful of this concern, and some components of such a policy were expressed in Secretary of State Cyrus Vance's important African statement on 20 June 1978. The Reagan administration, proceeding from a different set of premises, nonetheless shared aspects of this concern. But opportunities have been missed; policy has sometimes lacked coherence; and even when the implementation has been effective, there are lessons to be learned for the future.

Conflicts and Crises

In a consideration of conflicts, some definitions are needed. Writings on the subject usually draw an important distinction between conflict and crisis, which will be retained here.[8] In the following analysis, "conflict" will refer to the underlying issue in dispute between parties; and "crisis," to the active outbreak of armed hostilities. Although "crisis" is often construed to refer to a short period, implying a sudden flare-up, this restriction appears too narrow. Sudden flare-ups and variations in intensity may prolong a crisis whereas a focus on the short term alone prevents a full investigation of the dynamics of escalation. "Crisis," therefore, will apply here to such protracted disputes as the Saharan guerrilla war and the Ogaden guerrilla and then conventional war and also to brief outbursts such as the Shaba invasions.

A distinction should also be made between "conflict resolution" and "conflict management." "Resolution" here refers to the elimination of the causes of the underlying conflict, generally with the agreement of the parties. "Management" refers to the elimination, neutralization, or control of the means of pursuing either the conflict or the crisis. Conflict *resolution* is a tall order. It is rarely accomplished by direct action and is more frequently achieved only over long periods of time although the proximate aspects of conflict can sometimes be eliminated by agreement among the parties. As we will see, the basic causes of the rivalry between Angola and Zaire will remain seeds of conflict for a long time, but the immediate causes of tension have been largely eliminated.

By contrast, conflict, or crisis, "management" involves such measures as denying both sides the means of combat, neutralizing one party's means by slightly increasing the other's, separating the combatants in space or time, substituting conferences to talk for fighting, and so on. *Management*, then, seeks either to prevent conflict from erupting into crisis or to cool a crisis in eruption.

Another distinction concerns the terms "conciliator" or "mediator," which are used interchangeably here to refer to "good offices." Conflict resolution, in the situations described here, does not usually include formal mediation, and it certainly does not refer to a Kissinger-type of shuttle diplomacy with all the drain it imposes on foreign policy resources. Nor does it refer to a Camp David or Korean type of three-party negotiations in which the United States is a participant. Such involvement would be incompatible with the argument advanced here in favor of limited engagement by outside powers.

The lengthy debates that occupy legalists over the distinctions between mediation, conciliation, and good offices are irrelevant to the political process under study here. It is not the degree of formal authority to decide that determines the relative effectiveness of third-party conflict resolution, but the informal power to make the parties decide. Some attention will be devoted to that power, often referred to generically as "leverage," in the cases and conclusion that follow.[9]

Finally, it is useful to observe a distinction between escalation and intensification although the difference is a matter of feel rather than of statistics. The distinction lies between changes in nature and changes in degree.[10] These are not, of course, always easy to see. Was it escalation when SWAPO started assassinating tribal authorities or when it assassinated the leading Herero chief and rival nationalist leader or when it attacked a South African army base? Did Polisario (Popular Front for the Liberation of Saqiet al-Hamra and Rio de Oro) escalate in attacking a Moroccan army base in the Western Sahara or an obscure village in pre-1975 Morocco or a major base and administrative center in pre-1975 Morocco at Tantan? Ambiguity remains, but the concept is clear: Escalation is not just a matter of degree, a smoother, ever-rising curve or an intensification, but it involves distinct—even if debatable—steps.

The special nature of escalation, however, relates to the nature of crisis itself. Etymologically, crisis refers to a turning point or a decisive moment, as used by the Greeks, whose term it originally is, or by us today to refer to the critical peak of a disease. Most concepts of crisis in international relations include this decisive element involving a change in the nature of the relations between the parties or, more specifically, a shift in their power relations.

In this study, dynamics of a crisis will be discussed in terms of "ripe moments," viewed in relation to escalation of or to critical shifts in the intensity of a crisis. More specifically, such moments can be defined in three overlapping ways: (1) as mutual, painful stalemates marked by a recent or impending catastrophe; (2) as a time when both parties' efforts at unilateral solutions or "tracks" are blocked and bilateral solutions or "tracks" are conceivable; and or (3) as a place on a long slope where the "ins" start to slip and the "outs" start to surge. "First" and "second" tracks will be used here to refer to a party's pursuit of unilateral, as opposed to bilateral (or cooperative), solutions, respectively.

In the cases that follow, it may be helpful to think of a crisis as an earthquake along a fault line: There may be strains and pressures for readjustment between the two sides of the earth's crust over a long time, but at some moment they move into a new position vis-à-vis each other to the accompaniment of much disturbance and violence. Many indicators of seismic shifts have been studied. Although the indicators cannot predict the event itself, but only give warning, they do clearly show that pressures and their minor manifestations occur over a period of time before the change in relations strikes—just as conflict precedes crises. They also show that more than one seemingly decisive crisis may be required before the shift in relations is fully registered.

This analogy with seismic shifts is useful in understanding both the real weight of cold war confrontations and the nature of current African crises. The crust is only beginning to take form and harden in Africa, and power relations are only beginning to be worked out. Conflict and crisis is an emergent area like Africa are the equivalent in international relations of the struggle for power and independence on the domestic level. Now that the state units have been established, for the most part, they have to work out their relations with each other, not merely formally in the sense of diplomatic recognition and the exchange of ambassadors, but much more substantively in the sense of power relations, roles and ranks, and place in a power structure. Similarly, independence is far more than the formal matter of sovereignty. In more homely terms, a batch of new kids has come on the block, the parents (or the cops) have withdrawn, and some new relations and pecking orders will have to be established, with some bloodied noses. On occasion, there may even be calls for parents (or cops) to return briefly to break it up.

For all the similarities that this African situation bears to the crises of the cold war, there are real differences (beyond the obvious one of the levels of power).[11] To begin with, the cold war crises have, in part, turned out the way they did because there was a status quo side. The distinction between status quo and revisionist (or, in Kissinger's term, revolutionary) powers, however, does not exist in Africa. In most of the African crises, there is no status quo side—only different aims and different interpretations of change. Because the crises take place while African states are creating structures of relationship rather than, for the most part, maintaining or altering already established ones, no side can be identified as the party of continuity and order.

Secondly, the limiting conventions of the cold war are absent in the bush wars among Africans. One writer[12] has identified these conventions among the great powers as the exchange of "hostages" through mutually assured destruction, mutual surveillance, and a common strategic ideology. Africa has no equivalents. The power level of African disputants is still low enough so that there is no mutual threat of destruction. At most, some countries may be able to impose such strains on a neighbor's political system that its nature changes, possibly into a military regime. Not only is mutual surveillance absent, but a general intelligence capability to ascertain the other party's aims and abilities is usually lacking. States in conflict shadowbox and then are surprised by reality. In fact, they are often surprised by forces on their own side or by parties supposedly under their own control through usually quite independent, which play an autonomous role in the conflict. Then, too, a common strategic ideology is absent because the rules and behaviors applicable to African conflicts are themselves under challenge. The whole experience of working out a new continental power balance is new, and the ways in which conflict should be carried out are part of the matter to be decided in the conflict. Again, the situation is similar to the struggles for power on the domestic level, where both rulers and rules are being chosen as part of the same conflict.

Finally, the study of cold war crises generally focuses on hostile maneuvering short of violence (even if violence may occur as the crisis proceeds) and certainly short of all-out war between the great powers. African crises feature open hostilities and violence although, as seen, these wars do not eliminate the opponent. Part of crisis management in Africa, therefore, involves ending actual war, and part of it involves preemptive peacemaking.

What are the causes of current African conflicts? What changes these conflicts into crises? Why is Africa a "crisis-ridden continent, " where perfectly normal situations of conflict do not remain in the realm of politics but so frequently turn to violence, proceed from violence to a search for allies, and from allies expand to a cold war battlefield? The single response is that current African conflict arises from the inchoate and developing nature of African states, both on the domestic and international levels. As African states are being born and shaped, the stakes for the players are high and clear, but the rules of competition have not been established, and the limits and controls on the conflict are still part of the stakes. Twenty years, a generation, is a short time in which to expect rules, limits, and controls to be firmly in place, particularly if they have been changed several times in the interim. In fact, as development continues, the crises are likely to become more frequent than at the outset, for capabilities are outgrowing the initial fragile rules and controls. The first decade of competition within and among states may indeed be easier to control and less taxing on the capacities of the political system than the second. States in the first decade may live with a vague idea of their armies and their boundaries, but only in the second or third decade discover exactly where they meet their neighbor or overlap with it and how they can use their armed forces to pressure it. Because these circumstances are endemic and pervasive, conflict in Africa is on the rise, conflict resolution is a high and continuing challenge, and conflict management is a necessary area for the development of policy and skills.

The general causes of conflict can be broken down into six types or subcauses.

1. *Decolonization power struggles.* Independence—the right and ability to control one's own destiny—is the highest political value, and it is natural that there should be fierce competition and maneuvering among domestic groups and parties to participate in and control the process by which it is achieved. It is the exceptional situation to find all parties willing to share power with one another as the polity moves to self-government; it is far more normal to expect each party to be busy knifing the others in order to dominate the process and the outcome. Yet attempts to set up power sharing are not worthless even if they are an uphill effort, for the very way in which the power struggle is handled in preparation for independence is important in establishing the future rules by which power will be

used and passed among the parties thereafter. That makes the struggle all the fiercer. Angola, Zimbabwe, Namibia, and the Sahara all represent conflicts growing out of the power struggle that precedes and accompanies independence, and the cases clearly indicate that more than a presidency is involved. An ideological orientation in Angola, an ideological and racial orientation in Zimbabwe and Namibia, or the very nature of the polity itself in the Sahara—all are the stakes to be determined.

2. *New independent consolidation.* For all the struggles among Africans prior to independence, a colonial regime at least provided a common enemy against which to forge nationalist unity. With independence, that common cause is gone. The absence of a common enemy and the appearance of regional, personal, and programmatic divergences among the nationalists are the combined causes for the breakdown of the nationalist movement and the single party that often follows. The absolute nature of the anticolonial struggle, which allows the dominant nationalists to brand their opponents traitors, carries over the independence. Losers in the power struggle often go into exile, either in Europe or in neighboring African countries of a different ideological stripe. At times, usually when a previous commonality of experience has existed, leaders agree not to support neighbors' opposition movements, largely because everyone is vulnerable to the same threat. At other times, ideological differences arise to outweigh the common threat, or leaders perceive the threat being used against them first, and so they reciprocate. Where the control of national political space was first assumed at independence, it may actually break down or reach beyond national boundaries as the unity of independence collapses. Shaba, Ogaden, Angola, and Chad are all instances of wars over political space after independence as politics overflows national territorial limits and the state's control of its own territory runs afoul of rival protogovernments.

3. *Leftover liberation movements.* The struggle for national liberation has legitimized antistate politics and guerrilla movements; the successor states now have to live with their own legacy. National liberation movements have a presumption of authenticity. They are seen as the *pays réel*, in the anticolonial language of North Africa, against the *pays légal*, and legality must cede to reality. That is a heavy burden for the new legality of the independent state to bear when new antistate challenges need only show their reality to gain the presumption of legitimacy and call into question the legal order. More complicating problems arise thereafter. Specific national liberation movements are chosen over all other groups as the sole and

authentic representatives of their people by well-meaning supporters, moves that strengthen the movements but often make it difficult to deal with other elements of "the reality," such as rival movements and settler institutions, which still have power. Weaker national liberation movements find their reinforcement in neighboring states and, like many client bodies, become dog-wagging tails, turning conflict into crisis beyond the control of patrons.

Finally, national liberation movements have their own logic in regard to escalation. They have nothing to lose by fighting and nothing to do but fight. They have none of the problems of responsibility of a state, and their combat activities help them to build political solidarity and control their followers. So, unlike a state, they can only be defeated by being destroyed, a very difficult task. And, unlike a state, they cannot merely be persuaded to reorient their goals in regard to the conflict, for to change goals is to remove their reason for being. Again, unlike the situation with a state, recognizing their existence implies support for their case, and it becomes hard for other African states to withdraw recognition from them, particularly when they have been called the sole and authentic representative for their people.

The case studies that follow are filled with the complexity of this situation. Namibia's SWAPO, like the Patriotic Front of Rhodesia, is a real nationalist organization but not the only one. The Angolan FLNA and UNITA were legitimate nationalist organizations, but after their war was won by someone else, they remained and have served as runaway bargaining chips for outside parties. The Western Saharan group, Polisario, is a nationalist movement without a state, kept alive by Algeria's and Libya's support in their rivalry with Morocco, but Polisario would be difficult to get rid of if either supporter should want to end the war. Zaire's FLNC, like the many Frolinats in Chad, is a national liberation movement for the "second independence" (as the struggle against Mobutu's regime and its external allies is known in Zaire); this label attempts to stretch the legitimacy of a national liberation movement to a revolt against an independent government. Similarly, the Western Somali Liberation Front is presented as a national liberation movement, but now against the "colonialism" of an African neighbor; with its cause legitimized in the eyes of its sponsors, its influence—not on Ethiopia but on the Somali government—becomes hard to shake. A good deal of time will have to pass before the presumptive legitimacy of anti-state movements—and with it their power to give interstate conflict a violent expression—will wane.

4. *Ill-defined territory*. African states have been born under the OAU doctrine of *uti possidetis juris* ("as you hold possession by right"), whereby the colonial boundaries were declared unquestionably legitimate. From the beginning, two states—without, however, challenging the doctrine itself—declared their own case to be an exception: the Sharifian Empire of Morocco and the nation-state of Somalia. As with the ban against harboring other state's subversives, the boundary doctrine has held through mutual interest in not opening Pandora's box. But, with time, as African states grow into their "skin" and discover the problems, conflicts, claims, and overlaps associated with artificial territorial limits on human activity, the doctrine of *uti possidetis* has been challenged and will face even greater tests in the future. The Dahomey-Niger dispute over Lete island, the Mali-Burkina decenially recurrent border dispute, equally persistent claims for the Ewe border tribe's unity between Ghana and Togo, Libyan annexation of northern Chad and occupation of northern Niger, and Idi Amin's claims on his neighbors and his temporary annexation of the Kagera salient are all cases that have twisted the OAU doctrine, finding a competing *uti possidetis* in a different colonial treaty, a different interpretation of a badly drawn line, or, in the last case, for the first time in the continent, using "African" (that is, geographic) instead of colonial criteria for a new boundary. Generally, boundaries within the territory of a single colonizer are more likely to provoke disputes than the boundaries between colonizers because demarcation was less usual in the former. The difference is, however, only a matter of degree. Any state can have a boundary problem if it wants one; the real causes of conflict are present everywhere, and it takes a policy decision and effort not to pursue them rather than the reverse.

5. *Structural rivalries*. Just as African states are growing into domestic political patterns, so they are growing into roles and positions in the structure of inter-African politics.[13] During the 1960s, African states did not have the power to extend their influence far beyond the circle of their neighbors, and more ambitious attempts— Ghana's continental leadership pretentions, French African alliances—either collapsed or carried on at only a low level of effectiveness. By the end of the 1970s, however, both the distribution of power on the continent and the potential for its redistribution had become more evident. The evolving rivalry between Morocco and Algeria, the central position of Ethiopia in its region, the potential for dominance by Nigeria in West Africa and Zaire in central Africa, the front-line axis in south central Africa, and the polar position of

South Africa seeking allies to help remove its isolation—all began to give the continent some shape. If all other causes of conflict disappeared, if there were no problems of domestic maneuvering and development, the structural bases of conflict alone would be strong enough to shape domestic policies, differences, and forces.

These five causes of conflict are African, and they are primary. Their salience provides the proper context for the debate between the Africanist and globalist perspectives on Africa in world politics.[14] Global rivalries may tempt outsiders to capitalize on African causes of conflict, but external influence could not turn one state against another if these causes were not already present. The Africanist argument that Africans are so nationalistically independent that foreign subversion will have no lasting impact has validity, but only when that foreign subversion does not seize on African conflicts. The globalist argument that cold war influences are what make African conflicts serious is true, but only when the cause of these conflicts is understood as first and basically African.

6. *Runaway means.* Within this perspective, then, there is a final, secondary source of conflict that comes mainly from outside. African armies today have grown large enough to do more than overthrow their own governments. Although African power to pursue conflicts is limited, as we have noted, additional power comes from outside. External sources of power are activated primarily through alliances for political support and through arms for the military. Such support may be directly tied to a conflict, as in the Russian aid to Ethiopia in 1977. Alternatively, it may be present "only for potential dangers," like Russian arms for Somalia after 1963 (when no one was threatening Somalia—certainly not to the extent of the Soviet aid—and Russia had no interest in supporting Somalian claims on its neighbors).

In the Horn and in each of the crises studied in the following chapters, however, these arms would not have been used for war if there had not been a long-standing, deep-seated African cause for the conflict. This will continue to be true even though the general atmosphere of cold war competition continues to justify both reactive and preemptive arms sales and political support. It will be true as long as even lesser powers are eager to sell their arms for merely commercial reasons.[15] On the other hand, instability is so endemic in Africa that arms supplies are an invitation to crisis and hence to further great power intervention. The irony is that, once one side has provided arms or political support, the only way to bring the conflict to management, let alone resolution, may well be to provide enough countervailing support to bring about stalemate and negotiation.

When such conflicts and crises occur, the United States must have policies to meet them. The following chapters examine four African cases in which the United States had a role, different in each case according to the nature of the crisis. At this writing, the Shaba crises and probably even much of the underlying conflict have been resolved for the time being. The Ogaden crisis is also over, but the conflict rages on. The Namibia crisis is under treatment, as it has been for years, and the Saharan crisis may be heading toward a denouement on its own. Not only has American policy had different roles to play in these cases, but its role has also been the subject of intense internal debate. African conflict and the American response are the subjects of the following analysis in an effort to find out what opportunities are available for managing and resolving the conflict.

Notes

1. Richard Betts, *Soldiers, Statesmen and Cold War Crises* (Cambridge, Mass.: Harvard University Press, 1979); Ole Holsti et al., "Measuring Effect and Action: the 1962 Cuban Crisis," in I. William Zartman, ed., *The 50% Solution* (New York: Doubleday, 1976).
2. Richard Smoke, *War: Controlling Escalation* (Cambridge, Mass.: Harvard University Press, 1979); Ole Holsti et al., "Perceptions and Actions in the 1914 Crisis," in J. David Singer, ed., *Quantitative International Politics* (New York: Holt, Rinehart and Winston, 1971); Ole Holsti, *Crisis, Escalation and War* (Montreal: McGill, University Press, 1972).
3. Coral Bell, *The Conventions of Crisis: A Study in Diplomatic Management* (New York: Oxford University Press, 1971).
4. An important exception is *Controlling Small Wars* (New York: Knopf, 1969) by Lincoln Bloomfield and Amelia Leiss.
5. See the excellent analysis of the whole period in Saadia Touval's *The Peace Brokers: Mediators in the Arab-Israeli Conflict 1948-79* (Princeton, N.J.: Princeton University Press, 1982) and Alan Dowty's *Middle East Crisis* (Berkeley, Calif.: University of California Press, 1984), and on the 1970s in William B. Quandt's *Decade of Decisions* (Berkeley, Calif.: University of California Press, 1977).
6. See Madeleine G. Kalb, *The Congo Cables* (New York: Macmillan, 1982).
7. See Thomas P. Thornton, *The Third World in Soviet Perspective* (Princeton, N.J.: Princeton University Press, 1964); A. J. Klinghoffer, *Soviet Perspectives on African Socialism* (Rutherford, N.J.: Dickinson University Press, 1969). On Soviet friendship treaties, see Zajar Imam, *Towards a Model Relationship* (Atlantic Highlands, N.J.: Humanities, 1983).

8. See the chapters by Hermann, Pruitt, and McClelland and Hoggard, in James Rosenau, ed., *International Politics and Foreign Policy*, 2nd ed. (New York: Free Press, 1969); Philip Williams, *Crisis Management* (New York: Wiley, 1976); Ole Holsti, *Crisis, Escalation and War* (Montreal: McGill University Press, 1972; Daniel Frei, ed., *International Crisis and Crisis Management* (New York: Praeger, 1978); Daniel Frei, ed., *Managing International Crises* (Beverly Hills, Calif.: Sage, 1982); Charles F. Hermann, ed., *International Crises* (New York: Free Press, 1972); Alastair Buchan, *Crisis Management: The New Diplomacy* (Boulogne-sur-Seine: The Atlantic Institute, 1966); Oran Young, *The Politics of Force* (Princeton: Princeton University Press, 1968); Glen H. Snyder and Paul Diesing, *Conflict Among Nations* (Princeton: Princeton University Press, 1977); Richard Ned Lebow, *Between Peace and War* (Baltimore: the Johns Hopkins University Press, 1981); C. F. Smart and W. I. Stanbury, *Studies in Crisis Management* (Toronto: Butler Worth, 1978); Urs Schwarz, *Confrontation and Intervention in the Modern World* (Dobbs Ferry, N.Y.: Oceana, 1970); Ralph Starn, "Historians and Crisis," *Past and Present* 52:3-22 (August 1971).

9. For further discussion, see "Conclusion," in Saadia Touval and I. William Zartman, eds., *The Man in the Middle: International Mediation in Theory and Practice* (Boulder, Colo.: Westview, 1984).

10. Richard Smoke (in *War*) calls escalation crossing a "saliency." "Saliencies," of course, are a matter of debate. See Thomas Schelling, *Strategy of Conflict* (Cambridge, Mass.: Harvard University Press, 1960).

11. See Arnold Wolfers, *Discord and Collaboration* (Baltimore: The Johns Hopkins University Press, 1962).

12. Coral Bell, *Conventions of Crisis* and *The Management of Interdependence* (New York: Council on Foreign Relations, 1974); cf. Joanne Gowa and Nils Wessel, *Ground Rules: Soviet and American Involvement in Regional Conflict* (Philadelphia: Foreign Policy Research Institute, 1982).

13. On differential growth and "pecking order" as a source of strain in the international system, see Kenneth Boulding, *Stable Peace* (Austin, Tex.: University of Texas Press, 1978,) pp. 58 f.

14. See Helen Kitchen, ed., "Options for U.S. Policy Toward Africa" (special issue), I *AEI Foreign Policy and Defense Review* 1 (1979).

15. See Ali Mazrui, *Africa's International Relations* (Boulder, Colo.: Westview, 1979). In an interesting paper on "Dynamics of Military Rule in Black Africa," prepared for a conference sponsored by the Defense of Intelligence School on 16 September 1982 in Washington, D.C., Walter Barrows argues that increased military rule in the 1980s can be expected to lead to greater armaments and greater conflict in Africa.

2
Conflict in the Sahara

I against my brother.
                                    Maghrebi proverb

One drop of blood is worth a thousand friends.
                                    Another Maghrebi proverb

Boundaries at best are artificial matters.[1] The line that officially separates the "we" from the "they" rests comfortably only under ideal conditions—a long history of stability and good relations, separation of culturally different peoples, coincidence with economic and physical watersheds. Yet as the "skin" of the state, boundaries are so important that it is hard to find an equally appropriate way of determining or changing them. A simple momentary referendum may or may not reflect all the preceding considerations of stability. The problem is specifically exacerbated in Africa by four features— the recentness of the boundaries unsupported by a long historical evolution, the only gradual extension of state control to its sovereign territorial limits, the absence of determining physical features, and the many potential sources of irredentism that vie with colonial inheritance as a source of legitimacy.[2] Often the boundaries are held in place only by the African norm of territorial succession embodied in the 1964 OAU resolution on *uti possidetis*, a fragile support only as strong as the respect it draws.[3] The territorial basis of a state is so close to its independence, integrity, and identity that its definition and preservation constitute a vital interest, all the more delicate and touchy when it is not clearly established from the outset. Europe took centuries to work out its boundary lines; the New World was plagued by territorial problems during its first century of postcolonial independence, and many of these remain in the second century in Latin America. Africa follows suit.

Growing states are not all of the same weight and power, however, and therefore have politics of relation as well as of recognition. The appearance of a gap between African states with growing resources, influence, and ambition and those that have none of these is a major change that has arisen during Africa's two decades of independence.[4] Growing states feel a need to develop a sense of rank and relations with others; in the process, they also seek to fill voids, build buffers, and enroll allies. Such patterns of power or structural relations develop gradually, change slowly, and dominate other considerations of ideology, ethnos, and economics. They are, therefore, of tremendous importance in the motivation of foreign policy makers, nearly as much so as vital interest and second only to the definition of the policy itself. Rival influences run like water, overflowing into empty places, surging across space until they meet opposing forces; and, after the turmoil of the meeting, they settle down to fill the areas they occupy or to build up pressure for a new surge. The politics of structure needs to be worked out; the accompanying conflicts cannot be resolved, except with time. They can only be contained, by settling the component incidents and crises in such a way as to maintain a balance.

The Moroccan-Algerian conflict is such a structural rivalry between brothers and neighbors, fed by every incident that comes along between the two states and fueled into crises by territorial problems of boundaries and borderlands. The territorial conflict is grounded in the clash between two notions of the state: the historic Sharifian Empire, with a 300-year-old dynasty and a 1300-year-old history as a state, versus new colonially determined creations based on national liberation and self-determination. It is sharpened by the long absence of an established boundary along most of the distance between Morocco and Algeria. It was further heightened by the decolonization of the Western—formerly Spanish—Sahara, on which both states had designs, Morocco claiming it as its remaining irredenta and Algeria wanting it to be an independent but subordinate state blocking Morocco's path to the south. The border issue broke out into war in 1963, followed by successful conflict management and then resolution by 1972. However, the issue of the Western Sahara then arose to undo the border agreement and in turn to erupt into a war between Morocco and the Saharan national liberation movement (Polisario). This war rapidly escalated to stalemate and then gradually intensified despite various bilateral and mediated attempts to seize several periods propitious for resolution. Only when both strong and cornered in 1981 was Morocco able to turn toward a political solution, and only two years later was the newly consolidated regime of Algeria able to begin to take some hesitant steps to meet it. But the magic moment was drowned in miscommunications in 1983 and 1984, and the conflict escalated another notch. It took another five years before the stalemate forced the two states to bury their conflict in regional cooperation and pursue states' rather than insurgents' interests, after 1988, with a little help from some important mediators.

Background

The main channels of human movement and activity in the great African desert—*Sahara* in Arabic—occur around its edges, the western one of which is its Atlantic coast.[5] Here a series of inland plateaus manages to capture a bit of the moisture from Atlantic winds to provide enough seasonal vegetation for migrant grazing. Behind it lies a vast "empty quarter" covering northern Mali, southwestern Algeria, and northeastern Mauritania with huge dunes (Erg Iguidi and Erg Chech), pebbly plains (reg), and rocky plateaus (hammada). Dry as it is, the western Sahara forms an isthmus between Morocco and Senegal-Mali.

The long arc between the southern Moroccan mountains and oases and the Senegal and western Niger river valleys is sparsely inhabited by a mobile population of 1,500,000 or one per square kilometer, a quarter of whom are settled in the few colonial coastal towns and traditional inland centers but most of whom are pastoral tribes in movement. The Berber-speaking Tekna tribes, related to the Moroccans of the Anti-Atlas mountains, inhabit the northern part of this territory. The large nomadic and warrior tribes, notably the Arabic-speaking Ulad Delim and Reqeibat, are located along the coast and inland of the central segment—primarily the Rio de Oro of the former Spanish Sahara—but, in fact, roam from Tiznit in Morocco to Tijikja in Mauritania. Inland in the central part of Mauritania are other Arabic-speaking Moorish tribes who move seasonally north and south within their territory.

These people know no boundaries, and the straight lines that bounded Spanish Sahara, like those that separate Morocco, Algeria, Mauritania, and Mali, are unrelated to any features of human or physical geography.[6] The southeast points of the Rio de Oro border do touch the escarpment of the Adrar plateau, and the curved parts of the border in between arch at a distance of twenty kilometers from the valuable salt pan at Ijil, but the rest of the border corresponds to nothing. In the whole western Saharan region, only the Mali-Mauritanian border takes into account the nomadic patterns and watering holes. It stands as a unique example of the way borders should be regarded in Africa, for it was the subject of negotiations between independent governments in 1963 and was altered by common agreement to reflect pastoral and tribal needs.[7] But even here, the actual lines have no physical or human feature to follow. A more complicating situation is found in the area between Tindouf in Algeria and Figuig in Morocco, where no border existed at all because the French earlier had found that "a country which is without water is uninhabitable and a delimitation thereof would be superfluous."[8] In this kind of territory, any boundaries and territorial controls are difficult to apply, but a boundary or territorial dispute merely opens the area to its natural fluidity.

Not only is the economic and related social organization of the Saharan populations beyond state control, but they have also been in recurrent war among themselves and in rebellion against regimes on the edges of the Sahara. Both characteristics are typified by the actions of the famous prenationalist hero Ma al-'Ainain, who at the turn of the century delayed the French conquest of Mauritania with the help of the Moroccan sultan, and by his son Ahmed al-Heiba, who from his desert bases was the last pretender to the Moroccan throne.[9] Ibn Khaldun, the famous fourteenth-century Arab sociologist, had a theory about such activity; he saw North African history as a succession of regimes established by overflowing desert bands of militant religious reformers who softened as they adapted to city life beyond the mountains and fell prey to the next wave of fundamentalist warriors.[10] Such indeed has been the history of the Moroccan sultanate over the past millennium, and the present 'Alawi dynasty itself came from the Tafilalt oasis along the Algerian border region in the mid-seventeenth century.

The current Saharan crisis is part of the conflict arising from the different origins and natures of the states of Algeria, Mauritania, and Morocco. Within the central area of its kingdom—the so-called "government land" (*bilad al-makhzen*)—Morocco certainly qualified as a state-information in the Western sense by the time of the 'Alawi dynasty. But the traditional Islamic view of the state was not as a territorial unit but as a population entity, reflecting a centralized politico-religious focus within the common religious community (*umma*). At the beginning of the twentieth century, the Moroccan Empire extended southward beyond the Atlas and Anti-Atlas mountains for an indeterminate distance, with the sultan's religious position as *imam* and *khalifa* of the West recognized by tribes living throughout the great western arc of the Sahara, where grazing and commerce were possible.[11]

The central area of the kingdom fell under the colonial control of the French and Spanish in 1912, but as a protectorate, not as an outright colony. The continuity of the sovereign kingdom was internationally recognized, and the United States pursued an important case to the International Court of Justice in 1952 to reaffirm that continuity.[12] The western desert was not conquered until twenty years after the establishment of the protectorates, however, when the French took the Tafilalt and the Reqeibat base of Tindouf from the north and the Adrar from the south and the Spanish moved in from their few coastal posts to take their share of the Sahara.

In another twenty years, the tide of history was reversed and the colonial "protection" of the monarchy began to be removed. The French and Spanish protectorates were abolished in 1956, and Tangier was restored from international status to an integral part of the kingdom. The southern Spanish protectorate over Tarfaya, just south of the river Dra', was removed in 1958, and the coastal enclave of Ifni was returned to the kingdom in 1969.[13] It is not surprising that the Moroccans looked for the rest of their territory to be retroceded as colonial rule was gradually removed. The most articulate spokesperson of this view was not King Mohammed V or, after his death in 1961, his son King Hassan II. It was the Independence (Istiqlal) party, direct successor of the nationalist movement and Morocco's largest political party, and its charismatic president (until his death in 1974), the alim 'Allal al-Fassi, who had long led the call for the reunification of Tindouf and western Algeria, northern Mali, and all of Mauritania and Spanish Sahara and even the Canary Islands with the Moroccan Empire.[14] Even the other parties, notably the left oppostion offshoot of the Istiqlal—the Socialist Union of Popular Forces (USFP)— and the right groupings of independents and "king's men," adopted some form of irredentism, making it one of the fundamental themes of Moroccan politics.

But Morocco is rare among colonial territories in having a historic state that continued under colonial rule. More common is the colonially created state that then accedes to independence within its colonial boundaries, either through a territorial legislative act or through negotiations conducted by a combatant nationalist movement. Thus Algeria fought, negotiated, and voted in 1962 in a referendum for its independence, in which one of the points at issue was the very inclusion of the central Sahara and Tindouf.[15]

The crucible of Algerian political attitudes is quite different from the Moroccan experience. Whatever the status of Algeria's sovereign confederation of city states before the French conquest, it did not constitute a cohesive state. Algeria was the creation of 130 years of direct and intense colonization and of a revolutionary war of national liberation that won its independence. Its liberation struggle was a popular progressive cause of international dimensions, and its victory left it with feisty aspirations to Third World leadership and a penchant for supporting national liberation movements. But Algeria, the second largest state on the map of Africa (after Sudan), has a population slightly smaller than Morocco's but over twice its GNP (and per captial GNP) and a slightly higher economic growth rate— and thus a sense of sharp rivalry that is often created by the combination of a similar power base and a very different political system. Algerians frequently cite "the balance in the area" as the context for their policy toward Morocco and the reasons for opposition to Moroccan irredentism, reflecting a common misperception of balance of power in which the speaker must hold the edge of the balance. Moroccans have learned to respond in the same way in reverse. "The Sahara is part of Algeria's security zone," said President Houari Boumedienne of Algeria. "We have succeeded in establishing a certain balance in the region; we can't play with it."[16] Algeria has frequently been the spokesman for progressive, activist, confrontationist groups of African and other Third World states on continental and international—notably New International Economic Order—issues; Morocco has led similar groups of African states on an opposing, moderate stand. Finally, the 1963 border war between the two countries, despite subsequent reconciliation, has left a legacy of an unfinished fight, particularly among the military of both sides.

Mauritania was created as a territory of French West Africa (AOF) and became independent in 1960, its very existence contested at every step along the way.[17] Predominantly Arab in its population, it nevertheless has an important black (Toucouleur) minority related to the population of its southern neighbor, Senegal, and its existence was supported by its former AOF neighbors and by the larger moderate alliance of some of them, the African and Malagasy Union (UAM) and then the African and Malagasy Common Organization (OCAM). In 1965, however, Mauritania resigned from OCAM and began to develop ties with the more progressive Arab states, particularly Algeria, as a stronger counterweight to Morocco and in 1973 it completed its switch of alliances by joining the League of Arab States. In the process, Morocco changed its policy to recognize the existence of Mauritania at the Islamic Congress in Rabat in September 1969 and dropped its claims on Mauritanian territory. Mauritania's concern is, above all, the maintenance of its fragile independence—against Moroccan irredentist claims, against Senegalese "protection" of the black population, against Algerian dominance, against Libyan interference, against French dependency, and against internal collapse as a battlefield of traditional factionalism. Yet the very means of blocking each of these threats consist of using others among them as a counterweight, a most delicate piece of diplomacy.

During the process leading to independence, President-to-be Mokhtar ould Daddah articulated a different philosophy to face the Greater Morocco idea—the idea of a Greater Mauritania, a desert entity of similar people between the Senegal and Dra' rivers and hence including the then-Spanish Tarfaya and then-Spanish Sahara as well as Mauritania.[18] The return of Tarfaya to Morocco in 1958 and the continued presence of Spain in the western Sahara left little room for the realization of this idea during the 1960s and early 1970s, but later in the decade when he annexed part of the western Sahara, ould Daddah spoke in human terms of uniting families rather than state terms of balancing power. Later, from the other side of the desert, Libya's revolutionary leader, Muammar al-Qaddafi began to articulate another Greater Sahara idea for the whole area and put some of his large financial and military resources into support for sympathetic activists—in Chad, Niger, Mauritania and the Western Sahara.[19]

Thus, the western end of the Sahara is the arena of three overlapping conflicts: A Moroccan-Algerian rivalry of growing powers across a long inexistent border, a Moroccan struggle for national independence and integrity, and Mauritanian and Saharan efforts to find political forms for a desert society that the decolonization of the Spanish Sahara has brought about. It is only within these sets of relations that the conflict can be resolved—or even managed.

Conflict

The conflict in the Sahara is, above all, a power rivalry between two or more growing states in the region, fueled by interstate problems and incidents whose unusual seriousness is sharpened by the underlying power conflict. As colonizers and thereafter, the French played off their three North African territories of different status—two protectorates and "an integral part of France"—against each other and maintained the West African colony of Mauritania as a buffer area between black and Arab Africa. After independence, the same countries continued the pattern of relations. When Libya found that it contained oil, its power and aspirations grew apace, and it joined the pattern, completing the structure beyond its previous colonial limits. Once the parties were in place as sovereign units, the dynamic of their conflict was provided by a growth in resources and capabilities, a continuation of problems and incidents, and an evolution of differing policy directions. Thus, even when serious attempts were being made to calm the conflict, there was always one of these three elements present to revive it and to turn a perception, an incident, or a policy difference into a crisis.

Given this regional structure, a remarkable aspect has been not the occasional resort to ideology to color the spaces but its more general absence. To be sure, the Algerian press frequently refers to Morocco as a corrupt feudal monarchy, the Moroccans talk of Algeria as a leftist military dictatorship, and both tell how bad living conditions are in the other's territory. But a superimposed structure of ideologies—as in the Shaba crisis—or of allies—as in the Horn—has been absent in the Sahara. The reasons are that each state is strong enough in its own internal cohesion and national consolidation to be able to do without foreign ideologies and that the lines to foreign allies have been crossed and blurred. The cold war has not replicated or reinforced the conflict despite pressures to polarize in the 1980s.

America has strong interests in both leading parties in the region, in a regional stable balance, and in keeping the cold war out of the conflict; but the United States has not played a commensurably active role in reconciling the parties. The United States has been Algeria's leading trading partner, but it rarely sees eye to eye with Algeria on international political issues. The United States trades little with Morocco, but it has a history of common strategic concerns; both see a Communist threat to the African continent, Morocco partipated both in the United Nations Congo Operation (ONUC) in 1961 and in the Shaba interventions in 1977-78 (see the following chapter), and Morocco was the frequent supporter of Egyptian President Sadat's peace initiatives.[20] There is little direct American interest in Mauritania, but a good deal of perceived strategic interest in avoiding Libyan control over parts of the Sahara beyond its own boundaries because, whatever government Libya might have, its role could only be meddlesome and destabilizing.[21] It should, therefore, be equally clear that there is little interest in seeing additional states carved out of the Sahara, for they can only be further cases of African balkanization, needing financial and devel-

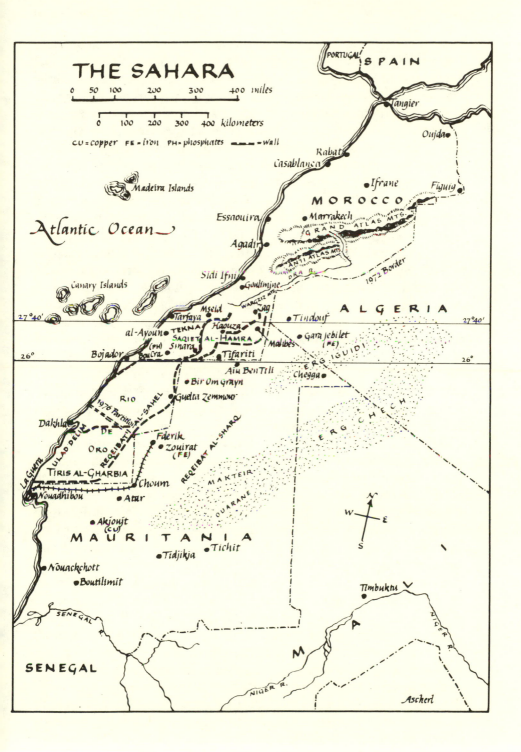

THE SAHARA

0 50 100   200   300   400 miles

0   100   200   300   400 kilometers

CU = copper   FE = iron   PH = phosphates   ——— = wall

PORTUGAL
SPAIN

Tangier

Oujda

Rabat
Casablanca

Ifrane
Figuig

Atlantic Ocean

Madeira Islands

MOROCCO

Essaouira
Marrakech
GRAND ATLAS MTS.

Agadir
ANTI ATLAS MTS.
DRA R.

1972 Border

Sidi Ifni

Canary Islands

Goulimine
WARGZIZ MTS.

Zag
Tindouf

ALGERIA

27°40'
Tarfaya
al-Ayoun TEKNA Haouza
SAQIET AL-HAMRA
Smara Malibes Gara Jebilet (FE)
(PH) Boucra
26°
Bojador Tifariti ERG IGUIDI 26°

Aïn Ben Tili
Chegga

Bir Om Grayn

1976 Partition RIO AL-SAHEL Guelta Zemmour
DE

Dakhla ERG CHECH
ULAD DELIM ORO Fderik
REGEIBAT Zouirat (FE)
TIRIS AL-GHARBIA REGEIBAT AL-SHARQ
La Guera Choum MAKTEIR
Nouadhibou Atar OUARANE

Akjoujt (CU) N
W   E
S

MAURITANIA
Tidjikja Tichit

Timbuktu
Nouackchott
Boutilimit
M A

SENEGAL R. NIGER R.

SENEGAL M
NIGER R. Ascherl

27

opment assistance, open to competing influences from neighbors, and a rising temptation to outside powers' interference. For a global power too often called on to play multiple political and economic roles in the region, one Mauritania is enough, with its weak economic base, social fissures, political rivalries, and security vulnerabilities.

Because of its interests on both sides of the Moroccan-Algerian border and its concern for balance and stability in the Mediterranean and Saharan regions, the United States has little advantage to seeing a one-sided victory in the continuing Saharan crisis or in the underlying conflict. But it does have a strong interest in seeing—and even helping—an end to the conflict on terms satisfactory to both sides. Nonetheless, there seems to be little middle ground between one-sided victories; a Polisario state is an Algerian victory, and the denial of a Polisario state is a Moroccan victory. As the prevention of an additional sovereign unit in the region is definitely in the interest of the United States, the problem of resolving the conflict lies in finding compensating elements in a final settlement that satisfy Algeria, preserve a balance of power in the region, and channel continuing Moroccan-Algerian competition into less conflictual directions. The American government has been most reluctant to embark on the this search, in part because of its difficulty and in part because of the standard mistaken judgment that the conflict is not hurting anyone enough to merit attention and will eventually go away.

French interests and goals are much the same, but the French role is more immediate, its concept of maintaining equilibrium is more direct, and its primary zone of interest includes the area. French policy has been to maintain its presence throughout the region, where it has long been the dominant power, and to do so it has tilted slightly to one side or the other according to the balance of grievances from the various North African states. French trade and cultural assistance to both countries, its investment in Morocco, and its strategic concern with the countries it faces across the Mediterranean underlie this continuing interest and balancing role. Between 1975 and the end of 1978, just before Algerian President Boumedienne's death, France was given a cold shoulder by Algeria and was more favorable to Morocco; after the death of Boumedienne, through the visit of the new foreign minister, Mohammed ben Yahya, in the beginning of 1980, it moved to a more neutral position. The 1981 election brought to power a Socialist administration with ties to Morocco but also with strong political sympathies with Algeria and a party commitment to support the Polisario. The result has been an ostensible French tilt toward Algeria, a flurry of diplomatic soundings on both sides of the Mediterranean, but a studied aversion to offending either side and, therefore, no greater activity on the Sahara than under the previous government.

By the same token, France has long sought to provide strong support behind Mauritania, to protect both its weak sovereignty against its neighbors and French cultural and economic interests. In the years 1973-74, Mauritania sought to replace French with Algerian support, but when Mauritania then turned to Morocco, France gradually returned to its former position, counterbalancing the Moroccan influence. At the end of the decade, Moroccan influence was removed, and French influence was greatly reduced, leaving Mauritania again a power vacuum to be fought over by Algeria and Libya. France is more directly interested in a balanced settlement in the region than even the United States, but also runs greater risks to its own interests in playing a mediating role that might offend some of the parties during its exercise.

Other parties have also felt an interest in the conflict, the most complex of which is certainly Spain. The former colonial ruler of the Western Sahara and also of other territories earlier returned to Morocco, Spain began to feel overburdened by its charge in the early 1970s and sought to withdraw while retaining its economic interests there. It found the best arrangement in an agreement with Morocco after an initial attempt with Algeria, but it was caught between the pressures that the two states could bring to bear on it: Morocco as claimant of the remaining Spanish Mediterranean enclaves of Ceuta and Melilla (on the same basis of contiguity that Spain claims Gibraltar); Algeria as an oil state and frequent supporter of the Canary Islands liberation movement; both states as part of the Arab region with which the new Spanish monarchial democracy seeks good relations.

In addition, the area is part of the maneuvering ground for inter-Arab politics, so that Egypt, Saudi Arabia, and the Palestine Liberation Organization (PLO) seek to pull particularly Morocco and Mauritania on one side or the other of the line of rejection, preserve Arab unity, and even provide financial support for economic or defense purposes. Among the Arab states within the region itself, Tunisia has an interest in seeing the balance between Morocco and Algeria maintained, even to the advantage of Morocco, lest an overwhelming Algeria become a threat to Tunisian autonomy. Libya sees an interest in developing the closest support for its radical policies, even to the point of unification with its neighbors, and in filling the geographic vaccum in Mauritania and the Sahara with forces with which it feels an affinity. Since the end of the 1970s, it has been a major rival for predominance in the North African region, challenging both Morocco and Algeria. In the end, it was Saudi Arabia that played the crucial mediating role, after having long been a major supporter of one of the parties in the conflict.

On the Soviet side, the interests have been less clear; and the role, less active. Russia was once a military supplier of Morocco and has maintained commercial relations with it, culminated in 1978 by a huge $2 billion phosphate and a $300 million fishing agreement; politically, the two countries are on very different wavelengths. Like the Americans, the Russians' position in regard to Algeria is quite the reverse of its Moroccan relations: Russia trades little with Algeria although it signed a $10 million iron mining contract for Gara Jebilet near Tindouf in April 1979, but it frequently has the same point of view on foreign policy issues. Russia has consistently supplied and twice remodernized Algeria's army. Its arms also reach the Polisario through Algeria and Libya although Russia has not made a major cause out of the Saharan national liberation movement, has not recognized it, and does not seem to have made ideological inroads into its membership. Soviet interest appears to be more closely tied to its various kinds of relations with Morocco and Algeria than to either the Polisario and its cause per se or to any particular kind of outcome in the crisis. A Polisario victory would contribute to the continuing instability on which Soviet presence seems to thrive although it would provide only a remote and unstable base for Soviet operations, ill-suited for a very doctrinaire application of Communist ideology— neither an Angola nor an Ethiopia nor even a Namibia.

Moroccan-Algerian relations have never been particularly good although they are always said to be fraternal, an example of the Arab adage that says: "My cousins and I against them [outside], my brothers and I against my cousins, I against my brother." Interspersing periods of attempted cooperation and coordination have been periods when they harbored each other's exiled opposition figures and movements, expelled each other's citizens, and recalled their own ambassadors. The worst problem in these conflictual relations, however, has been the long absence of an established boundary between the parties.

The evolution of the conflict has been a story of unresolved crises and unfulfilled promises that, like the conflict in the Horn of Africa and at roughly the same times, has run through two rounds of crisis escalation and deescalation without any resolution. Even before the independence of Algeria, in 1960, 1961, and 1962, Morocco received promises from the presidents of the Provisional Government of the Algerian Republic (GPRA), Ferhat 'Abbas and Benyussef Ben Khedda, to discuss the matter of the frontier; but when the GPRA was replaced by the government of Ahmed Ben Bella at independence in 1962, the commitment went out with its signatories.[22] Morocco pressed for the promised negotiations. Instead, border tensions continued over the following year, until an armed confrontation broke out in early October 1963.[23] The Moroccan army, with shorter communications lines, quickly turned the confrontation into a political statement by surrounding the westernmost Algerian city of Tindouf, which Morocco claimed. Ben Bella used the conflict to rally domestic political support and then began to negotiate a cease-fire. His army, however, felt that this was no position for a truce, and on the order of its chief, Colonel Boumedienne, launched a counterattack on the eastern (but uncontested) end of the borderlands, where its supply lines were shorter, surrounding the Moroccan town of Figuig. Thus mutually encircled at either end of the border and economically drained by the short but intense military effort, the two sides were ready for the mediation. Emperor Haile Selassie of Ethiopia and President Modibo Keita of Mali were effective in seizing on the ripe moment and negotiating a cease-fire in early November while channeling the conflict into an ad hoc OAU committee, where it could be pursued by diplomatic means.[24]

The war produced reconciliation and frustration. Hassan II and Ben Bella met at Cairo in July 1964 under Tunisian President Habib Bourguiba's good offices and then at Saïdia in April 1965, where Ben Bella finally made the GPRA promise to study the border his own. But he also began a military modernization program through large Soviet arms purchases, and both sides nursed their wounds, spoiling for another round that each was sure it could win. Ben Bella's army never forgave his concessions at Saïdia nor his premature truce while they were fighting the war and cited both as reasons, among others, for his overthrow in mid-July 1965.[25] The military regime of Boumedienne did improve relations with King Hassan in its turn over the rest of the decade, however, just as the disposition of the Spanish colony in the Western Sahara began to appear on the international agenda.

After initial disagreements reflecting conflicting long-term goals, the three states neighboring on Spanish Sahara joined forces in the pursuit of immediate aims. The campaign for the decolonization of the territory began with a United Nations General Assembly (UNGA) resolution of 1965 calling for negotiations, but the annual resolutions thereafter called for self-determination through referendum.[26] Throughout the 1960s, Morocco and Mauritania pursued their claims to the territory while Algeria led the campaign for a referendum and Spain periodically announced plans for one, each hoping for a weak Saharan state that it could dominate. Once Morocco recognized Mauritania in 1969, however, the three neighbors started coming together, shifting their competition for territory to cooperation against Spanish rule. Meanwhile, King Hassan had made his first trip to Algiers to attend the OAU Summit in September 1968 and, in return, Boumedienne had paid a state visit to Ifrane to draw up a Treaty of Solidarity and Cooperation with Morocco on 15 January 1969. On 27 May 1970, the two heads of state met in Tlemcen to coordinate their Saharan strategy and settle their border, and at the OAU Summit at Rabat on 15 June 1972, they signed a treaty that finally established a common frontier. Morocco also signed a friendship treaty in June 1970 with Mauritania that formally ended its claim on that country; and Hassan, Boumedienne and ould Daddah met in September at Nouadhibou to plan a joint campaign against the Spanish.

The most extraordinary component in this *renversement des alliances* was accomplished by Morocco. The early 1970s were difficult years for the monarchy, which had just lifted a five-year state of emergency, established two constitutions in rapid succession in 1970 and 1972, faced two barely unsuccessful military coups in 1971 and 1972, and had to contend in March 1973 with an extraparty left-wing opposition that found sanctuary in neighboring Algeria. The wisest policy was to mend fences on the Algerian side, and the best way to mend fences was to fill in the inexistent border. The 1972 border agreement essentially followed the Algerian terms: a line to be demarcated along the hammada escarpment south of the Dra', Moroccan renunciation of claims over Tindouf, cooperation in evacuating the iron mined at Gara Jebilet through Moroccan ports.[27] However, the agreement won Morocco one point: Algerian support for Moroccan claims over the one remaining piece of the irredenta, the Spanish Sahara. At the same OAU Summit, Boumedienne called in ould Daddah and told him to come to terms with Morocco.

Cooperation continued over the next two years. The day after the border convention was signed, Hassan told the OAU of Algeria's withdrawal from interest in the Sahara, and two years later, on 29 October 1974, Boumedienne explicitly blessed the Moroccan-Mauritanian solution for the territory at a meeting of heads of state (of which the Moroccans made a recording) of the Arab League in

Rabat, as did Algerian Foreign Minister Bouteflika in Rabat as late as July 1975. In July 1973, the three heads of state met at Agadir to coordinate their policy further. Presumably, in the first discussions at this point, Morocco was to receive Saqiet al-Hamra, the smaller part that contained the rich phosphate deposits of Bou Cra' first mined in 1973 and inhabited mainly by the Tekna; and Mauritania would receive the larger and poorer Rio de Oro inhabited mainly by Reqei-bat and Ulad Delim.[28] It was a Moroccan mistake not to maintain this colonial division along the 26th parallel.[29]

By 1974, the year of the Portuguese decolonization, pressure on Spain had begun to be effective, and events accelerated. Spain announced its intention to comply with the 1973 UNGA resolution and to hold a referendum in early 1975 in the territory. Faced with this challenge, the Moroccan and Mauritanian strategy finally jelled, and at the end of the year the two introduced a resolution in the UN General Assembly calling for an advisory opinion from the International Court of Justice on the precolonial legal ties of the territory to the Moroccan Empire and to a Mauritanian entity. When the court's opinion was rendered, in October 1975, it recognized such legal ties but declared them insufficient for current claims of territorial sovereignty; self-determination, not history or society, was the only acceptable basis for territorial disposition, as the UN resolution had declared for the Spanish colony from 1966 to 1973 and as stipulated in the original UN resolution 1514 (XV) on decolonization of 1960. Morocco, however, seized on the first phrase of the court's opinion and immediately massed 350,000 civilians on its southern border for a "Green March" into the territory.[30]

Under this threat, with Generalissimo Franco on his deathbed, Spain agreed to negotiate with Morocco and Mauritania. Morocco called off the Green March, and the three countries soon arrived at the Tripartite Agreement at Madrid on 14 November 1975, transferring administration of the territory to its two neighbors by 28 February 1976.[31] On 14 April 1976, the two administering countries concluded an agreement partitioning the territory, the northern two-thirds becoming the three Moroccan provinces of al-Ayoun, Smara, and Boujdor and the southern third becoming the Mauritanian province of Tiris al-Gharbia. Six months later, the Tiris voted for ould Daddah in the Mauritanian presidential elections along with the rest of the country and sent its eight representatives to the National Assembly. In November the Moroccan provinces elected their local councils along with the rest of Morocco, in June 1977 sent independent and Istiqlali representatives to the Moroccan National Assembly in the national elections, in May 1980 voted to accept two constitutional amendments on the monarchial succession and the parliamentary mandate, and in September 1984 again elected deputies from the Istiqlal, Democratic, Constitutionalist, and Popular parties. Morocco considered self-determination to have been expressed, reinforcing history.

Like other African colonies, the Western Sahara also had its transitional representative body under colonial rule. The Spanish instituted an assembly or *jama'* (*yemaa* in Hispano-Arabic) in 1967, elected for a second time in 1971, with 36 directly elected seats and 46 tribal chiefs; in 1973 membership was increased to 102.[32] This was the body that corresponded to the territorial assemblies and legislative councils in other African territories that often legislated the independence of their countries. In Spanish Sahara, the *jama'*'s resolutions frequently favored cooperation with the colonial power (as did other territorial assemblies on occasion) with bursts of individual independence; Hajj Khatri ould Sidi Said ould Jumani, chief of the leading Reqeibat Leguacem tribe, was arrested in an important nationalist demonstration in 1970 but elected president of the *jama'* in 1971, an example of the shifting loyalties common to the region. On 28 November 1975, 67 members of the *jama'* met under the aegis of the national liberation movement at Guelta Zemmur to declare themselves in favor of the movement and then to dissolve the body.[33] But on 22 December, 72 members endorsed the Tripartite Agreement in writing, and on 28 February, 65 members—including some 40 who had met at Guelta Zemmur—again supported the Moroccan administration at al-Ayoun. However, UN Secretary Waldheim refused to attend any of these meetings to certify them as providing self-determination.

A number of nationalist movements had appeared during the 1960s, usually initially under the patronage of one of the neighboring countries. The most important—because eventually most independent—arose in 1968 among conservative Muslim students in Rabat who formed the Saharan Liberation Front and in 1967 among local youths with some education who organized a widespread nationalist demonstration in al-Ayoun on 18 June 1970.[34] Pursued by the Spanish army, the leaders and sympathizers fled to Mauritania and in May 1973 began the first in a series of attacks on Spanish troops under the name of the Popular Front for the Liberation of Saqiet al-Hamra and Rio de Oro (PoLisaRio). The Polisario gradually shifted its patronage from Mauritania to Algeria, and when Spain withdrew, incorporated 3,000 Saharan auxiliaries from the Spanish army, with arms and equipment, plus nomads from elsewhere throughout the Sahara from as far as Mali and Libya. When the UN Visiting Mission came to the territory in mid-1975, it found strongest sentiment behind the Polisario and its option for independence.[35] When the Moroccan army entered the territory with the vindictiveness that "liberating" armies often show for "friendly" people, it was the Polisario that organized as much of the nomadic population as it could and carried them to refugee camps in Algeria, between Tindouf and Gara Jebilet. When a Sahrawi Arab Democratic Republic (SADR) was declared on 26 February 1976, it was the Polisario that made the declaration, before the more usual interval of guerrilla successes had taken place.

In the tradition of the area, the Polisario-SADR leadership has come from all over.[36] One group was born in southern Morocco: Prime Minister Mohammed Lamine, Information Minister Mohammed Salem ould Salek, Secretary General Mohammed 'Abdul 'aziz and his predecessor Mustafa al-Ouali, killed in June 1976, Deputy Secretary General Bachir Mustafa Sayed. Another group comes from Mauritania and was once active in Mauritanian politics: Foreign Minister Hakim Brahim and the politburo member Ahmed Baba Miske (who returned to Mauritania and was charged with plotting a coup in 1980). Others came from the Spanish territory itself. These groups of origin in turn redivide into groups of followers: pro-Algerians, pro-Libyans, and other factions, where the lines are more fluid and change with the season, according to the custom of the area. Above all, by 1978, the Polisario had developed a life of its own, independent of its primary Algerian sponsors and difficult to extinguish by fiat just as its political character is, above all, independent.

It is not certain when or why Algeria changed its position from publicly commited support to active opposition against the Moroccan-Mauritanian solution. It has been suggested that hard-liners in the Algerian Council of the Revolution eventually convinced Boumedienne or that he realized on his own that he had given up a strategic position or that he felt a Morocco-Mauritania-Spain agreement to be so unlikely that he could agree without any danger of realization. Any of these interpretations could be correct. It has also been suggested that he changed position after Algerian ratification of the convention on 17 May 1973 because he felt that nonratification by Morocco effectively annulled the treaty, but it is likely that the ratification issue was coincidental to more important causes, and in any case Algeria still considers the convention to be valid. It is most probable that the determinant event was the entry of a Saharan national liberation movement into action in the mid-1970s, where before there had only been names and claims of nationalist activity. When, in 1974, Morocco and Mauritania turned to the International Court of Justice (ICJ) for its advisory opinion, Algeria appeared before the court as a contesting rather than a supporting party. There are reports of a secret agreement between Algeria and Spain the same year to set up a pro-Algerian independent state under the Polisario, which Spanish policy then reversed.[37] In any event, by 1975, Boumedienne was personally committed to a defeat of the Moroccan position by all means and for a number of reasons: personal sense of umbrage at the successes of Moroccan diplomacy just when Algerian leadership was at its height; a personal sense of disdain for ould Daddah, whom he regarded as a renegade progressive who turned against his mentor; and a personal commitment to the desert warriors of the Saharan national liberation movement. When Bouteflika tried to cool the conflict and condone Moroccan policy in the joint communiqué of July 1975, he was purely and simply reversed by Boumedienne in the Algerian Council of the Revolution. On 10 November 1975, Boumedienne summoned ould Daddah to Bechar, threatened to throw 50,000 to 100,000 Algerian volunteers behind the Polisario, and told him that Algeria could annex Mauritania whenever Boumedienne liked; the Mauritanian president replied that the land could be annexed but never the people, and he walked out.[38] The war was on.

Prior to November 1975, the Saharan situation was fluid, with a number of competing parties pursuing different aims. With the signature of the Tripartite Agreement, conflict crystallized. There was an occupying power claiming sovereignty in each part of the territory, united in their efforts after mid-April 1976 by a treaty of mutual cooperation. Between 1976 and 1979, 9,000 Moroccan troops were stationed in Mauritania, in addition to the 40,000 Moroccan troops in southern Morocco and the three Saharan provinces; the Mauritanian army of 1,500 in 1975 was rapidly brought to 17,000, an increase that eloquently symbolizes the burden of the conflict. The war has followed three phases—the war against Mauritania until 1978, the war against Morocco until 1981, and the diplomatic war thereafter.

During the first phase, it was the Polisario strategy that determined the course of the conflict. Initially, the Polisario undertook direct attacks on the occupying Moroccan and Mauritanian armies as they took over the territory, and it was defeated. In early 1976, it withdrew to its Algerian sanctuary to prepare a new strategy. From then on, until mid-1978, both for tactical reasons and because of the nature of its leadership, the Polisario threw the main weight of its Fabian attacks against Mauritania. Each success engendered a military escalation, however, until the weight of escalation became too heavy for Mauritania to bear. In June 1976 a daring raid of some 500 Polisario troops in 100 vehicles under the leadership of al-Ouali struck 1,000 miles into Mauritania at the capital itself. The Nouakchott column was defeated, and al-Ouali was killed, and the Mauritanian army developed a more sophisticated defense against long-range raids, including counterattacks around preidentified cache points. A year later, in May 1977, another deep raid interrupted mining operations at the iron mine at Zouerate and carried off six French technicians as hostages. While Paris negotiated for their release, it also sent six Jaguars from France's Dakar base to harass Polisario units and protect its nationals. But even with such support, the war became an unbearable strain on Mauritanian society.

Mauritania's war was limited from the start by a weak domestic base. Despite ould Daddah's Greater Mauritanian dream, the Saharan issue never had much domestic appeal to cushion the economic burden of the policy. By 1977 defense took up 60 percent of the Mauritanian state budget and a 25 percent war tax was imposed on salaries. Still this was not enough, and by 1979 Mauritania had received $400 million from Saudi Arabia and the Gulf States and additional loans from France, Libya, and Morocco. The largely rural and partly nomadic population grumbled because the war was diverting money from rural development, the youth complained because it was undermining Mauritania's socialist option, and the businessmen protested because it limited their prosperity. A special congress of the Mauritanian People's Party (PPM), the single party of the regime, in January 1978 endorsed the Saharan policy but provided no enthusiasm to support the regime. Many of the new conscripts were blacks from the Senegal valley, who had no interest in the affair (except to prevent a Polisario takeover of Mauritania itself, for the liberation movement was remarkably scornful and even racist about the black population). In real terms, in the division of the territory, Mauritania received a potential iron mine at Agracha, rich fishing grounds off the coast, a fine port at Dakhla, a reunification of some families, and final settlement of the Moroccan irredentist threat; but in the process it also found itself occupied by Moroccan troops, burdened by a military budget, and torn by aims that had no benefit for many. As a consequence of all these burdens of the wartime situation and in accordance with some of the basic theorems of military coups, the

Mauritanian army overthrew ould Daddah on 10 July 1978 and put in a moderate military government under Colonel Mustafa ould Mohammed Salek.

The Polisario response was to declare a unilateral cease-fire with Mauritania, beginning a process that culminated, thirteen months later, in the signature of a provincial peace agreement between the two parties.[39] The new Mauritanian Military Committee of National Salvation (CMSN), set up in April 1979, was torn among pro-Libyan, pro-Moroccan, and pro-Algerian factions, each with different tribal attachments in the country, and did not find it easy to reconcile its aims of good relations with Morocco (to avoid revival of the irredentist claim) with peace with the Polisario (to avoid further military and economic drain). Four internal military coups followed before the new nationalist strongman, Lieutenant Colonel Khouna ould Haidalla—himself a Requeibat from the Western Sahara—became president and chairperson of a new Military Committee in January 1980. In July 1979, on the anniversary of the original announcement, the Polisario had announced the suspension of their unilateral truce and the capture of Tichla in the Tiris, providing enough military pressure for Mauritania to renounce its territorial claims and abandon its war against the Polisario in an agreement signed on 5 August.[40] Morocco immediately reinforced its garrison in the Tiris capital city of Dakhla and announced that the territory had reverted to Moroccan sovereignty while, in Dakhla and Rabat, crowds and notables proclaimed their allegiance to the king. There has been little military activity in the former Mauritanian part of the territory (renamed Wad el-Dahab for Rio de Oro).

Because the war was designed by the Polisario to extract a political decision from Morocco and not to conquer territory, the defection of Mauritania did not immediately prove to be a conclusive event. However, after 1979 the hardening of the Moroccan defense and rising rivalry between Algeria and Libya in their support of the Polisario returned military pressure to Mauritania, compounding its political instability. On Christmas Eve of 1980, a pro-Libyan coup in Nouakchott failed; in mid-March a pro-Moroccan coup also failed. A month later, in Tripoli and Nouakchott, Colonel Qaddafi urged the Mauritanians to form a union with the SADR and to join the 1975 Algero-Libyan defense pact (Treaty of Hassi Messaoud). In reaction, nationalist Mauritanian officers forced the removal of the Mauritanian civilian prime minister, the cancellation of a referendum on return to civilian multiparty rule, and the appointment of an anti-Libyan premier and other ministers.[41] Algerian personnel and supplies in Mauritania became more numerous during 1981, but the Libyans effectively took over the function of arming the Polisario with increasingly sophisticated matériel. During the year, Polisario camps began to move from the Tindouf region into northern Mauritania. Then, at the end of 1983, Moroccan defenses effectively cut the Western Sahara in half by running along the border for 25 kilometers along the northwest corner of Mauritania, thus forcing the Polisario to cross Mauritanian territory if its people were to reach Rio de Oro. The conflict began to reach its full Saharan dimension as a struggle for control of the entire western Sahara between the Dra' and the Senegal rivers, with Moroccans, Algerians, and the visionaries of distant Libya vying with Maritanians as well over their national existence. Militarily, the collapse of Mauritania is a doubly dangerous eventuality: It not only extends the conflict over a much larger area, but it also invites Moroccan hot pursuit and Algerian protection in an area where restraints on a direct Moroccan-Algerian war no longer obtain. As these possibilities of escalation increased, through the opening up of the whole Mauritanian battlefield, efforts at conflict resolution needed some powerful outside reinforcement if they were not to be pushed aside.

The second phase of the war has turned out differently from the first, essentially because of the different domestic foundations of the Mauritanian and Moroccan strategies. For both countries, the Saharan issue has been as popular as its success and as unpopular as its burden, but Morocco has far greater latitude in pursuing success and bearing its burden than Mauritania, and in Morocco the cause has been a popular national issue. For Morocco, the economic cost is high, but the political usefulness of the issue as a common bond and creed of the political system since 1974 is great, to the point where it imposes real constraints on the policy latitude of the incumbent or any other government. If the king were to be overthrown on the issue, it would be for weakness or tactical errors in pursuit of the cause, not for the pursuit itself, and the new government would be even more harshly attached to an anti-Algerian, pro-Saharan policy. In the meanwhile, the effect of popular commitment is to restrict severely the bargaining range of the king, as seen, for example, in his inability to secure ratification of the 1972 treaty (assuming he wanted to, which amounts to the same thing) and possibly also in his use of the "empty chair" approach to diplomatic occasions.

The Saharan issue is the final campaign in the struggle for political independence and territorial integrity. The king is outflanked on the issue by the Istiqlal party, and the other parties—including the

Communists—feel the cause to be so unquestionable that they can only situate themselves in the narrow space between king and Istiqlal. At best they can call—as has the USFP[42]—for an active pursuit of a political solution and not an "empty chair" policy at diplomatic meetings. The Green March was a remarkable feat of mobilization as well as logistics, and the belt tightening that has accompanied the continuing Saharan conflict is generally seen as an unfortunate national necessity.

There are obvious limits to this popular commitment; belt tightening for any national cause becomes unpopular after a while, but the while can be very long if the cause is well played and does not appear to be a losing one.[43] When, on top of the war effort, the international demand for phosphate fell in the mid-1970s and the country was hit by exceptionally severe droughts, the king canceled the Five-Year development Plan (1978-82) in its first year and imposed an austerity plan instead. The public has twice erupted against this austerity—in June 1981 in Casablanca and other cities and again in January 1984 in Tetuan and other places in the north—and has gone so far as to criticize the monarchy as well as the price rises, but never the Saharan campaign.

Moroccan strategy during the first phase was to occupy and defend the new provinces, bringing as much normalcy and prosperity as possible. This meant, above all, a policy of sedentarization to create conditions for both control and development, bringing a sudden and probably irreversible revolution to the lives of the 100,000 Sahrawis behind the Moroccan lines. From the north, Morocco brought a $230 million development program, civilian technicians and administrators, and new settlers, including Saharans who had fled Spanish and French territories in 1958 and thereafter. Successful occupation and normalcy have been necessary to restore the economic worth of the area by bringing the mining and transportation facilities back into operation. At the turn of the decade, in the second phase, Moroccan strategy changed: Population was gathered into the "useful triangle" around the towns and was assured normalcy and security while the desert hinterland was left to the Polisario or to search-and-destroy encounters. In the third phase, a normal life was assured behind the walls and the war was limited to the borderlands.

Militarily, the original strategy was to establish defensive points at strategic positions, a strategy of immobility compounded by a highly centralized command structure, which left decisions to Rabat and no initiative to the field. For the first few years, this strategy was successful in occupying and defending settlements and even in keeping open transportation routes, and it was able to keep attacks away from the settled core area of Smara, Bou Cra', al-Ayoun, and Boujdor in most cases. However, it was not able to occupy the vast stretches of desert or to interdict them to enemy use, and both outposts and units in the field were sitting ducks for the Polisario strategy of encirclement and attack. As a whole, the strategy was essentially defensive and depended on being able to hold on. By 1979, Morocco found holding on difficult.

Once Mauritania was knocked out of the war, the Polisario strategy changed. It threw its weight against Morocco, particularly increasing its attacks on southern Morocco proper (pre-1975 and even pre-1958), and it declared its goal to be a "military solution" not by conventional military victory but by destroying enough costly military matériel to break the Moroccan military machine—in reality, an "economic solution" as in Mauritania. The salient events of this campaign were the January and June 1979 raids on the commercial center and military base of Tantan, in Tarfaya, where the Polisario suffered heavy losses but where it also showed its ability to penetrate defenses and wreak havoc in Moroccan territory. The first Tantan attack was also important, however, as a concerted effort to impress and commit the new Algerian leadership of Col. Chadli Benjedid, meeting at the moment in party congress, whose devotion to the cause was rumored to be less firm than Boumedienne's. The Polisario inflicted two more Moroccan defeats in late August and mid-September (just as the Nonaligned States and the UN General Assembly were meeting). First the armed camp of Lebouirate fell with heavy losses, and then a Moroccan unit was ambushed near the camp of Zag. Changing fortunes led both sides to escalate in the battle of Smara in early October.[44] The Polisario attack on the holy city marked the first major attempt to penetrate the central perimeter of Moroccan forces and attack one of Sahara's principal towns; heavy casualties were inflicted on both sides, but the Polisario never got to the town. It did, however, move the Moroccans to use the new French Mirage F-1 as the fighting on both sides shifted from guerrilla to conventional warfare.

As Morocco began to lose fortified points in the eastern part of the desert and suffer attacks within its own (pre-1975) territory, it finally changed tactics in two ways, improving both the mobility of its military and the defense of the useful triangle in the northwest half of the territory. Early in November 1979, the Moroccan army launched Operation Ohoud, a 6,000-person drive across the territory to sweep out the rebels and recover lost positions. The campaign was only

partially successful, for the conventional Saharan army merely became guerrillas again and melted into the countryside or its Algerian
sanctuary. But the Moroccan army did regain its mobility and some
of its outposts. Ohoud was followed by two other mobile columns,
Zellaqa and Arak, during the first half of 1980, which took the
initiative from the Polisario and, even if not eliminating the guerrillas, gained an upper hand.[45] The Polisario had pushed the conflict
into a conventional war where the Moroccan army was stronger, and
the Moroccans pushed it back into guerrilla warfare, where a second
change has enabled them to keep it under control.

The other change was more unusual: erection of a six-to-nine-foot
wall and minefield diagonally across Saqiet al-Hamra protecting the
populated parts of the territory, around Smara, al-Ayoun, Bou Cra',
and Boujdor.[46] Construction was delayed in late 1980 by fierce Polisario attacks, but they were defeated, and it was completed in May
1981, with the walls around various sectors joined together a year
later. Behind the wall, the Royal Army could defend outposts, repulse attacks, and assure security; to the east, the mobile columns
could continue their counterguerrilla operations. Unable to stop the
wall, the Polisario shifted its attacks to foreign fishermen at sea,
punctuated by some highly publicized raids just before international
meetings—UN General Assembly, OAU Summit, and Non-aligned
States' sessions. Between March and October 1981, it engaged the
Royal Army in a major series of battles against Moroccan installations in Guelta Zemmur, along the eastern border where its positions
were once strong, finally causing Moroccan evacuation of the post in
early November after the use of SAM 6s to bring down a Moroccan
C-130 and two F-5s. This was Polisario's last military success, and it
too abandoned Guelta Zemmur as too vulnerable. The Polisario
launched heavy attacks against the wall in January and July 1982,
but suffered heavy losses and was unable to penetrate the barrier.
There was an effective cease-fire for a year, and the series of attacks
on the wall between July 1983 and January 1984 involved smaller
units and longer breathing spells. There was little military activity in
1984 except for one heavy attack against the wall in October, just
before the OAU Summit, that penetrated the defenses but was pinned
against the wall and repulsed. Morocco was even able to reopen the
phosphate mines at Bou Cra' and the conveyor belt to the sea since
July 1982. In the beginning of 1984, the wall around Smara was
expanded, and in April a new wall was built diagonally from Zag to
the Mauritanian border near Amgala, enclosing two-thirds of Saqiet
el-Hamra (and the Polisario "capital" of Haouza). A new wall was

added in January 1985 to enclose more than half of the remaining territory, from Mahbes, 30 kilometers from Algeria, southwest to Amgala. In August 1985, a fifth wall was built along the eastern border of Wad el-Dahab, around Guelta Zemmur, and then west to the sea south of Dakhla; and in April 1987, the sixth wall, built in record time, continued southward to the southern border before heading west (leaving the entire Cap Blanc to the Mauritanians).

After 1979 the Polisario was no longer in control of the strategy of the war; after mid-1982 it practically ceased military operations. The change in military fortunes had its effect on the political sympathies of the population behind the wall and on the morale of the population in the refugee camps near Tindouf. Between 1980 and 1984, the Polisario fighting force dropped from an estimated 10,000 to from 3,000 to 5,000 as fighters became harder to find. Still, despite reversals in Polisario fortunes, there was no likelihood that Morocco could win by military means alone as long as Polisario had sanctuary and political support outside of Moroccan reach, any more than the Polisario could win militarily against the entrenched Moroccans.

These developments were accompanied by a series of outside events that gave heart to the Moroccan side, even though not providing a decisive advantage. On 22 October 1979, the U.S. Administration decided after long debate to respond favorably to Morocco's request for helicopters and low-flying aircraft. Although the decision was made after months of gradual reevaluation of administration policy, it was made less on the merits of the case or the trends of the war than as a result of rising Saudi interest and of decreased congressional opposition. The decision was prepared by congressional hearings in July, which showed the beginnings of a changed attitude in both branches of government, and it was followed by visits of Under Secretary of State Warren Christopher to Rabat and National Security Advisor Zbigniew Brzezinski to Algiers to indicate that American support was designed to check military victory by one side (Polisario, in the event) and to prepare for a political solution.[47]

A year later, a new American administration more favorable to Morocco was elected. Even before its full foreign policy machinery was set up, Moroccan representatives approached Secretary of State Alexander Haig and received approval for the sale of 108 M-60 tanks at a crucial moment just before the assembly line on the tanks was to be shut down. The tanks were not to be delivered for three years and were not of primary use in the Sahara (although they were needed by an army that had only a tenth the number of heavy tanks in neighboring Algeria and was faced with a Polisario also newly equipped with Soviet tanks), and indeed the order was suspended the following year when Morocco was unable to pay for them. But they indicated an increase in diplomatic support, and they were accompanied by accelerated deliveries of the OV-10 reconnaissance planes and F-5 fighters, by official Defense Department visits and cooperation in providing electronic surveillance of the wall, and by the removal of the Carter administration's insistence on a linkage between arms deliveries and "progress toward a peaceful negotiated settlement."[48]

The third phase of the war has been primarily diplomatic and is closely associated with Algeria's efforts on behalf of the Polisario. The Algerian strategy has been complex. It has consisted of enough military support to keep the Polisario alive and bleed the enemy, and diplomatic support for the SADR to keep the issue alive and eventually win, applying the lessons of the Algerian revolutionary war. At the end of 1975 there were some 20,000 Algerian troops in the Spanish Sahara and the Tindouf area, and in January 1976 there was a direct clash between Moroccan and Algerian troops at Amgala. The battle was crucial, for it set one of the constraints of the conflict: no more direct contact between the two major adversaries. But the Polisario operated by crossing the border into pre-1975 Morocco and returning to retrain and refuel in its Algerian sanctuary. In February 1976, in some frustration, Hassan publicly called on Algeria to come out and fight or negotiate; Boumedienne did neither.[49] In 1978 some further clashes in southern Morocco were said to involve Algerian troops, and the atmosphere tightened again, but nothing was proved. As a result of such attacks, King Hassan in early June 1979 declared the right of hot pursuit into Algerian bases and urgently requested a meeting of the UN Security Council. Both measures were without effect: Hot pursuit has not been used for fear of setting off a Moroccan-Algerian war, and the UN Session on 20–25 June ended in adjournment for lack of proof of Algerian involvement in the attacks.[50] In July 1980, Moroccan planes crossed the border in pursuit of the Polisario. Again, in April 1981, Moroccan troops pursued Polisario units into Algeria after the Polisario had broken an agreement negotiated with Algeria in September barring attacks on pre-1975 Morocco from Algerian sanctuary.[51] Such incidents served to reinforce rather than weaken the Amgala understanding.

There are repeated stories about the active role of Algerian troops with the Polisario, but no proof, and, above all, no prisoners since Amgala. In the summer of 1975 and again in October 1978, Boumedienne told the king that no Algerian soldiers had or would cross the 1972 Moroccan-Algerian border[52] although this does not cover their presence in the Western Sahara. In the absence of evidence of direct participation, Algeria can be said to advise, logistically support, and train the Polisario using Russian weapons, having delegated to Libya the military supply function following the Treaty of Hassi Messaoud at the end of 1975. In addition, Algeria has provided sanctuary for the four groups of refugee camps, which, under the constraints against direct military contact, has been crucially protective.

Politically, Algeria has disclaimed any interest in the territory so often as to be suspect but has repeatedly insisted on the procedures of self-determination. Although it has forgotten that most African countries were not born through a referendum, contrary to Algerian experience, it has pressed the self-determination resolution through a number of international organizations as part of its campaign. The UNGA has long (but not initially) been on record in favor of a referendum, equating referendum with independence, but, under Algerian pressure, abandoned referendum for direct negotiation with the Polisario, implying recognition. In 1975 it passed two contradictory resolutions, one on an Algerian initiative calling for self-determination and the other favorable to Morocco taking note of the Madrid Tripartite Agreement; in 1978 it again passed two contradictory resolutions, one on an Algerian initiative calling for self-determination and independence and the other expressing confidence in the OAU ad hoc committee; in 1979 it unambiguously supported the Polisario as representative of the Saharan people and called on Morocco to withdraw; in 1980 it defeated a moderate motion on OAU efforts to pass an Algerian motion calling for self-determination and independence; in 1981 it passed both an OAU resolution supporting a referendum and an Algerian resolution calling for direct Moroccan-Polisario negotiations; in 1982 it called for direct negotiations, self-determination, and independence; after 1983 it adopted Algerian resolutions calling for negotiation between Morocco and the Polisario. The Arab League was earlier won over by Moroccan diplomacy,[53] a process completed by Boumedienne's endorsing speech at Rabat in 1974, and for long the only other Arab state besides Algeria that recognized the SADR was South Yemen (not even Libya and Syria until 1980).

It is in the OAU that Algeria has sought to recoup its diplomatic leadership and where the major diplomatic battle has been waged until it nearly destroyed the organization. Each year until 1979, the battle ended in a draw, but by its very continuation it provided a sense of an unresolved problem that has been useful to the Polisario. Morocco and Mauritania (the prestige of ould Daddah being important) were long able to block discussion of the problem in the annual OAU Summit with a threat to withdraw from the organization if it gave any recognition to the Polisario although they lost the vote in the preliminary Council of Ministers in 1976. The OAU Summit that year decided to submit the problem to a special summit, which Morocco accepted on condition that all heads of state be present; the meeting was scheduled for Lusaka in 1976 and then for Libreville and understandably never took place. The African heads of state had no desire to be torn publicly between Morocco and Algeria, two major OAU members. Finally, in 1978, the problem was handed to an ad hoc Committee of Wisemen, whose report in the Monrovia Summit of 1979 (discussed later) was the occasion finally for a vote supporting self-determination, passed with some Algerian procedural artifices. As of the OAU meeting in 1979, fourteen African states besides Algeria had recognized the SADR: Angola, Benin, Burundi, Congo, Ethiopia, Equatorial Guinea, Guinea-Bissau, Madagascar, Mozambique, Rwanda, São Tomé and Principe, Seychelles, Tanzania, Togo, and Botswana (plus North Korea, Vietnam, Cambodia, Laos, and Panama outside the region).

By 1980, as the military conflict began to be locked in a stalemate, the diplomatic conflict took the forefront. By the time of the OAU meeting in July, twelve more African states—Cape Verde, Ghana, Uganda, Lesotho, Zambia, Mali, Chad, Swaziland, Sierra Leone, Zimbabwe, and Libya—had joined in recognizing the SADR, plus nine non-African states.[54] Faced with admission of the SADR and the split of the organization by the withdrawal of Morocco and an undetermined number of its friends, the heads of state agreed to suspend the admission until the Committee of Wisemen had a final chance at an agreeable solution. The decision was reaffirmed in the OAU midterm Council of Ministers meeting in February. The committee spent the year in a desultory search but could only reaffirm its earlier recommendations. When the OAU president, Siaka Stevens of Sierra Leone, announced that the SADR had the necessary votes for admission at the 1981 OAU Summit at Nairobi, King Hassan proposed the Committee of Wisemen's solution of a referendum, and the conflict appeared finally to have shifted to a decision by legitimate means.

Although this effort will receive greater attention later as conflict resolution, it is important to note that referendum does not mean an end or abatement of the conflict, but merely its transferal to another means of determination. Unlike a negotiated solution, where each side presumably receives something in exchange for its agreement to drop hostilities, the referendum is a zero-sum winner-take-all proposition, at least as defined by the OAU. Discussions on the referendum made good progress in the seven months after the June Summit, but the nearness of an apparent diplomatic victory was too much for the SADR supporters. At the mid-term Council of Ministers meeting in Addis Ababa in February 1982, generally reserved for administrative and budgetary matters and unqualified to make political decisions, the SADR was seated by the outgoing administrative secretary general, Edem Kodjo, under pressure from the radical states—Algeria in the region and more distant radicals with only an ideological stake in the decision such as Zimbabwe, Mozambique, Seychelles, Congo, and Benin.[55]

The admission of the SADR had catastrophic consequences for inter-African relations. The February Council of Ministers meeting was canceled for lack of a quorum when nineteen states—Cameroon, Comoro Islands, Djibouti, Gabon, Gambia, Guinea, Equatorial Guinea, Ivory Coast, Liberia, Morocco, Mauritius, Niger, Central African Republic, Senegal, Somalia, Sudan, Tunisia, Upper Volta, Zaire—walked out of the meeting, leaving the OAU without a budget, although the remaining states declared the meeting to have been held anyhow. Subsequent OAU meetings were boycotted by one side or the other because the SADR was present or absent. When the 1982 Summit was to meet in Libya, under the controversial aegis of Qaddafi, the meeting was twice boycotted by enough states to prevent a quorum, leaving the OAU without a secretary general or a new president. Only a year later and in another capital, on 7 to 10 June 1983 in Addis Ababa, was the organization able to hold its nineteenth summit—and that only when the threat of a continued Moroccan-led boycott of more than nineteen states brought the Polisario's supporters to make it "temporarily suspend its membership in the OAU." The result of the nonsolution of the Saharan conflict was the temporary destruction of the African regional organization, of its activities, and of its progress toward conflict resolution. The twentieth summit of the organization was postponed until 12 November 1984 because of the death of its president-designate, Sekou Toure of Guinea; but when it met, Mauritania, Chad, and Nigeria had joined the majority in recognizing the SADR, which was seated as the fifty-first member of the OAU. Morocco withdrew from the organization, and the deadlock was complete. One party had recognition but no territory; the other had the territory but no recognition.

Thus, the conflict has gone through several phases: first a sudden, carefully controlled escalation that removed Spain from the territory, then a stalemate among the remaining parties until one of them could not stand the weight of the stalemate any longer and dropped out; after that, the remaining parties returned to their stalemate, gradually escalating their choice of arms and use of tactics until a new stalemate came, held, and then was gradually extended by Moroccan territorial control; then the conflict shifted to the diplomatic arena, where another stalemate occurred. By 1985, possibilities for escalation had either been exhausted or implied such a rise in the stakes as to be excluded. On the ground, each side is safe in its home territory, the Moroccans secure behind the wall and the Polisario secure behind the Algerian border, although Moroccan territory still was open to isolated terrorist attacks whereas Algerian sanctuary was still inviolate. The completion and advances of the Moroccan wall throughout the 1980s extended Moroccan "home territory" by extending the "mountains" of Southern Morocco. In the process, it left eastern fringes of the Sahara a no-man's-land. Although reduced to a stalemated war of positions, the conflict continued, not just for territorial control and inviolability, which can never be fully achieved as long as each enjoys sanctuary, but over international recognition and legitimization. The question now was whether the stalemate would hold until one of the parties collapsed internally or would be turned to conflict resolution.

Yet holding out was still preferable for both sides and remained their first track strategy. For Morocco to win completely, Algeria would be required to cut loose the Polisario—end its arms or gasoline supplies and Libyan transit, its military activities from the refugee camps, and its use of Algiers as its political or diplomatic platform—or the Polisario would have to collapse internally—run out of troops and splinter into rival factions. Thus, beyond defense of the wall and short of an unlikely war and victory over Algeria, Morocco's military victory over the Polisario would depend on its diplomatic ability to win away Algerian support. Morocco might also win by simply holding onto the wall, keeping the Polisario on the other side, and hoping it would fade away into irrelevance as recognized Moroccan territory gradually came to include the inhabited Sahara and then its inhospitable hinterland. For Polisario to win, it would need an overwhelming wave of diplomatic recognitions leading to membership for the SADR in the UN and other international organizations and also a string of military conquests across the wall and some spectacular raids over the mountains deep into Moroccan territory, forcing Moroccan withdrawal from the Saharan territory. But the Polisario could also win by simply being active enough to deny Morocco either of its victories and eventually causing internal unrest and a political breakdown in Morocco.[56] Neither is very likely in its entirety, but each contains some likely elements. It is this contradiction that kept each side on its initial policy track in search for an unlikely victory and that long prevented a second track or negotiated solution from coming into view. Yet, in the absence of total military victory, a solution requires some negotiation. War is military effort to force a political decision, and it is on the political level that war has to be ended.

Conflict Resolution

Attempts at resolving or even managing conflict in North Africa have been strikingly unsuccessful and show some rather curious characteristics. There has been no lack of procedures and formulas that appear to bridge the conflicting points of view, but even when these are attained, they are aborted somewhere along the way, sometimes even after having been agreed to. This is approach-avoidance behavior in its extreme,[57] where parties bog down in the cross-pressures of conflicting drives, and might be explained by a cultural attitude toward negotiation rather than by the inadequacy of the solution itself. Although there is little corroborative evidence from other sources, a close reading of the various negotiations indicates a "banking" attitude toward concessions, in which the parties ask that they be twice paid, first by a countercession, which is then banked, and then by a second concession. This attitude extends even to concluded agreements, which must then be the source of further payments before being ratified; and when the payment is naturally refused (because it, too, would require two concessions), the ratification or the implementation is withheld. The attitude is compounded by a growing distrust among the parties and an increasing inability to communicate—to read each other's signals correctly.

Taken to its extreme, the approach leads to a neglect of real goals and a fixation on reaction to means. Appointments are missed—however useful they may have been to the furtherance of goals in the conflict—because of a detracting incident—a military incident, a position on another issue—that is treated as if it were a substantive and unacceptable position on the other side, not merely a wayward means. All these traits add up to a fixation on the process to the exclusion of meaningful goals and position, suggesting that such goals are not clear in the parties' minds. Algeria has not seemed sure whether it wants to win independence for the Sahara or to topple the

Moroccan monarchy, and Morocco has not conveyed much assurance that its aims are limited to part of the Sahara alone and do not still extend to parts of Algeria or Mauritania or that it would fairly seek and accept the verdict of self-determination. If this analysis is correct, North African states need help more than most in finding suitable ways to extricate themselves from their conflict and will also be more difficult than most to deal with in mediation. But mediation will also be worth the effort because some tendency toward accommodation is already present.

Each of the two territorial crises in Morocco-Algerian relations—1963 and 1975 onward—was accompanied by attempts at conflict management and resolution. Some failed because the moment was not ripe and others for more complex reasons, including a lack of skill in taking advantage of moments that were ripe. The two phases of the first crisis were simple and well executed, involving first a successful attempt by conciliators to manage the conflict by bringing about a cease-fire and agreement to investigate and then a lengthy multilateral investigation process, which gradually contributed to a bilateral settlement of the conflict. In the cease-fire, the mediating leaders, Keita of Mali and Haile Selassie of Ethiopia, were assisted by the prestige of the newly formed OAU within which they operated. But, above all, they took advantage of a stalemate on the battlefield in which two weeks of fighting produced mutual encirclement of military positions and military-economic exhaustion. Hands around each other's neck and panting, as it were, the two fighters were ready to be separated in a draw.[58]

The mediated cease-fire was accompanied by an agreement to establish a committee within the OAU, composed of Mali, Senegal, Ivory Coast, Nigeria, Sudan, Tanganyika (to become Tanzania), and Ethiopia, in order to examine the grievances (but not actually to establish a border). At the end of the process in 1967, the committee nearly ruled in favor of Algeria, but was called to order by Nigeria, which reminded the other members that its charge was to mediate and reconcile, not to arbitrate.[59] Rather than ruling on the causes of the war and the solution of the boundary dispute, the committee started a process that allowed the parties to move on toward a settlement of their own (as it could not have done had it acted as an arbitrator). The Ifrane Solidarity and Cooperation Treaty of 1969, the Tlemcen framework agreement of 1970, and the Rabat border convention of 1972 were the result. The moment was ready for settlement in the early 1970s because of the pressures on both sides to lessen tension between them and because of the unattainability of any major changes. Moroccan irredentism was worn down to size.

Why these elements were not retained as a settlement of at least part of the conflict is still somewhat of a mystery. Morocco made a monumental error in not ratifying the Rabat convention of 1972 although the border is no longer in dispute. Algeria defaulted, too, on the other parts of the agreement regarding the Sahara, but Morocco would have been in a far better position to call in its commitments and even to pursue the structural rivalry if it had followed through with its own part of the agreement rather than holding out for twice-paid concessions. Instead, both parties let incidents and opportunities stand in the way of commitments.

Although the Western Sahara was apparently covered in the margins of the 1970-72 agreements, it was bound to be swept up to the surface again by the underlying structural conflict between the two neighbors. There have been six phases to the conflict resolution efforts in the Saharan crisis: an initial flurry of contacts from outside states in 1976; a long period to let the stalemate ripen, during which the parties to the conflict kept in touch; a brief time for conciliation in July-September 1978 (between the overthrow of ould Daddah and the illness of Boumedienne) that was grasped both by the OAU and by other would-be mediators but then let slip; and then repeated attempts to bring Hassan and Boumedienne's successor together that finally began to work in 1983, but then foundered on further misunderstanding; and finally a revival of meetings in 1987-88 under the auspices of King Fahd, the pressure of the deadlock, and the activity of the UN Secretary General, with prospects for an accord and a referendum.

During the first half of 1976, the heads of state or other top officials of Saudi Arabia, Tunisia, Iraq, Kuwait, Egypt, Senegal, Guinea, Gabon, the Palestine Liberation Organization, the Arab League, and the OAU visited or otherwise contacted one or both parties to ascertain possibilities of reconciliation. They rapidly ascertained that there were none. At this point, no extraregional state was interested either. Four attempts, however, were especially serious.[60] One was the weeklong shuttle of Hosni Mubarak, Egyptian vice-president, in late January and early February, proposing a cease-fire, foreign ministers' meeting, and then summit among the three states in the conflict; Algeria demanded Moroccan evacuation of the Sahara before the summit, however, and Morocco agreed only to the first two steps. The sides had not yet tested their strength and established a stalemate. Another was the effort, between February and May, by President Senghor to meet the form of all demands by proposing a referendum that would confirm the partition and occupation of the territory, as in the case of Irian Barat, along with joint exploitation of Gara Jebilet and Bou Cra'. In March, on Saudi and Yemeni request, an Arab League mission worked out an agreement among the parties not to use force, but it did not include the Polisario. At the end of 1977, the Saudis again sought to mediate, and a summit in Riad was rumored but never materialized. Only the latter attempt was tied to the evolution of the conflict, for it was a response to the escalation produced by the Zouerate raid and the intervention of French Jaguars. But neither the escalation nor the stalemate was serious enough during this period to produce a will to negotiate among the parties. Each side at this point expected victory, if not easy victory: The Moroccans were surprised by the resistance of the Polisario, which they had discounted, and the Algerians and Polisario were true believers in their cause.

In 1977 and 1978, there were continuing contacts among parties. Polisario approached Morocco and Mauritania separately in September 1977 to inquire about a separate peace against the other party; unfortunately for the proposer, the two allies exchanged intelligence reports.[61] Again, in early 1978, Polisario again suggested a separate peace with Mauritania, and in May Mali tried to bring the two together; in fact, at first Mali sought a whole Saharan summit, with the participants in the Chad conflict invited as well.[62] The summit never materialized, for other talks were going on without the Polisario. In November 1977, the king approached Boumedienne about a political solution, and talks began in Fes in November and in Lausanne in December between Presidential Adviser Ahmed Taleb Ibrahimi and Ambassador (Princess) Lalla Aicha, later replaced by Royal Adviser Ahmed Redha Guedira as the talks continued into 1978.[63] They were to culminate in a meeting of the king and the president in Brussels on 6 June—according to some sources, to complete the details of a Moroccan-Polisario division of the territory—but the king stayed home; another meeting in Brussels scheduled for 24–25 September was canceled by Boumedienne's illness. The initiative has been termed by the king[64] one of the three moments when the two sides were close to an agreement, and the time was indeed ripe.

The overthrow of ould Daddah was the culmination of the Polisario's Mauritanian strategy; but when it occurred, they did not know how to take it. The unilateral cease-fire was a clever move, for the new military rulers of Mauritania were torn between their desire not to lose face as the military and as nationalists—and hence to pursue the war—and their desire to end the war, which they blamed on ould Daddah. The cease-fire removed the need to prove their continuing respectability as warmakers, and they could concentrate on their ability as peacemakers. France, Libya, and Mali saw the importance of the moment and offered venues, projects, and good offices. A meeting between Mauritanians and Polisario in Bamako was also attended by two of the Moroccan king's closest collaborators, Guedira and Colonel Ahmed Dlimi, but the report of the meeting reached the king at the same time that the news of Boumedienne's illness did; and he is reported to have declared that as long as Boumedienne was dying, talks were no longer necessary. On the Algerian side, Boumedienne had lost interest just at the moment that the Mauritanian coup seemed to open opportunities; the Polisario was doing well on the ground, the king's support for Sadat's peace initiative ran counter to Boumedienne's best efforts for the PLO at the Damascus summit of the Arab League, and the king had dropped a promising opening. The ripe moment had passed.

If the Moroccan-Algerian conflict was not properly seized for settlement, the Polisario-Mauritanian conflict was becoming ever riper. In the midsummer and then fall of 1978, a new formula appeared, associated with, but denied by, the French and also associated with Algeria. The original form involved handing the Tiris to the Polisario, who would then federate with Mauritania. Hassan then threw cold water on this proposal in an enigmatic speech on August 20, when he declared that he would not permit a state "of a different ideology" on Morocco's southern border. In response, a variant on the formula was put forward: a "Gambian solution" involving a slight retraction of the southern border of the Moroccan Sahara so that the Polisario-Tiris would be completely surrounded by Mauritania. The Polisario turned this down at its IV Congress in late September 1978, requiring recognition, cession of the Tiris, and a withdrawal of Mauritanian troops as preconditions for any negotiation.

The primary obstacle in the 1978 round of proposals and contacts and for a long time thereafter was the fact that the ripe moment for some was not ripe for others: Any solution was wasted as long as the status of Boumedienne and, eventually, his successor, was unsettled. Thereafter, a decent interval was also required so that the new team of Colonel BenJedid could settle into place and any policy changes not have the appearance of a public disavowal of his popular predecessor. The moment was, therefore, not ripe for a new Algerian position until after BenJedid's consolidation of power in the party congress of June 1980. Unfortunately, even after the consolidation, the government still contained hard-liners, for whom continued support for the Polisario was the last symbolic test of fidelity to Boumedienne's legacy as the regime went about reversing most of the other aspects of his previous policy. Thus, a top level personal commitment to national liberation under Boumedienne was institutionalized as an inflexible policy against negotiations under BenJedid even though there was no deep interest or feeling behind it. Moreover, there was little cost in the Algerian policy, but great cost to Algerian prestige in its abandonment.

Observers have generally agreed, perhaps too optimistically, that the advent of a new leadership in Algeria provided an opening for a settlement, but they have missed this element of timing and cost. A new administration, its positions not yet crystallized, could benefit from a decisive move properly presented to augment its prestige. Initially, the context tended to be propitious, too, because of the stalemate and the danger of war between the two neighboring armies that further escalation would bring, but the mutual observance of the Amgala understanding reduced that danger and stabilized the stalemate. It would have been even more propitious if the stalemate had already been more apparent in 1979—if the Moroccan military organization had been better adapted to the conditions of conflict by being allowed greater mobility and initiative in the field and if Morocco had not felt abandoned by its customary arms supplier at a moment when it needed support. Both conditions were later remedied, by Operation Ohoud and then by the wall and by the American decision in late 1979 to release counterinsurgency arms. But in the meantime, Algeria's position had been allowed to harden, the mediators made some crucial mistakes, and the king missed his appointments again on the weakest of pretexts.

The most promising mediation effort was set up before Boumedienne's death at the 1978 OAU Summit in Khartoum by reviving the seven-state ad hoc committee of 1964–67 as a Committee of Wisemen. Its composition was the subject of intense conflict from the beginning: Ivory Coast's President Félix Houphouët-Boigny dropped in and out of its membership,[65] Algeria objected strongly to OAU President Ga'faar Nimeiry of Sudan for his positions on issues of Arab politics and to Senegalese President Senghor for his sympathies for Morocco, Tanzanian President Julius Nyerere was actively partisan in favor of the Polisario, and Hassan II cited his objection to Nyerere and Malian President Moussa Traore as a reason for missing one of the appointments. The work of the committee of the presidents of Mali, Guinea, Nigeria, Ivory Coast, Tanzania, and Sudan was, therefore, carried out essentially by a working group of Traore and the Nigerian president, first Olusegun Obasanjo and then Shehu Shagari, constituted at the end of November 1978.[66] The committee met in Khartoum at the end of June 1979 to consider the report of the working group, which was then forwarded to the foreign ministers' and summit meetings of the OAU in Monrovia. The mistake of the committee lay in its charge to adjudicate rather than to mediate the dispute (although, by the same token, the weakness of the OAU and the alternatives before it meant that it had no power to oblige both sides to accept its mediation). King Hassan indicated that he would attend the Monrovia Summit if President BenJedid did, too. However, when the committee report called for a cease-fire and an exercise of self-determination in the Western Sahara and ordered a referendum (under unspecified conditions), Hassan reneged again, claiming that a recent Polisario raid on Southern Morocco from Algerian bases made a meeting impossible.[67] The committee scheduled another meeting in early December in Monrovia in response to the king's declaration that he would meet BenJedid anytime, but again he stayed home at the last minute. The committee resolution was nonetheless moderate, calling for a Moroccan withdrawal only from the Mauritanian part of the territory.

The OAU meeting of 1980 was even more propitious for some progress toward settlement: Not only was it the "rain date" for the missed meeting of the previous year for the heads of state, with better conditions of physical security in Freetown than had obtained in Monrovia, but it was also the date of the conflict deadline, when the SADR would have enough votes to become a member of the OAU. But because twenty-six of the fifty-one members of the OAU had recognized the SADR by 3 July, in the middle of the summit meeting, the recognition vote was no longer a threat but a reality. Attention, therefore, swung away from the Wisemen's attempt to conciliate and turned to the recognition issue. Holding in reserve its last card— the threat to pull out of the organization with an undetermined number of its supporters—Morocco called for a decision as to whether the SADR filled the OAU definition of a "state," a challenge of charter interpretation requiring a two-thirds vote. At the same time, it agreed to "open discussions with all interested and concerned parties," a major concession but one that also brought in the elected and tribal representatives of the territory and members of the Association of Natives of Saqiet al-Hamra and Rio de Oro (AOSaRio) as

well as the Polisario and Algeria. Such contacts were pursued by the
Wisemen, and in another meeting in Freetown in early September the
further small concession was obtained that a referendum need not
require the withdrawal of the Moroccans.[68] The paradoxical problem
faced by any would-be conciliator was that neither side seemed in
danger of losing and, thanks to outside support—Saudi Arabia for
Morocco, Libya for Polisario—neither side was even hurting very
badly. Conceivably, the conflict could go on forever.

It was the deadline of admission to the OAU that brought the
Wisemen's mediation to fruition. To the pleased—if skeptical—surprise of the OAU members, the king at the 1981 Summit at Nairobi
on 27 June reversed his position and agreed to a "supervised referendum" in the territory. The OAU leaped at the occasion and immediately turned the Wisemen into an Implementation Committee of
Kenya (then OAU president), Sudan, Nigeria, Guinea, Mali, Sierra
Leone, and Tanzania to organize a cease-fire and referendum with
the help of the UN. The Polisario's conditions before the meeting
included direct negotiations with Morocco over a cease-fire, withdrawal of Moroccan administration and armed forces 150 kilometers
north of the 1956 border (thus withdrawal from Tarfaya as well) and
their replacement by an international administration and peacekeeping force, and a vote for or against independence[69] from lists supplied
by the Polisario. Morocco's position opposed direct negotiations or
Moroccan withdrawal or international administration, but did not
oppose a peacekeeping force or military consignment to the bar-
racks; it called for use of the Spanish census list and voting on a
single question of approval of allegiance to the kingdom—"a referendum of confirmation" as the king presented it to his people.

Between these positions, the committee meeting in Nairobi at the
end of August ("Nairobi II") was able to establish a good deal of
common ground.[70] The referendum would take place in the Western
Sahara; voters on the Spanish list over eighteen years of age, including those documented by the UN high commissioner for refugees in
the refugee camps and those included through normal population
growth (20,000 by 1982 at 3 percent), would vote for either independence or integration with Morocco. A cease-fire would be negotiated
under the auspices of the committee, followed by the installation of a
peacekeeping force and an impartial interim administration working
in collaboration with the existing administration structures while
existing troops would be confined to their bases. The five months
following Nairobi II were filled with intensive consultation with the
UN Secretariat over implementation of the points decided and those

remaining. In early February 1982 the committee finally met again ("Nairobi III") to work on the cease-fire, but the best they could do was to annul some pro-Polisario attempts to change the terms of the Nairobi II agreement. Two weeks later, the Addis Ababa Council of Ministers' meeting admitted the SADR to its rump session, suspending the OAU mediation.

In political terms, as the Addis Ababa session showed, the parties were far from agreement, but—and in part because—in technical terms many of the conditions for a fair and free referendum had been established. Other points remained. There was no decision as to whether the results would be announced for the whole territory or whether a split (as, for example, along the colonial boundary between Saqiet al-Hamra and Rio de Oro on the twenty-sixth parallel) would be allowed, although the presumption was in favor of the former. The matter of the peacekeeping and administrative forces accounted for much of the delay between Nairobi II and III and was still not resolved; the OAU at the same time was engaged in the costly and politically divisive task of setting up similar forces in Chad, with encouraging results. The cease-fire was theoretically a simpler matter that could be proclaimed by the Implementation Committee (as the UN Security Council had done on various occasions in the Middle East), but the Polisario was more interested in the recognition that its precondition of negotiations implied than in the cease-fire itself. The electorate was the most complicated matter, for fitting names to faces in a nomadic society is an exercise in uncertainty. Yet this uncertainty should not be exaggerated, as it often has been: It is quite possible for a panel of Saharan tribal authorities—even with sympathies divided—to identify individuals on the basis of lineage, which is well known to them.

But behind these questions is the normal politics of the exercise. It is in each side's interest to establish an electorate favorable to it although some favorable to the other party may be included as long as they are in the minority. Therefore, the mediator can obtain agreement to an electorate with sectors expected to be favorable to each side plus an undetermined sector in between as long as each side feels it has a winning chance with that sector. The process is then one of adding on segments until a total electorate is reached that each side feels it is likely to win. Obviously, one will be wrong in the end. If, however, the process of constituting an electorate takes a turn that seems irretrievably hostile to one side, it will break off negotiations and quit the process. That is what happened. With its bird nearly in hand in the OAU and the two in the bush fading before committee decisions that left Morocco a good chance at winning, the Polisario opted for immediate recognition for its government-in-exile. The fault was not that of the mediators, who had done a conscientious job of putting together fair conditions for a settlement.[71]

The OAU has played a number of roles at the same time in the conflict, only some of them supportive of its efforts at mediation. Its most disruptive role was as an arena for the conflict itself, an alternative place where victory was within grasp when it was out of reach on the battlefield. Yet there was no avoiding this situation, for refusal to mark a Polisario victory would be a Moroccan victory and refusal to face that test would remove an important element from the stalemate that compelled negotiation. The diplomatic victory of the Polisario in 1984 counterbalanced Moroccan military predominance on the ground and brought about an unmatched stalemate. Another role of the OAU, as seen, was that of a would-be mediator, either to provide an alternative path to a decision through referendum or to serve as a catalyst for bilateral negotiations. Unfortunately, the purely technical problems involved in holding a referendum—identifying the electorate, providing an interim administration, installing a peacekeeping force—are simply beyond the capabilities of the organization and are not particularly attractive opportunities for UN involvement either (although OAU resolutions did call for UN assistance). A third role of the OAU is that of legitimizer. In a situation where Moroccan-organized votes were suspect and no other organ or party was available to certify free and fair voting, the OAU became the necessary stamp of legitimacy for any popular expression of will, whether decisive or merely confirmatory. The OAU was, therefore, condemned to sponsor a process of resolution that was a strain on its political capabilities and was at the very edge of, if not beyond, its technical capacities.

France and the United States have long indicated that they do not wish to mediate, but they could lend weight and good offices to the OAU and help channel the conflict in its direction. The U.S. arms deliveries to Morocco and its signals to Algeria in favor of a political solution from a position of a military balance have been of some help, but they would have to be accompanied by even stronger pressures toward mediation than have been forthcoming. When the United States refused to deliver the requested arms to Morocco, it was too slow and too faint in signaling Algeria that this was not a permanent position but one that could be revised if a political solution were not sought. An inept and overly principled congressional attitude during Carter's first Congress helped keep such signals faint.

Similarly, instead of treating Morocco to moral debates about American foreign policy, the same refusal could have been conveyed to Morocco as reversible on the condition that OAU—or any other—mediation be accepted. In January 1980, the United States finally began some mild pressure for a political solution, an appropriate complement to its arms decision,[72] but this was explicitly dropped with the change in administrations in Washington the next year.

Beyond the fuzzy perceptions of those who saw Hassan as an Arab shah and those who considered anticommunism in one country as the sole criterion of American policy, the real debate was between those who saw U.S. arms sales as a concomitant to negotiation and those who saw them as an obstacle. Considered alone, arms aid does not lead to negotiation, but, coupled with pressure for a political solution, arms give a party the necessary strength and assurance to make concessions. It took nearly five years for the United States to develop an active coherent policy based on these two elements, having long been paralyzed by its internal policy debate. Then in 1981 a new administration threw away the linkage policy. Not only did the United States proclaim that it was no longer attaching to its arms deliveries some pressure for a search for a political solution, but it also then negotiated with Morocco for contingent use of military facilities—former American bases evacuated in 1963—in connection with the Rapid Deployment Force in the Middle East. An agreement was signed on 27 May 1982, giving Morocco enough leverage over the would-be mediator to disarm all pressures.[73] The United States has never addressed the problem of pressure on Algeria at all.

In addition to the OAU and the United States, other mediators tried their hand. Although they had no success, they testified to the complex structure of the conflict. Both King Khalid of Saudi Arabia in July 1979 and Yasir Arafat of the Palestine Liberation Organization (PLO) in September made concerted efforts, backed in the former case by the manipulation of financial support,[74] to bring about a solution acceptable to Morocco in exchange for Moroccan opposition to the Sadat peace initiative with Israel. Morocco indeed softened its support of Sadat and withdrew its ambassador from Cairo in order to keep the majority members of the new Arab League in Tunis behind it on the Saharan question. But the mediations failed because they had no solution to offer and no pressure to bring to both sides. Tunisian President Bourguiba worked hard in October and November 1979 to bring BenJedid and Hassan II to the Arab League summit at the end of November in Tunis to settle their differences, as Iran and Iraq had done—temporarily—at a similar summit at Algiers in 1975. In the event, neither head of state attended. Saudi Crown Prince Fahd and Tunisian Premier Mzali renewed their efforts in June 1980 with no more success despite the more propitious moment, and the Polisario called on Saudi King Khalid to intervene in December 1981. The Arab League has no special advantages over the OAU and little of its background in the conflict.

Hassan has singled out two other occasions that he felt were promising for an agreement until they collapsed, both during 1981, when the military stalemate and the OAU mediation contributed to a ripening moment. One was at the Islamic Summit at Taif in January, where the small gesture of a handshake passed between the two heads of state in the midst of some very tentative contacts at lower levels. Again, in November, at the stormy Arab League meeting at Fes, Algerian Foreign Minister Mohammed ben Yahya asked the Moroccans for a meeting of heads of state on the border with the maximum publicity. But when Moroccan Foreign Minister Mhamid Boucetta met him a few days later in Paris to arrange the meeting, ben Yahya demurred, indicating that BenJedid had too much opposition at home. Such contacts are the usual and proper way to move toward a political settlement, but their collapse indicated that there were still basic obstacles to the readiness of the parties to move to settlement.

Algeria is the key to any settlement. Both a party and a potential mediator, it can make or block solutions. Within Algeria, a gradual internal evolution continued under BenJedid, and as 1982 passed, the "Boumediennistes" within the government found themselves in an increasingly weaker position. In May 1982, ben Yahya was killed in an airplane crash during an attempt to mediate the Iran-Iraq war; and his replacement, former presidential adviser Taleb Ibrahimi, was a more moderate, flexible, and pro-Maghrebist figure. President BenJedid's consolidation efforts moved into core areas of power in 1982 as he brought military regional commands under his control.[75] Algeria began to pull away from its alliance with Libya in foreign policy, deserting the Steadfastness Front in the reconvened Fes Arab summit in September, with Ibrahimi subsequently joining the Arab delegation to Washington that was headed by King Hassan II. In late November, Saudi King Fahd visited Algiers (with a quick side trip to Rabat) to press for reconciliation on the Saharan affair. Algerian delegates attended an Arab Interparliamentary Union meeting in Rabat in January 1983, and two months later there was a shoot-out between Algerian army units and a Polisario group bringing Libyan matériel across Algerian territory.

The result of this evolution was a long-awaited meeting between Hassan and BenJedid on 26 February 1983 at the village of Akid Lotfi on the border.[76] Meticulously prepared, the summit concerned improved bilateral relations and led to the partial reopening of the common border and plans for restoration of diplomatic relations. The meeting showed that BenJedid could break away from those about him who considered a Saharan settlement to be a precondition for any contacts between Morocco and Algeria. But aides of the two heads of state also discussed the Saharan conflict at the same time, beginning to examine a compromise that could form the basis of the OAU resolution at the Addis Ababa summit in June: Morocco would meet Polisario representatives (indeed, such meetings had occurred secretly but inconclusively in the past), and Algeria would keep Polisario from insisting on OAU membership but would press for an early referendum, agreeing to recognize any results including a vote favorable to Morocco. Autonomy, federation, and other outcomes less than independence were discussed. Morocco felt that Algeria was offering its good offices to prepare Polisario for a fruitful encounter. The entire arrangement was to take place within the context of renewed economic cooperation among Maghrebi countries and within the framework of a North African confederation of the vaguest nature.

During the same period, Algeria gave form to its Maghreb initiative by preparing a Treaty of Peace and Friendship with Tunisia that was signed and ratified in an exchange of presidential visits in March and April 1983 and to which Mauritania also acceded in December. Between the presidential visits, at the beginning of April, the promised meeting was held secretly in Algiers between Guedira, Boucetta, and Moroccan Interior Minister Driss Basri, and three members of the Polisario's Political Bureau; Mahfoud Ali Beiba, Bachir Mustafa Sayed, and Salem ould Salek. Morocco advanced the possibility of a solution of autonomy that could meet the needs of both sides, which the Polisario representatives rejected. Morocco left the meeting feeling that it had met the conditions agreed at Akid Lotfi, although disappointed that the Algerians had not better prepared Polisario, and Polisario left expecting to press for further and more public meetings.[77]

The promising opening of 1983 foundered on miscommunications and erroneous expectations that rapidly degenerated into self-confirming views of bad faith. At the beginning of June, the OAU Summit was held in Addis Ababa. Algeria helped hold Polisario to its previous agreement not to attend the meeting and worked for a resolution favoring a referendum by the end of the year. But it also pushed to the forefront of the resolution a clause "urg[ing] the parties to the conflict, the Kingdom of Morocco and the Polisario Front, to undertake direct negotiations with a view to bringing about a cease-fire," thus advancing the claims of Polisario to equal status with Morocco; and it revealed the secret April meeting to Morocco's allies to show that Morocco had no basis for refusing to treat Polisario as a direct negotiating partner. Morocco felt that Algeria all along had merely been seeking recognition of Polisario to legitimize its claim to sovereignty and victory.

Soon after Qaddafi left Addis in a huff in June on being refused the OAU presidency, he showed up in a surprise visit to Rabat to propose and consummate another reversal of alliances with Morocco:[78] Libya agreed to end all material and political support for Polisario in exchange for Moroccan support for the Libyan position on Chad, favoring the rebels under former President Goukouni Weddei and the Libyan claim over the northern Aouzou strip of the country. The agreement, concluded at the beginning of July, held for more than a year, much longer than a similar attempt in mid-1981. Algerian officials were furious, seeing fulfillment of their fears of "encirclement" and a repetition of Moroccan connivance with former allies, as practiced with Mauritania in 1975. A month after the end of the OAU Summit, the Polisario launched a major attack against Mseid in southern (pre-1975) Morocco, using tanks and artillery, followed by similar attacks in early September against Smara and December–January in the Amgala sector. Although the attacks were designed to show that the Polisario was still alive after the OAU and before the UN sessions, the July offensive was too heavy not to have been planned before the OAU meeting, and it had the effect of reminding Morocco to expand the protective walls and reduce vulnerability. Hassan, feeling betrayed at Addis, announced on 20 August that even if the Polisario won the referendum, Morocco would not give up its territory on a silver platter,[79] while BenJedid in mid-September began a theme he was to reiterate through the FLN Party Congress in December that Maghreb unity would have to be built out of six states (Algeria, Tunisia, Mauritania, Libya, Morocco, and the Sahara) and would not take place at the expense of the Saharan people's struggle. A week following BenJedid's speech in September, the OAU Implementation Committee met in Addis Ababa, where Morocco rejected a proposal to meet in the committee face-to-face with the Polisario; rather than seek proximity talks to get on with the cease-fire, Mengistu canceled the meeting. A committee mission to Rabat, Algiers, and the Polisario camps and a simultaneous mediation by Sheikh Zayed of the Arab Emirates at the end of November ran up against the same impasse, and the committee efforts collapsed on the secondary clause of direct negotiations rather than pursuing its primary task of declaring and monitoring a ceasefire and organizing and conducting a referendum.

The final twist of the reactive spiral that had begun in mid-1983 and had buried a propitious moment for conciliation in acrimonious misperceptions escalated the conflict to a pair of hostile, interlocking alliances splitting the region. In response to the Algerians' overly clever Maghreb initiative, which isolated the two states on Algeria's flanks, Morocco and Libya made their own counteralliance on 13 August 1984 in the Treaty of Oujda, consolidating their informal cooperation of the previous year. Morocco had many interests in the arrangement, including hopes of Libyan financial support for the Moroccan budget and employment for Moroccan workers; not the least of Morocco's interests was the formal annulation of Libya's engagements to Algeria and Polisario under the 1975 Treaty of Hassi Messaoud. For Libya, the Treaty of Oujda meant a reprieve from its international isolation. For Algeria, it was the height of insult and offense. By the end of 1984, the Saharan conflict had lost its specific focus on a piece of territory and had become a clash of alliances in the Maghreb. Ironically, the alliances had no ideological content; both aimed at friendship and cooperation in North Africa.

The escalation of the conflict to the level of political alliances within the Maghrib meant that the battle had to be pursued until one of the alliances broke down or an effective and hurting stalemate registered between the two groups. The situation raised the danger of direct hostilities between Morocco and Algeria again, as the two sides' attempted to test each other's (and their own) alliances. The two weak points were Tunisia, on the Algeria side, and Libya, on the Moroccan. Algeria immediately attempted to undermine the Libyan alliance with Morocco. Falling oil prices and moderating Arab positions provided occasions for Algeria and Libya to work together during 1985, but they were not strong enough to overcome the outstanding grievances (in addition to the Oujda treaty) on issues such as Chad and the common Algerian-Libyan border. It was not until the end of January 1986 that BenJedid and Qaddafi finally met at Ain Amenas along the disputed frontier.[80] A reversal of alliances was not produced, but the meeting showed that the rival treaties did not keep the two ideological neighbors from discussing commalities. Algeria also got a little help from an unexpected quarter—the United

States. Washington continued to press Morocco on its "pact with the devil," at the same time that it took more direct measures against Libya, culminating in the Tripoli airraid of mid-April. When Israeli Prime Minister Shimon Peres met with King Hassan in mid-July and Qaddafi criticized the visit, Hassan used the occasion to denounce the Oujda treaty on its second anniversary. The way was open for Algeria to win over Libya to its alliance and isolate Morocco. At the beginning of December, BenJedid was in Syrte, stopping off in Tunis on the way home to report on the many measures of economic cooperation and transborder integration agreed to. However, Algeria did not allow Libyan revival of arms transshipments to the Polisario, preferring to maintain its own control over the Sahrawis. At the end of June 1987, Qaddafi was in Algiers, calling for a military alliance and bilateral union. Conflicting communiques from top Algerian party councils in mid-July spoke of Libyan entry in the 1983 friendship treaty, on one hand, and a national referendum on a bilateral union on 1 November, on the other. Algerian dominance of North Africa and the isolation of Morocco seemed complete and tightened the pressure on Morocco in the Sahara.

Morocco, on the other side, maintained its good relations with Tunisia, whose interest was in good relations with its two counterbalancing neighbors but not in a close alliance with either of them nor in a close alliance between them. The more Algeria tightened ties with Libya, the more it troubled Tunisia. As early as 1984, when the two camps began to crystalize and the tension mounted in the region, Tunisia rose to wave the banner of Maghrib unity and call for a summit of all the state leaders. By the end of the year, it had brought the parties to an agreement in principle on a regional summit, but no agreement on the date, since there was no agreement on how many states there were in the region—6 with the SADR or 5 without. At the beginning of July 1987, BenJedid flew to Tunis after Qaddafi had left Algiers and was confronted with a Tunisian veto on further union or alliance steps with Libya. Furthermore, Tunisian leaders insisted that Maghrib unity must not be used to isolate Morocco but rather to provide a context for solving the Saharan conflict. November began without a referendum on an Algerian-Libyan union, and continued a week later with the replacement of Bourguiba by his prime minister, Zine Labidine BenAli with an active pan-Maghribi policy.

While Tunisia was turning the inter-Maghribi alliance conflict in more productive directions, the stalemate on the Sahara began not only to harden but to hurt. The new pain was primarily economic. Morocco had always been under budgetary constraints in its pursuit of the war, with a cost roundly estimated at $1 billion per year, only a third of which was borne by Saudi Arabia. But the late 1980s brought two new constraints. Algeria lost the economic cushion previously provided by high oil prices and began looking seriously for ways of cutting expenses; the Saharan war, never deeply popular, was increasingly seen as a costly relic of a dead Boumedienism. At the same time, the entry of Spain and Portugal into the European Common Market, putting products competing with North Africa within the economic community, and the decision to remove all internal tariffs by 1992, meant that North Africa's largest market was about to become its economic adversary. Maghribi economic cooperation and integration was a pressing necessity, but any progress toward regional unity was blocked by the Saharan affair.

Furthermore, progress for the Sahrawi cause became more and more evidently blocked on the diplomatic as well as the military front. After the OAU victory, the SADR tried for entry into the Non-Aligned Movement meeting in Harare in September 1986 but its candidacy was informally discouraged by the host country among others. The same year, the United States, Japan and some European countries refused to receive the OAU/ECA document prepared for the special UN session on economic redress for Africa if it included the SADR as a signatory. Not only was the way to recognition by broader international organizations blocked, but only one new recognition was gained inside Africa (Liberia) and few outside, and some of those who had already granted recognition lost their fervor as they saw that Sahrawi entry into the OAU solved no problems. Militarily, Morocco continued to consolidate its hold on the terrain behind an ever extending wall.[81] Through mid-1985, the secure area included only 80% of Saqiet el-Hamra, the northern sector, plus the southern coastal enclave of Dakhla. But in August 1985, the fifth wall was thrown up diagonally across Rio de Oro, and on 20 April 1987 the sixth wall was completed, enclosing some 60% of the southern province and running along two thirds of the length of the southern border with Mauritania. The action meant that the Polisario had only the southeast corner of Saqiet el-Hamra and the eastern part of Rio de Oro, the latter a flat and often sandy terrain without easy cover, and the two territories were connected only by passage through Mauritania. Now the Polisario's supply lines were stretched as far as were Morocco's. The Polisario fought hard to disrupt construction, thus ending nearly two and a half years of inactivity in mid-February 1987 in the northern sector and again throughout March in the south. The southern wall was built in a record two months, and heavy attacks which penetrated the wall in the north could cause casualties but could not last more than half a day inside the perimeter. The Polisario's military activity, wildly inflated for the press, was good for headlines but not for holding terrain; new recruits became harder to find, morale dropped, and dissatisfaction and defections increased.

Pieces of the conciliatory track were kept in repair in the aftermath of the Akid Lotfi summit. In September 1983, the king told the UN General Assembly that Morocco would abide by any results of a referendum. Ibrahimi and Guedira exchanged secret visits to each other's capitals in April 1984 and again in January 1985 to keep communications open, but then contacts stopped. As the gradually hurting stalemate set in and ways of escalation other than direct war were ruled out, it became clear that what was required was a mediator who would be able to help the parties with a second track of conciliation and keep them from being distracted by their mutual proclivities for conflict, mistrust and one-upmanship.

Two mediators were ready to assist. During the period of the three Nairobi meetings, in 1981-82, the UN Secretariat had performed valuable services for the Implementation Committee by preparing reports on technical details about the holding of the referendum. Those plans were set aside when the SADR was admitted to the OAU. When Senegalese President Abdou Diouf became president of the OAU in 1985, he spent an unusually active year trying to revive the Organization's role and relevance in resolving African problems. King Hassan had called for a UN organized referendum in a speech in March but UN Secretary General Javier Perez de Cuellar had rejected the proposal as long as there were no negotiations with the Polisario, as resolutions 104 of the OAU (June 1983) and 40-50 of the UNGA (October 1985) stipulated, when he visited Rabat after the OAU summit. At the beginning of October, the Secretary General issued a report offering UN assistance in the eventual organization of a referendum; Hassan repeated his call later in the month and declared a ceasefire. The General Assembly turned a deaf ear to the proposal and called again for negotiations; instead, Perez de Cuellar and Diouf began to consort on ways to cut through negotiations to referendum. In March 1986 in Dakar, they agreed that Senegalese Defense Minister Medoune Fall would assist the Secretary General's initiative, and immediately upon his return to New York, Perez de Cuellar talked with the Moroccan and Polisario representatives to begin a process of proximity talks between the two, with Algeria and Mauritania as observers. These meetings took place on 9-14 April and 5–9 May, with little progress. Following the soundings, led by UN Undersecretary General for Special Political and Decolonization Affairs Abderrahim Farah, the two parties were given a technical questionnaire and then the debate shifted to the question of sending a UN mission to the territory to investigate the conditions for a cease-fire and a referendum. As the discussion turned to practical conditions, the divergence between the two sides became clear: Morocco continued to press for a referendum by the rules developed in the Nairobi rounds but refused the precondition of direct negotiations, which would have implied recognition of the SADR, whereas the latter refused any referendum except under conditions of total Moroccan withdrawal but insisted on the recognition of direct negotiations, as called for in the Algerian-sponsored OAU and UN resolutions since 1983. It was only in September 1987 that the Polisario finally accepted the principle of a UN mission, but with restrictions. Two months earlier, the King had declared that "if the Sahrawis join Morocco, they will be welcome; if they decide to secede, we will be the first to open an embassy in their capital," a statement the Polisario termed a "constructive spirit." The UN mission of 15 UN and 2 OAU experts, led by Farah, met the king in Rabat on 20 November and then moved on to the Sahara, Mauritania, and Algeria, until 9 December. The mission issued its report on 19 January and sent it to Zambian President Kenneth Kaunda, current OAU president, where it awaited action. A month later, Kaunda made a last attempt to press for an OAU solution in an appeal to Morocco to withdraw its troops. At the same time, however, Perez de Cuellar indicated that a UN-administered referendum was possible on the basis of the 1974 Spanish census, corrected and augmented for population growth, at a cost of $300–$400 million. The technical report was then issued to Morocco and the Polisario in May, summarising technical details of the situation.[82] The UN Secretariat, with skill and perseverance born of a deep sense of calling in conflict resolution, played a vital role in moving the dispute away from a political deadlock to a level of technical possibility. But even when a referendum between Morocco and the Polisario was shown to be technically possible, it was still necessary to bring the parties out of a hurting stalemate to a political settlement between Morocco and Algeria.

There had been no contact between Algeria and Morocco since January 1985. Two years later, following the efforts of Tunisia, Ibrahimi and Basri met in Tunis and decided on a subsequent meeting of Basri with Gen. Larbi Belkheir, President BenJedid's cabinet director. The followup meeting never took place, for indeed the moment was particularly inhospitable to peacemaking efforts. Morocco was completing its final wall along the Mauritanian border, leaving little room for the Polisario and provoked Polisario attacks against the northern wall in February from their bases around Tindouf with Algerian support. In March, the Polisario accused Morocco of attempting to assassinate their president. The pressure of the stalemate was beginning to produce discomfort on the Algerian side and a desire to somehow put an end to the conflict. Into this situation stepped Saudi Arabia, the Arab treasurer, supporter of Morocco and potential aid source for Algeria. King Fahd visited Algiers in preparation for the coming Islamic Conference and continued on to Rabat in mid-March from which he left speaking of a "Saudi plan" and a coming summit. On 4 May 1987 the principals in the negotiations once again met on the border, with BenJedid's military tent at Akid Lotfi, Hassan's royal tent at Zouj Bghal just across the border, and Fahd's airconditioned tent across the frontier. The two sides clung inflexibly to the two questions of any likely referendum—independence or integration—and the two neighboring heads of state met directly for only one of the six scheduled hours of the meeting. The only agreement was to renew the vows of non-aggression and eliminate the possibility of a direct war. The meeting did not produce the expectation of peace that followed the 1983 meeting.

However, second-level meetings revived, with six exchanges in as many months including a visit by Foreign Minister Ibrahimi to the king in mid-July. Behind the zero-sum choice of the referendum in these discussion lay another question: should Moroccan-Algerian relations be restored before a Saharan settlement or was the settlement a precondition? Although Algerian hardliners, including Ibrahimi and party secretary Messaadia, clung to the latter condition, the restoration of relations prior to a Saharan settlement might have provided a point of initial agreement in the absence of an agreement on the referendum. Then in mid-November, the Tunisian succession cleared the air and opened the way for renewed Tunisian pressure to include Morocco in the construction of the Maghrib. Moroccan Foreign Minister Abdellatif Filali met his Algerian colleague to announce the creation of a bilateral commission, which had been discussed but never implemented in the previous summit, to study all of the problems of common interest, including borders, migration, and diplomatic relations. Once again, second level delegations resumed their visits. Again, in the first three months of 1988, the increasing attempts to resolve outstanding problems of interstate relations while bypassing (or preparing for) the sovereignty question

in the Sahara were disrupted by an outbreak of polemics over as-
sorted claims and charges, and the momentum faded. At the end of
March, nonetheless, Messaadia and Belkheir met with Hassan II,
Guedira and Basri in Marrakesh to resolve the sequence of the
reconciliation: diplomatic relations were to be restored first. But
once more, nothing happened, because hardliners in Algiers emphasized the absence of an appropriate occasion.

Outside events finally forced the pace of negotiation attempts. On
10 May, Messaadia and Belkheir returned to Rabat, this time to
assure the presence of King Hassan at the special Arab summit
scheduled in Algiers the following month. The Arab summit was a
serious diplomatic concertation on the Palestinian uprising to which
Algiers attached the highest importance. Hassan agreed but called
for diplomatic relations first. Within the week Basri and Guedira
were returning the visit to draw up an agreement which was finalized
by a quick return trip to Hassan in Rabat, an audience with Ben-
Jedid, and a telephone call between the two heads of state, on 16 May
1988. The agreement marked the beginning of a composite compromise between the two questions of the referendum, based on the
renewal of interstate relations before the referendum on sovereignty
in the Sahara. Relations were to be restored, the border opened, "the
full validity of all treaties, conventions and agreements" between the
two parties reaffirmed, and an engagement made to "favor the success of international efforts undertaken to hasten the process of good
offices for a just and definitive solution of the conflict in the Western
Sahara through a free and regular self-determination referendum
taking place in the most total sincerity and without any constraint."
In other words, the third clause reaffirmed the 1969, 1970 and 1972
treaties which provided close integration of the two economies, including joint exploitation of certain mineral deposits and established
a boundary. The last clause, crafted with delicate diplomatic ambiguity, indicated a referendum as arranged by the UN Secretariat but
without the pre-condition of direct negotiations.[83] The way was
opened for a direct search for a formula on the Sahara itself. Not
only did the agreement provide for specific exchanges for the first
time in nearly twenty years, but contrary to the practices of 1983 and
1987, the provisions were immediately implemented. Diplomatic relations were immediately restored, transportation lines were reestab-
lished, the border was opened to a large influx of neighbors eager to
do business and meet their families, and the King attended the Arab
Summit. At Algiers, the five heads of state of North Africa held their
own meeting and set up a Maghribi committee to meet in Algiers in

mid-July and work out the procedures of integration. The return of Morocco to the OAU and its entry (with Libya) into the 1983 Friendship Treaty were discussed, for a later agenda.

With the political context of interstate relations restored, the Saharan issue could return to a determination of sovereignty. On 11 August, Perez de Cuellar handed Morocco and the Polisario a proposal for holding a referendum. The procedural provisions were a compromise. Following an early ceasefire (by the end of September), two thirds of the Moroccan troups (variously claimed to be 90,000 to 167,000) and the Polisario troops (5–8,000) would be withdrawn and then remaining Moroccan troups would be confined to UN-supervised camps. Moroccan administration would remain; the UN would administer the referendum. Although the proposal repeated the conflicting choices of independence or integration, it also sought to translate the real situation of Moroccan control over the territory and Polisario political existence into a third choice of loose autonomy within Morocco. It would be left to the parties to work out the details and conditions of the referendum, as well as a pre-referendum agreement on the selection of the third option as the ultimate choice, or else one of them would face a surprise. At the end of August, Morocco and the Polisario accepted the Secretary General's proposal, and in January 1989 they began the process of discussing the conditions of the referendum.

The need for a mediator provided a potential role for several countries. It is a role that fitted one of Algeria's chosen foreign policy images: Algeria has mediated a number of disputes involving Middle East countries and movements.[84] The mediator role could allow it to negotiate both with Morocco and between Morocco and the Polisario. But its role as a party, which it was not willing to admit, prevented this. The need for a mediator also provided a role for the United States. It could have not only acted as a mediator close to Morocco but could also have confirmed Algeria in its own mediator role by acting in concert, much as the Western Contact Group and the African front-line states did in Namibia (as discussed later). This role was never played. After the opening of 1983, the United States was content to stand behind Moroccan policy but without helping to provide the good offices that would help that policy move to a political settlement and keep Morocco and Algeria on the conciliatory track that they themselves had laid down. In playing this role, the United States could have benefited from the cooperation of Saudi Arabia and Tunisia, who were willing, and France, who was less so. The Saharan conflict was so deep-seated and multilayered, the parties were so intimate with and distrustful of each other, and the unilateral prospects of simply holding out were so attractive and so perilous for each, that they badly needed some help from their friends to seek a political settlement and reconciliation. In the end, it took Saudi King Fahd, Tunisia, and UN Secretary-General Perez de Cuellar.

The negotiated outcome will require an acceptable formula, something for each party, a softening of all parties' perception of the acceptable, and static-free open communications, four elements that need a third-party role. The only three dimensions of the conflict where compromise is possible are territory, status, and personnel: The territory can be split, half going to Morocco and half to the Polisario; it can be treated as a unit, but autonomous within or federated with Morocco; or Saharan leaders can be given special positions in a united state. A Polisario Tiris or Rio de Oro, federated with Mauritania, joint exploitation of the area resources, and local autonomy for the Moroccan Sahara were all possible elements in a package that might grow out of a conciliation process. The pre-1975 division into Rio de Oro and Saqiet al-Hamra (repeated in the wall and the Polisario name) could make separate districts for referenda to protect the OAU norms on boundaries if a special status for the territory or its representatives cannot be agreed on.[85] A precedent for special status is found in the experience of Italy, Spain, Ethiopia, and Cameroon, among others. Above all, a solution to be effective must respond, not to the rightness or wrongness of Morocco or Polisario or anyone else, but to the three sets of conflictual relations across the Sahara that underly the issue.

Seen as a boundary dispute, the Moroccan-Algerian case is hard to replicate, for everywhere else there has been at least an established boundary. The next most serious case—the other exception to the 1964 OAU norm—is the Somali border with Ethiopia (see the next chapter). Other boundary problems of lesser standing in international law may nonetheless have serious implications. One case that has already arisen is the justification found in a treaty prior to the current one in force. Libya has based its occupation of a northern strip of Chad and Niger on a Vichy French treaty with Italy that was never ratified. The real conflict here is not over an uncertain boundary, but one posed by an aggressive state drawn to a power vacuum. Seen as a problem of disputed regions and structural rivalries over powerless areas, the Moroccan-Algerian case is merely an introduction to many possible successors even though—except for Namibia (see following chapter)—the origins of the Saharan case in the decol-

onization process can no longer be replicated. Different origins can
underlie similar conflicts. One can be the presence of anomalies of
statehood, small enclaves that have their excuse only in now-irrele-
vant colonial history. Lesotho (1.3 million people in 30,000 km.²),
Gambia (0.6 million in 11,000 km.²), Guinea-Bissau (0.5 million in
36,000 km.²), Swaziland (0.5 million in 17,000 km.²), Djibouti (0.3
million in 28,000 km.²), and Equatorial Guinea (0.3 million in 28,000
km.² including islands) are all sovereign anomalies with an uncertain
future, not to speak of the South African Bantustans, whose sovereignty is uncertain as well.[86] Nonsovereign enclaves isolated from the
main country, such as Angola's Cabinda or—at least for the moment—South Africa's Walvis Bay, are also coveted by the surrounding state. Whether these small entities will go the way of Ifni, Zan-
zibar, or Ouidah and be incorporated in their neighbors or whether
they will become the Luxembourgs, Liechtensteins, San Marinos,
and Andorras of Africa and live on depends on the strength of
African norms, the tactics of their neighbors and their own cost-
benefit analysis of integration.

Another source of territorial problems can be unabsorbed minorities, their traditional nationalism awakened by disruptive modernization and their restiveness expressed in national liberation movements
waving the banner of self-determination. The problem is already in
. full explosion in Eritrea (see the next chapter) and can be expected to
flare up again elsewhere along the Sudan-Ethiopian border. It will
continue to trouble Zimbabwe and also many of the states in the
Saharan or sahel region, such as Sudan, Chad, and Cameroon, with
ethnic minorities living in the poorer parts of the country. As internal
problems, such troubles require help and sympathy, but they run the
danger of not remaining internal as national liberation movements
find external support and justification in principles.

The broadest sources of further conflicts like the one between
Morocco and Algeria concerns power vacuums between growing
powerful states. Both types of countries exist in Africa, often danger-
ously juxtaposed. Mauritania's future, between Morocco, Algeria,
and Senegal, is not assured; nor is Swaziland's, Botswana's, or Namibia's autonomy (see a following chapter). Djibouti represents a fragile solution to a conflict between Somalia and Ethiopia (see the next
chapter). Zambia, at the crossroads of southern Africa, is also open
to conflict (see a following chapter). But the vacuums need not be
absolute, as Chad or Niger between Nigeria and Libya show. They
can also include a Tunisia between Algeria and Libya in the turmoil
of Bourguiba's succession or Sudan between Egypt and Ethiopia in a

crisis of cold war dimensions or even a Libya between Algeria and Egypt on Qaddafi's overthrow. In all these cases, a solution that preserves the balance in the area and protects the independence of viable entities will be necessary but hard to achieve. A useful guideline would be for parties to discourage further balkanization and the perpetuation of ministates, with all their problems of instability and interference, and work for the creation and preservation of larger, stronger entities.

Notes

1. In addition to referenced sources, material for this chapter has been gathered during regular visits to Morocco and Algeria for discussions with government figures and Polisario officials. I am grateful for the help of Fatih Bouayad Agha, Mhamid Boucetta, Ahmed Redha Guedira, Mohammed Abdulaziz, Omar Hadrami, and Moktah ould Daddah. I am also grateful for the insights of King Hassan II, Abdelaziz Dahmani, John Damis, and Stephen Solarz.

2. There are a number of good studies of African boundary problems; see, above all, Saadia Touval's, *The Boundary Politics of Independent Africa* (Cambridge, Mass.: Harvard University Press, 1972); Carl G. Widstrand, ed., *African Boundary Problems* (Uppsala: Scandinavian Institute of African Studies, 1969); and also I. William Zartman's *International Relations in the New Africa* (Englewood Cliffs, N.J.: Prentice-Hall, 1966), chap. 3b; Société française pour le Droit international, *La frontière* (Paris: Pedone, 1980).

3. Reprinted in Martin Minoque and Judith Molloy, eds., *African Aims and Attitudes* (New York: Cambridge, University Press, 1974), p. 199.

4. There is some recognition of this phenomenon but not much discussion of its implications; see I. William Zartman et al., *Africa in the 1980s* (New York: McGraw-Hill, 1979), chap. 2, and Timothy Shaw, with Malcolm Grieve, "The Political Economy of Resources: Africa's Future in the Global Environment," *XVI Journal of Modern African Studies* I:1–32 (1978); Timothy Shaw, with Don Munton, "The Future(s) of Africa: A Comparison of Forecasts," in Shaw, ed., *The Futures of Africa* (Boulder, Colo.: Westview, 1981); and Timothy Shaw, with Kenneth Heard, eds., *The Politics of Africa: Dependence and Development* (New York: Africana, 1979), chap. 14.

5. The best general treatment of the Western (formerly Spanish) Sahara is John Mercer's *Spanish Sahara* (London: Allen & Unwin, 1976); John Damis' *Conflict in Northwest Africa* (Stanford, Calif.: Hoover Institute, 1983) is the most balanced presentation of the political issues of the conflict. A briefer treatment is David Lynn Price's *The Western Sahara* (Beverly Hills, Calif.: Sage, 1979, VII Washington Papers, 63). Virginia

Thompson and Richard Adloff, in *The Western Saharans* (Totowa, N.J.: Barnes & Noble, 1980), also include Mauritania but omit Algeria's role. See also Alfred Gerteiny, *Mauritania* (New York: Praeger, 1967). An unusual and thorough Spanish treatment is Francisco Villar, *El Processo de Autodeterminacion del Sahara* (Valencia: Torres, 1982). Tony Hodges, *Western Sahara: Roots of a Desert War* (Westport, Conn.: Lawrence Hill, 1983); Suresh C. Soxena, *The Liberation War in Western Sahara*, (New Delhi: Vidya, 1981); Maurice Barbier, *Le conflit du Sahara occidental* (Paris: Harmattan, 1982); and Elsa Assidon, *Sahara Occidental* (Paris: Maspero, 1977) are briefs for the Polisario. Robert Rezette, *Le Sahara occidental et les frontières marocaines* (Paris: Nouvelles Editions Latines, 1975), and Attilio Gaudio, *Le dossier du Sahara Occidental* (Paris: Nouvelles Editions Latines, 1977), take the opposite view. See also Tony Hodges, *Historical Dictionary of Western Sahara* (Metuchen, N.J.: Scarecrow, 1982).

6. See I. William Zartman, "The Sahara—Bridge or Barrier?" *International Conciliation* 541:1–62 (1963); Philippe Husson, *La question des frontières terrestres du Maroc* (Paris: CIB, 1960); Maurice Flory, "La notion du teritoire arabe et son application au problème du Sahara," *Annuaire français de droit international* 3:73–91 (1957); Germain Chauvel, *Notions d'état et de nationalité au Maroc* (Casablanca: Farraire, 1937); Ian Brownlie, *African Boundaries* (Berkeley, Calif.: University of California Press, 1979), pp. 59–84, 149–159, 436–444.

7. I. William Zartman, "A Disputed Frontier Is Solved," *VIII Africa Report* 8:13–14 (1963) and correction *IX Africa Report* 3:31 (1964); *Geographer*, Department of State, International Boundary Study no. 23 (1963).

8. Treaty of Lalla Maghnia, 18 March 1845.

9. Henri de la Bastide, "Une grande famille du Sud marocain: Les Ma elainain," *Maghreb-Machrek* 56:37–39 (1973); Hodges, *Western Sahara*, chap. 5.

10. Abdurrahman ibn Khaldun, Charles Issawi, ed., *An Arab Philosophy of History* (London: Murray, 1950), chap. 6.

11. See documentation submitted to the International Court of Justice, Advisory Opinion of 16 October 1975.

12. *International Court of Justice Yearbook 1952* (Leyden: Sejtoff, 1953), pp. 69–74.

13. See I. William Zartman, *Problems of New Power* (New York: Atherton, 1964), chap. 3.

14. See Attillo Gaudio, *Allal al-Fassi* (Paris: Alain Moreau, 1972); Allal el-Fassi, *Livre rouge et documentaires* (Tangier: Peretti, 1960) and *La vérité sur les frontières marocaines* (Tangier: Peretti, 1961).

15. On the vote in Tindouf, see Zartman, *Sahara*, p. 48. The Algerian Provisional Government negotiating the Evian independence agreement

repeatedly refused a separate referendum in the Algerian Sahara; Tahar Ben Gelloun, *Monde*, 3 March 1976.

16. *L'Humanité*, 21 November 1975; see also the statement of Mauritanian Foreign Minister H. Ould Mouknass, *UNGA* 32:368–369 (13 October 1977).

17. See Gerteiny, *Mauritania*; I. William Zartman, "Mauritania's Stand on Regionalism, *XI Africa Report* 1:19–37 (1966); Virginia Thompson and Richard Adloff, *The Western Saharans*; William Eagleton, Jr., "The Islamic Republic of Mauritania," XIX *Middle East Journal* 1:45–53 (winter 1965); Clement Henry Moore, "One-partyism in Mauritania," *III Journal of Modern African Studies* 3:409–420 (1965); Christine Garnier and Philippe Ermont, *Desert fertile, un nouvel état: La Mauritanie* (Paris: Hachette, 1960).

18. See Garnier and Ermont, *Desert fertile*, p. 219; Mokhtar ould Daddah, *Discours et Interventions* (Nouakchott: Government of Mauritania, 1966), pp. 9–11. Such pronouncements are typically Saharan. See also the statement of *jama'* president ould Jumani that Sahrawis would claim their rightful lands within neighboring states' borders after independence; *West Africa*, 24 February 1975.

19. See Hervé Bleuchot, "La pensée de Muammar Qadhdhafi" et I. William Zartman et Auriliano Buendia, "La politique étrangère de la Libye," in Maurice Flory, ed., *La Libye nouvelle* (Paris: CNRS, 1975); René Otayek, "La Libye révolutionnaire au sud du Sahara," *Maghreb-Machrek* 94:5–35 (July 1981).

20. Until its own need for allies on the Saharan issue reduced its freedom to support the policy of Egyptian-Israeli negotiation, which it helped create, when Morocco hosted the original Dayan-Touhami meetings in 1977; see Saadia Touval, *The Peace Brokers* (Princeton, N.J.: Princeton University Press, 1982), pp. 288, 291, 295.

21. See I. William Zartman, ed., special issue, *XXIX Focus 4* (March–April 1979), based on a State Department conference on the Sahara.

22. I. William Zartman, *International Relations* . . . , p. 110; *Le Monde*, 12, 15 October 1963; Nicole Grimaud, *La politique extérieure de l'Algérie* (Paris: Karthala, 1984), chap. 6.

23. Zartman, *International Relations* . . . , pp. 89 f.

24. See Saadia Touval, "The Organization of African Unity and African Borders," *XXI International Organization* 1:102–127 (1967); Touval, *The Boundary Politics* . . . , pp. 255–269; Patricia Wild, "The OAU and the Algerian-Moroccan Border Conflict," *XX International Organization* 1:18–36 (1966).

25. Houari Boumedienne, "Proclamation du Conseil de la Révolution," 19 June 1965, in *Documents: Les discours du Président Boumédienne* (Algiers: Information Ministry, 1966), p. 6.

26. See Touval, *The Boundary Politics* . . . , pp. 262–268. UN resolutions

from 1966 to 1978 are included in Stephen Solarz, ed., *U.S. Policy and the Conflict in the Western Sahara.* Hearings of the 96th Congress, 23–24 July 1979. The 1965 resolution is, of course, not included.

27. *Le Monde*, 18 January 1969; *Jeune Afrique* 421:24, 27 January 1969, on Ifrane. *Le Monde*, 27 and 29 May, 1970; *Jeune Afrique*, 492:27 f., 9 June 1970, on Tlemcen. The text of the Rabat treaty is found in Brownlie, *African Boundaries*, pp. 73–78. Algeria ratified the treaty on 17 May 1973. Morocco did not, ostensibly because it had no parliament at the time, but more realistically because the ratification, announced by the king in April 1973, was cut short by the discovery of an Algerian-supported plot against the king. The king stated on 1 June 1981 that the treaty stood and there was no longer a border conflict with Algeria.

28. There is no arrangement that will leave local tribes on the "right" sides of the border, including an arrangement for territorial independence as well. Tribes no longer act as political units or organization or allegiance although they still do have social cohesion. Furthermore, some of the tribes, notably the Ulad Delim, have also settled hundreds of miles away in central Morocco. See discussions in Mercer, *Spanish Sahara*, and Damis, *Conflict in Northwest Africa* . . . , chap. 1; on boundaries and tribes in Africa, see Zartman, *International Relations* . . . , p. 108.

29. Some African states, however, such as Guinea, opposed the 1976 partition because it was a partition although a division of the two colonial territories may not be seen in the same way. See Sékou Touré, "A Conversation with Sékou Touré," *CSIS Africa Notes* 2 (15 April 1982).

30. Jerome B. Weiner, "The Green March in Historical Perspective," *XXXIII Middle East Journal* 1:20–33 (1979); Mohammed Maradji, *La Marche verte* (Paris: SEFA, 1976).

31. The Madrid Treaty is found in Damis, *Conflict in Northwest Africa*, pp. 149–150.

32. Mercer, *Spanish Sahara.*

33. The text is published in *Statement Addressed to the President of the 24-Members' Committee on the Occasion of the 31st Session of the United Nations*, Polisario, p. 11.

34. Some of the Saharans who were to form the nationalist organizations were of the families of those—Saharans and Mauritanians—who took refuge in independent Morocco in the late 1950s. On the origins of Saharan nationalism, see Mercer, *Spanish Sahara*; I. William Zartman, *Problems of New Power*, chap. 3; Ahmed Baba Miske, *Front Polisario, l'âme d'un peuple* (Paris: Rupture, 1978), pp. 112–118. "Ligue française pour les droits et la liberation des peuples," *Sahara occidental: un peuple et ses droits* (Paris: Harmattan, 1978); Hodges, *Western Sahara*, pp. 149–156.

35. Report of the UN Visiting Mission. A former founding member of the Polisario in exile in the Netherlands, Sid Ahmed Mohammed Larose,

complained that little of the leadership by 1981 was Saharan; *Pourquoi Pas* (Brussels), 8 December 1981.

36. No one has analyzed Polisario internal politics although some raw material is found in Hodges, *Historical Dictionary*.

37. *Le Monde*, 16 February 1978. The best review of the Algerian decisions is found in Grimaud, *La politique extérieure . . .* , chap. 7.

38. Mokhtar ould Daddah, "La genèse d'un affrontement," *Jeune Afrique* 790:24–27 (27 February 1976); *Jeune Afrique* 880: 76–83 (18 November 1977).

39. *Washington Post*, 7 August 1979; *Washington Star*, 14 August 1979. Text of the agreement is found in Stephen Solarz, *Arms for Morocco? U.S. Policy Toward the Conflict in the Western Sahara*, House Committee on Foreign Affairs, January 1980, appendix, and in Colin Legum, ed., *Africa Contemporary Record 1979–80* (New York: Africana, 1981), p. B571.

40. The 1979 agreement between Mauritania and the Polisario was also to have contained provisions for continued Polisario use of its base at Chegga in northern Mauritania (on the same parallel as Bir Moghrein) and continued Mauritanian occupation of LaGuera (next door to Nouadhibou); *Jeune Afrique* 989:35 (19 December 1979). Nouadhibou became a port of entry for Libyan supplies for Polisario in the 1980s and was the site of heavy Polisario concentration.

41. *Jeune Afrique* 1061:20 f. (6 May 1981).

42. In September 1981, the USFP criticized the king for softness on the Sahara issue after he agreed to a referendum in the OAU, and its leaders were jailed and sentenced. Some interpreters have suggested that the USFP position was only tactical and that it sought to embarrass and weaken the monarchy, but even this tactic shows the power of the issue in Moroccan politics. For USFP statements, see *Maghreb-Machrek* 94: 105–109 (October 1981).

43. Like most such efforts, the CIA input into the State Department interagency intelligence report on the stability of the monarchy, which was leaked in late October 1979 as part of the intergovernmental maneuvering over the renewed arms supplies to Morocco, erred by underestimating the resiliency of the monarchy and even of the army. It predicted that if the "ineffectual leadership displayed . . . since mid-1978" (when the Mauritanian opportunity was lost) continued, Hassan "will lose control of events—probably within a year—and eventually his throne," an evasively worded contingency. The State and Defense Departments' assessments were more realistic about the king's political skill and also about the relation of the conflict to political stability in Morocco. See *International Herald Tribune*, 1 November 1979.

44. *Le Monde*, 10, 11, 16, 19 October 1979.

45. *Jeune Afrique* 1038:28–32 (26 November 1980).

46. *Jeune Afrique* 1052:21 (18 February 1981); 1061:21 (6 May 1981). The

only concentrations of population outside the wall were at Dakhla and LaGuera, on peninsulas on the coast.

47. House Committee on Foreign Affairs, Africa Subcommittee, Hearings 23–24 July 1979. See also V *Strategic Mid-East and Africa* 30:1 ff. (1 August 1979). The decision to supply arms was extremely hard-fought, carried even to the media through leaks, and the fallout of the leaked debate included investigations and resignations. For the leak of the Policy Review Committee session, see William Branigin, *Washington Post*, 18 October 1979.

48. *The New York Times*, 26 March 1981.

49. See King Hassan's account and the text of the letter in Hassan II, *The Challenge* (New York: Macmillan, 1978), pp. 166–168.

50. UN Security Council s/PV 2151–2154, 20–25 June 1979.

51. *Jeune Afrique* 1061:21 (6 May 1981); *Marches Tropicaux et Méditerranéens*, 17 October 1980, p. 2543.

52. Speech to Algerian People's National Assembly, July 1978, repeated in a letter to Hassan II, 4 October 1978, UN Document A/33/289, annex, p. 2; Hassan II, *The Challenge*, p. 166. On the Libyan supply function, see Grimaud, *La politique extérieure* . . . , pp. 213, 326 f., and Ania Francos and J. P. Serini, *Un Algérien nommé Boumediène* (Paris: Stock, 1976), p. 341.

53. The Arab League was an early supporter of Moroccan irredentism; see Jamal Sa'd, *The Problem of Mauritania* (New York: Arab Information Center, 1960, Information Paper no. 4).

54. Meanwhile, Equatorial Guinea withdrew its recognition following its military coup.

55. The United States played its most active diplomatic role of the conflict at the time of the OAU meeting, when it provided the communications (which the Ethiopians tried to block) needed to coordinate the walkout of the nineteen. For Kodjo's explanation of his controversial action, see *Jeune Afrique* 1105: 18–22 (10 March 1981); although he acted within his administrative powers in a normal situation, his action circumvented both the prior political decision by the heads of state and the constitutional challenge by Morocco as to what constitutes a state.

56. Polisario Secretary General Mohammed 'Abdul'aziz said, on 27 February 1984, "the solution of the Sahara problem will come with the downfall of Hassan II."

57. North African students at New York University displayed this type of behavior in a simulated negotiation, quite different from other behaviors observed in repeated tests. On approach-avoidance behavior, originally a social psychological term, see Lloyd Jensen, "Soviet-American Behavior in Disarmament Negotiations," especially p. 314, in I. William Zartman, ed., *The 50% Solution* (New York: Doubleday Anchor, 1976); Bernard Berelson and Gary Steiner, *Human Behavior* (New York: Harcourt Brace, 1964), p. 272.

58. Berhanykun Andemicael, *Peaceful Settlement Among African States* (New York: UNITAR, Study No. 5, 1972), pp. 5–8; Touval, *The Boundary Politics* . . . , pp. 257–268.
59. The momentum of conflict management overrode an important incident in 1966, when Algeria nationalized the iron mines of Gara Jebilet, claimed by Morocco; see Touval, op. cit., p. 260.
60. *Maghreb-Machrek* 72:30 (April 1976).
61. *Jeune Afrique* 880:78f. (18 November 1977).
62. *Le Monde*, 11 November 1979, 19 April 1979.
63. Interviews with M. Guedira; *Jeune Afrique*, 926:34 (4 October 1978); 970:47 (8 August 1979); *Le Monde*, 11 November 1979.
64. In an interview, 21 May 1982.
65. Houphouët-Boigny was to have been the source of a compromise plan just after the Mauritanian coup, involving four-party talks, a UN mandate for the territory for a few years, and a UN referendum following a cease-fire and evacuation of all troops; *Afrique-Asie*, 4 September 1978. The proposal met no favor with the parties. For a discussion of Houphouet as "the forgotten Wiseman," see *Jeune Afrique*, 970:42 (8 August 1979). Revolutionary Ethiopia was never a member of the 1970s' Wisemen, until Mengistu assumed the OAU presidency in 1983.
66. Committee Records, *Jeune Afrique*, 970:40–53 (8 August 1979). Nigeria under General Mohammed Buhari resigned from the Committee in August 1984 in order to be able to recognize the SADR and thereby force a referendum.
67. Hassan II interview with Edouard Sablier, *France-Inter*, 17 July 1979.
68. *Jeune Afrique* 1030:33 (1 October 1980); see also text of resolution of Nairobi II.
69. *El-Moudjahid*, 17 June 1981. On comparison of the two positions, see *Jeune Afrique* 1079:21 (9 September 1981). The Algerian position called for an entirely new census of Saharans, a process of several years; see Memorandum presented to the OAU Implementation Committee by the government of Algeria, August 1981.
70. For the speeches and resolutions of Nairobi I and II, see *Maghreb-Machrek* 94: 99–104 (October 1981).
71. On the 1982 aborted OAU Summit in Tripoli, July attempt, see CSIS *Africa Notes*, no. 3 (1 September 1982); *Jeune Afrique* 1124 (21 July 1982) and 1127 (18 August 1982); also Yassin el-Ayouty and I. William Zartman, eds., *The OAU After 20 Years* (New York: Praeger, 1984).
72. *Le Monde*, 11 October, 22 November 1979; 11 June 1980; *International Herald Tribune*, 17 September 1980.
73. See House Subcommittee on Africa, Hearings, *Review of U.S. Policy Toward Conflict in the Western Sahara*, 15 March 1983, and the appended study by the Congressional Budget Office on the U.S.-Moroccan Agreement and its Implications for U.S. Rapid Deployment Forces, March 1983.

74. The amount of annual Saudi support for Morocco is unconfirmed, but
$1 billion seems likely. This probably includes the $232.5 million bill for
the 1980 supplies of reconnaissance planes (OV-10), fighters (F-5E), and
helicopters, which Saudi Arabia agreed to pay for. Saudi aid was
interrupted during 1978 to signal displeasure with Hassan's support for
Sadat and was restored when Hassan criticized the Camp David process. See James Markham, "Hassan's Quagmire," *New York Times
Magazine*, 27 April 1980; *Washington Post*, 29 October 1979; *le Monde*,
31 March 1980.

75. For details of this consolidation, see the annual reports on Algeria in
Africa Contemporary Record 1979–1980 to *1983–1984* (New York:
Africana, 1980–1984); I. William Zartman, "La consolidation de pou-
voir de Ben Djedid," *Maghreb-Machrek* 106 (October 1984); John
Entelis, *Algeria* (Boulder, Colo.: Westview, 1985); Nicole Grimaud, *La
politique estérieure* . . .

76. See James Dorsey, *Christian Science Monitor*, 28 March 1983; *Figaro*,
31 March 1983; XXIV *Africa Confidential* 8:6 (13 April 1983)—interviews. Reports that a territorial split based on the 1975 boundaries,
organic ties between the southern (Polisario) section and Mauritania,
and subsequent plans for a Moroccan-Mauritanian-Algerian meeting to
work out details were discussed but have (unfortunately) not been
confirmed.

77. Interviews with participants.

78. Unconfirmed reports indicate that the deal was prepared during Qaddafi's surprise vist to Saudi Arabia immediately after Addis Ababa and
that Guedira first went to Libya just as Morocco was considering
sending troops to Chad to support the government of Hissene Habre
and offered to cancel these plans in exchange for Libyan support for
Morocco in the Sahara. In any case, Hassan II did refer understand-
ingly to the Libyan claims in an interview with *Figaro Magazine* in
September 1983. For a perceptive view of the situation created by the
Libyan rapprochement, see Bechir ben Yahmed, "Le deuxième round a
commencé," *Jeune Afrique* 1235: 18–23 (5 September 1984).

79. Selective communication to different audiences has also been a problem, typical of many conflict resolution situations. Hassan II has repeatedly told Moroccan audiences that the referendum would be "confirmatory" to sell the idea of a referendum; this decreases his own
maneuvering room but also has created doubts in the minds of outside
observers about the honesty of the referendum. Yet domestic policy
change does require skill and latitude in domestic communication to
ensure domestic support. Guedira (in an interview) has indicated that
the king's statements to international audiences—as in his UN assurances in September 1983—are authoritative rather than his domestic
speeches—such as the "silver platter" statement of August. However,

matters may not be that simple: The "silver platter" speech was directed to Algeria and the Polisario as a petulant rebuff to the Mseid attack.

80. *Jeune Afrique* 1354:44f (12 December 1986), 1386:32–35 (29 July 1987), 1406:32f. (9 December 1987).

81. *Jeune Afrique* 1368:34f. (26 March 1987); *Le Monde* 13 and 17 March 1987.

82. *Report of the Technical Survey Mission to the Western Sahara, November–December 1987* (UN Secretariat); also Kingdom of Morocco, *Résponses aux questions relatives à l'organisation d'un référendum au Sahara*; Sahrawi Arab Democratic Republic, *Mémorandum administratif à la Commission technique de l'ONU et l'OUA sur le Sahara occidental.*

83. *Jeune Afrique* 1430:18–22 (9 June 1988), 1433:32–37 (22 June 1988), 1434:12f. (29 June 1988); *Algérie-Actualitiés*, 15 June 1988; *Le Monde*, 20 November 1987; *New York Times*, 31 August 1988; *Washington Post*, 12 and 31 August 1988.

84. See chapters by Gary Sick (American hostages in Iran) and Diana Lieb (Iran-Iraq border dispute) in Saadia Touval and I. William Zartman, eds., *The Man in the Middle: International Mediation in Theory and Practice* (Boulder, Colo.: Westview, 1984); Grimaud, *La politique extérieure . . .* , chap. 11.

85. On territorial divisions, see Damis, *Conflict in Northwest Africa*, chap. V; I. William Zartman, "Referendum and Negotiation in the Western Sahara," paper presented to the African Studies Association meeting in Boston, December 1983. Morocco already created some measure of autonomy; in March 1982 a special consultative council for Saharan affairs of 182 Saharan members was installed, including the 12 elected deputies from the Saharan provinces and 85 tribal representatives elected in August 1981.

86. Whatever its population, the Western Sahara is smaller than any of these. The curious list attached to Solarz, *Arms for Morocco? . . .* , showing states with fewer than 230,000 people, contains 12 island states, 6 city states and other historic anomalies, and Qatar, scarcely a convincing justification for a new ministate.

3
Conflict in the Horn

War and drought, peace and milk.

Somali proverb

It is better to be the cub of a live jackal than of a dead lion.

Ethiopian proverb

A fundamental problem of national consolidation is found in the need to bring nation and state into coincidence.[1] Generally, one element comes into existence first, so that certain periods of history are marked by widespread efforts to bring the other into focus with it, as in the attempts to create nation-states in nineteenth-century Europe or state-nations in twentieth-century Africa and Asia. Sometimes these efforts clash, however, either within a single country or between countries applying different criteria. A particularly sharp conflict occurs when a multinational state wants to maintain its boundaries against the claims of a multistate nation, and empire faces irredentism, army faces national liberation movement, capital faces provincial rebellion.[2]

Most new states in the current era are trying to weld a number of component traditional nations into a new and modern nation coterminous with the state, and they face resistance to these efforts from ethnic minorities. Resistance grows when resources and rewards are slim and the new nations get neither psychic nor material benefits from their restructured identity; conditions of the economy, such as terms of trade or weather, have rapid political repercussions. Sometimes these minorities are a spillover from a larger group of relatives across the border and so have a natural ally and sanctuary to support their grievances. Others find support and sanctuary next door for political reasons. In the worst case, the whole next-door neighbor is an irredentist nation, creating a zero-sum conflict of identities with no easy way out.

The two concepts of state and nation need not necessarily clash. They could exist on separate levels without any need to be coincident and without component nationalisms being regarded as treason or different sovereignties being regarded as domination. There are many national groups in Switzerland, France, England, Senegal, Ivory Coast, and Nigeria, among many others, and these states' citizens live as national minorities in other countries. But in the uncertainty of profound sociopolitical change, of national liberation and revolution, both state and nation will be new and insecure enough to feel that they have to control each other or lose hold of events.

The Somali-Ethiopian conflict is a clash between nation and state, or between nation-state and multinational empire. On another level, it is the expression of a literally legendary hatred between two ethnic groups in the region, one of them in the midst of a historic volkerwanderung. Thus, the conflict is a long and constant part of history, evolving through different forms. First it was a clash of tribes or traditional nations; then it became part of the process of imperial consolidation and religious war, soon compounded by the intrusion of foreign colonialism with its need to draw geographic boundaries. Then it burst out as part of the politics of newly independent and highly expectant states, complicated by cold war superpower support and most recently by revolution.

In its contemporary form, the conflict has erupted twice, but the two cases were too far apart to have a reinforcing effect toward conflict resolution. In the early 1960s immediately after its independence, Somalia fought with Kenya and Ethiopia; the conflict was defused by a promise to deal with the political issues, but the Ethiopians forgot their promise as danger of war receded. So war flared up again when the empire apparently collapsed, in 1977, and superpower military intervention was required to restore the status quo. But the superpowers came to stay, the Soviet Union moving in on revolutionary Ethiopia and the United States obtaining use of the former Soviet bases in Somalia, making resolution difficult and even management unpromising as the conflict burns on. By the end of the 1980s, management was again possible but resolution remained elusive.

Background

The Great Rift Valley—where Africa is very slowly pulling apart[3]— cuts diagonally across Ethiopia. The southwestern half of the valley lies high up in the Ethiopian highlands, pocked with lakes. The northeastern half opens into a large lowland fan, in the middle of which lies the Republic of Djibouti along the Bab al-Mandab coast

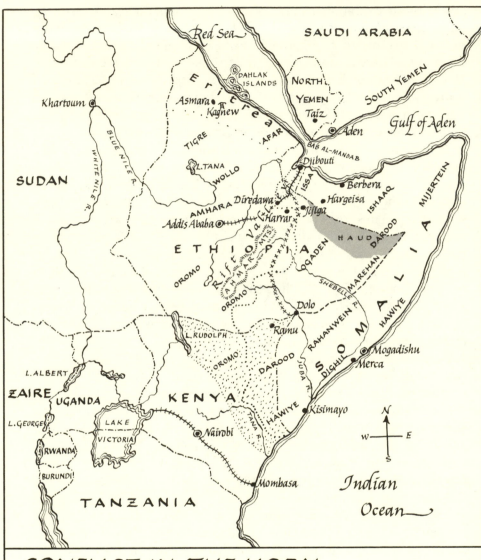

Red Sea

SAUDI ARABIA

DAHLAK
ISLANDS

NORTH
YEMEN

SOUTH YEMEN

Gulf of Aden

Khartoum

Asmara
Kagnew
Taiz

Aden

BAB AL-MANDAB

Djibouti

Berbera

Hargeisa

ISHAAQ

MIJERTEIN

SUDAN

TIGRE

AFAR

WOLLO

L.TANA

ISSA

Diredawa

AMHARA

Harrar

Jijiga

HAUD

DAROOD

Addis Ababa

Rift
Va
AHMAR MTS.

ETHIOPIA

OGADEN

MAREHAN

HAWIYE

SOMALIA

OROMO

OROMO

SHEBELLE R.

Dolo

RAHANWEIN

JUBA R.

Mogadishu

Ramu

DAROOD

DIGHIL

Merca

L.RUDOLPH

OROMO

L.ALBERT

ZAIRE

UGANDA

KENYA

TANA R.

HAWIYE

Kisimayo

N

L.GEORGE

LAKE
VICTORIA

Nairobi

W   E

RWANDA

S

BURUNDI

Mombasa

Indian
Ocean

TANZANIA

CONFLICT IN THE HORN

- - - - - Provisional Administrative Line established by British Military Administration 1950
xxxxxxx Maximum Somali Advance 1977-1978
HAUD and Reserved Area returned to Ethiopia 1955
Former Northern Frontier District seeking secession from Kenya
. . . . Western Limits of Somali Habitation

0   200   400 mi.   0   200   400 km.

Ascherl

of the Gulf of Aden, and the southern edge of the fan is the Ahmar Mountain chain running parallel to the gulf, with its coastal plain a continuation of the low-lying fan. From the Ahmar Mountains the land gradually slopes southward through Somalia to the Indian Ocean. This great shield from the mountains to the ocean is scrubby and arid but contains the watercourses that provide the basis of widespread grazing and the limited coastal agriculture of the region. The land is desert by some counts and subdesert steppe by others, closer to the sahel in its soil and vegetation than to the Sahara.

In such land the population must be nomadic, forced to move to find the next source of water and nourishment when its current pasture is worn out.[4] Four out of every five inhabitants of this great shield are nomads, continually in movement, migrating outward (north and east) toward the coast in the June–September and January–March dry seasons and inward toward the highlands during the spring and fall rains. The entire area may have 5 million inhabitants (although there are some wilder claims), with only the city of Mogadishu over 200,000, and four more cities—Merca and Hargeisa in Somalia, Diredawa and Harar in Ethiopia—over 50,000 population. There are no raw materials in the area at all despite some hopes of oil, and, except for some coastal farming, all economic activity has to do with the nomadic grazing. The shepherds' markets lie principally in the coastal lowlands of the shield whereas the economic area of the three mountain towns—Diredawa at the edge of the mountains in the Rift Valley, Harrar and smaller Jijiga in the mountains guarding the passes—is much smaller and is self-centered.

With three exceptions, all the inhabitants of this shield are Somalis, that is, people who identify with a common (probably mythical) ancestor, who regard other such people as kinfolk, who share the same Muslim religion and speak the same Somali language. One exception concerns the settled inhabitants of Harar and Diredawa, most of whom are ethnically different from the surrounding countryfolk.[5] The second concerns the western upland area of the shield, which is inhabited by related Cushitic-speaking Muslims known as Galla or Oromo although they share the same economic orientations as the rest of the region.[6] The third concerns the "foreign" settlers brought in periodically by the Ethiopian regime from elsewhere in the empire to counterbalance the Somalis.

The Somali nation is not a historic kingdom or a centralized social unit, but a segmented identity and kinship group that tells its members who they are, who their friends and rivals are, and who is the enemy stranger.[7] Identity does not prevent strife between cousins, but it does distinguish such strife from war against foreign enemies and especially against neighboring attempts at domination. Somalis have occupied the entire region since the end of the seventeenth century, having gradually expanded to present limits from an original tenth-century beachhead on the northern (Gulf of Aden) shore. The heartland of the nation lies slightly inland from the shore, in the central piedmont of the shield inhabited by the Ishaaq and Darood clans, where the nomads could move about to take advantage of both seasonal rainfall and permanent waterholes. As population has grown, however, the Somalis have gradually expanded in the only directions possible—westward where the Oromo already do their best on poor land and southward where the land is even poorer but even less populated.

The region was colonized at the end of the nineteenth century, with the French fully established in their part of the Somali Coast (Djibouti) by the Congress of Berlin in 1885; the British completed their control over the northern coast along the Gulf of Aden two years later, and the Italians completed their hold on the Indian Ocean coast by two years after that, the same year that they consolidated control over their Red Sea colony of Eritrea. At the same time, the historic but territorially fluctuating Ethiopian Empire, reconstituted out of warring baronies by Emperor Tewodros (r. 1855–68), was undergoing its modernizing consolidation under Emperor Menelik II (r. 1889–1913).[8] Crossing the Rift Valley, the empire spread across the shield in the 1880s and 1890s until it met the colonizing Europeans along the coast. At that point, boundaries became necessary, a concomitant of the territorial state that the Somali nomads had neither needed nor encountered before.

The boundaries of the three European colonies with Ethiopia were established by agreement between the parties in 1897; and the boundary between the French and British territories, in 1888.[9] The French treaties are refreshing reminders that it was not impossible to draw a boundary in the region. For the rest, the multiple agreements and disagreements are scenes in a situation comedy of errors in which treaty texts were lost, wording was couched so as to establish boundary lines but avoid recognition of sovereignty on either side, precise agreements were made by parties who did not control the territory they divided, boundary lines were hung on nonexistent points, and frontiers were established along the "territorial boundaries" of nomadic pastoral tribes and clans. The British Agreement had the wisdom of specifying transit rights for tribes grazing on either side of the border, subject to the jurisdiction of the territorial authority, although conflicts among tribes and between authorities continued to create problems. Another source of problems was finally eliminated in the years 1932–34, when the British frontier was demarcated by joint agreement.[10]

The Italian boundary, however, was never demarcated, nor do the 1897 treaty nor the 1908 convention, which corrected it, even delimit the boundary by any recognizable references. In 1935, as a pretext to invade, the Italians branded Ethiopia an "aggressor" for being on its own territory, and after their conquest of Ethiopia they moved the Somali boundary westward to include the Ogaden, the Ethiopian portion of the shield named for a major Somali clan. When the British replaced the Italians in 1941, they maintained this boundary, adding on their own protectorate to unite almost all the Somali-inhabited shield under one administration. Such unity was only tantalizing, however, for in 1948 Somali territory was restored to its prewar components: British Somaliland to its 1897/1923–34 boundaries and British Kenya to its 1925 boundaries, and Italian Somaliland separated from Ethiopia by a provisional administrative line based on an interpretation of the 1908 agreement. Furthermore, in 1954, the reserved areas for grazing in the Ogaden (the Haud area) were returned from British to Ethiopian administration, and the boundary became a barrier to pastoral migration, giving a powerful spur to Somali protest nationalism. Provision was made for border negotiations between the Italians and Ethiopians, but by the end of the decade, negotiation, mediation, and arbitration had all been exhausted, as both parties met claims with counterclaims and concessions with demands. Throughout these attempts at conflict resolution, Ethiopia was arguing a legal case over where the border was, and the Italians were arguing a social-moral case on behalf of the Somalis over where the border should be. In 1960 the British Protectorate and the Italian Trusteeship territory united in independence and in the fervent pursuit of, not a historic, but a social irredenta.

The symbol of Somalia irredenta floats over the country in the form of the five-pointed star in the middle of the flag, one point for each of the Somali-inhabited territories. In addition to Somalia, made up of the British and Italian colonies, and the Ethiopian Ogaden, there is also the French Somali Coast, later known as the Territory of the Afars and the Issas, which became independent in 1977 as the Republic of Djibouti, and the Northern Frontier District, later known as the Northeastern Province, of Kenya. The Somali position has been that these are "Somali territories" (read: "territories inhabited by Somalis"), parts of the Somali nation that should comprise the Somali state. More frequently heard than this substantive position is its procedural expression—a demand for self-determination for the populations in the area. And one step back from such formal demands for national reunification is the more usual position of a state suffering from ethnic overhang into its neighbor's territory—the demand that it be admitted as spokesman for its people who are suffering ill treatment across the border.

It is important to emphasize both the social reality of this position and its consequent reasonableness in Somali eyes. The socioeconomic unity of the Somali-inhabited shield (this partially excepting Djibouti) is such that the region is unimportant to Ethiopian or Kenyan society or economics.[11] Moving the next step to more subjective realities, the Somali sense of nationhood is uniquely strong in Africa, and many postwar events of importance—from the British and Italian espousal of postwar Somali causes, even if it concerned *their* Somalis and therefore expanded their power, to the impetus toward reunification given by partially united Somalia's independence—have reinforced this sense with international approval.[12] Finally, within this nation, the poverty of the country reinforces the overwhelming predominance of a pastoral economy, the cultural sentiments of superiority associated with nomadic grazing alongside a sense of condescension toward sedentary agriculture, and the importance of the central piedmont in the social structure of the nation. Within the vigorous clan democracy of the Somali sociopolitical system, government is responsible to the nation for articulating and attenuating the needs arising from its poverty and divisions.

If the Somali perception and attitude is tied to the concept of "nation," the Ethiopian is linked with the notion of "empire."[13] The Ethiopian position on the respect of international boundaries is straightforward and easy enough to understand. But behind it lies a combination of ingredients that is highly complex. One component has been historic status, associated with the Solomonic descent of the emperor and hence of the empire. Another is modernity, paradoxical as it may seem, for the parallels between the "oldest Christian kingdom" and the European modernizing (and eventually revolutionized) monarchies are frequently cited to the point where Haile Selassie appearing before the League of Nations in 1935 was seen to be acting as the head of a modern state, not an African developing nation (a term not then yet in vogue). Indeed, the Somali charge that Ethiopia is a colonizing power of the 1880s like any (other) European state only reinforces this notion. A third component is the Christian mountain fortress holding out against Muslim encirclement, a notion reinforced by the very isolation afforded by the highland battlements. A fourth idea is that of military sacrifice; fighting and dying for the state is a compelling occupation in Ethiopia, even if not always done with the greatest technological sophistication, and the Ethiopian army units are distinguished by a high ability to suffer casualties and a low rate of surrender. Finally, there is the notion of African leadership, symbolized by Addis Ababa as the founding site and permanent seat of the Organization of African Unity and expressed for a decade by the frequently effective mediating role of the emperor in African disputes, a king of kings and presidents and the oldest elder statesman in a continent where ancestors are worshipped.

These components are capped since the mid-1970s by the updating element of revolution. Curiously perhaps, none of the previous components disappeared in 1974 with the emperor. Instead, they were adopted by the successor regime, either directly or even as a challenge to the new leadership. But the revolutionary military government also added its own nature to the Ethiopian complex of perspectives. Ethiopia was no longer governed by a venerable anachronism but by a revolutionary socialist regime, automatically allied with the progressive forces of the continent and the world, intrinsically endowed with answers to the problems that felled the enfeebled emperor.

Of these, the most striking is the national question. The collapse of central authority in the last days of the emperor gave the opportunity to the national minorities of the multinational empire to make a break for self-determination, and the new revolutionary government that struggled to fill the power vacuum could not afford to fail before the challenge. Indeed, if there was one issue between 1974 and 1978 over which rivals for leadership (General Aman Andom, General Teferi Bante, Lieutenant Colonel Atnafu Abate) were successively liquidated, it was not the ideological issue but the national question. The most violent case of national insurgency was in Eritrea, where a number of competing left-leaning national liberation movements had nearly succeeded in wresting the province from Ethiopian control by 1978.[14] No Ethiopian government after Haile Selassie could afford to give in to any dissident minority lest it end up with a country the size of Tewodros' tribal kingdom a century before.

This study will not discuss Eritrea because it is a chapter in itself and because it is a parallel but not a part of the Somali irredentist conflict with its neighbors. The Eritrean question was slightly different in form from either the international irredentist issue of the Ogaden, Djibouti, and northern Kenya or from the other issues of national awakening among the Oromos, Tigreans, and others in

Ethiopia. Eritrea had been an Italian colony from 1882 to 1941 and then was federated with Ethiopia from 1952 to 1962, when the emperor made the great tactical error of abolishing its privileged status. The Eritreans broke out in revolt, led by a number of faction-ridden but highly effective Marxist movements and by 1978 had nearly defeated the Ethiopian army. The fact that by that time the Ethiopian government had declared itself to be Marxist, too, made no difference to the developmentally and culturally different Eritreans. To the rulers of the Ethiopian Empire, whether monarchists or Marxists, the Eritrean rebellion is the touchstone of the national question, the key to the perpetuation or dissolution of the empire, showing that, even without the support of an irredentist neighbor, a provincial rebellion can threaten the center.

Another element in the Somali-Ethiopian conflict is the former French territory of Djibouti. It was regarded by Somalia as another piece of the national territory that would join the nation-state when colonial rule was removed, but it is also the railhead of the only railroad in Addis Ababa and, therefore, regarded by Ethiopia as vital to its existence.[15] Furthermore, its inhabitants are divided into roughly equal numbers of Somalis of the Issa clan and Rift Valley Danakils of the Afar clan, with Djibouti city with its port and rail terminal lying within the Somali-inhabited part of the territory. Thus, unlike the Ogaden, Djibouti is part of the Ethiopian economy. Because there was little chance of the territory's joining Ethiopia, which had never ruled it, both Ethiopia and France had an interest in continued French rule in order to hold off the Somali claim. In 1958 the population voted overwhelmingly in favor of colonial association with France under the Gaullist constitution (although many of the Djibouti Somalis appear to have abstained), and the mandate was renewed by a closer vote in 1967.[16] By refusing to offer the alternative of union with the other Somalis in the other Somali lands, however, France was able to establish the framework for politics within the territory itself, and the Djibouti politicians sought to establish a winning coalition through biethnic alliances seeking cooperation with the colonizer. The winner in 1958 was Hassan Gouled Aptidon, an Issa who dominated Djibouti politics thereafter into the 1980s. As late as January 1973, French President Georges Pompidou visited Djibouti and then Addis Ababa, where Emperor Haile Selassie supported his intention to continue French colonial rule over the Territory. Through the mid-1970s there was a growing current in favor of independence although up to a point this option was synonymous with the Somali claim rather than separate existence as a successor state to the colony.

The southernmost part of Somali irredenta concerns Kenya.[17] In the early 1840s, the Somali migration crossed the Juba River and by 1910 reached the Tana River in British East Africa, the furthest point of their population movement to the present time. In recompense for Italy's participation on the Allied side in World War I, Britain ceded it nearly half this territory between the two rivers in 1925 to create the present Somali border with Kenya. Nonetheless, the rest of the territory, comprising the Northern Frontier District (NFD) of Kenya, has been regarded by Somalia as an integral part of its irredenta; and, after 1960, as Kenya, too, moved toward independence, Somalia expected that the removal of British rule would mean unification of the Kenya Somalis with Somalia. Ethnic Somalis in Kenya joined the preparations for independence with a successionist campaign of their own in the hopes of then negotiating favored treatment from Somalia in exchange for unification of the Somali nation. In recognition of the district's different nature, Britain sent a survey commission to the area in 1962, which reported overwhelming support for unification with Somalia.[18] But Kenyan pressure for state territorial unity was too strong; in March 1963, Britain announced it would grant independence in December to a Kenya as colonially constituted, and Somalia broke off its diplomatic relations with Britain. In July the plot was formalized in Somali eyes by the negotiation of a boundary and defense treaty between Kenya and Ethiopia before Kenya was even a sovereign independent state. Irregular attacks within and across the border by Somali "*shiftas*" (bandits) followed, intensifying in 1964 and 1966 until 2,000 Somalis (some of them *shiftas*) were killed in Kenya by 1967.[19] Kenyan Somalis and other Kenyans tend to look down on each other, the Kenyans being considered inferior black Africans and the Somalis inferior nomads, respectively.[20] As a result, there is some social discrimination against Somalis in Kenya to refer to when a cause is needed.

The Somali conflict had gone through a full round of escalation and management in the 1960s before the second round of the 1970s. Upon the independence of the formerly British and Italian Somalilands, their newly united inhabitants shared the general hope that cousins still under French and British rule would soon join them. This hope was even more fervently extended to Somalis living under Ethiopian rule because of the past fluctuations of the provisional boundary and because the area included the homelands of the Da-rood clan and the core area of the Somali nation. As in the NFD, harassment of sedentary and official installations by irregular guerrillas in the Ogaden rose after 1960 to the point where it finally drew a direct riposte from the Ethiopian army on 13 October 1963 and spilled over into conventional war until a cease-fire on 1 April 1964.[21] The Somali army was still small at that time, and the Ethiopian army cleared the territory to its border without difficulty; the OAU Council of Ministers called for a cease-fire and President Ibrahim Abboud of Sudan brought it into effect through mediation, to be followed by further discussions in the OAU. The guerrillas, organized under a number of names after 1960, continued their raids through 1966, however. The Somalis had wanted an army of their own to face the large Ethiopian armed forces and had received modest military aid from Great Britain and Italy in late 1961. But the Western assistance seemed more of a palliative than a program, and when the United States, Germany and Italy offered a larger, $10 million package in mid-1963, tied with strings against use for irredentist purposes, Somalia rejected it as being too little and too restrictive and at the end of the year contracted for Soviet military aid three times as large instead.

The irredentist issue has been both the fire and the safety valve of Somali politics. After the 1964 Ogaden war, the debate on the conflict paralyzed the country for the rest of the year and a no-confidence vote of the newly elected National Assembly left the country without a government from March to September. Because there was no government, the discussions with Ethiopia scheduled for the OAU Summit meeting in Cairo in July could not be held, and instead the OAU reinforced its charter provisions in favor of territorial integrity by passing a firm resolution supporting colonial boundaries. Underlying the Somali debate—and indeed underlying all Somali politics—was the competition among Somali clans for public benefits—and specifically the pressure exerted by Darood politicians from the core area of the shield for the inclusion of their clans at the public trough.

Two events upset the dynamic equilibrium of this Somali political system in the late 1960s. In 1967, following the second presidential election, a new government headed by Ibrahim Egal brought in some new policies, a new approach to the irredenta by trying to settle secondary grievances (including the guerrilla attacks themselves) as a way to get the other parties to agree to discuss the primary (territorial) issue, normalized relations with Kenya where the problem was secondary, and a reduction in the growing military forces and military budget. Two years later, the third National Assembly elections started with sixty-three parties—largely clan representatives—and ended effectively in the installation of a single-party system as all but one opposition figure crossed the aisle. As a result of these events, the political system became overburdened with demands, but the irredentist safety valve was clamped shut, and the military—once honored as a means to achieve the national cause and expanded as a result—now found its belt suddenly tightened.[22]

The triggering incident in this ripe situation was the assassination of President Ali Shermarke by a dissatisfied policeman in October 1969 and his imminent replacement by a lesser politician through the same discredited system of clan competition. On 21 October the army under General Mohammed Siad Barre took over, abolished the parties, suspended the constitution, inveighed against tribalism and corruption, tightened relations with the Soviet Union, and established a system dedicated to socialism and covered by slogans of revolution.[23] In the following years, to the surprise of many observers in light of the events causing the coup, little was heard of the irredentist issue although the military budget grew steadily. However, the government that came to power was half Darood (primarily, Marehan Darood) in origin, representing the core area of the nation in the Ogaden, and two other fifths came from the Hawiye Somalis from south Somalia and Kenya and from the Ishaaq Somalis from western Somalia and Djibouti.[24] In comparison to the civilian governments of the 1960s, this change moved the clan representation heavily out of balance, favoring the irredentist factions and removing the representations of the Mijertein Darood and the Saab Somalis, who came from the coast away from the borders. The point is not that particular individuals are ascriptively oriented by birth but rather that in the responsive democracy of Somalia, individuals are particularly vulnerable to pressure from their clans, who are collectively oriented by the conditions of their area of habitation.

In sum, the Horn of Africa is the site of a complex conflict between nation and state, or between an incomplete nation-state and a multinational empire. The core area of the conflict is not only the historic and present core of the Somali nation, but also an important part of the Somali economy, even though under internationally recognized Ethiopian rule. The "wings," the Djibouti and Kenyan territories, occupy a very different position within the Somali nation and economy. From the other side of the established, even if contested, border, however, Somali nomads are considered merely another case of restive minority nationalities, and attempts to support them are aggression. For the OAU, guardian of the basic norms of inter-African relations, the boundary is sacred, even if approximate, and the irredentism is illegitimate.

Conflict

The irredentist conflict in the Horn of Africa came to a head in the 1970s just as the fluid geopolitical structure of the area was undergoing major changes. The fluidity is symbolized by the uncertain location of the Horn. Geopolitically, we do not know where it is. It is an exclusive part of neither northern Africa nor black Africa nor East Africa nor the Middle East nor the Indian Ocean area, but is partly in all of these.

Although the size, military strength, and geographic position of Ethiopia would tend to make it the dominant state in this region, its prevailing underdevelopment and its tenuous national unity have kept this role out of its reach. Instead, relations around the Horn of Africa are structured, in perception and in operation, around a Muslim encirclement of the Ethiopian fortress-empire, through a potential and sometimes actualized alliance among Sudan, Eritrea, and Somalia, backed by various other ready sources of support across the Red Sea and the Gulf of Aden, including the Yemens and Saudi Arabia, but also Libya, Egypt, and Iran. This pattern has been dominant for at least three decades, even overriding cold war alliances. Nonetheless, within this potential regional alliance pool, there is also a global dimension along which partners are chosen.

In this structure, the strategic imperative for Ethiopia is to break out of the encirclement, which is possible by a number of means. One is to turn isolation into self-reliance and develop the largest army and other independent elements of power to make alliances unnecessary. Thus, after the revolution, the military force was increased sixfold by the creation of a 200,000-person army of mobilized peasants. Another means is to capture the other element besides ethnicity that determines the solidity of the Arab alliance by being radical or conservative enough to attract the support of some Arabs across a crosscutting ideological dimension, as Mengistu has done by cultivating radical Arab support from South Yemen. Yet another is to consolidate the breach in the encirclement by solidifying the alliance based on common defensive interests with Kenya, as expressed in the 1963 defense treaty and its reaffirmation in 1979. A fourth is to vault the encirclement by becoming a sacred continental—not just subregional—leader, as Haile Selassie did through his position in the OAU. And a fifth is to neutralize neighbors individually by blackmailing them with their own problems, as Ethiopia has done to Sudan on occasion by giving sanctuary to its opposition groups and as it has tried with Somalia.[25]

On the other side, Somalia alone is no match for Ethiopia, and therefore it must find allies for itself by invoking principle ("self-determination"), ideology ("scientific socialism"), and nationality (Arab League membership since February 1974 although it is not Arab). The result has been ineffective in Africa, where Somalia's irredentist cause is highly illegitimate and has alienated any potential support; but in the Mideast, Iraq, Syria, the PLO, Egypt, Saudi Arabia, and the shah's Iran have given Somalia military support. Djibouti has depended on French support for its separate status, first as a colony and after 1977 as an independent state; its membership in the Arab League added additional allies. The Eritrean liberation movements have benefited from Sudanese support and Somali ties, but have at various times enjoyed assistance from Egypt, Saudi Arabia, and Syria according to the Arab ideological constellations of the moment. The Somali irredentist conflict is, therefore, only one front of a broader ethnic and ideological conflict.

Overlaying this regional structure is a cold war battle line that also appears to coincide with, and even be determined by, the irredentist front.[26] For the most part, throughout the 1960s, Ethiopia and Somalia were left alone in their conflict relationship by neighbors who were themselves preoccupied either with internal rebellions, as in Sudan, or with evolving regional relationships, as in East Africa. Much of this changed in the 1970s. In the beginning of the decade, the Muslim encirclement of Ethiopia also looked like an encirclement of an American-supported regime by Soviet allies. The radical military regime of Sudan, supported by Soviet-armed Egypt, and the radical military regime of Somalia, tied to Russia in 1974 by a treaty of friendship, were joined by two or more competing Marxist nationalist movements in Eritrea.

But the cold war dimensions began to change as the decade moved on. The gradual Egyptian shift from the Soviet to the American side of non-alignment after 1972 was both prepared for, and followed by, a similar Sudanese disenchantment with both domestic and foreign Communist allies, terminating in Sudan's expulsion of Soviet military advisers in May 1977 and the concomitant American decisions to sell Sudan arms. Somalia expelled its Soviet advisers and closed down its Soviet base in Berbera and port facilities at Kisimayo in

November, as will be examined in greater detail later. In each of these three countries, a military regime came to power in 1969–70; initially it attracted Soviet support, but then turned to the United States as it began to perceive a serious need for development assistance and as its opponents began to be the recipients of Russian support (a pattern, incidentally, not followed by the region's other 1969 military regime in Libya). In May 1977 the encirclement appeared to be reversed as Sudan, Somalia, Saudi Arabia, and both North and South Yemen met in Taiz to discuss common Red Sea concerns.

Some states in the region are more important than others because of their continental role, their development potential, and their strategic positions although none has the importance of Egypt for regional security concerns or of a Saudi Arabia for energy matters. The United States has an interest in Ethiopia for its central position in the region and its possibilities for further development in agriculture and light industry and has had such an interest for a long time.[27] Russia is attracted to Ethiopia for the same reasons, with an even older historic interest dating from the Czars. American interest in the other states is, above all, relational, that is, determined by the state's relation to third parties and areas, not by their intrinsic nature. In Sudan and Somalia, American interest lies primarily in keeping out a hostile presence, such as the Soviet Union, and in keeping both the neighbors of Saudi Arabia and Egypt and the Red Sea, Aden Gulf, and Indian Ocean coasts neutral and free of enemy forces. Because of their poverty and their low development potential, both Sudan and Somalia bring as many burdens as advantages to a close relationship with a great power although their positions differ slightly. Sudan has a great possibility for agricultural development after a sizable initial investment, and it has a strategic location on the Nile valley, between Egypt and Ethiopia. Somalia suffers from unrelieved poverty and irredentism, making it a drain and an embarrassment for its foreign assisters, but it does have an extensive coastline with possibilities for a port development along the classic lifeline to the East and the Indian Ocean. Thus, an alliance with Ethiopia provides a great power with some tempting opportunities for internal political and economic cooperation, as well as for a regional power base, whereas an alliance with Somalia is of interest primarily for geostrategic reasons whatever the fine verbiage of human and ideological solidarity to the contrary. Furthermore, Somalia's coast is one among many—a "strategic redundancy" alongside Oman and Kenya for the United States and a duplicate of Aden for the U.S.S.R.—whereas Ethiopia's position is unique. So in Ethiopia there is a directly competing interest between the United States and the USSR whereas, in Somalia, America's interest, above all, is in seeing the Russians out, more than seeing itself in.

The most favorable moment for American interest would have been a time when the Russians were out of Somali but not yet in Ethiopia in strength, if such a moment ever existed. American—and indeed Western and African—interest in resolving and managing the conflict in the Horn is also relational in that it aims at reducing needs and hostilities that will draw in outside powers. But once a hostile great power is already "in," as Russia was in Somalia and came to be in Ethiopia, resolution of local conflict and pursuit of global competition become mixed up and get in each other's way. Even when interest is clear, policy is often less so, for it depends on timing, available means, and other parties' positions, as well as on appropriate goals. Were there then times when local conflict could have been resolved and cold war conflict reduced in the Horn of the 1970s and 1980s?

The dramatic reversal of the alliances in the Horn of Africa, as in the case of the Ethiopian Revolution, has been discussed from many angles. Indeed, it was the first battle in the policy war that tore the Carter administration and culminated near its end in the resignation of Cyrus Vance as secretary of state in May 1980 over the Iranian affair.[28] The debate between Vance and National Security Adviser Zbigniew Brzezinski concerned the use of pressure to get the Russians out of Ethiopia. It came to a head in a duel of communiqués on 1 March 1978 linking and delinking SALT and Ethiopia. The outcome was ineffective in its impact on the Horn, but, what is more serious, the debate was years too late.

The first important question is this: Could the United States have acted earlier to keep its position in Ethiopia and to manage the worsening conflict while the hope of negotiating "the major issues" was still alive? In Ethiopia, the United States had a long history of political cooperation with Emperor Haile Selassie, beginning with a friendship treaty of 7 September 1951, when Ethiopia was the only independent state in the region; it also established a steady military relationship with the Imperial Army, beginning with the Korean War and formalized in May 1953 by a comprehensive base and arms agreement for a quarter of a billion dollars over the next two decades and nearly the same amount in development aid.[29] The base involved was the communications installation at Kagnew in Eritrea, a major link in U.S. global military communications until the development of satellites. In 1973 the United States provided $11 million in spare parts, ammunition, training, and limited replacements—about the same annual level as over the previous decade. A trip by the emperor to Washington in April 1973 to plead for a matériel modernization program failed. Instead, in September, four months before the revolution began and five years before the American lease ran out, he was told of the U.S. decision to phase out Kagnew communications station, the specific element that gave Ethiopia military importance in American eyes. Up to this point, American pressure on the emperor to live up to the implications of deescalation agreements negotiated with Somalia between 1964 and 1968 under the auspices of the OAU and seek a settlement on the Somali border was conceivable, although not easy and not prompted by much incentive as long as the Russians were in Somalia. But after mid-1973 there was no American leverage left on the emperor.

A military modernization program either at this point or the next year might have occupied and satisfied the army, probably not forestalling some form of revolution but possibly maintaining both America's position and a moderate military leadership during its course. After 1974, military sales and assistance did continue, amounting to $80 million or a third of the total since 1953, but not as a purposive program to maintain political relations. In 1973 the United States was losing interest in a country viewed as less strategic with a government taken for granted; in 1974 it saw its longtime friend being overthrown by a movement that it assumed to be irrevocably hostile rather than open to influence. Admittedly, however, the cost of such a purposive policy, if successful, would most likely have been to keep Russia in Somalia, for it was the Russian support for Ethiopia against Somalia that caused the latter to expel its former ally.

The second question is this: Could the United States have acted later to maintain its position or manage the conflict? The blood of the old regime's supporters and the moderate military leaders flowed in November 1974; the blood of the revolutionary rivals flowed during the first half of 1977. In between, the Ethiopian government on several occasions asked for American arms and $34 million requested in February 1975 was pared to a $7 million sale of parts and ammunition in March; a $22 million replacement program began in the beginning of 1976. But the United States also protested the November 1974 political assassinations and in May and June 1976 put heavy diplomatic pressure against the use of an untrained peasant militia in Eritrea. A secret Soviet military assistance agreement for $100 million of Korean-War vintage arms was signed in December 1976 during Mengistu's first visit to Moscow. In February 1977, after Mengistu's shoot-out to power, the Carter administration placed Ethiopia on a list of human rights violators ineligible for its $6 million military aid (although still eligible for the projected $10 million military sales), reaffirming a decision made but never announced by the Ford administration the previous year. The scaling down of Kagnew base was met in April by the Ethiopian demand for the closing of consulates and embassy sections and, in turn, by the suspension of arms shipments by the United States (announced retro-actively in July) just as Ethiopia was running out of American ammunition in its efforts to hold the empire together against Eritrean and Somali insurgents. Even thereafter, there were discussions in mid-September over the resumption of arms transfers and occasional inviting contacts and speeches by Ethiopian officials in their time of dire need until November 1977, when the Russian airlift began and Cuban and Soviet preponderance in Ethiopia was assured.

From the Russian side, documented steps toward the Friendship Treaty include the cultural exchange and sports agreements of January and December 1975 and the arms agreement of December 1976, the latter probably the Russian down payment on a pact with Mengistu.[30] When Mengistu consolidated his control in February, he announced that Ethiopia would seek its military supplies in Communist countries rather than simply seeking arms source diversification as previously indicated. His next visit to Moscow, in early April, was followed by the arrival of the first Cuban military advisers and increased Soviet military aid of $400 million in May.[31] The airlift of $1 billion of arms ran from 26 November till the end of the year, and the Friendship Treaty with Russia was signed a year later, on 20 November 1978, after the Eritrean and Ogaden battles were won for the moment. The major question, still unanswerable, is whether the Soviet shift of interest to Ethiopia was assured by the end of 1976, as promised to Mengistu before he completed his control of power, or whether the last clear option for the United States was at some later moment. But by mid-1977 the Soviet decision to make Ethiopia a major target of penetration seems to have been made. The resumption of arms shipments to Somalia from early August 1977 to their announced termination on 19 October, the new economic and cultural protocols of August and October, and other continuing relations show that until they were expelled in November, the Soviets expected to retain their ties with Somalia as well.[32]

It does appear that the United States, with an ambassador in post in Addis Ababa and a different spirit in Washington, could have maintained a stronger position in Ethiopia by providing better military assistance and other political attentions in 1974–76 if it had tried to understand the dynamics of revolution and ride them out. Instead it focused on human rights in the midst of a revolution, and it limited arms shipments at the same time that it opposed the Derg's favorite project, the people's peasant militia, then about to march in Eritrea.[33] Ethiopian needs by 1977, however, were for tangible support from "the most communist country" for its revolution and for several thousand troops to lead its new people's army, needs that were simply outside American capabilities by definition. After 1976, it was too late for an American role in Ethiopia or in the resolution of conflict in the Horn.

The United States has been accused of inciting Somalia to aggression with promises of arms and then abandoning it in characteristic indecision.[34] The new Carter administration was attracted to the idea of developing better relations with Somalia despite its Russian ties, as the American embassy had been urging as well.[35] The president instructed his advisers to "move in every possible way to get Somalia to be our friend" in April and in a speech in June indicated that his "own inclination is to aggressively challenge, in a peaceful way of course, the Soviet Union and others for influence in areas of the world that we feel are crucial to us now or potentially crucial 15 to 20 years from now."[36] Dr. Kevin Cahill, a friend of Siad, was sent to Somalia at the same time to prepare contacts, indicating a possibility of military assistance, and the Somali ambassador was "encouraged" by talks with the president in May and June.[37] On 15 July, the decision was made in principle to sell defensive arms to Somalia; a week later, Somalia regular army units were reported in the Ogaden; a week thereafter, the arms offer was suspended.

The American process of policy formulation may have been ill-informed in the light of the well-established irredentist campaign and the earlier presence of Somali soldiers within Ethiopia, as discussed later, and it may have fueled the Somali capabilities for wishful thinking. But military invasions are not launched in a week, and the Somali attack was under preparation for a much longer time, as will also be seen, leaving little role for the United States in the process. When, in mid-November, Somalia abrogated its Friendship Treaty with Russia and sent home the last remaining Soviet advisers, the Somali move was at the same time a punitive reaction to Russia's lack of support and a desperate attempt to imitate Sadat's Egypt in a bid for American assistance.[38] Again, the American position was misread, for American—and, generally, world—opposition to a Somali armed presence in Ethiopia was stronger than to a Russian presence in Somalia. In sum, little of the conflict escalation can be attributed to American policy, but much misperception of other states' policies can be laid to Somalia's self-justified pursuit of the conflict.

The third question is this: When, if at all, could Russia and its Cuban partner have acted to manage the conflict?[39] The Russians had the same assured position in Somalia as the Americans held in Ethiopia at the beginning of the conflict escalation and the same territorial limitation clause in their military aid agreements as the United States has, and they apparently suffered from the same weakness of taking their client for granted. A third of a billion dollars of military assistance had been provided since 1963 and over 4,000 advisers were in civilian, security, and military positions, down to the battalion level; in exchange, Russia received communications, missile, and port facilities at Berbera for its Indian Ocean operations. The ideological training given to the Somali guerrillas from the Ogaden, organized into the Western Somali Liberation Front (WSLF) in 1976, responded not only to Siad's notions of control but also to his desire to ensure Soviet support for his adventure. Until mid-1977, despite its rapprochement with Ethiopia, Russia apparently kept the expectations of unshaken relations with Somalia and also of seeing the Ogaden campaign maintained at a guerrilla level; it had no interest in restraining the campaign below that level as long as Ethiopia was an American ally, although there are indications that it urged Somalia not to escalate above that level either. In a particularly clumsy attempt at heralding principles, the United States helped support Soviet expectations in May 1977, when it labeled Somalia a supporter of international terrorism for its activities in Djibouti. Nevertheless, meetings between Siad and Cuban Premier Fidel Castro and Russian President Nikolai Podgorny in March–April, like Siad's attempt to meet Premier Brezhnev in August, were steps in the worsening of Somali relations with Communist countries; and Soviet advisers were noticed going home on leave without replacement after the spring meetings, Soviet arms were reduced in May and suspended in July, and Soviet oil shipments to Somalia stopped in August. At the same time, after the spring meetings, Russia apparently gave Ethiopia assurances from Siad that he would not attack, a source of embarrassment three months later.

The Soviet Union had, therefore, less than half a year (February to July 1977) during which it enjoyed palatable relations with both sides. Even this was not a position from which conflict could be restrained, for Russia was more concerned with maintaining access while changing sides than in complicating its delicate position with conciliation during the period. The Somali decision to expel all Russian advisers in mid-November may have crystallized the Russian decision to airlift troops to Ethiopia two weeks later, but the latter was certainly prepared by previous steps in Soviet Ethiopian relations even if it represented a dramatic escalation in the war.

There was a moment when a policy of arms limitation would have favored conflict resolution, but it would have required major East-West cooperation. In July 1977, both parties were beginning to run low on their military stocks to the point where a refusal by Russia on one side and by Egypt, Saudi Arabia, and China on the other to replenish them could have produced a stalemate. Instead, Russia made the massive escalating move, changed sides, and left the United States a helpless bystander, clutching its scruples. The cold war relations of the Horn, based on the parties' perceived interests, were those of conflict, not of conflict resolution.

Among the countries of the Horn themselves, at the beginning of the 1970s, the cycle of escalation and detente that had characterized the civilian years of Somali government was still in the resting place of detente where Egal had left it, awaiting a discussion of "the major issues." It is not known what the military regime's long-term plans or grand strategies were on the irredentist issue beyond simply building up its own corporate interest group, the army, with massive Russian support. If the distant goal of Somali unification still remained on the military's horizons, it is likely that the regime was simply busy elsewhere in consolidating its control, restructuring the political system, trying to define and implement a Socialist notion of society, and making some tough decisions on internal political, economic, and social issues—a point on which the regime of Siad Barre certainly outshone his civilian predecessors. Moreover, in line with the OAU-induced detente between Somalia and Ethiopia and as part of its general efforts to consolidate control over its segmented society, the Siad regime reduced arms supplies to the Ogaden guerrillas and arrested several members of the Western Somali Liberation Front (WSLF) upon coming to power. The major WSLF leader surrendered to the Ethiopian authorities in March 1970 and was pardoned and given a title by the emperor.[40] There seems to be no evidence for a Somali grand strategy other than awaiting the fruits of the local detente at this point.

The detente was fragile, however, because, as a product of conflict management rather than conflict resolution, it regulated the means for pursuing the conflict but not its ends. This fragility was shown in March–April 1973, when Somali troops challenged Ethiopian troops guarding a Tenneco drilling team that had recently struck gas north of Dolo, 35 miles inside Ethiopia near the Ethiopia-Somalia-Kenya tripoint.[41] Reinforced by heavy Soviet arms supplies, which began pouring in in ever-doubling amounts after 1971 and continued at about $100 million a year in 1974–77, Somalia took the conflict to the OAU in May 1973 in Addis Ababa. Ethiopia rejected the agenda item at the Council of Ministers, and Nigeria (the OAU president) sought to defuse the issue by proposing a Good Offices Committee (on the model of the Moroccan-Algerian committee). Somalia began to realize that it had only Arab African support for its cause and that OAU diplomacy was an unpromising means of pursuing the conflict. The following year, Siad Barre, the OAU host and new president, sought to raise the issue again and win African support, but even Nigerian efforts on behalf of the Good Offices Committee were checked by the two parties' vetoes as the contacts disintegrated into a shouting match reaffirming conflicting claims rather than coming to grips with the major issues.

The major event of 1973, however, was not conflict over territory but the resurgence of the great drought that devastated the sahel and the Horn in 1969–71 and continued its depredations over the next years. In Somali-inhabited territory, the poor conditions of the grazing lands in the interior were exacerbated, and nomads moved to southern Somalia from the Ogaden and even from northern Somalia. By 1975, over 200,000 Somalis—many of them permanent or seasonal inhabitants of Ethiopia—were resettled, some along the Aden Gulf and more along the Indian Ocean coast, and a million Somalis with no way of earning their own subsistence became dependent on Somali government support for medical assistance and food for themselves and their flocks.[42] Some of these Somalis found employment in Somali government activities, including the police and the army, and those in the camps and even in the resettlement projects longed to return to their old place and way of life when the rains again would appear.

In Ethiopia, the effects were even more serious. The drought and the imperial government's inability to handle it, even in its own Amhar provinces such as Wollo, were triggers of the revolution.[43] Rapidly moving leftward on its own momentum, through the imperial governments of Endelkatchew Makonnen (February–July 1974) and Michael Imru (July–September 1974) and the miltary governments of General Aman Andom (September–November 1974),

General Teferi Bante (November 1974–February 1977), and Colonel Mengistu Haile Mariam (thereafter), the revolution presents all the characteristics of a classical sociopolitical upheaval accompanying the collapse of the old order under a centralizing feudal monarchy. That context makes the dynamic trend of events understandable. But it also makes it predictable that the national question would again come to the fore as traditional forces seized on the breakdown of central authority to combine both ideological and national goals.

The initial Somali reaction to the revolution was hesitant and even hopeful. Locked in their own perception of the problem as one of imperial colonialism, the Somalis expected the weakening and fall of the emperor to be accompanied by a fraternal recognition of injustice on the part of the new regime and, therefore, by negotiation to meet Somali demands (although these were never very clearly formulated). Expectations for a favorable settlement of the core issue were raised, based on the notion first that the revolution would accelerate and then that it would render unnecessary the negotiations. Until early 1975, communications were open between the two countries through an effective Ethiopian ambassador, and Somali missions were sent to Addis Ababa. On one occasion, Siad announced that he would not "stab Ethiopia in the back" and take advantage of the collapse of order by taking territory with force.

As 1975 proceeded, it became evident that these hopes were empty. This disappointment, as well as the refugee pressure and the opportunity that continued through Ethiopian military infighting, seems to be the main element in the Somali change in tactics. Like Egal, Siad was under pressure to do something different and more successful than his predecessor; like Sadat, Siad portrayed himself as a man of decision and action. By January 1976, when he went to Addis for the OAU Summit on Angola and talked with Teferi, Barre floated a number of ideas, including a federation of the two states (no longer impossible with the passing of the emperor) but received no encouragement. When he sent official greetings to Ethiopia on the second anniversary of its revolution and when he made a policy speech on the Muslim holiday of 'Id al-Fitr later in the year, he downplayed Ethiopia's claim to having a socialist revolution, berated it for sabotaging a reconciliation on the territorial problem, and called on Communist and African countries to mediate. But a policy decision on a second track had already been made.

In January 1976, Siad met with Darood leaders from the Ogaden and reorganized the Western Somali Liberation Front, attempting to reinforce his control and give ideological content to the nationalist organization by putting some younger socialist leaders in control.[44] In the course of the meeting, as Barre tried to promote the socialist cause, the tribal leaders pressed the nationalist cause, reproaching him for neglecting their homelands in the Ogaden. During the summer, the organization was further modified to provide for two separate but coordinated bodies, the WSLF of Somalis in the Ogaden and the Somali Abo Liberation Front (SALF) of Oromos to the west under Waqo Gutu, the formerly pardoned leader of the earlier revolt. Military training was pursued along with ideological education, apparently with the help of foreign—including Soviet— instructors.[45] Passive control over much of the Ogaden countryside was quickly established through contacts with the Somalis living there; and a complex system of provinces and local, central, executive, control and inspection and coordinating committees were set up throughout the Ogaden and in liaison with Mogadishu. Guerrilla attacks against Ethiopian installations and activities increased during 1976. At the same time, a successful organization was created with a life and a following of its own, as capable of pressuring and committing the Somali government as it was of harassing and defeating the Ethiopians.

The new strategy was successful enough that at some moment in late 1976 it reached the point of its own undoing by requiring a new round of escalation. As the guerrilla forces moved against conventional army installations and toward control of territory, they invited greater Ethiopian army response and, in turn, required direct Somali army support. Although it is possible that in the beginning, in 1976, the guerrilla strategy was seen purely as a way of forcing Ethiopia to negotiate, by the following year—especially after the meetings with Castro in March—military means had been chosen as the way to a solution of the territorial issue. Somalia's well-trained and over-equipped 31,000-person army compared favorably at the beginning of 1977 with the factionalized 65,000-person Ethiopian army (not counting the militia) tied down throughout the country. Whether there was a conscious Somali policy of provoking Ethiopian attacks that would justify a Somali response or whether the Somalis simply followed their own actions progressively up the ladder of escalation is not clear. It is clear that by July 1977 Somali army units were operating with WSLF units in a conventional invasion of Ogaden. The question of official Somali participation is complicated. Throughout the whole Ogaden affair—from 1976 through 1979— Somali soldiers from Ogaden or with families in the Ogaden returned home to "fight for the 'farm,'" with official Somali permission (leave, detachment) or without, but not on military assignment per se or in army units. This is in the nature of the family relationships across the invisible border. From June or July 1977 until March 1978 and again in late 1978 to 1980, Somali army units were ordered to the Ogaden to fight alongside WSLF guerrillas, a different matter from the individual military participation.

Another round in escalation occurred in May 1977, when Somali forces (probably the WSLF) cut the railroad near Diredawa.[46] An impromptu attack on Diredawa itself in April tested its defenses, and more orderly assaults occurred in July and August. Jijiga was surrounded by this time but did not fall until the end of September. Once Jijiga had been taken, the siege of Harar began and continued until February 1978. At the end of the year, at the highpoint of the Somali attack, the entire shield up to the mountains was in the hands of the WSLF and SALF, with Somali army support, except for Harar and some of the highland area in the western (Oromo) part. Having conquered a third of Ethiopia while the Ethiopian army was busy elsewhere, in Eritrea and generally throughout the northern half of the country, the Somalis were unable to consolidate their hold on their territory.

The denouement was rapid, the result of a final unanswerable escalation that moved the territorial conflict back to the positions of early 1976 and the mentalities of the early 1960s. Between November and Feburary, 11,000 Cubans and 1,000 Soviet advisers were brought into the conflict area with $1 billion worth of new arms and the counterattack began. After a month of pounding by Cuban-piloted planes and Soviet artillery and attacks by Russian-driven tanks and human waves of Ethiopian militia, the siege of Harar and Diredawa was lifted, and Jijiga was recaptured on 5 March. The Ogaden was then open to Ethiopian troops, and the Somali army withdrew in haste to defend its contested border. It took the Ethiopians and their allies three years to reach the border in many places, however. After the spring rains of 1978, the WSLF began its activities again, pinning the Cuban and Ethiopian troops to their camps, ambushing garrisons and convoys and causing constant Cuban and Ethiopian losses, interdicting roads, even continuing to hold towns near the border; and by the end of the year Somali troops were back again in the Ogaden. In late 1978 and 1979, foreign visitors were taken by the WSLF throughout much of the Ogaden without detection by the Ethiopians.[47] In response, the Ethiopians destroyed settlements, poisoned wells, decimated herds, and stationed a third of their now 250,000-person army in the area, reinforced by three Cuban brigades cantoned at Jijiga, along the northern end of the railroad, and on the western end of the Somali border. By August 1980, Ethiopian troops had reached the border and began to clear out resistance in the area, launching attacks across the border into central and northwest Somalia throughout the fall of 1980. The Somali army continued to make harassment raids into Ethiopian territory. WSLF activity continued on its own throughout 1980 and then after a six-months' pause was renewed from June 1981 into 1982. The war has never ended, merely taken new forms.[48]

The nature of the second (1975–78) round of the conflict was thus a series of escalating moves on a challenge-and-response or escalation spiral, in which a "final scenario" or grand strategy was probably not present in the mind of either party at the beginning. When the penultimate escalation, by Somalia, was almost successful, Somalia found itself strained and worn out by the effort. It took one more raise by Ethiopia to win the hand.

It is worthwhile spending a moment in defining the reasons for failure, for they have much to do with the components of a winning mentality and the goals of escalation. First, for a number of minor reasons of military operations, the entire campaign went a bit more slowly than expected, so that by the rainy season in September 1977, when the WSLF planned to proclaim the unification of Ogaden with Somalia, the tricity area of Harar, Diredawa, and Jijiga was still in Ethiopian hands.[49] Doubtless the Somalis were misled by their belief that the Ethiopian army had collapsed from within. Second, the Somali army was logistically overextended and, at the end, worn out, also as a function of its mistakenly short timetable. As in any operation of this kind, the deeper one drives into enemy territory, the more vulnerable one becomes to the enemy's enhanced ability to attack, and the Somalis had made inadequate provision for resupply and reinforcement. Finally, ironically, the Somalis lost air control, for their MIGs were no match for the Ethiopian's F-5s.

The problem for Somalia was that it had an overextended definition of winning, forcing it to overextend its means. The only way for Somalia to win is to take Addis Ababa and force a capitulation, an impossibility, or to liberate a defined territory—never clearly identified by the Somalis—and enable the proclamation of an independent secessionist state. For that it remained to capture Harar, a necessity, and to attain the geographic limits of the shield, notably to the west in Oromo lands, another impossibility. Thus, Somali goals were a manifest overrun of legitimizable ends and available means. Unfortunately for the Somalis, there is no natural or salient frontier between

Somali and Oromo territory, and the two liberation movements are linked in fact and history as well as organization.[50] The conflict was thus defined in an unwinnable way for the Somalis.

Yet Ethiopian attempts to consolidate its victory have only succeeded in exacerbating the conflict. Enforced population movements have reinforced pressures rather than creating solutions. Ethiopia attempted to resettle Amhars from the central provinces in the Ogaden but was only partially successful because of local animosity and the drought; 350,000 Amhars and Tigreans were resettled in the Oromo area in 1979–80 against rising local hostility. By 1979, half a million Ethiopian Somalis had fled to Somalia, according to the UN High Commission for Refugees, the largest group of refugees in all Africa; by 1981 and thereafter, they were 1.5 million, pressuring the Somali government for welfare and return.[51] The Ogaden had temporarily lost many of its Somalis without finding a solution for its status.

The Ethiopians also appropriated the Somalis' weapon by fostering their own "eastern Somali liberation front." They encouraged the activities of former army officer Abdullah Yussef, who had been gathering Somali dissidents (particularly fellow Mijertein clanspeople) into a Somali Democratic Action Front (SoDAF) or a Somali Salvation Front (SoSaF) in preparation for an Ethiopian-supported attack.[52] Indeed, since early 1979, Somalia professed fear over a "Cambodian solution," that is, a Cuban- and Ethiopian-supported attack on Somalia, pushing a force of "friendly" Somalis in front of it to put in place as a government that could come to terms with Ethiopia. The past unwillingness of Russians and Cubans to violate African land boundaries, the occupation of the Ethiopian army in other more serious regional dissidence, and the bitter enmity between Somalis and Ethiopians of any ideological color long worked to render a "Cambodian solution" unlikely.

Continuing incidents in the Ogaden made the opportunity for the Ethiopians to attack too tempting, however. In October 1981, SoSaF and the Aden-based Somali Workers' party formed the Democratic Front for Somali Salvation (DFSS), joined in October 1982 by the London-based, largely northern Somali National Movement to form a broad opposition coalition against Siad. At the beginning of July 1982 the attack finally came, in retaliation for continued WSLF activity. With the DFSS as a screen, Ethiopian forces and Cuban advisers brought the war into Somalia, occupied two central border salients for over six years and further postponed any possibilities of conflict management. The Ethiopians and Somali dissidents remained in the area even after 9,000 Cuban troops withdrew from the border and from Ethiopia in mid-1984, leaving only a brigade near Addis Ababa to protect the capital.

In its turn, the Somali National Movement (SNM) entered into action at the beginning of January 1983 and at its November central committee meeting in Jijiga, its military faction took over leadership. A new civilian leadership under Ahmed Mohammed Silanyo, a former Somali minister, was installed in late 1984, just at the time when the DFSS was torn with clan politics and turning against its own leader. Within a year the SNM had announced new attacks in the central part of southern Somalia and in 1986 began planning its major offensive against the north where its own Ishaaq clansmen predominated. The SNM is somewhat more independent of Ethiopia than is the Marxist DFSS and is decidedly a regional movement. It is not clear whether northern secession or a takeover of all Somalia from the Siad Barre regime is its preferred goal.

Conflict Resolution

Conflict resolution during the second-round crisis of the 1970s was difficult not only because of incompatible perceptions of a solution, which is assumed in the notion of conflict, but also because the time was perceived by both sides as being ripe for winning, not for resolving, and because the potential conciliators themselves were more interested in keeping a position than in finding a solution. The Ethiopian Revolution provided the great Somali opportunity to redeem the unfulfilled Ethiopian promise, but it also provided the context in which any Ethiopian government could least afford to be "soft on secession." Beneath these important considerations of moment were more constant zero-sum perceptions of conflict resolution itself. These had been temporarily overcome by a change in perception of appropriate tactics in the 1960s, leading to conflict management but leaving the major issues unresolved. Thereafter, no potential mediator had an unambiguous interest in conflict management, no ripe moment arose on which they could seize, and no mutually intolerable stalemate occurred.

The Somali, Ethiopian, and Kenyan positions are basically rather simple zero-sum perceptions with little in the positions themselves or in the cultures on which they reside to favor negotiation.[53] In a typical debate (in the 1977 UN General Assembly during the Ogaden war), the Ethiopian foreign minister announced, "The root cause is the expansionist ambition of successive Somali regimes, based on an untenable and absurd assumption that any land on which ethnic Somalis live must be part and parcel of the Republic of Somalia";[54] the Somali representative answered that, although the situation is complex, its sole root is Ethiopian colonialism,[55] and his president pursued the argument by indicating that the situation constituted a threat to the peace because of Ethiopian denial of self-determination.[56] In a caricatural sense, both sides were accurate.

In the direction of conflict resolution, the Ethiopian chief of state, Mengistu, proposed Somali cooperation in resources development in the region, common infrastructure to promote trade, and joint development of the Juba and Shebelle basins, a proposal that was not only predicated on recognition of existing sovereignties but also would help Ethiopia take care of its Somalis.[57] The Somali president, Siad Barre maintained that durable peace could be achieved only by a political solution based on the right of self-determination, and he offered his good offices to help the parties to the conflict—the WSLF and Ethiopia, in his view—enter into direct negotiations.[58] During the same time, Siad said that he would not welcome OAU mediation until all Ogaden was liberated and that Somalia would negotiate with Ethiopia, but not about Ogaden sovereignty;[59] as late as January 1978, he called on Ethiopia to undertake a "genuine dialogue" with the WSLF.[60] None of these were even openers for discussion.

Underlying these positions are national cultures that do little to favor direct negotiation or conflict resolution outside of segmentary conflicts within the same identity group. The Somalis, who are the aggrieved or revisionist party, have often shown themselves to be particularly awkward spokespersons for their own cause, with a fine sense of debate, a disregard for established facts, and an inability to present positions in terms attractive to the other party. For example, Somalis blandly ask how they can meet the Kenya demand of renouncing their claims on the Northeastern Province when they have never made such claims, and then they talk about "Somali territory" in Kenya, admitting only under insistent pressure that they mean "Kenyan territory inhabited by ethnic Somalis." Somalis have indicated that, in this system of values and procedures, legal award and actual possession may be two different things, and the challenge of winning litigation may often be great enough that, once legal title is established, actual ownership can be given over to the other party;[61] but such legalistic delights are applicable only to disputes among brothers and cousins, not with foreigners.

Ethiopians and Kenyans, the status quo parties, simply deny that there is a problem outside of the one caused by Somalia. However,

Ethiopian attitudes toward conflict resolution in general are no more helpful than Somali attitudes. Amharic culture relishes litigation and glorifies violent conflictual behavior, exhibiting attitudes character- ized by deception, suspicion, secrecy, and domination. "While it is true that Amhara culture provides means and a certain amount of moral pressure for the reconcilation of conflict, it appears to place greater emphasis on the acting out of aggression . . . Similarly, ver- bal aggression is encouraged by the inclusion of excellence at litiga- tion and insulting in the domain of proper male behavior . . . If the Amhara is by disposition inclined to bestow insults, he is still readier to take offense at the slightest hint of one directed at him . . . Argumentation, litigation, insulting and revenge comprise the hard core of social interaction among Amharas. . . . Most of the time, however, deception is obviously being used to further one man's interests at the expense of another's. . . . The natural complement of so much deception is pronounced suspiciousness. Amhara are con- stantly on the lookout for latent meanings and hidden motives."[62] Such traits obviously make Ethiopians fitting opponents of their Somali neighbors, whom they regard in addition as being weak and unworthy enemies, feeble for having fallen to colonialism and phony in their professions of socialism and Arabism.

Throughout the dispute over the Horn of Africa, it is sharp identity terms that have prevailed; in the era of young states and unstable regimes, possession, relation, and identity are perceived as insepara- ble. As Touval[63] has noted, "Somalia, Kenya and Ethiopia had regarded their disputes as involving 'core values' concerning the definition of the 'national self.'" Even in simulations of conflict resolution on the Horn, identity terms predominate: "We [Somalis] are a free people." "I *am* [sic] an Ethiopian." "As a Kenyan national- ist . . ." "Somalis are suffering from ethnocentrism." "Somalis are warriors," and so on.[64] The same characteristic was directly observed by Levine in Ethiopian behavior: "The Amhara . . . seeks to maxi- mize the opportunity for self-assertion through litigious disputes. . . . The identity of Amhara males is very much bound up with their capacity for aggressiveness, by both violent and verbal means."[65] When identities are seen as being so closely related to the core issue, it becomes hard to move away from the zero-sum problem of sover- eignty and turn to the more subtle issues of relations either as a basis for conflict resolution or as a means of making the sum of the outcome more positive.

Yet Somali irredentism has changed: Some of the points of the five-pointed star have been blunted. The clearest expression of the different status of the various irredenta comes from the Second (Extraordinary) Party Congress of the Somali Revolutionary Socialist Party (XHKS) in January 1979, which resolved to "consider with an open mind political solutions to problems of the Horn, while reaffirming support to Somali liberation forces in Ogaden." Somali irredentism remains unabated in regard to the Ethiopian part of the shield, but in reality has accepted the status quo in regard to the other two territories on the wings.

In addition to the negotiations preceding Somali and Kenyan independence, there have been a number of attempts at conflict resolution and management in the Horn.[66] Sudanese good offices at Khartoum brought a cease-fire on the Ethiopian border in March 1964 after inconclusive clashes between the Somali and Ethiopian armies. President Julius Nyerere of Tanzania was less successful in facilitating an agreement between Somalia and Kenya in Arusha in December 1965; the initiatve came from Somalia, but the stalemate was not hurting the parties enough to force reconciliation, and neither the Somalis nor the mediator seem to have been able to overcome underlying Kenyan suspicions. Attempts at conflict management with both Ethiopia and Kenya in the period 1967–69 and the removal of Djibouti and Kenya from the conflict in 1977 and 1981, respectively, all were at least temporarily successful for reasons to be examined later.

It has been shown that the Kenyan-Somali question is simply less important to Somalia than the Ogaden; it involves fewer people, poorer land, little economic integration with Somalia, and an area of Somali (Darood and Hawiye) emigration, not a core area of the Somali nation. The dispute, as conducted with Kenya, involved two issues: relations between the states and allegiance of the people (a better way of putting it than "sovereignty over the territory" because Somalia has not explicitly claimed the territory, only the people). Reference to the conflict in terms of the people provides the basis for a formula for reconciliation, for it permits Kenya to retain sovereignty while accepting Somalia as an interested spokesman for the population in their grievances. This formula was accepted by Kenya in 1962, rejected after the *shifta* war of the 1960s, but is still available for revival. The conflict management agreements of the years 1967–69 became possible when Somalia and Kenya agreed to come to terms on the relations between states before resolving the question of sovereignty/allegiance, and this decision in turn appears to have been possible because a new group of Somali leaders were able to see a way of perceiving the issue as one of population's grievances rather than territorial sovereignty. It would be begging the question to leave the explanation of the conflict management of the 1960s simply with the arrival of a new Somali government, however, for most of the new team had been prominent in Somali government and politics before. It is more important to ask why they changed their minds, why their views fitted the times and the public mood, and how they obtained results.[67]

Conflict management of the Kenyan dispute was possible in mid-1967 first of all because the new government of President Shermarke and Prime Minister Egal was under a number of pressures to change Somali policy. As a new team in a fluid Somali party arena, they had to show their difference from their predecessors. The previous policy of diplomatic hostility and guerrilla attacks was both expensive and unsuccessful; its renunciation could be temporary, if unsuccessful, and in any case would be less costly. Somali's Soviet arms supplier approved of the new policy and may even have urged it in the aftermath of the June war in the Middle East, where Russia was held accountable for its client's losing.

Conflict management was also possible because the Kenyan government, although unchanged since the abortive mediation attempts of the years 1963–66, was also now under more subtle pressures to accommodate. The same expensive failure marked the antishifta policy, which had only caused the attacks to escalate the choice of weapons from small arms to explosives to landmines.[68] Kenya was also more secure in its independence and identity than it had been in the earlier 1960s.

Finally, conflict management was possible because of the choice and skills of the mediator, President Kenneth Kaunda of Zambia, leader of an East-Central African state noncontiguous to the conflicting parties (replacing Julius Nyerere of Tanzania from the 1965 round, who had some problems of his own with his neighbor, Kenya). After Egal had prepared the contacts by ceasing hostile propaganda against his neighbors, he approached both Haile Selassie and Kenyan Vice-President Daniel Arap Moi at the OAU summit meeting in Kinshasa in September 1967 and then called in Kaunda to help his talks with Arap Moi overcome an initial Kenyan precondition for further negotiations. It was not until July 1968 three meetings later, that Kaunda was finally able to leave the two parties to meet on their own without his conciliatory presence. These meetings produced a gradual deescalation of hostile measures over two years; a mutual recognition of sovereignty and territorial integrity; and a mutual recognition of, and agreement to discuss, the "major issues" of allegiance. The outcome was possible because a gradually grinding stalemate that had produced only worse conditions for everyone had been traded in for a promise to negotiate the basic issue instead.

Thus managed, however, the conflict was susceptible to being revived whenever it was posed in territorial terms. During the Ogaden war, especially in June 1977, Somali troops made several incursions into the northeast desert corner of Kenya at Ramu, probably through a local commander's zeal to get to Ethiopia. Unfortunately, it was just at the time of the OAU meeting, where the Kenyans made much of the incident. Somalia denied and apologized and agreed in July to a border commission to normalize the area, thereby taking the problem out of the area of sovereignty/allegiance and putting it back into interstate relations.

But the context of events in the Ogaden refused to leave it there, and relations worsened between Somalia and Kenya during 1977 and the three years thereafter. Both Britain and Saudi Arabia sought to facilitate communications between the two—without avail. Kenya still had the impression that Somalia wanted its territory, and it demanded a public renunciation of territorial claims; Somalia replied that it could not renounce what it had not advanced. From a strategic point alone, the most obvious policy for Somalia was to come to terms with Kenya, showing Ethiopia (relevantly or not) that its territorial claims could be overcome and isolating Ethiopia from its only contiguous ally. Throughout the 1970s the Somalis were incapable of such a strategy and were unable to remove the suspicion of the Kenyans and replace it with some actions inducing trust. Instead, in February 1979, new President Arap Moi of Kenya made Ethiopia the site of his second African state visit, reaffirming the Kenya-Ethiopian Defense Treaty of 1963. His purpose was as much to liberalize Kenya's image with a visit to a Socialist revolutionary country as it was to enforce Kenya's security, but the gesture symbolized the basic suspicion that inhibits conflict resolution. In December 1980, Mengistu returned the visit, and the two heads of state again reaffirmed their intention to coordinate their action against Somalia.

Other than a clear reading of his solution and the hopelessness of the cause, it is not certain what prompted Siad to change his policy toward Kenya the following year; the U.S. government had felt that pressure to accommodate would have little chance of success despite the entry it enjoyed as ally to both parties, and other mediators were not notably active. Nonetheless, at the OAU summit meeting in Nairobi in July 1981, Siad announced that Somalia had no territorial claims on Kenya and called for an end to the dispute. Kenya received the announcement with some skepticism, but border incidents abated and, more important, were not considered an expression of Somali national policy by Kenya.[69] Although the full force of reconciliation did not occur immediately, a promising opening to resolution had been made, making management of incidents easier. The incipient detente with Kenya shows that conflict resolution can begin when local issues are no longer considered national issues.

The Somali-Kenyan opening of 1981 was consummated over the next three years. Siad Barre simply and finally recognized the hopelessness of his demands and the unproductivity of the campaign. In addition, the Somalis in Kenya were an embarrassment to Somalia and the Somali government was unable to help them despite its claims; Northern Frontier District Liberation Front (NFDLF) leaders had taken refuge in Somalia as Kenya extended its control over the region and Somalia had little control over its "own" people. A sensitive test of Siad Barre's disclaimer occurred in February 1984, when Kenyan soldiers and police participated in killing several hundred members of a Somali-related tribe in Kenya, the Degodia; the Somali government made no protest, and the matter was forgotten. In July, Arap Moi made the first visit of any Kenyan president to Somalia to hear Siad Barre repeat his disclaimers and to sign an agreement on border administration and economic cooperation. An interministerial meeting of the two countries worked for a week in November, and at the end of the year the two presidents signed a border peace and security agreement that ended the dispute. Siad Barre was able to rationalize the distinction between territories by recognizing that Kenya had had its self-determination (whereas Ogaden had not) and therefore the formal expression of the Somali demand was met. When President Moi visited the eastern region in September, he announced a general amnesty and welcomed home 18 NLDLF leaders from their exile in Somalia. While scattered incidents still occur, they are no longer seen as statements about the sovereignty/allegiance issue. Siad Barre ended the Kenyan conflict because he no longer had the means to carry it out nor the hope of its ever succeeding, and Kenya was worth more to him as a friend than as an enemy. Over the years, through ordinary diplomacy, the United States was helpful in bringing out this perception of things.

Djibouti is another successful case of conflict resolution, but paradoxically one that is no more stable for all that. In 1976, France changed its policy in the Afar and Issa Territory, and shifted from reliance on loyal Afar support to cooperation with the Issa politicians calling for independence. Yet the previous policy had operated for so long that it had succeeded in creating a nationalist context of its own in Djibouti, and independence—curiously perhaps, considering the region—has come to mean separate sovereign existence rather than unification with Somalia. A referendum and an election on 8 May 1977 registered an overwhelming vote in favor of independence, meeting the Somali criterion of self-determination, and elected a single-party largely Issa government, later headed by President Gouled.[70] An external solution was made possible only after an internal solution. Although it was born in the very midst of the Ogaden war, Djibouti has remained unshaken, and its independence has become an accepted reality, for the moment.

Djibouti is a good example of the classic compromise formula of nul possession in response to conflicting claims. When parties discover that their maximum goal of possession is unattainable, their minimum goal takes the form of denial of possession to the other party, and then buffer state agreements become possible. In Djibouti's case, each party has agreed to respect the independence of the state as long as the other does, a formula that is successful as a basis for conflict resolution but manifestly unstable. The nul possession formula provides for a vacuum, which normally would add to its instability. However, in the Djibouti case, the problem of vacuum has been skillfully taken care of by a continued French presence in the form of 5,000 troops, reduced two years after independence to 4,500. This force is a deterrent and is effective as such; whether it would be used against Africans in cases of attack is uncertain, but not uncertain enough to reduce its deterrent effect. It is certain, however, that the deterrent force is the linchpin of the buffer formula and that without it the agreement would be the easy prey of an incident, a much more likely eventuality even than in the Kenyan area. Initial French expectations of gradual force reductions in Djibouti were reversed in 1980 because of events in Iran and the Gulf, and a five-year military guarantee was made, with revised expectations of renewal into the 1990s.

The Ogaden is a tougher nut to crack because it is so important to Somali society and economy. It is much more difficult to bypass the sovereignty/allegiance aspect of the conflict and simply concentrate on interstate relations over the core of the conflict. Conflict management of this issue will always remain fragile without conflict resolution. Past attempts to deal with the issue by conciliation have all collapsed on this distinction.

The detente inaugurated by Egal's government in 1967 concerned relations with Ethiopia as well. Its evolution was similar to the

Kenyan detente. Preceded by a unilateral propaganda truce, it began with direct Somali contacts with the emperor at the Kinshasa OAU meeting in September 1967 and continued through the following September. The provisions for a demilitarized frontier zone and the end of hostile propaganda, among others, as included in the 1964 cease-fire agreement, were renewed in 1967; and new efforts in the following years identified specific grievances and sought to eliminate them. However, progress was slower than in the Kenyan discussions, and contacts were direct, unmediated by any helpful catalyst. The purpose was to eliminate sore points and create trust as a new context for discussing "major issues" (the sovereignty/allegiance question). The military government reaffirmed its attachment to Egal's policies but never got to the "major issues," and the Tenneco incident demonstrated how fragile detente on means alone was.

After the Ethiopian Revolution began, a number of mediators were invoked but were powerless before the sweep of events. The OAU Commission of Eight was created in 1973 to investigate the conflict, but Ethiopia maintained that there was nothing to mediate, and Somalia maintained that there was nothing to manage. On the model of the recent (1972) Moroccan-Algerian agreement, the commission empowered Sudanese President Nimeiry and Nigerian President Gowon to investigate the possibility of joint development of an autonomous Ethiopian Ogaden, which, however, had few resources to develop. During the preparation for guerrilla war, Siad called on East African and Communist states to mediate. When Castro did so in Aden in March 1977, it was to urge Somalia to let Ethiopia proceed with its Socialist revolution and not trouble it with the national question, an approach that led Barre to walk out of the meeting, convinced that he had only a few months to complete a military solution before Soviet arms arrived in Ethiopia and that the negotiation track was closed. In August the OAU Commission attempted to hold hearings, but Somalia again walked out when they refused to recognize the WSLF as a principal, independent party. Ethiopia then called for a special OAU Council of Ministers, but the request was never endorsed by a quorum for fear that Somalia would leave the organization and carry the Muslim member states with it. Along the other dimension of international politics in the Horn, the radical governments of Madagascar and Congo proposed their good offices, but the moment was not ripe, and the mediators were powerless to influence the parties' alternatives. In early February 1978, the Nigerian foreign minister came again to Mogadishu for the OAU Commission just as the Ethiopian counteroffensive began to roll, clearly an unpropitious moment. As long as Russia and Cuba were willing to help Ethiopia win, no mediation was possible because the means of stalemate-breaking escalation were at hand. In its meeting at the end of August 1980 in Lagos, the committee reaffirmed the territorial status quo and called for normalization of interstate relations as a step to conflict resolution.

For a brief moment in early 1978, American policy tried various forms of conciliation with limited success that was probably more apparent than real. By the end of 1977, rapprochement between Somalis and Americans was blocked by American insistence on Somali withdrawal from the Ogaden, for it was precisely for arms in support of its invasion that Somalia sought the rapprochement. When an apparent stalemate arose at the turn of the year, U.S. policy tried to seize an apparently ripe moment in mid-January to propose the OAU formula for a solution: Somali return to the border in exchange for Ogaden autonomy, with an international aid program for the Somali inhabitants of the Ethiopian territory. The Ethiopian response in mid-January was categoric: "No negotiations before victory,"[71] as the Soviet and Cuban airlift provided the escalated means for a unilateral rather than a negotiated solution. By early February Siad was worried instead that the Ethiopian drive would continue across the border and retake Berbera for the Russians as punishment.[72] The ostensibly ripe moment vanished with the Somali ability to hold the stalemate.

American policy then shifted to conflict management, seeking to extract an Ethiopian commitment to respect the border just as it had earlier sought to use its arms sales policy to keep Somalia within its side of the border. In November and December 1977, when the possibility was not evident, Mengistu and the Russians announced they had no intention of entering Somalia. Secretary Vance on 10 February called for a cease-fire and Somali withdrawal in exchange for a withdrawal of Cuban and Soviet troops, who would then no longer be necessary, and confirmed Soviet assurances that the border would be respected. By the beginning of the following month, the United States apparently thought it had an agreement on at least a substantial Cuban withdrawal once Somali troops were removed,[73] but this assurance evaporated. Throughout February, assurances received from Russian, Kenyan, and also Ethiopian sources that no border crossing was intended began to be contradicted by Ethiopian public statements about the right of hot pursuit.[74] During the same month, substance was given to the assurances by both sides: The Soviets offered their influence to ensure that Somali forces would be allowed to withdraw without being attacked (a promise that was partially kept, to the annoyance of the Ethiopians), and the Americans promised that Somalia would be armed only if the border were crossed (a promise that was kept in the negative in 1978 and in the positive in 1982). To back up the exchange of promises with a threat, the National Security Council considered but eventually rejected moving an American aircraft carrier from Singapore to the western Indian Ocean as well, a major item for the linkage debate between Secretary Vance and Adviser Brzezinski.[75] The U.S.S.R., in return, turned down an American suggestion that the matter be taken to the UN Security Council and insisted again on a Somali withdrawal before any political discussions. Then, on 19 February, in order to make sure that the local parties not create a situation where their external allies would be obliged to enter the fray and confront each other directly, Deputy National Security Adviser David Aaron was sent to Addis Ababa to establish a better understanding with Ethiopia and confirm assurances that the border would be respected. The assurances were repeated but it was not until 2 March that the United States was able to transmit a Somali agreement to withdraw and announce Soviet Foreign Minister Gromyko's promise to stop at the border in return. In the absence of a mutually intolerable stalemate, the moment was propitious for nothing more than a cease-fire, which took place on its own on 15 March at the border. Six weeks of intense diplomacy ensured that the Great Powers were able to change local partners in the midst of a local war without a higher escalation and confrontation, but the local conflict itself only returned to its starting point in aggravated form.

American policy thereafter returned essentially to the prewar position of 1977 with greater intensity. The withdrawal of the Soviets from Somalia and the rising concern for facilities for a Rapid Deployment Force in the Middle East provided the opening for a closer military relationship between the United States and Somalia, which both sides wanted. The United States, however, also attempted to use this new relationship as a means of extracting a Somali promise not to commit its troops to the Ogaden. The assurance was necessary to the United States in order to avoid an appearance of support for Somali irredentism, but it tied the very hand for which Siad hoped to have help through his American connection. Discussions on arms supplies and respect of the border began with the visit of Assistant Secretary for African Affairs Richard Moose to Mogadishu in mid-March; the use of Berbera was offered to the United States at the end of the following year, two years after its evacuation by the Russians;

and a military and development aid and base facilities agreement including the use of Berbera was signed on 22 August 1980.[76] In the process, however, Somali assurances were repeatedly given in the face of contradictory evidence concerning the presence of troops in the Ogaden, and it was not until the end of 1980 that Somali statements that their army was out of Ogaden appeared to be true. To be sure, U.S. pressure can be said to have been effective, at least for the moment, in making Somalia keep its army on its own side of the border, but that appears to have been the limit of American influence on Somali Ogaden policy in the aftermath of the 1977–78 war.

The problem has been to find a ripe moment and a conceivable formula for a solution to the sovereignty/allegiance issue. One way would be for Ethiopia to hold firm and through time wear down Somali irredentism, as in Kenya and Djibouti, before making accommodations on the interstate relations aspects of the issue. Firm, even harsh, measures might make Somali support for the WSLF costly and inconclusive. Ethiopian measures to expel Somalis and to occupy pieces of Somali territory are examples. Once Somali perception of the issue changed, questions such as grazing or frontier crossing could be discussed without difficulty. It is obvious that this is a long and unsure process that can easily fall victim to the inevitable recurrent incidents. Yet the fact that it remains theoretically possible, with examples from the wings to support it, removes any possible Ethiopian interest in a compromise solution. At the same time, Ethiopian interest in the lesser concessions on interstate relations that would make this solution work depends on the more important national question of Eritrea and its solution on Ethiopian terms.

Another possibility lies in the pursuit of ingenious schemes of association, as tried by the Italians in 1935, by British Foreign Minister Ernest Bevin in 1946,[77] by the Pan-African Freedom Movement in East, Central, and South Africa (PAFMECSA) in 1961–62, and by Fidel Castro in 1977. Haile Selassie noted that unification of the entire region made economic and social sense, but he was thinking of a particular, imperial type of unification. The emperor's passing has removed an obstacle to federation or commonwealth among equal partners. But such an arrangement can come only as a distant result, not a cause, of reconciliation—and indeed of a degree of reconciliation not yet seen in the continent of young states.

The only diplomatic possibility for strengthening the Somali side and equalizing the parties prior to mediation would have to involve legitimizing the Somali claims. Flatly challenging the OAU norms on boundary revisions is unwise, if not impossible, but recognition of the

1964 OAU resolution in the terms in which it was passed could emphasize that two states—Somalia and Morocco—accepted the resolution but declared their case to be an exception to it. Because both cases are indeed unique in that they have involved unresolved boundaries, they could be supported without challenging the principle, and because the Moroccan-Algerian border agreement has already produced a negotiated solution, the disruption of precedent is limited. Such a demarche would involve more skillful diplomacy than the Somalis have shown a capability for thus far, a greater willingness than OAU members have shown to take on a tough case, and an agreement to challenge Ethiopia head-on.

Negotiated solutions come when there is a will and a perceived means to end a situation judged intolerable by both parties, or when parties have something to exchange. Intolerable as the situation may be to Somalia, it is not intolerable to Ethiopia, and the more Somalia adopts policies of detente, the less intolerable to Ethiopia it becomes. Continued guerrilla harassment and continued danger of conventional war might perhaps produce a situation where Somalis and Ethiopians can exchange peace for territory,[78] but Somalia has a long way to go to legitimize its cause and to make harassment and war appear reasonable to African and other states. Cession of the reserved area of the Haud or return to the 1935–41 Italian border (paralleling the coast 600–700 miles in the interior) is unlikely because these old colonial frontiers no longer have any legitimacy. A new border rectification, such as cession of the point of the Ogaden east of 45° East or more to Somalia, has no justification in society or history and would require more power than Somalia has had since 1977 or is likely to have in the future.

In sum, territorial adjustment is a long shot, conflict resolution of the core issue is unlikely, and the best to be expected would be an achievement of conflict management of the interstate relations several steps behind a Somali-Kenya and an Ethiopia-Eritrea detente of a similar type. In the late 1980s, after a few years of revolutionary consolidation and party implantation in Ethiopia, a policy of regional autonomy (already vaguely foreseen by the 16 May 1976 proclamation of the Derg),[79] the opening of the Haud border, and an effective Somali renunciation of force can be steps toward which the parties move as the moment ripens. In the end, if Ethiopia is to remain a multinational empire, then it must allow national autonomy, if not frontier permeability, for its members. Similarly, if Somalia is to remain a nation-state within OAU-legitimized boundaries and come to terms with Ethiopia on an agreed version of the border, then it must dull its irredentism in the Ogaden as it has in Kenya and Djibouti. Wise Ethiopian and Somali statesmen, skillful mediators, and time will be required to find the way.

The structure of relations in the Horn favors one possible scenario for conciliation, especially for a Great Power linked by defense agreements with both Somalia and Kenya. It is in Somalia's interest to complete the process of coming to terms with Kenya, reducing the security threats between the two countries, bringing autonomous Somali bandits in Kenya under control, exchanging final recognition of the border for recognition of its position as concerned neighbor, and thus, as in the case of Djibouti, dulling another point on the five-pointed star. Such a step would serve to isolate Ethiopia by reducing its need for an alliance with Kenya but would also show Ethiopia that Somali irredentism can be reduced, under proper conditions. Optimally, moves for setting up an eventual resolution of the conflict would include a parallel activity by a Communist conciliator—as Russians and perhaps others have already tried—to arrange a settlement in the Eritrean conflict, providing a test case for autonomy. Such a mediation is very much in Soviet and also Ethiopian interest, independent of its effect on Somalia. As a third move, the autonomy precedent and the reduced irredentism precedent could be combined to provide conflict management and eventually conflict resolution in Ogaden. The Ethiopian military control of the entire region achieved during 1980 facilitates such a solution, for autonomy and the return of migrant grazers cannot be accomplished when sovereign control is in doubt; the Ethiopian salients on Somali territory may actually favor a solution, too, for they give Ethiopia something to give up. Such three-step diplomatic maneuvers, involving two rival Great Powers, are too complicated to execute with any chesslike precision. But that should not hinder the first steps from being taken, for they are in the interest of all parties (an unusual situation) and can leave the parties in position for the next steps when they can be taken.

In fact, some of these considerations and scenarios were realized in the second half of the 1980s. It was the drought, catalyst to the earlier war, that brought together the state leaders of the Horn, at the invitation of Djibouti, to organize common measures against the natural catastrophe. The Djibouti summit on 16–17 January 1986 established an Inter-Governmental Authority on Drought and Development (IGADD), but during the meeting there was a three-hour tête-à-tête between Mengistu and Siad Barre, largely the result of Italian instigation, and at the state banquet they publicly shook hands. Weakened by drought and the burden of refugees and faced with effective, if not complete, Ethiopian control of its eastern terri- tory, Siad shifted his goal from military takeover of the Ogaden to an opening of its frontiers to natural population movements—in fact, from the sovereignty/allegiance issue to that of state relations. He proposed a study of grievances and adoption of mutual measures to reduce local tensions. In accordance with established positions, the Somalis refused to refer to "border," since they claim there is none as yet, and the Ethiopians insisted on discussing the border first of all, since they consider recognition of the provisional administrative line as a precondition to progress on other issues. An interministerial committee of foreign ministers met in Addis in April, long sessions were spent discussing whether one should discuss "the common boundary," but an exchange of prisoners was also discussed as well as an agreement to continue discussions. Subsequent meetings were as unproductive. Instead, like Kenya, Ethiopia took measures to test Somalia's commitment. In June occasional air strikes against Somali settlements in Ethiopian planes resumed, but Somalia responded that even the fatalities would not affect the atmosphere of the talks. In addition to the continuing occupation of two localities by the DFSS and the rise of SNM activity, Ethiopia and Somali armies clashed directly for the first time since the Djibouti summit in mid- February 1987 on Somali territory north of the border. Yet inter- ministerial meetings continued, without result.

It was clear that a decision from the heads of state was necessary to break the deadlock over precedence between confidence-building measures and boundary determination, between interstate relations and sovereignty/allegiance. Ethiopia's next response was a positive unilateral signal but not part of a multilateral exchange: in mid- September 1987, the new Ethiopian National Assembly adopted legislation providing for 5 autonomous provinces including Ogaden and Dire Dawa. Half a year later, the two heads of state met again in Djibouti. Mengistu was under heavy pressure to recover army units from idleness in Ogaden and send them to help on the Eritrean front. Thus, he finally agreed to Siad's proposal for the initial establish- ment of confidence-building measures, leaving the interministerial committee to work out the details. In the ensuing agreement of 3 April, the two states renounced the use of force and interference in internal affairs in their mutual relations, agreed to withdraw their armed forces 10–15 kms from the border by mid-May (in accordance with the Khartoum ceasefire 24 years earlier!) and agreed to estab- lish a joint military committee to supervise the disengagement, pre- vent all acts of destabilization, subversion and hostile propaganda, repatriate all remaining prisoners by the end of July, reestablish diplomatic relations, and charge the interministerial committee with preparing recommendations to settle the boundary question. Implementation of the agreement proceeded apace.

The Djibouti accord is a conflict-management measure, stable in nature, and neither side has any incentive to go back on it nor forward from it. It also has some ironic twists. The Somali army immediately recovered the two DFSS salients at Balambale and Guldogob as the Ethiopians withdrew in May 1988, then the Somalis withdrew in their turn. In the northern sector, when the troops were withdrawn from the border, instead of losing its protection, the SNM was suddenly freed of constraints and began its long-planned offensive. By July, a rebel army of 10,000, causing as many deaths, had aroused northern resentment against the government and laid siege to the major towns of the North. Over 25,000 Somalis fled (back) into Ethiopia to escape the fighting, and, in a reversal of role, the Ethiopian foreign minister flew to Mogadishu to assure the Somali government that this was not Ethiopia's doing. Just at the time when reconciliation seemed to be making its way, the campaign for the succession of aged, ailing Siad opened to push aside other considerations and destabilize planned progress. Domestic stability and strength is necessary to the making of concessions, and accomodation must be functional to domestic politics if it is to be possible. The confidence-building measures of 1988 were functional to Siad's and probably Mengistu's regime, but less certainly so to the various participants in the struggle for Siad's succession.

The Horn of Africa is clearly a case where the local conflict dominated global politics. Historic opponents sold themselves to global competitors for armaments, then evicted their suppliers and offered themselves again for further military support to carry on their conflict. The global contestants, too eager to respond and too self-assured of their ability to master the conflict, found themselves dragged into the fray, unable to demur or disengage. When the crisis burst out, they found themselves faced with an opportunity they could not resist as the parties offered themselves once again. The global powers ended up not noticeably better or worse as a result of the switch: Russia had a better partner but a worse military base whereas the United States inherited the better base but it is hosted by a more troublesome partner. Neither side had its grand design; both acted incrementally as they tried to keep their balance during the shift; neither showed much control over the events that pulled them along.

But in the process, the conflict was not resolved, and it lives on to trouble global politics in the future. The crisis did not help the historic conflict, but, if anything, worsened it. The Somalis did not learn the limits of their power, nor the Ethiopians the extent of their responsibility. Only prolonged deescalation can lead to conflict resolution; in the absence of a military stalemate at the end of 1977, there was no ripe moment for mediation in the Ogaden war, and 1969 was a better year for conciliation than at any time until fully twenty years afterward. That is why it is important to keep on encouraging deescalation and preparing for a proper time for conciliation. Otherwise the conflict will continue to impose its own dynamics, drawing its victims from local refugee populations, governments of the region, and outside powers with a stake in regional presence and stability.

Notes

1. In addition to citations, material for this chapter has been gathered from discussions in Mogadishu and Addis Ababa in January 1979. I am particularly grateful for the help of Dr. Hussein Adan and Ambassador A. B. Clark. I am also grateful for the assistance of the American embassies in Addis Ababa and Mogadishu and of INR in the State Department in Washington.
2. On matters of nation-state consolidation, see Karl W. Deutsch and William B. Foltz, eds., *Nation-Building* (New York: Jossey-Bass, 1963). The conflict is closer to the problems analyzed in the classic treatment of Alfred Cobban, *National Self-Determination* (Chicago: University of Chicago Press, 1947), than to those of the more recent classic of Rupert Emerson, *From Empire to Nation* (Cambridge, Mass.: Harvard, 1960).
3. See the report of the first Rift Valley Congress, *Le Monde*, 5 March 1980; also William Hance, *The Geography of Modern Africa* (New York: Columbia University Press, 1964), pp. 354 et passim.
4. The leading work on the Somali nomads is done by I. M. Lewis, *Peoples of the Horn of Africa: Somali, Afar and Saho* (London: International African Institute, 1955); *A Pastoral Democracy* (New York: Oxford, 1961); *The Modern History of Somaliland* (New York: Praeger, 1955); "Modern Political Movements in Somaliland," XXVIII *Africa* 3:244–261, 4:344–363 (1958); also T. Beshah and John Harbeson, "Afar Pastoralists in transition and the Ethiopian Revolution," V *Journal of African Studies* 3:249–267 (1978). A good summary appreciation is found in Bentzil M. Kasper, "Internal Determinants and Consequences of Conflict Resolution of the Somali Border Dispute," paper presented to African Studies Association, 1972. See also J. S. Trimingham, *Islam in Ethiopia* (London: Oxford University Press, 1952); I. M. Lewis, "The Dynamics of Nomadism: Prospects for Sedentarization and Social

Change," in Theodore Monod, ed., *Pastoralism in Tropical Africa* (London: Oxford University Press, 1975); Thadis W. Box, "Nomadism and Land Use in Somalia," XIX *Economic Development and Social Change* 2:220–225 (1971). For a clear portrayal of the transhumant movements, see Lee V. Cassanelli, *The Shaping of Somali Society* (Philadelphia: University of Pennsylvania Press, 1982), chap. 2, especially map, p. 45.

5. On Harrar, see Wolf Leslau, *Ethiopians Speak* (Berkeley, Calif.: University of California Press, 1965), pp. 62–75.

6. On Oromo, see P. T. W. Baxter, "Ethiopia's Unacknowledged Problem: the Oromo," DXXVII *African Affairs* 308:283–296 (1978), and Patrick Gilkes, *The Dying Lion* (London: St. Martin's, 1975), chap. 7. For an excellent treatment of shifting identities, see David Laitin, "The Ogaadeen Question and Changes in Somali Identity," in Donald Rothchild and Victor Olorunsola, eds., *State Versus Ethnic Claims* (Boulder, Colo.: Westview, 1983).

7. On the politics of the Somali nation, see, above all, Saadia Touval, *Somali Nationalism, International Politics and the Drive for Unity in the Horn of Africa* (Cambridge, Mass.: Harvard, 1963); E. A. Bayne, *Four Ways of Politics: State and Nation in Iran, Israel, Italy and Somalia* (New York: American Universities Field Staff, 1965); I. William Zartman, *Government and Politics in Northern Africa* (New York: Praeger, 1964). An exhaustive study of Somali clan politics and conflict is found in A. A. Castagno, "Somalia," in James Coleman and Carl Rosberg, eds., *Political Parties and National Integration in Tropical Africa* (Berkeley, Calif.: University of California Press, 1964). An excellent study of the whole problem is Tom J. Farer, *War Clouds on the Horn of Africa*, 2d ed. (Washington, D.C.: Carnegie, 1979). The most exhaustive but conceptually complex treatment is Volker Matthies, *Der Grenzkonflikt Somalis mit Äthiopien und Kenya* (Hamburg: Institut für Afrika-Kunde, 1977), and another very thorough study with an overly heavy conceptual framework is Robert F. Gorman, *Political Conflict in the Horn of Africa* (New York: Praeger, 1981). New and conflicting light on the origins of the Somalis is found in Bernd Heine, "Linguistic Evidence on the Early History of the Somali People," in Hussein Adam, ed., *Somalia and the World* (Mogadishu: State Printing Press, 1980).

8. See Mordechai Abir, *Ethiopia—The Era of the Princes* (New York: Praeger, 1968); D. Crummey, "Tewodros as Reformer and Modernizer," X *Journal of Modern African History* 3:457–469 (1969); Robert Hess, *Italian Colonialism in Somalia* (Chicago: Univerity of Chicago Press, 1966).

9. The treaties are found in Sir Edward Hertslet, *The Map of Africa by Treaty*, 3d ed. (London: HMSO, 1909), II, pp. 630 ff., 726 ff.; also

Hubert Deschamps, *Côte des Somalis* (Paris: Berger-Levrault, 1948). Then also see Abdi Awaleh Jama, *Basis of the Conflict in the Horn of Africa* (Mogadishu: State Printing Agency, 1978), and Mesfin Wolde Mariam, *The Background of the Ethio-Somalia Boundary Dispute* (Addis Ababa: Berhanena Salem Press, 1964). See The Geographer, *International Boundary Study* no. 87 (Djibouti-Somalia) (1979), no. 134 (Kenya-Somalia) (1973), no. 152 (Ethiopia-Kenya) (1975), no. 153 (Ethiopia-Somalia) (1978), no. 154 (Ethiopia-Djibouti) (1976), State Department; and Ian Brownlie, *African Boundaries* (Berkeley, Calif.: University of California, 1979) pp. 753–851.

10. In 1935 the British offered to exchange the Aden Gulf port of Zeila for the Ogaden, which would have solved so many problems by giving Ethiopia its own ocean port, separating Djibouti from Somalia-to-be, and bringing the Ogaden to eventual Somali rule. The offer was refused. James Dugart Launce-Laforte, *Days of Emperor and Clown* (New York: Doubleday, 1973), p. 131; Touval, *Somali Nationalism*, p. 158.

11. See Gundrun Dahl, *Suffering Grass—Subsistence and Society of Waso Borana* (Stockholm: Studies in Social Anthropology, 1979) for trade flows, and Matthies, *Der Grenzkonflikt*, pp. 251–254 for an evaluation of oil prospects.

12. Ethiopians hold that the Greater Somalia idea is solely a foreign creation; Wolde Mariam, *The Background . . .* , p. 48.

13. On post-1955 (second constitution) Ethiopia, see Richard Greenfield, *Ethiopia* (New York: Praeger, 1966); Christopher Clapham; *Haile Selassie's Government* (New York: Praeger, 1969); Peter Schwab, *Decision-Making in Ethiopia* (Rutherford, N.J.: Fairleigh-Dickinson University Press, 1972); and John Markakis, *Ethiopia: Anatomy of a Traditional Policy* (New York: Oxford University Press, 1974).

14. Eritrea and the northern Ethiopian regional insurrections are not treated in this chapter. On Eritrea, see Gerald Trevaskis, *Eritrea: A Colony in Transition 1941–1952* (New York: Oxford University Press, 1976); Patrick Gilkes, *The Dying Lion*; Barakat Habte Selassie, *Conflict and Intervention in the Horn of Africa* (New York: Monthly Review, 1980); Richard Sherman, *Eritrea: The Unfinished Revolution* (New York: Praeger, 1980); and Haggai Erlich, *The Struggle over Eritrea 1962–1978* (Stanford, Calif.: Hoover Institute, 1983).

15. On Djibouti, see Deschamps, *Côte des Somalis*; Virginia Thompson and Richard Adlof, *Djibouti and the Horn of Africa* (Stanford: Stanford University Press, 1968); Touval, *Somali Nationalism*, chap. 10.

16. Touval, op. cit., p. 126.

17. The problem is peripheral to most works on Kenya. The best treatment is found in Dahl, *Suffering Grass*, and Anders Hjort, *Savannah Town: Rural Ties and Urban Opportunities in Northern Kenya* (Stockholm: Anthropology Department, 1979).

18. Report of the Northern Frontier District Commission, presented to Parliament by the Secretary of State for the Colonies by command of Her Majesty (London: HMSO, 1962).

19. Dahl, *Suffering Grass*, p. 200, clearly expresses the overlaying layers of conflict typical of the crises studies here: "Local tensions were partly the expression of a conflict with wider ramifications. . . . But it was also a local conflict, with roots in local fears of interference with the traditional pastoral forms of production, in Muslim-Christian rivalry, and to a high degree in the security of land rights experienced by the so-called 'alien-Somali.'"

20. See Hjort, *Savannah Town*. Local perceptions were often transmitted to other African states to form a view of the general conflict; thus, East African states, above all, saw Somali activities as a form of Arab expansion, backed by the Arab–oil-consuming West. Clement Cottingham, "Conflict in the Horn of Africa" (mimeographed), January 1978.

21. There is a good report on this phase of the conflict by Ted Gurr, "Tensions in the Horn of Africa," in Feliks Gross, *World Politics and Tension Areas* (New York: New York University Press, 1966).

22. This period of politics is covered in Christian Potholm, *African Political Systems* (Englewood Cliffs, N.J.: Prentice-Hall, 1970) although he misjudges the subsequent coup.

23. See I. M. Lewis, "The Politics of the 1969 Somali Coup," X *Journal of Modern African Studies* 3:383–408 (1972), and David D. Laitin, "The Political Economy of Military Rule in Somalia," XIV *Journal of Modern African Studies* 3:449–468 (1976); Gary D. Payton, "The Somali Coup of 1969: The Case for Soviet Complicity," XVIII *Journal of Modern African Studies* 3:493–508 (1980).

24. Comparative figures are found in I. M. Lewis, "Kim Il-Sung in Somalia," in William Shack and Percy Cohen, eds., *Politics and Leadership* (New York: Oxford University Press, 1979).

25. There is no good analysis of Sudanese-Ethiopian relations except in occasional reports in, for example, *Africa Contemporary Record* (New York: Africana, yearly) and *Africa Confidential* (London, weekly). See series of dispatches by John Darnton, *The New York Times*, 21 June 1977, 28 July 1977. Interestingly, these strategies are all echoed in the smuggled Ethiopian foreign ministry policy paper, "What Should Ethiopia's Guiding Foreign Policy be at the Present Time?" (11 August 1977).

26. The conflicting alliances of the Horn were well presented in *Jeune Afrique*, reproduced in II *An–Nahar Arab Report and Memo* 6:4 (6 February 1978). The region including Sudan is discussed in J. Bowyer Bell, *The Horn of Africa* (New York: Crane, Russak & Co., 1973), albeit not too profoundly.

27. An excellent statement of American interests was given by Matthew Nimetz, then under secretary of state for security assistance, on

16 September 1980 to the House Subcommittee on Foreign Operations, State Department, Current Policy Statement No. 221.

28. See Cyrus Vance, *Hard Choices* (New York: Simon & Schuster, 1983) esp. pp. 87–91, 274, et passim; Zbigniew Brzezinski, *Power and Principle* (New York: Farrar, Strauss & Giroux), esp. pp. 178–190; Michael Samuels, ed., *White Paper: The Horn of Africa*, special supplement, *The Washington Review of Strategic and International Studies*, May 1978; Elizabeth Drew, "Washington Report," *The New Yorker*, 1 May 1977; "Cy vs. Zbig," *Time*, 12 May 1980; *Manchester Guardian*, 15 February 1978. Interesting questions are raised by Constance Holden in "Ethiopia: Did Aid Speed an Inevitable Upheaval?" CLXXXVI *Science* 1192–1226 (27 December 1974). See also Philip LeBel, "Economic and Social Predictors of the Ethiopian Revolution," I *Horn of Africa* 2:53–59 (1978).

29. See "Ethiopia and the Horn of Africa," hearings before the Senate Foreign Affairs Committee's Africa Subcommittee, 4–6 August 1976; Paul B. Henze, "Arming the Horn, 1960–1980," Washington, D.C., The Wilson Center Working Paper no. 43 (July 1982), is the best discussion of the armaments issue.

30. See Dimitri Simes, "Imperial Globalism in the Making," in Samuels, ed., *White Paper*. Two excellent chapters analyze the incremental Soviet decision; Richard Remnek, "Soviet Policy in the Horn of Africa: The Decision to Intervene," in Robert Donaldson, ed., *The Soviet Union in the Third World* (New York: Praeger, 1981), and Robert Patman, "Ideology, Soviet Policy and Realignment in the Horn of Africa," in Adeed Dawisha, ed., *The Soviet Union in the Middle East* (London: Heinemann, 1982).

31. David Ottoway, *Washington Post*, 24 March, 8 May, 25 May 1977.

32. David Ottoway, *Washington Post*, 7 August, 21 October 1977; Richard Remnek, "Soviet Policy in the Horn of Africa: The Decision to Intervene," in Robert Donaldson, ed., *The Soviet Union and the Third World* (Boulder, Colo: Westview, 1981), p. 138.

33. It is the thesis of Erlich's detailed work, *The Struggle over Eritrea*, that the militia was the decisive issue that parted ways between Ethiopian revolutionaries and American military suppliers; see also Sherman, *Eritrea*, pp. 86f.

34. As in Tad Szulc, *New York Magazine*, 27 February 1978; Donald Rothchild et al., *The Eagle Entangled* (New York: Longman, 1979), p. 329; *Washington Star*, 14 January 1978; Selassie, *Conflict and Intervention* . . . , p. 140.

35. On similar attitudes from an earlier period, see former Ambassador Raymond Thurston, "The United States, Somalia, and the Crisis in the Horn," I *Horn of Africa* 2:11–20 (1978).

36. See Arnaud deBorchgrave, *Newsweek*, 26 September 1977, and *Department of State Bulletin*, 11 June 1977.

37. See Gorman, *Political Conflict in the Horn of Africa*, pp. 70–73 and deBorchgrave, *Newsweek*, 26 September 1977. For a statement by Cahill, see *The New York Times*, 18 July 1977.
38. For another discussion as a Saudi condition, see Gorman, *Political Conflict in the Horn of Africa*, pp. 116–123; and Patman, "Ideology, Soviet Policy and Realignment," pp. 50, 53. On congressional opposition to the invasion, see Representatives Don Bonker and Paul Tsongas, *War in the Horn of Africa: A First-Hand Report on the Challenge for U.S. Policy [by a] Fact Finding Mission . . .* , 12–22 December 1977 (Washington, D.C.: House of Representatives, 1978).
39. Kruschchev offered to mediate the Somali-Ethiopian crisis of 1964.
40. Gilkes, *The Dying Lion*, p. 218.
41. The incident is reported in detail in Farer, *War Clouds*, and Colin Legum, *Ethiopia: The Fall of Haile Selassie's Empire* (New York: Africana, 1975), pp. 19f. On the 1973 and 1974 OAU meetings, see Colin Legum, *Africa Contemporary Record 1973–74*, "Somalia," "Ethiopia," and "The Tenth Anniversary of the OAU" (New York: Africana, 1975); and Laitin, "The Ogaadeen Question," 333 f.
42. Basil Davidson, "Somalia in 1975: Some Notes and Impressions," V *Issues* 1:19–26 (1975); Richard Greenfield, *The Wretched of the Horn* (New York: Lilkan Barber, 1984). The rising numbers of refugees are periodically catalogued by the UN high commissioner for refugees (UNHCR); see the UNHCR's *Refugees Magazine* and also the *World Refugee Survey 1983* (New York: U.S. Committee for Refugees [USCR] 1983), pp. 61–64.
43. The best work on the revolution is Marina and David Ottoway, *Ethiopia: Empire in Revolution* (New York: Africana 1978).
44. Hussein M. Aden and Bobe, "The Western Somali Liberation Front," I *Halgan* 11:5–8 (1977); interviews with WSLF leaders in Mogadishu, "An Interview with WSLF," I *Horn of Africa* 2:7–9 (1978); "Interview with Abdullahai Mohammed Mahmud," *France Pays Arabes* 79:18 f. (1978–79). An earlier meeting in January 1975 prepared the process of WSLF reorganization. The Ethiopians were not in error in their January 1976 memorandum, imitatively entitled "War Clouds in the Horn of Africa," which they sent throughout Africa in their charge that WSLF had been active in the early stage of a planned escalation since November 1975; see Ottoway and Ottoway, *Ethiopia*, pp. 163–64; Selassie, *Conflict and Intervention . . .* , p. 119.
45. Arnaud deBorchgrave interview with Siad, *Newsweek*, 1 February 1978.
46. The military events of the following year, in all their confusion and imprecision on the ground, are well covered in newspaper accounts, as in *The New York Times*.
47. See, for example, Nicholas Proffitt, *Newsweek*, 3 December 1979; Kirsty Wright, *Egyptian Gazette*, 17 January 1980; and from the other side, David Ottoway, *Washington Post*, 23 November 1980.

48. See David Ottoway, *Washington Post*, 23 November 1980; Jay Ross, *Washington Post*, 23 November 1980.

49. Colin Legum and Bill Lee, *The Horn of Africa in Continuing Crisis* (New York: Africana, 1979), p. 76.

50. In addition to the Somali Abo Liberation Front, there is also a left-wing Oromo Liberation Front (OLF), which distrusts the Somalis but which does not enjoy some of the sources of international support that the Somalis are able to muster; the OLF has received arms and training from the Eritrean People's Liberation Front. *The Dying Lion*, chap. 7, gives some of the tangled history of these organizations, but the internecine maneuvering goes on; *Christian Science Monitor*, 12 October 1980.

51. David Ottoway and Jay Ross, *Washington Post*, 23 and 24 November 1980; Gregory Jaynes, *The New York Times* 3 and 6 November 1980; Richard Greenfield, "The OAU and Africa's Refugees," in Yassin el-Ayouty and I. William Zartman, eds., *The OAU After Twenty Years* (New York: Praeger, 1983), especially pp. 215, 220 f.; 1983 figures of 500,000 (USCR) to 700,000 (UNHCR) are cited, but an equal number of unregistered refugees are claimed.

52. *Le Monde* 23 September 1979; *Jeune Afrique* 1051:48 f. (25 February 1981); *Jeune Afrique* 1125:44 f. (28 July 1982); see Abdullahi Yussef interview on 1 August 1981 in *FBIS*, MEA, 81–148, R 2–4.

53. The parties' positions can be conveniently located in any plenary debate of the annual UN sessions, where they are invariably expressed. Statements associated with the crisis of the early 1960s are found in Catherine Hoskyns, ed., *The Ethiopia-Somalia-Kenya Dispute 1960–1967* (New York: Oxford University Press, 1969, case studies in African diplomacy no. 11). The telling debate from the 1964 OAU session is found in I. William Zartman and W. Scott Thompson, "The Development of Norms in the African System," in Yassin el-Ayouty, ed., *The Organization of African Unity After Ten Years* (New York: Praeger, 1975), esp. pp. 31–35.

54. Gedli Georgis, *UNGA* 32/Plen 27.125–153/10 October 1977.

55. Warsame, *UNGA* 32/Plen 27.306–322/10 October 1977.

56. General Siad Barre, *UNGA* 32/PLEN 33.163 ff./13 October 1977.

57. Gedli Georgis, *UNGA* 32/Plen 27.150/10 October 1977.

58. Siad Barre, *UNGA* 32/Plen 33.165/13 October 1977.

59. Barre representative in Nicosia, 20 September 1977.

60. Barre, 7 January 1978.

61. Richard E. Walton, "A Problem-Solving Workshop on Border Conflicts in East Africa," VI *Journal of Applied Behavioral Science* 4:453–489 (1970) at 466.

62. Donald Levine, *Wax and Gold* (Chicago: University of Chicago Press, 1966), pp. 248–253.

63. Saadia Touval, *The Boundary Politics of Independent Africa* (Cambridge, Mass.: Harvard University Press, 1972), p. 212.

64. Walton, op. cit., pp. 466, 472 ff.
65. Levine, op. cit., pp. 248 f.
66. In the following pages, analysis of the conflict management negotiations of the 1960s is based on the exhaustive treatment found in Touval, *The Boundary Politics . . .* , especially chap. 9. Relevant documents are found in Hoskyns, ed., *The Ethiopia-Somalia-Kenya Dispute.*
67. See especially Touval, op. cit., pp. 230–245; and also John Drysdale, "The Situation in December 1967—Review and Prospect," in Hoskyns, ed., op. cit.
68. Dahl, *Suffering Grass*, p. 201.
69. An Eastern Kenya Liberation Front remained in Mogadishu in 1983 but under Somali control. Kenyan Somalis' local problems were sometimes resolved in Somalia if the clan leader who resolved disputes lived on the Somali side.
70. See the John Darnton series, *The New York Times*, 24 May, 28 May 1977; Said Yusuf Abdi, "The Mini-Republic of Djibouti: Problems and Prospects," I *Horn of Africa* 2:35–40 (1978); Bentzil Kasper, "The Viability of Independence for the French Territory of the Afars and Issas," paper presented to the African Studies Association, 1976. Both Ethiopia and Somalia were poised to pluck Djibouti if its transition to independence were to fail, in mid-1977, although the coincidental timing was not a cause of the Ogaden war. Djibouti independence (and its subsequent duration) was a remarkable exercise by the French, the result of a gradual evolution rather than of a specific conflict resolution move.
71. *Ethiopian Herald*, 15 January 1978; *Addis Zemen*, 17 January 1978. A good analysis of American efforts in this phase of the war is found in Larry C. Napper, "The Ogaden War: Some Implications for Crisis Prevention," in Alexander L. George, ed., *Managing U.S.-Soviet Rivalry* (Boulder, Colo.: Westview, 1983). Curiously, Secretary Vance, who did not feel that "the moment had yet arrived for a Western mediation effort" in November 1977, felt that the time was ready "for a negotiated settlement' in late January after a coordinating meeting with Britain, France, Italy, and West Germany: Vance, *Hard Choices*, pp. 74, 85–86.
72. Siad press conference, 8 February 1978. Ethiopian troops attacked Somali villages in the Borma-Hargeisa region on occasion in December and January.
73. *The New York Times*, 9 11, 12, 16 March 1978.
74. President Carter to the National Press Club, 2 March; Secretary Vance, 10 February 1978, cf. *Ethiopian Herald*, 14 February 1978. On earlier assurances and the February–March diplomacy, see Napper, "The Ogaden War," 235 ff.
75. See Vance, *Hard Choices*, 86–87, 91; Brzezinski, *Power and Principle*, pp. 182 f. The most the United States could do was to suspend talks

with the Soviets over the security of the Indian Ocean, in early 1978
(*The New York Times*, 19 June 1979). The movement of naval forces to
the Indian Ocean did not occur until 1979, in connection with the
Iranian revolution (*The New York Times*, 10 July and 25 December
1979).

76. *The New York Times*, 17 and 24 March 1978, 3 April 1978; *Le Monde*,
25, 28 December 1979; *Washington Post*, 27 and 30 August, 6 September 1980.

77. Bevin's explanation before Parliament, Hansard, 4 June 1946, col. 1840,
of a proposal for a UN Trusteeship Territory for all Somali-inhabited
areas is reproduced in Hoskyns, *The Ethiopia-Somali-Kenya Dispute . . .*, pp. 9 f. On PAFMECSA's call for a wide federation, see
Touval, *The Boundary Politics . . .*, p. 214. The Italian and Cuban
plans are discussed earlier.

78. The Fermeda Workshop encounter group elaborated a "Free Zone" of
Joint Administration Area concept (Leonard Doob, ed., *Resolving
Conflict* [New Haven: Yale University Press, 1970], pp. 51, 166–71). The
idea did not take hold on the participants, in part, because it was felt
that "Somalia has nothing to offer in return" (p. 166), showing the
Somalis' problem in putting across the idea of exchanging peace for
territory. When they did make gestures toward accepting autonomy, in
late 1981, the moment was overtaken by an Ethiopian shift to destabilizing the Somali regime (Edward Girardet, *Christian Science Monitor*,
15 December 1977). For a comparative study of such "intermediate
status," see Yoram Dinstein, ed., *Models of Autonomy* (New Bruns-
wick: Rutgers University Press, 1981).

79. Ottoway and Ottoway, *Ethiopia . . .*, p. 158 and Appendix A. Communist countries tried to mediate between Ethiopia and the Eritreans in
spring 1977 in East Berlin and in 1979 in Moscow; Ethiopian intransigence ended the first meeting, and Eritrean intransigence ended the
second. See also Erlich, *The Struggle . . .*, p. 113, and David Albright,
"Low Intensity Conflict in Ethiopia," in William Taylor and Steven
Maaronen, eds., *The Future of Conflicts in the 1980s* (Lexington,
Mass.: Heath, 1983).

4

Conflict in the Heartland

He who opens the fish's belly must eat it.
Angolan proverb

What you have eaten is yours.
Bantu proverb

Of all the broad concepts associated with independence—territoriality, sovereignty, consolidation—the most elusive is legitimacy.[1] Philosophers and kings alike have puzzled over the sources of the right to rule, the means by which they can be cultivated, and the way to separate legitimacy's decline from its disappearance.[2] African states' legitimacy is particularly fragile because it is new and because it is vulnerable to attack from its own sources. New, legitimacy is up for grabs, and those who have gotten a hold of it on the basis of ostensibly irrefutable nationalist credentials have often been either removed, discredited, or obliged to constrain the opportunities for demonstrating legitimacy so stringently that their claims on it become meaningless. Vulnerable, incumbent governments find themselves under attack by new nationalists wielding the same kind of weapons that they themselves had used against their colonial rulers—notions of collaboration, unrepresentativeness, corruption, parasitism, in a word, illegitimacy. The struggle for power that accompanies the struggle for independence leaves the losers scattered about the political scene, waiting for the winners of the moment to make a false move and trip. Even when they do not, their need to think of power consolidation before they think of citizen welfare and the need to come to some terms with Great Power sources of support and power lay them open to sniping and assault.

This continuing struggle for legitimacy in the early decades of independence often forces politics to be played on and from neighboring territories, quite independent of any boundary problem or irredenta. Neighbors adopt different ideological positions either because of different histories or simply to distinguish themselves from each other, and so they become natural havens for opponents of each other's regimes, with high level justifications for a contest of each other's legitimacy.

The conflict between Angola and Zaire, which goes back to the beginning of the 1960s, and the crises of 1977 and 1978 in Shaba province of Zaire, concern legitimacy, with personal, ideological, structural, and global ramifications. Zaire's attempts to dominate the Angolan nationalist movement and then Angolan independence were set back when the Popular Movement for the Liberation of Angola (MPLA) came to power in 1975. A formal truce between the two states was signed but not observed. Instead, both countries harbored exile movements of the other's nationals who tried to disrupt their home politics—with their host's approval but beyond its control—from the other side of the border. While Zaire sponsored or allowed sporadic attacks on Angola, Angola permitted—and its Cubans seem to have at least partially trained—two specific invasions into the copper country of Shaba, causing increasing disruption and casualties. Each host country hoped that the attacks from its territory would cause the other government to collapse. The pattern of escalating crises by runaway national liberation movements that distorted the political space of the two countries finally led to management and probably resolution of the conflict under threat of a third, even more catastrophic crisis to come. Properly handled, however, the conflict probably could have been managed one year and one crisis earlier.

Background

The terrain itself is less important a factor in the central African conflict than in northeast and northwest Africa. The region where Zaire, Zambia, and Angola meet is part of the south-central African plateau, a flat highland that is the region of origin for some of Africa's important rivers—Zambezi, Lubilash (a Kasai River confluent), Lualaba (eventually becoming the Zaire River). There is no problem in defining the border between Zaire and its neighbors.[3] It is demarcated throughout. For part of the way between Angola and Zaire it follows the Kasai River itself, and for another part and for much of the way between Zaire and Zambia it follows the watershed between the west central (Zaire) and east central (Zambezi) river systems. The land is covered with tropical savanna with spots of tropical forest and swamplands, the vegetation thriving on a heavy rainy season from November to April. The boundary pays no particular attention to ethnic distributions in the region, but the area is lightly populated, and movement is unimpeded across a recognized but permeable border. In fact, unlike the Ogaden and the Sahara, the territory would be unimportant if it were not for what lies underneath.[4]

In the heart of central Africa lies the copper belt, site of a fifth of the world production of copper; two-thirds of the production of cobalt; and lesser but important amounts of gold, silver, manganese, and zinc. There is also some supportive industry in the area. Transportation systems reach out to both coasts of the continent. The most direct port link—closed since August 1975—is the Benguela railroad running due west across the Angolan highlands to Benguela and Lobito, and the next shortest rail line—also closed from 1977 to 1980—runs circuitously through Zambia and Zimbabwe to Beira and Maputo in Mozambique. A heavily traveled rail line also runs south from Zambia and Zimbabwe to South Africa, others are the Tanzam railroad (TaZaRa) and the Lake Tanganyika crossing to Dar es Salaam, and a final one connects through the Zaire River system northwest to Matadi. With the natural wealth has come an island of European population, centered on the southern Zaire's province of Katanga, renamed Shaba, and bringing with it all the accoutrements of a European expatriate life-style. Well after independence the expatriate population dominated the politics as well as the economics of the region; it made the extractive industry run, and its consequent political role is more a matter of global links than local dominance.

The roots of the Shaba conflict are not deeply historic, for they go back only to the events of independence. Zaire and Angola both had similar problems in establishing a stable government in control of the national territory during the first years of independence, and both had to resort to foreign military assistance to keep the government in its seat. Zaire's initial instability lasted five years, covering its first half of the 1960s, and the effectiveness of government control in a serious challenge continues to be doubted by observers. The reasons are many: Zaire's size, its ethnic rivalries, its terrible internal communications, and above all its early independence given the absence of any preparation for self-government by the colonial power, resulting in the absence of effective political organization and ideology by the nationalist leaders, and the weakness of their legitimacy.

Zairean efforts at national consolidation can be categorized along two crosscutting dimensions—federalist versus unitarist on governmental structure, and radical versus conservative on policy direction—although these policy labels cover a host of different political personalities.[5] None of Zaire's politicians has been able to mobilize enough power by himself, or even with others, in order to accomplish the goal of national consolidation, and so each in turn has been impelled to seek outside allies (who have needed no begging to come to the aid of acceptable Zairean politicians).

After the elimination of the radical unitarist, Patrice Lumumba, and his National Congolese Movement in the first year of independence, the conservative federalist, President Joseph Kasavubu, with his strength in the Bakongo tribal area, sought to overcome the secessionist efforts of the rival conservative federalist, Moise Tshombe, with his strength in the separatist Katanga province of the copper belt. An attempt at national consolidation under a government of national unity headed by the conservative unitarist Cyrille Adoula in mid-1961 was able to overcome Katangan secession with the help of UN forces at the end of the following year but gradually lost its control over politics and its direction over the economy. When the radical unitarist and deputy prime minister Antoine Gizenga was arrested, other members of his African Solidarity party began organizing the current economic, social, and political dissatisfaction and joined with other opposition leaders to form a Committee of National Liberation (CNL). Tshombe, in exile in Madrid, negotiated with the CNL as with other Zairean groups to set up a new national unity government replacing Adoula. In the event, in July 1964, the new government was dominated by Tshombe without the support of the radicals, who continued their local rebellions against the conservatives and their foreign international supporters. Upon his installation in power, Tshombe recalled his former provincial army, the Katangan gendarmerie, from its exile in Zambia and Portuguese Angola, and proceeded with it and mercenary support to overcome the radical dissidence to the humiliation of the regular national army. Tshombe's success again placed him in a position to challenge President Kasavubu, the competing conservative federalist, for control of the state. To forestall this rivalry and finally establish a unified national polity, General Joseph-Désiré (now Sese Seko) Mobuto, a conservative unitarist, took power in November 1965.

From the point of view of the internal structures of politics, Mobutu's reign has in some ways been typical of military rule and in some ways quite different.[6] Unlike the ideal type of radical military leader, Mobutu did not sweep out the old system and "freeze" politics until a new generation of civic politicians could rise within newly created institutions. To the contrary, he has used the independence politicians, wearing out their popular support by skillfully playing them off against each other, buying them off personally with a national system of corruption, creating a direct system of local control, co-opting popular local leaders and drawing them to Kinshasa away from their local bases, and then keeping the capital (scarcely "national") politicians and technicians off balance and dependent on his favor. He created a party, the Revolutionary Peoples Movement (MPR), in 1967 by incorporating all the bits of regional parties in a national organization, but when this parallel channel brought up mainly complaints, he saw only incoherence in it and "rationalized" the system into a single downward channel. The strength of such an approach was its ability to create stability where there had been none in a country whose size, geography, ethnic composition, and lack of national sense and purpose have all favored centrifugal strains and instability. But the cost of stability is stagnation. The weakness of this approach typical of many military—and some civilian—regimes in their more static moments is its tendency to focus on control rather than on movement, on position politics rather than on productive politics, and on the elimination of rivals rather than on the mobilization of competitive groups and regional clienteles into an accountable national system.

Katanga enjoyed the worst aspects of this system.[7] Renamed Shaba by Mobutu (who renamed everything and everyone in Congo-Zaire), it was treated not so much to punish as to remove all its secessionist tendencies. Its strong regional leaders were eliminated by death, exile, or corruption. Instead, either minor tribal representatives were chosen to speak for the province, as in the 1977 Political Bureau elections, or Shabans in the capital were so identified with the central government as to be unrecognizable to their constituency, such as Mobutu's sometime lieutenant Nguza Karl-I-Bond (Tshombe's nephew). But the party regional commissioner or the local military leader has always been a "foreigner" to Shaba and close follower of Mobutu, and this plays on the strong local tribal rivalries while the General Mining Company (Gecamines) and the central government appointees run the province.

Soon to be eliminated when Mobutu came to power were the military supporters of Tshombe, but only after they had completed the job of putting down the radical regionalist secessions. When Mobutu's promises of nondiscrimination and integration of the Katangan gendarmes into the army went unfulfilled, 3,000 gendarmes mutinied at Kisangani in mid-1966. The following year, in the same area, at Kisangani and Bakavu, 2,000 gendarmes joined a mercenary revolt, which was savagely repressed, and—in a tactic frequently used by Mobutu—even those who surrendered were killed; the gendarmes have thereafter been understandably suspicious of offers of amnesty.[8] The gendarmes dispersed, mainly back to Zambia and Angola. In Angola, they were first used by the Portuguese to separate Angolan nationalist groups and were actually in control of the border rail town of Texeira de Sousa during the Angolan civil war. Others later joined the Popular Movement for the Liberation of Angola (MPLA), the Angolan nationalist movement most opposed to the Angolan allies of Mobutu; and those who supported the Portuguese before 1975 were "handed over" to their new allies, the MPLA, by the radical military governor, Admiral Rosa Continho. In Texiera de Sousa, the gendarmes and younger cotribesmen and other younger recruits formed a Congolese National Liberation Front (FLNC) in mid-1968 under the leadership of General Nathanial Mbumba, a former Katangan police commissioner, who then entered into contacts with other exiled opposition groups.[9] FLNC developed the reputation of being the strongest opposition group, and it was this body of errant mercenaries that was to be the immediate cause of the 1977 and 1978 crises.

After the Katangans, all the other political groups and leaders have been played off and worn down under Mobutu's political system and then eliminated as a political force, and still others have merely been removed from politics. There are two effects of this system: One is the isolation of Mobutu through the removal of anyone with skill and visibility, and the other is the exportation of Zairean politics to other African countries and Europe as exiled politicians wage campaigns against Mobutu from abroad. In an attempt to bring Zairean politics under state control, Mobutu has accomplished the opposite by forcing it far and wide, keeping abroad the groups that try to tap domestic discontent in Zaire. To replace domestic support, by the same logic, he has sought the closer involvement of foreign allies, and to replace domestic resources he has sought ever greater injections of foreign aid.

In the political vacuum that has been developing in Zaire, the only remaining support of the president has been his nominally 60,000-person army and, above all, his Israeli-trained 500-person pretorian guard, kept fat and loyal by the corruption system. In such situations, the janissary effect frequently appears, in which the guardians, seeing that no one stands between them and power, seek to replace the unpopular incumbent. In mid-1975, Mobutu carried out a preemptive purge of the army and again the following year removed some of its top officers after an abortive coup. During the Angolan civil war, the Zairean Armed Forces (FAZ), the largest black African army south of Nigeria, was not only ineffective and under its complement by as much as 50 percent; in many cases, its members preferred the security of jail for desertion rather than the risks of fighting the declared enemy.

The enemy of the time on the southwestern frontier was not the Portuguese colonist but the MPLA. Ever since 1960, when Angola's national liberation struggle broke out along its northern border, Zaire gave sanctuary and support to the National Liberation Front of Angola (FLNA), later organized as the Government of the Angolan Republic in Exile (GRAE) under Holden Roberto. In the early 1960s, this movement was seen as the natural prolongation of Congolese independence and of Kasavubu's Bakongo tribe; after the military coup of Mobutu, it became the Angolan arm of the Zairean army and foreign policy and from 1963 to 1968 was recognized by the OAU as the legitimate Angolan national liberation movement. Zaire worked for and expected to see an independent Angola under its aegis. But as time passed without bringing independence, the FLNA lost its vision and fell into internal scrapping, and the war of national liberation became a civil war. After the MPLA started recruiting Katangan gendarmes, in April 1975, the FAZ crossed the border to support the FLNA, but they fought a losing war and gained a hostile neighbor.[10]

The mid-1970s were also a time when even Mobutu's foreign allies were questioning their degree of commitment to their client for the same economic reasons that underlay local discontent.[11] The price of copper fell suddenly to a third its value between mid-1974 and early 1975 as the price of oil rose apace—and with it the world prices on food and manufactured items, Zaire's two largest imports. State investment projects launched in the boom years of 1970–73 now became a drain on resources, and officials' corruption further absorbed and exported parts of the treasury. State indebtedness rose; by 1975, Zaire had the largest foreign debt in black Africa and the eighth largest debt-service ratio in the world (almost all the others being in Latin America), but the same year it began a four-year run of nonpayments on its debts. Between March and November 1976, the government was obliged to meet with its major foreign public and private creditors and agree to begin paying back interest; forced to renegotiate standby arrangements by the International Monetary Fund (IMF), Zaire warned of bankruptcy and received additional payments facilities instead. "Doesn't this mean that Zaire is holding the principal hostage to continued credit?" Senator Frank Church correctly observed. "Doesn't this indicate that a debtor country has its creditors over a barrel?"[12] Nonetheless, the relations of dependency were beginning to bear their obligations. Thus, 1977 was a time when the domestic political vacuum and the strains in the foreign political support of the Zairean regime combined to provide a good opportunity for its opponents abroad to strike.

A decade and a half after Zaire, neighboring Angola underwent a similar series of events accompanying its independence.[13] Although the Portuguese provided almost as little preparation for independence as the Belgians, the Angolans had created their own preparation through thirteen years of sporadic guerrilla warfare against the colonizer and internecine conflict among themselves. After the military revolution in Portugal in April 1974, the Angolan nationalist movements faced a colonial government that would negotiate the conditions of independence, and an agreement was finally put together at Alvor, Portugal, in the following January. By March–April 1975, the Alvor Accord among the parties had collapsed in open fighting over the capital Luanda, triggered by a massacre of an MPLA village by the FLNA moving in from Zaire. Almost immediately, starting with Russian arms to the MPLA in April and American (CIA) arms to FLNA and UNITA in July, the external allies of the three major nationalist movements began a cycle of escalation that continued throughout the summer until the MPLA finally captured Luanda in early August. As the formal date of independence on November 11 grew near, a more serious escalation occurred; in September, South African and mercenary troops moved north in conjunction with combined units of the National Union for the Total Independence of Angola (UNITA) and the FLNA, already helped by some FAZ troops, while Cuban troops joined the MPLA, beginning in October. The OAU met in extraordinary session in January 1976 and split in half over whether to continue to support the tripartite arrangement of the Alvor Accord or to give all support to the MPLA, the liberation movement untainted by South African support. The issue was gradually decided by the MPLA on the ground as its Cuban allies consolidated its control over the more heavily populated core of the country in the west coast and central highlands, pushing the other two allied movements into the interior along the Zairean, Zambian, and Namibian borders, by February 1976.

Like the Zaireans, the Angolans can be seen along the same two dimensions. All three movements are regional organizations, the

MPLA being a Mbundu party of northcentral and eastern Angola, the FLNA being a Bakongo party from northern Angola, and UNITA being an Ovimbundu party from southern and eastern Angola. Only the MPLA had a unitarist base in addition to its regionalist character, in the *mestiço* "tribe" that provided a number of its leaders, including Agostinho Neto, Angola's first president. The movements also had an ideological dimension, like their Zairean counterparts, but this sometimes proved as flexible as their foreign support and more so than their regional-ethnic basis; FLNA may or may not be "conservative," but it had support from the United States, Zaire, and China; MPLA is a radical or Marxist party with Russian and Cuban support; and UNITA has presented many self-images and once had Chinese and later American, French, South African, Moroccan, and Saudi support.

This is not the place to repeat the debate on the escalation of foreign support in the Angolan civil war, but only to indicate the background of conflict, escalation, intervention, and then continued foreign client relations and incomplete territorial control that characterized Angolan independence.[14] Nonetheless, once military victory had been achieved by the MPLA and Cubans over the FLNA and UNITA with their American, South African, and Zairean support, Neto and Mobutu rapidly came to terms and at the end of February 1976 signed an agreement at Brazzaville normalizing relations between their two countries. As in the Horn, this was crisis management without conflict resolution. The two parties agreed to end support to each other's opposition movements and establish normal interstate relations, including reopening the Benguela railroad for Zairean copper exports. None of this occurred.

Instead, each of the successive years was marked by a sudden, brief invasion of Zaire from Angola, not only a dramatic escalation of bad relations but an escalating series of conflicts in which the second was much more vicious than the first and the third was expected to be catastrophic. The conflict has been one of political boundaries—not over lines on the ground but rather over the establishment of territorial limits to national politics or political space.[15] As long as Zairean politics was played in Angola and Angolan politics played by Zaire, conflict was likely to continue. Conflict resolution, which occurred in 1978, involved an agreement to respect each other's political space. In such a situation, it is important to determine whether the settlement of 1978 is final and whether it oc21d not have been achieved in 1976 or 1977.

Conflict

Like Ethiopia and Algeria, Zaire is a potentially dominant power in its region, whose potential makes outsiders covetous and its leaders ambitious. Zaire is the heartland of the continent, comprising the immense basin of the Zaire River within Africa's third largest country, with its fourth largest population and its sixth largest army and GNP. Zaire links Arab African Sudan with southern African Zambia, and Atlantic Congo with Indian Ocean Tanzania. One out of every five African states lies on its borders. For the moment, however, Zaire's power is only potential. Its size is a strain on its communications, its population is a burden on its resources, its army is incompetent, and its political machine runs on corruption. Until 1974, Zaire was held in a front-line position by the fact of its border with Portuguese Africa. Only after the mid-1970s did it find itself surrounded by independent African states, some with hostile ideologies, and only then did it become necessary to start conceiving of a structure of relations among sovereign actors to replace the structure imposed by the anticolonial battleline. The more it develops, the more Zaire—now a vacuum of attraction—will become a major pole of attraction and reaction of central African relations.

There is a second element that gives structure to the relations in the area, and that is the network of ideological attachments that serves as the basis for common action in "camps" and protoalliances on occasion but that also provides a perception greater than reality, much like the Muslim encirclement of Ethiopia or the mutual encirclement of Morocco and Algeria.[16] Zaire's encirclement is a product of the radical states on half of its borders since 1975, when Angola joined the Congo Republic and Tanzania in independence; there has been enough active cooperation between the two Atlantic radicals and between Angola and Tanzania as front-line states to give credence to the perception. Like many Africa-watchers, Mobutu also sees the development of a "radical belt" across to its south, from Angola to Mozambique, and if this belt has noticeable gaps—notably in Zambia—that only demonstrates a pressure that reinforces the perceived trend. By the same token, radical states saw Zaire and Zambia as conservative regimes tied by their extractive industry to a world structure that includes South Africa. This "axis" was geographically complete while Zimbabwe was Rhodesia, but developed a gap after 1980.

Not only is this interlocking structure of "camps" and "axes" a perception of the parties, but it is also a way of committing their external supporters and assuring the African parties a place and a backing in the larger world. The perception is useful, manipulated, and self-reinforcing. Because there is no other system of relations in place, ideology is the pervasive element in imparting structure. The central area where the two ideological "axes" cross, therefore, becomes a major area of conflict because the stakes are defined in terms that identify and enhance their importance. The parties no longer perceive themselves fighting for a mere piece of terrain or even for its underground riches, but rather for the "fate of the progressive alliance" or against "Communist encirclement." Points in this ideological crossroads include Rhodesia/Zimbabwe and Katanga/Shaba.

The parties' perception of the forces that locked them into relentless struggle was formulated in terms of great and global strategies that could have been used by the most fervent cold warrior on either side of the iron curtain. The perceived unit of action is the state, inchoate though it may be in central Africa, but behind and through the state powerful forces were seen to be operating. The debates in the United Nations throughout the period and even after the crises were past reflected this perception.[17] Angolan Foreign Minister Paulo Jorge in the General Assembly debate of 1977 depicted his country as being caught between a Zaire that had contracted itself out as a missile-testing ground for West Germany, sending NATO cruise missiles and reconnaissance satellites over Angola, and a South Africa that used its illegal colony of Namibia as a training and staging base for armed infiltrations into Angola. "The consequences of such designs are the full responsibility of certain governments of Western powers and of certain French-speaking African countries." Happily, he could reaffirm his profound gratitude for the militant solidarity of the Socialist countries, particularly the Soviet Union and Cuba, and of progressive African countries. Clearly, the new state of Angola was not alone but had an important place in the great confrontation of Manichaean world forces.

Perhaps because of its slightly longer independence and different ideological cast, Zaire's perception is made of smaller pieces although they add up to a similar picture. In the special UNGA session on disarmament in 1978,[18] the Zairean ambassador cited new Latin American-type guerrilla tactics within Zaire, new East German and Russian weapons to the region, new Soviet missiles on the Angolan border with Zaire, Katyushka rocket launchers near the Zairean border, large shipments of Russian arms seized in the recent years' border incursions, and the presence of Cuban troops who were never on hand when Portuguese colonialism was the enemy—all to show

Angolan collusion in the Machiavellian world plan to unsettle certain African regimes. Although less explicitly grateful to the Great Powers standing behind Zaire, lest he feed the conspiratorial perceptions of his neighbors, the spokesman for Zaire showed, too, how he perceived his country as the central focus of a global conflict.

There is nothing African or "Africanist" about these nearly mirror-image perceptions. Instead, they represent a cold war projection on an African screen. Unlike the conflicts of northeast and northwest Africa, there is no place in these views for local social problems (other than the plight of refugees from the conflict) or for traditional perceptions of conflict resolution. In northern Africa, the states and their conflicts have some history, from which they can escalate their perceptions into global dimensions, but the newness of political structures on both the state and international level in southern Africa leads the parties to think immediately in ideological terms.

Because people often make up for knowledge with beliefs, another reason for the ideological outlook is the absence of intelligence. The two neighboring states themselves had their own biased sources on events in the border area and neighboring provinces, but even their own provinces were not under their own control, and their knowledge of local events or of events in each other's capitals was incomplete. "One can see that the presence of an Angolan ambassador in Kinshasa [and a Zairean in Luanda] would have helped dispel misunderstandings and clear up illusions," the Zairean ambassador told the UN.[19] There were almost no FAZ units stationed on the border in 1977. During the invasions, even foreign news correspondents were kept out of the province.

Interested external allies were in no better a position as the situation of the United States clearly shows. The only major Western country with an ambassador in Luanda was France, and its relations and sources of information were not very good: the United States had more diplomats in Havana, where diplomatic relations were broken, than in Luanda, where it had none at all, not even the sort of liaison officer it had in Rhodesia before independence. For the United States, the whole region of conflict was what is known as an "intelligence deprived area," and reports were based on very secondary sources—other diplomats, other countries' agents, prisoners. The debate over the degree of Cuban involvement is instructive in this regard. In neither Shaba invasion were Cubans known to have crossed the border although evidence to the contrary would have been useful to the United States: during the same period, Cubans were known to be in the part of Angola from which the invaders

came. Between these two facts lay the gray area on which information was elusive. The nuances of Angolan thinking and the details of
their action were beyond direct sources of information, leaving only
broad lines and suppositions.

The United States has long seen its interest in central Africa as
being directly focused on Zaire, and it defines these interests in
simple geopolitical terms. Zaire's size and location give it a com-
manding position, and its mineral wealth, already noted, comes from
the lodes of the Copper Belt and contains important strategic minerals for the West. American predominance in Zaire was part of the
Congo settlement of the 1960s and was generally accepted, at least as
long as it remained short of direct military implantation or, otherwise stated, as long as it remained compatible with general notions of
nonalignment. However, the relatively large expatriate population
brought by the economic interests of the West in Zaire meant that the
West required a government capable of assuring its security without
Western military presence.

Unfortunately, the weak spot of Western interest in Zaire is the fact
that the government corresponds very little to a Western image of a
popular democratic polity and instead is frequently a downright
embarrassment. Mobutu's legitimacy is under attack. No matter how
large the ministrations of the West designed to put the government
on a stable footing to meet the needs of its people, Zaire has a way of
swallowing all aid within the swamps of corruption and, pleading the
catastrophic effects of being set adrift, asks for more. Yet there is no
promising or legitimate replacement for Mobutu among the opposition,[20] no one who can hold the country together or bring a better
system of government, and Zaire's closest partners—United States,
France, Belgium—have generally felt it better to work with or on him
than against him.

The independence of Angola complicated this Zaire-centered view
of geopolitical Africa. The southern part of the continent no longer
shaded into the domain of South Africa but instead was interrupted
by a number of genuinely radical states such as Angola and Mozambique. American interest in Angola is not very strong, and apart from
protection of oil operations (in Cabinda, not even in the main part of
Angola), U.S. interest is, above all, in keeping the Angolan revolution contained and even satisfied so that it is not impelled by domestic frustrations to seek outside diversions or support. Not all American observers have seen it this way, of course, but even if one
somehow manages to conceive of Angola as the only problem in an
otherwise moderate southern Africa, it seems hard to justify a policy

of siege rather than support, for siege only increases the justification
for foreign assistance against it. On the other hand, it is also hard to
justify the continued presence of 20,000 Cuban troops as an element
of stability. They are not only a reversal of the troop withdrawals of
decolonization but also challenge the implicit restrictions on direct
military implantation in the region established in the Congo crises.
Civilian technicians would be a different matter. Thus, as in many
other parts of the continent, American interest in Angola is in keeping out a hostile foreign presence on a strategic shore and in attenuating relationships across the southern African battleline in order to
avoid an escalating search for external military support.

The complicating factor in Angola has been the continuing presence of a popular guerrilla force in the Ovimbundu areas of central
and eastern Angola, the National Union for the Total Independence
of Angola (UNITA) of Jonas Savimbi.[21] Ten years after independence, the Cubans have still not been able to make a dent in this
opposition, and yet the tenacious and growing presence of UNITA is
a continual justification for their presence. However, because the
components of American interest in the area have changed with the
removal of Portuguese colonial rule, a discussion of the policy implications will have to be pursued in the historical context, and that is
the larger story of the Shaba conflict.

Other Western powers also have a strong interest in Zaire. The
Belgians' postcolonial economic interests have been whittled down
by Zairean nationalizations, but their concern for their former colony remains strong and is whetted by the growing French efforts to
include Zaire in its French-speaking club of Africans. Thus the 2,500
Europeans in Shaba during the crises included 400 French and 2,000
Belgians (compared with 83 Americans), and the rescue and intervention operations were as much an exercise in Franco-Belgian rivalry as
in their cooperation. In May 1974, France and Zaire had signed
technical and military cooperation agreements, but these do not seem
to have provided for military intervention and were not yet ratified
four years later.[22] West Germany also sees opportunities for economic and political cooperation with Zaire.

Russia, on the other hand, recognizes Zaire to be firmly enough in
the Western area of interest to be outside its realistic concern. Angola, to the contrary, is Russia's Zaire in central Africa: a rich
country that has a recognized Marxist-Leninist party in control, a
Friendship Treaty with the Soviet Union signed in October 1976, and
an observer status in Comecon. Soviet aid to the MPLA is long-
standing. Angola is doubtless of continuing importance to the Soviet

Union not only because of the recognizable attempts at revolutionary transformation but also because of Angola's own mineral wealth and its position among the front-line states, though these perceptions have paled under Gorbachev.

Russia had little role in the conflict and apears to have had little in its management.[23] Cuba's role in the conflict was indirect, a product of its presence in Angola. Its interests there are parallel to Russia's; Angola represents a fellow revolution with racial and linguistic similarities as well and also a chance to develop a firm partner in its pretensions at "nonaligned" leadership. Even more than for Russia, Angola was for Cuba a target of opportunity.

Angola became independent and was declared a People's Republic at the beginning of November 1975, but the new MPLA regime did not control the majority of the urban centers until the following February. During this period, as during the previous year, the troops of the MPLA and their Cuban allies fought the Zairean army as allies of their FLNA and, to a much lesser extent, UNITA enemies.[24] Although Neto and Mobutu signed their agreement at Brazzaville for settling interstate problems at the end of February, the joint standing commission that it set up turned out to be an occasion to parade grievances, not to resolve them. Mobutu called on Neto to reconcile all factions into a government of national unity as Mobutu himself claimed to have done; Angola refused to discuss any bilateral problems until Zaire recognized its MPLA regime, which Zaire wanted to do only as part of the package of reconciliation between the two regimes.

The underlying problem was the continuing insecurity in western Angola as a result of forces that were literally beyond either party's control. Zaire wanted the Angolan sanctuary to be denied to the exiled Katangan opposition, and Angola wanted to reassert its control over the territory occupied by UNITA—which Zaire was supplying. Nearly half a million Angolan refugees were camping in Zaire along the border, most of them in the Bas-Zaire region, whereas a quarter of a million Zaireans—primarily Lundas—were taking refuge in northeast Angola and the Katangan gendarmes were making sporadic raids and appeals into the Shaba region to impress local youth into FLNC ranks. In a situation where neither party could control the remnants of rebellion on its territory, both judged it better to blame the other rather than proceed to normalization when normalization would not yield control.

Not only were relations across the border in a constant state of deterioration, but relations among Zaireans in Shaba were worsening

since Angolan independence. In the summer of 1976 a series of
strikes began, starting with miners and railway workers and continuing to the students; this was the only possible form of protest against
the continually worsening economic situation as all other political
expression was under government control. In the fall, strikes were
compounded by a mounting crime wave of murders, rapes, robberies,
and flagrant fraud; although soldiers and officers were active participants in the crime wave, an informal martial law was declared by
General Bumba in mid-December to "restore honesty and order"
until Mobutu contradicted him in early 1977. As both the farthest
and the richest province, Shaba required special attention from the
government and was a tempting hostage for the political opposition
abroad.

At the beginning of 1977, Mobutu tried a new tack and publicly
recognized Neto's regime, meeting Angola's conditions for normalized relations. Angola, however, scorned the gesture, claimed it never
received notice of the recognition and that recognition "had not been
put into practice," and charged Zaire with harboring military training camps from which "Plan Cobra 77" for a South African-Zairean
invasion of Angola would be launched.[25] Later, in February, while
Mobutu repeated assertions that the FLNA office in Kinshasa had
been closed, that the FLNA members in Zaire had been disarmed
and were living as refugees, and that no action against Angola would
be permitted, Angola protested against a FLNA massacre in a northern Angolan village, presumably UNITA sabotage of the Benguela
railroad near the Zaire border, and renewed attacks across the border
on Cabinda. On March 8, several hundred—and eventually about
2,000—Katangan gendarmes and their followers invaded Zaire, following the railroad from Texeira de Sousa to Dilolo toward the great
Gecamines mining center of Kolwezi and also taking two towns
north of the railroad. Shaba I had begun.[26] The invaders' aim, according to Mbumba, was "to chase Mobutu from power and to
create a government of national unity."

The first Shaba invasion falls into two phases. During the month
of March, the disorganized, undisciplined, and poorly supplied
Zairean army units in Shaba fell back and fell apart before the
Katangan FLNC advance. Most FAZ planes were down for lack of
maintenance and parts, Zairean soldiers deserted to avoid fighting or
to join the Katangans, and a munitions train and diesel fuel stocks
fell into the hands of the invaders at Mutshatsha (the highpoint of the
invasion two-thirds of the way to Kolwezi) at the end of the month.
The second phase began in early April, when a contingent of 1,500

Moroccan troops arrived in response to Mobutu's appeal and began to push the FLNC back, standing behind reorganized FAZ units. The Moroccans' deadline was the end of June, for they wished to be out of Zaire before the OAU meeting at that time in Libreville.[27] In fact, the job was accomplished a month before the deadline although the FLNC flow did not start to be reversed until Mutshatsha was recaptured at the end of April, three weeks after the Moroccans arrived. By the end of May, the Katangan gendarmes had melted back into their Angolan sanctuary. The campaign had involved about 2,000 Katangans, who had benefited from some Angolan and Cuban support and training and Russian arms in Angola, and, on the other side, several thousand FAZ troops, 1,500 Moroccans flown in by the French, 80 Belgians, 20 French, a number of Egyptians, and two emergency injections of American noncombat military supplies.

Mobutu's domestic reaction to this evidence of dissatisfaction was characteristically harsh and flexible at the same time.[28] At the beginning of July, he announced sweeping structural reforms in the party and government. Part of the Political Bureau of the Popular Movement of the Revolution (MPR) was to be directly elected and geographically representative; a quasi-parliamentary Legislative Council was to be directly elected, as were municipal councils; and a prime minister was to be appointed. The move allowed an appearance of democracy and a sharing responsibility without any real dilution of centralized power or structural change, for, in the event, most of the Politburo and Legislative Council members as well as the prime minister, Mpinga Kassenda, were political and business figures who had already benefited from the system. On the other hand, in February and March 1978, twenty-seven leaders of lesser opposition uprisings and conspiracies were executed in a return to political repression and suspicion. A large number of middle-level officers from rebellious regions were purged, and even the foreign minister, Nguza Karl-I-Bond, Mobutu's closest lieutenant at times, was convicted of treason in September 1977.[29] The reactions of liberalization, accompanied by suspicion and repression, were not unnatural in the situation, but they resulted in no change in the nature of Zairean politics, like so many of Mobutu's reforms.

Nothing was resolved by the invasion or its defeat. Relations between Angola and Zaire continued to be as unfriendly as before throughout the rest of the year, and an attempt to discuss grievances in interstate relations at the beginning of 1978 collapsed in short order over the inability of either party to meet the other's demands. These demands continued to focus on exiled opponents' raids across

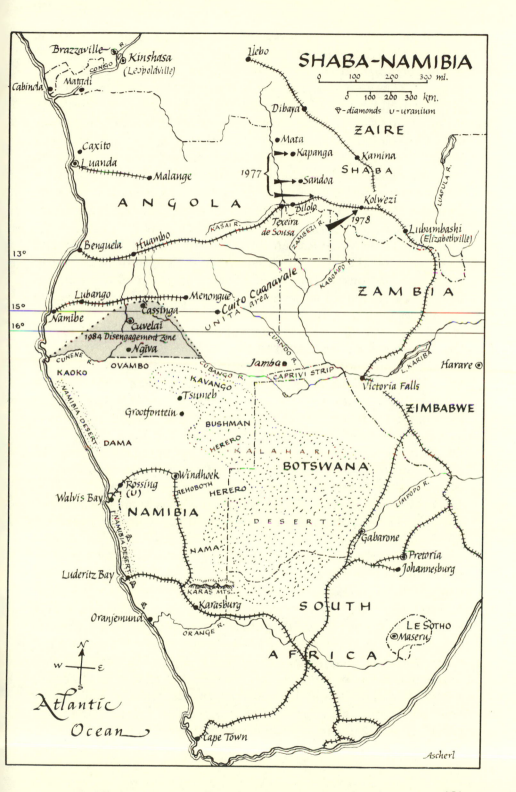

SHABA-NAMIBIA

0   100   200   300 mi.

0   100   200   300 km.

♦-diamonds u-uranium

Brazzaville
Kinshasa
(Léopoldville)
Cabinda
Matadi
Ilebo
Dibaya
ZAIRE
Mata
Caxito
Kapanga
Kamina
Luanda
1977
Sandoa
SHABA
Malange
ANGOLA
Dilolo
Kolwezi
1978
Texeira
de Sousa
Lubumbashi
(Elizabethville)
Benguela
Huambo
KASAI R.
ZAMBEZI R.
KASOMBO
13°
Lubango
Menongue
Cuito Cuanavale
ZAMBIA
15°
Namibe
Cassinga
UNITA area
16°
Cuvelai
CUANDO R.
1984 Disengagement zone
CUNENE R.
Ngiva
Jamba
CAPRIVI STRIP
L. KARIBA
Harare
OVAMBO
CUBANGO R.
Victoria Falls
KAOKO
KAVANGO
Tsumeb
ZIMBABWE
Grootfontein
BUSHMAN
DAMA
HERERO
KALAHARI
Windhoek
BOTSWANA
Rossing
(U)
REHOBOTH
Walvis Bay
HERERO
NAMIBIA
LIMPOPO R.
DESERT
NAMA
Gabarone
Pretoria
Luderitz Bay
Johannesburg
KARAS MTS.
Oranjemund
Karasburg
SOUTH
ORANGE R.
LE SOTHO
N
Maseru
W   E
AFRICA
S

Atlantic
Ocean

Cape Town

Ascherl

151

the border: There were rumors of a second Shaba invasion in the fall of 1977; FLNC troops infiltrated the border after mid-December; Angola complained to the UN of raids on its villages by Angolan refugees, Zairean troops, and South African, Moroccan, and French soldiers. UNITA and FLNA continued to run across the border in the north and sabotage the Benguela railway in the south; and at the end of March 1978, Zaire retaliated to FLNC raids with attacks on a border town just south of the site of the previous year's Shaba invasion, where UNITA claimed Cubans and East Germans were training recent Shaban refugees. After April, the Angolans felt even more threatened by revelation about a Zairean lease two years earlier of a large tract of land in northern Shaba delivered with full sovereign right to a West German missile firm, Orbital Transport und Raketan AG (OTRAG), suspected of making cruise missiles instead of communications satellites and of sending spy satellites over Angola.[30] At a number of moments during this period, Zaireans readied themselves for a new Shaba invasion as Angolan statements fell into the same pattern of invective that had preceded the attack of 1977.[31] One 13 May 1978, the second Shaba invasion began.

United States policy was an essential element in the conflict. The new Carter administration inherited a Manichaean notion of the border confrontation from its predecessor.[32] Official policy was dominated by the fact of the Cuban presence, whose withdrawal as a precondition for American recognition had been escalated by the State Department from "substantial" to "complete" during the course of 1976. The other major fact of Angolan politics—the MPLA victory—was not considered to be a valid basis for U.S. recognition because that victory was perceived as being twice incomplete: the People's Republic did not control the entire territory, and the Cubans rather than the MPLA were seen as the agents of control where the People's Republic was effective. In this view, Cuban withdrawal was to be achieved through pressure or purchased by some appropriate gesture, but neither the means of pressure nor the terms of trade were very clearly perceived. If American policy was to play on divisions in the Angolan polity, it was the territorial division between MPLA and UNITA (FLNA being considered unimportant) rather than the ideological divisions for and against exclusive reliance on Communist allies within the MPLA itself that was to be the subject of manipulation. This policy view was realistic and reasonable, but so were alternative policies. Although appropriate for the period of the civil war, it became less and less so for its aftermath. The other side of the policy context was found in the broad American commitment to Mobutu as the man who brought order and stability to Zaire after a traumatic period in American African policy. Although few American officials were likely to have had any illusions about the attractiveness of Mobutu's regime (he had already expelled the American ambassador and denounced alleged CIA intervention against him in the mid-1970s), he was at least "our" Mobutu, and no alternative appeared more viable or more attractive.

Shaba I provided the new American administration with an occasion to put some nuances into its Zairean policy without as yet undertaking a revision of its policy toward Angola. Instead of running to Mobutu's aid, the United States kept its distance from events, made two responses of limited "nonlethal" aid of $2 million and $13 million, and commented on the background support and only indirect involvement provided by the Angolans and Cubans.[33] The needs of military support were supplied by the Moroccans, transported by the French, reinforcing both countries' notion of their role in African affairs; and American aloofness was underlined by Mobutu himself in his repeated appeals for greater U.S. aid during the invasion and his castigation of the United States for its unresponsiveness afterward.

An initiative to change the Manichaean view of Zairean-Angolan relations came from within the State Department after Shaba I, in November–December 1977.[34] Draft memoranda laid out four options, including a hard line involving renewed Zairean aid and transit for French aid to UNITA to combat the Katangan FLNC; and three variants on a softer line: warnings to Zaire against continuing its support to UNITA because such support only legitimizes Angolan support to the FLNC; warnings as well to France, Morocco, and Saudi Arabia against making the Angolan-Zairean border a battlefront because the conflict only reinforces Angolan reliance on the Cubans; and attempts to stimulate negotiations between Angola and Zaire to solve the continuing problems and remove the dangers of a second Shaba attack, although with no guarantee of success. The memoranda favored the softer line or within it the last option (or alternatively a combination of the last two). Congo and Nigeria were to be encouraged to resume mediations, and carrots and sticks were suggested: possible Cuban withdrawal in the case of successful reconciliation, renewed but tapering military aid to the FAZ, reduced military aid if UNITA support continues. After much refinement, the memorandum was sent to Secretary of State Vance with additional Belgian proposals on economic and military aid to Zaire and a covering note indicating that there was no urgency. The initiative was abandoned on the doorstep, in its very presentation, reportedly because of a feeling that it would not be well received in the White House and that the case was hopeless.

The second Shaba invasion was something different than the first.[35] It was a better planned and more direct military attack, coming through Zambia from the south directly into Kolwezi rather than losing time moving eastward along the railroad, and it was carried out with a viciousness absent in the first. Again its purpose was national insurrection rather than regional secession, "dedicated to overthrowing the fascist, neo-colonialist Mobutu regime," according to the FLNC Brussels spokesman. The attack fell into three phases: the first week during which 4,000 FLNC invaders occupied most of Kolwezi against some active FAZ resistance; the second period of ten days during which 1,500 French and Belgian paratroops repulsed the invasion, to be replaced in the third period beginning on June 1 by an inter-African force of 1,500 Moroccans, 600 Senegalese, 390 Central Africans, 110 Ivorians, and token numbers of Togolese and Gabonese. The invasion had a traumatic effect on the white technicians associated with the mining operations and their families, about 120 of whom were massacred during the fighting or as FLNC hostages.

It is a widely debated issue whether the hostages would have been killed had the paratroops not appeared or whether they were killed in panic as the fighting turned against the invaders. But the debate smacks of casuistry: The Europeans were killed by the invaders and in the subsequent fighting to repel the invasion. The invasion also left a heritage of bitterness among the Africans, some 1,000 of whom were also killed during the fighting, including equal numbers of civilians, rebels, and Zairean troops. The FAZ conduct was often anarchic and vengeful, the paratroopers were arrogant, and the rebels were bent on showing the unpopularity and ineffectiveness of Mobutu's regime. There was no joy in Kolwezi when the invaders were driven out.

In 1977 it had been easy for a new American administration to experiment with new approaches to Africa and see the Shaba invasion as merely a hangover from the Angolan civil war and from a previous administrations' crisis fixation, requiring no firm globalist response. In 1978, after the Russians and Cubans made their second decisive appearance on the continent, in Ethiopia, it was easy to fall off the other side of the road and see Shaba II as part of a Russo-Cuban grand design and even to see the first invasion in retrospect as a test of Western reflexes in preparation for the Horn. Happily, the administration's actions did not fit its words, and its response was to shore up the state under attack while moving to overcome the sources of the conflict. The United States wisely used Shaba to press Zaire—probably not enough—for reforms. The response did not need to be justified as good global policy for it to be good African policy. The Shaba invasions disrupted the Zairean and indirectly the Western economies and cost African and Western lives, and continued conflict wasted Western attentions and Zairean resources and justified continued Cuban presence and Russian preponderance in Angola. The idea that either Shaba was part of a Communist grand design depends on a greater Cubo-Russian role in the invasions than it has appeared possible to establish. Fidel Castro admitted that he knew of the invasion plan a month before and tried to stop it but denied any complicity, and a Democratic congressman after a CIA briefing said, "I think an impartial jury would acquit Castro for lack of evidence."[36] The idea that Shaba prepared the way for Ethiopia misses the chronology of events in the Horn (see the preceding chapter) and also forgets that the lessons of Angola in 1975 were more applicable to Ethiopia than were the lessons of either Shaba invasion.

The conflict represented by the Shaba invasion went through an escalating series of crises. Each crisis was more intense than its predecessor, and each called for an intensified response. A third crisis, expected by some observers, would either be a deplorably pointless repetition of the same bloody event or would follow the escalatory trend and be more intense, more direct, and more massive in its response and, therefore, more easily prepared for. Shaba I came as a surprise to many participants who should have expected it; Shaba II was less of a surprise, and indeed some French spokesmen have indicated that it provided a welcome and anticipated opportunity to make a necessary, demonstrative intervention; the very predictability of Shaba III has made it unlikely. It is that same predictability and the foreseeable magnitude of the next round that made the time ripe for conflict resolution following Shaba II—the balance of terror or impending catastrophe effect.

The Shaba crises were highly irrational events, indicative of the anarchy of conditions in the area. The crises were irrational in that they were inappropriate means to chronically vague ends, a triumph of runaway capabilities over any sense of attainable goals.[37] All levels of policy-making—the opposition movements, the neighboring states, their great power mentors—participated in this irrationality. The opposition movements did what they were able to do—invade, disrupt—without any notion of clear and attainable purpose. UNITA and FLNC alike have proclaimed the end of their respective regime opponents but are unable to make good on their proclamations, no matter what the level of outside support they receive. Zaire and Angola were unable to control the opposition movements against their neighbor, but also unable to give them enough support to assure them victory. France and Cuba, with no effective dissuasion from the United States and Russia, were able to support these movements, and the two pairs of Eastern and Western allies were able to buttress their client states. The sum of their efforts was to maintain a balance in the ability to inflict and withstand damage on both sides, not to either change or resolve the conflict. The Shabas were relics of past policies worn out when future policies were needed.

To recognize this direction is not to imply that the conflict was easy to resolve. The conflict involves a number of dimensions: a conflict among Angolans for control of the Angolan political space, a conflict among Zaireans to bring Zairean political space back into Zairean borders, a conflict between Zaire and Angola over outstanding interstate problems over the control of their own political space and the sorting out of their own structural relations, and a contextual conflict among the great power patrons of the parties.

Conflict Resolution

Each crisis in the conflict has been accompanied by attempts at conflict resolution, and the escalatory nature of the crises has a close relation to the effectiveness of these attempts. The first round of bilateral reconciliation, in 1976–77 after the Brazzaville Accord, turned into a phase of the conflict itself.[38] The accord provided for the repatriation of refugees from both countries, the end of military activity against the other, the cooperation on jointly used communications (notably the Zaire River and the Benguela railroad), the implementation of measures of trust and security along the border, and the normalization of relations. The joint standing committee that it established met in March and then again in December 1976, limiting its discussions to an enumeration of points in the agreement that were not achieved. Underlying the continued conflict was the fact that many of the conditions were beyond the capability of the parties to achieve, and so each used an unwillingness to perform the remaining commitments as an attempt to bargain for the other's performance. When Zaire dropped one of its voluntary obstacles and recognized the MPLA government in January 1977, the pattern of conflict was deeply enough entrenched for the gesture to be lost in the smoke.[39]

During the first Shaba invasion, Nigeria sought to provide the first good offices necessary to resolve the underlying problems.[40] Initially, in mid-April, Mobutu felt that a successful military response to the invasion was necessary before the parties could enter negotiations on an equal footing, and he excluded the other Angolan-Zairean issues of contention outside of the invasion itself from the scope of the discussions. By the end of the month, when Nigerian Foreign Commissioner Joseph Garba came to Kinshasa and the prospects of Moroccan intervention appeared, Mobutu became more amenable to mediation and asked for an inter-African observer force along the border. Angola reversed the Zairean tactics of the preceding year and declared that it would only consider the observer force as part of the subjects to be negotiated, not as a precondition. The "peacekeeping formula" for a solution collapsed on this disagreement, and Nigeria gave up. When Garba renewed attempts to normalize relations at the OAU Council of Ministers at Libreville, he found his Angolan counterpart uninterested.

At this time, both parties found they could live with their conflict, and neither wished to give up the foothold on the other's political space that the conflict gave them—whether it was in their power to give it up or not. Indeed, Mobutu emerged from Shaba I stronger than before. He had shown those who thought his regime to be on its last legs that even a concerted invasion in a weakly held part of his country did not trigger a vast popular uprising, and he had shown that Africa—in the person of Morocco—was ready and willing to come to his aid. Neto, on the other hand, suffered nothing from the affair. He had no reason to reconcile, Mobuto could give him nothing that he wanted, and, if anything, he saw from a narrow reading of the American response to the crisis that Shaba I was not a step in the wrong direction, just too weak a step. A weak response without a move to reconcile and without something to offer was not a policy. Had the United States pressed Zaire and had it established diplomatic contacts to press Angola to pursue the Nigerian demarche during Shaba I, the ripeness of the moment could have been tested.

In November 1977, Mobutu invited Neto to attend his inauguration at the end of the year, beginning the second round of attempts at bilateral reconciliation. Neto did not appear, but at the turn of the year the two sent each other pleasant New Year's greetings, followed by more substantive speeches: Neto complained of Zairean border incursions, particularly by the FLNA, whereas Mobutu called for normalized relations and border observers. An element that facilitated contacts was the existence of African states that were friends of both parties; Zambia, Congo, and Nigeria all played a role, and behind them, France, East Germany, and eventually the United States also urged reconciliation and warned against adventure. During his visit to Nigeria, Neto particularly urged the Zaireans to plan a meeting.

The meeting of the joint standing commission finally took place a year later in January 1978 in Kinshasa, only to discover that things had not changed since the last meeting.[41] Zaire proposed border observers, Angola rejected this, neither side agreed on the nature of political refugees, and not even a final communiqué was possible. The following month the two presidents exchanged public messages, pledging respect for the other's sovereignty and urging a new meeting, but Shaba II was on them before they could meet.

There is probably no clear-cut answer to the Angolan role in Shaba II, but rather an incremental situation in which Cuban training, Angolan foreknowledge, and Katangan initiative all have a part. Neto was known to have been angry over the timing of the invasion, which came just five days after the South African raid on Cassinga (see the next chapter) and undercut his ability to protest. His hand may have been forced by the FLNC, to be sure, but it is unlikely that the attack alone upset a chance for conciliation. The 1978 meeting shows that not enough change in the situation had occurred for fruitful talks to begin.

An American initiative at conflict management—such as proposed in the November-December State Department memoranda—could have made the difference. Instead, Shaba II provided the change. It showed Mobutu that the second escalation was worse and Neto that the second response was worse, providing a trend to future escalations. As time passed, too, both sides developed a somewhat greater control over their own territory and a lessened notion that the opposition groups were useful instruments of policy. Until Shaba II, neither government was persuaded that its aims could not be accomplished by force alone, and indeed both sides cradled a lingering hope that aid to opposition groups could trigger the process of eliminating the other from power. The goal of changing the government of Zaire and of Angola was still present as a favored track for the other party during the period even though the parties also considered the means to this end (to the extent that they controlled them) as matters to be bargained off against each other, as a second-track position. For Angola and Zaire, the FLNC and FLNA-UNITA were bargaining chips with a life of their own. The presence of a first-track policy of changing the other party meant that both parties could be tough in the bargaining process, would lose nothing by not giving in, and would actually retain a possible instrument of national policy by doing so.

The mechanics of the last and apparently successful round of conflict resolution in 1978 show a coincidence that testifies to the overripeness of the moment. At a meeting of Presidents Carter and Giscard d'Estaing on May 26 during the latter's visit to Washington, it was decided to hold a small meeting on June 5 among American, French, German, Belgian, and British officials to discuss the general situation prior to the larger economic conference in Brussels a week later. Initially, there was no agreement on the approach, the United States seeking to stress the economic aspects of the problem and the French insisting on security as a precondition for economic stability. Once the matter was posed as a question of "how to stabilize Zaire after last month's invasion . . . without getting bogged down in African rivalries or in any new East-West confrontation,"[42] the natural answer appeared to be to call off the threat to Zairean stability. This was to be done both externally and through measures dealing with internal Zairean reform, the alienation of Shaba, and other domestic problems to be discussed with some insistence with Mobutu.

A week after the Paris conference, Ambassador Donald McHenry was sent to Luanda in response to repeated signals from Angola inviting contacts.[43] When the mission arrived, it found that the Angolans had arrived independently at the same conclusions and were interested in discussing the Zairean border problems, the negotiations with Namibia (see the following chapter), and the diversification of relations with the West to counterbalance those with Cuba and Russia. They were told, in turn, that control of the FLNC and less reliance on the Cubans would produce the improved relations that they sought with the West, and there was doubtless also some discussion of the Angolan requirement that the West give up its support for UNITA.

The change was overdue all around. As was already evident a year before, Neto was interested in developing relations with other countries to dilute his dependence on Russia and Cuba and indeed needed some payoffs for pursuing this option because it was a point on which his opposition scored him. The chances of a MPLA-UNITA government were long gone; the chances of a more flexible MPLA regime were in need of support.

The reconciliation occurred on 19–20 August 1978, when representatives of both sides met to reaffirm the solutions to the outstanding problems provided for originally in the Brazzaville Accord, but now with greater ability and intention to perform on the part of the two sides.[44] The two presidents met in Luanda two months later to confirm the agreement and then in Kinshasa in mid-February 1979 to take stock of the status of the measures taken. They found some of the problems of refugees and the railroad hard to resolve rapidly but vowed to pursue their efforts. The Kinshasa meeting was followed up by another summit in June and then, after the death of Neto in September, was reaffirmed by a meeting between Mobutu and the new Angolan president, Eduardo dos Santos, in mid-October in Ndola. The reconciliation meetings broadened as they continued: The Zambian prime minister was present in Kinshasa in February and Zambian President Kenneth Kaunda made the Ndola meeting a tripartite summit. Economic cooperation was added to the agenda items of refugees and railroads, a bilateral monetary agreement to promote trade was signed in December, and a trilateral nonaggression treaty in October. The reconciliation was signed, therefore, in repeated engagements at the highest level, sealed by a continuing search for outstanding problems and a search for new areas of cooperation, and delivered through specific measures to implement the general agreements and reduce the sources of interstate incidents.

The reconciliations held as bilateral policy for more than a decade even though all the problems were not yet eliminated. The Benguela railroad was finally opened for one symbolic trip in April 1979, but it took so long that it was judged uneconomic, and the line has been closed under UNITA attacks ever since. The movement of over 200,000 refugees in each direction was conducted effectively, and a tripartite agreement was signed with the UN High Commission for Refugees in September 1980 to organize continued voluntary repatriation.[45] The number of Zaireans in Angola and Zambia was down to 18,000 and 6,000 respectively in 1981 and stayed there at an almost residual level beyond which accounting is difficult. But over 300,000 Angolans still remained in Zaire, in part because of the ongoing civil war in Angola. After the Ndola meeting and the initial Zairean and Angolan amnesties and receipt of refugees, FLNC and FLNA leaders were expelled from their former host countries; Mbumba went to Guinea-Bissau (although there was a later rumor of his return to Brazzaville), and Roberto to Paris after having been refused asylum in Senegal. Expatriates in the Copper Belt were initially concerned over their security after the Inter-African Force pulled out in August 1979, but they have gradually learned to live with their concerns and with the new Belgian-trained army brigade, backed by a new French-trained intervention brigade of paratroops, which replaced it. After

Shaba II, the number of Europeans in Kolwezi dropped from 2,000 to 300, where it has stayed since then.

The threats of worse escalations have been avoided: the United States did not refurbish the Kamina base, the FAZ was not involved in Angola, the Angolan army has not (or has not been able to) exercised hot pursuit into Zaire. The agreements of the late 1970s were reinforced in the mid-1980s: during President dos Santos' visit to Kinshasa in early February 1985, following a meeting of the Zairean-Angolan joint commission, agreements were signed on border trade and customs, natural resources, medical cooperation, defense and security, circulation of persons and goods, and a joint border security commission. At the state dinner on the occasion, Mobutu summarized the spirit of the reconciliaton with a pledge that "the territory of one will never serve as a bastion for the destabilization of the other." But by the end of the 1980s, the fortunes of instability had shifted, reconciliation between Zaire and Angola had become subservient to the politics of national reconciliation in Angola, and Shaba was now on the other side of the border. In an effort to combine both reconciliations and stay on the good side of any Angolan government while keeping a hand in Angolan political space, Mobutu in May 1988 offered to serve as mediator in the Angolan civil war.

The Shaba crises are unique in that they involve the first instance of African collective defense and the first use of an inter-African force for peacekeeping. An African collective security force has been part of the African unity idea since before the founding of the OAU and has its place in the OAU Charter, but has never been realized because of disagreements among the members over its use and dangers of its misuse. The role of Morocco in Shaba I actually precipitated the formation of an African peacekeeping force after Shaba II because Morocco did not want to take on a permanent role as the African gendarme—or at least not without other African support. Whereas the proponents of an African army in the 1960s were the radical states, such as Ghana, in the mid-1970s it was the moderate French-speaking states such as Senegal, Gabon, Ivory Coast, and Zaire who favored the idea, supported by Arab African moderates such as Morocco and Egypt. Not only had the concern for defense against an external enemy shifted from the radical to the moderate camp by the second decade, but by 1978 the idea of an African peacekeeping force had developed strong support in the West, for the same reason as expressed by Morocco. In May, during Shaba II, both France and Belgium began to urge the creation of an inter-African force; the United States lukewarmly supported the idea, but felt it must be within the framework of the OAU.

The very Western support that rendered the idea possible also made it unacceptable to the OAU. The idea was raised at the Franco-African summits of 1977 and 1978, the latter fortuitously scheduled on May 22–23 during the Shaba crisis, but was blocked formally by Mali's expressing the reticence of some of the military regimes.[46] It was also defeated by uncertainty as to its exact form: mutual defense and nonaggression act (proposed by Niger for West Africa), Pan-African or French-speaking African intervention force, or Franco-African or even French-speaking "Commonwealth" (Francophonia) defense force—all had their supporters and opponents. When the idea was carried—personally, against the decisions of the meeting—to the OAU summit at Khartoum by OAU President Bongo of Gabon in July, the weight of the French role in it killed it. Many Africans saw it as necessarily dependent on, and therefore an extension of, NATO. Nonetheless, the general idea of an inter-African security force under the aegis of the OAU was again repeated in OAU Secretary Edem Kodjo's annual report to the 1979 summit, a tantalizing idea as attractive and almost as inaccessible as African unity itself.

Instead, in response to the personal appeal of the OAU president, Morocco and five other African countries formed a peacekeeping force outside the OAU to replace the French and Belgian intervention force after Shaba II. The force operated well, without incident, and when it withdrew fifteen months later,[47] it had accomplished a greater restoration of a sense of security in the province than any of the comments of the moment indicated was possible. It is worthwhile to press African states to establish continental observer forces, as the need requires, and to learn from experience rather than shying away from imagined difficulties. The success of a "friendly" peacekeeping force may help convince OAU members that a "neutral" peacekeeping force is possible although, as the experience of the UN and of other regional organizations has shown, it is a long way from a peacekeeping force to a collective security force. The inter-African force in Shaba helped pave the way for an OAU force in Chad the following year and again in 1981–82, where the experience was less positive. Many of the problems of finance and logistics in Chad were already present in Shaba and did not receive adequate attention; other military and political problems in Chad were new, just as the situation was different, and were probably both foreseeable and insurmountable. Both Shaba and Chad provide experience with which to confront the problem of an inter-African force, the biggest lesson of which is that it is easier to defend a governmental authority than it is to create it through collective action.

Relations between Kinshasa and Luanda have become acceptable, and future border incidents are likely to be handled as detailed events, not as parts of some larger strategic plan. Political space has been brought more closely in coincidence with sovereign space, and the challenges to legitimacy have been weakened. But UNITA remains in Angola, where its rising fortunes in the late 1980s could tempt Zaire to provide it greater support and civil war is likely to persist in some form in Zimbabwe as the examples of Zaire and Angola move southward. In Zaire, the problems of national consolidation, particularly strong in Shaba, have become internal problems unless the instability of Zambia allows a Shaba III from the south.[48] But in the rest of the front-line area—Angola, Zambia, Zimbabwe, Mozambique—the problems of territorial control and of leftover national liberation movements remain as tangible expressions of the problem of legitimacy, and the ideological view of structural rivalries is present to give them greater shape. South Africa stands ready to assist and exacerbate these problems or simply to benefit from them. The defeat of the FLNC probably also defeated the chances for an anti-Mobutu movement to mobilize radical states' support for the "second independence" of Zaire, but the second independence of Zambia or Malawi could be difficult to keep an internal affair.

But "Shabas" are not only found in the more recently independent states of southern Africa. A similar series of incidents already took place in Uganda during the first three years of the 1980s, as leftover members of Idi Amin's army invaded from their areas of refuge in Zaire and Sudan.[49] Sudanese and Ethiopian political refugees in each other's territory present the same situation. In January 1980 and March 1982, Tunisians trained in Libya made raids on southern Tunisia in the hopes of triggering a revolution against President Bourguiba.[50] Libya hosts and trains similar refugees of discontent from a number of other countries.[51] Usually, as in the case of Uganda or Tunisia, the proper response is one of support for the country under attack; in the Tunisian case, the United States and France reacted swiftly with military support when the regional organization—in this case, the Arab League—was unable to take a stand. An additional problem for conciliators, therefore, is to separate out such cases from the rarer but more important ones where grievances are legitimately bilateral and conflict can be managed and resolved.

The American response in the two Shaba affairs was frequently criticized from many quarters, but particularly for its interventionist aspects. Yet it was intervention in the most positive sense—limited, coordinated with Africans, and used to achieve domestic reforms and international conflict resolution. Furthermore, the agreement that was finally achieved has stuck. Built on a ripe moment, it responded to the readiness of the parties to the conflict for a resolution of their differences. Within the American administration the policy debate was over the degree of support to give to Zaire and the degree of opposition to adopt toward Angola. When it combined the two questions in an effort to improve its position toward both countries, the administration produced a constructive policy response that was clearly in its interest. But by the same token, that response could have been tried a year before, with a good chance of the same process. Even if it had failed, it would have left the United States in a more attractive position among African states and would have facilitated a second attempt the next year.

Notes

1. In addition to citations, material for this chapter has been gathered through consultation of State Department records and from interviews during a field trip to Shaba in 1976. I am grateful for comments from Michael Schatzberg, Ilunga Kabongo, and Richard Moose.
2. See, for recent discussion, a series of writings by Robert Jackson and Carl A. Rosberg, *Personal Rule in Black Africa* (Berkeley, Calif.: Univerity of California Press, 1982), especially chap. 2; "Why Africa's Weak States Persist," XXXV *World Politics* 1:1–24 (October 1982); "Political Legitimation in Africa's Multi-Ethnic States," paper to the International Political Science Association, Rio de Janeiro, 1982; "Empirical Statehood in Sub-Sahara Africa," paper to the Defense Intelligence School Conference, 1982.
3. On the boundary, see the *The Geographer, International Boundary Study* no. 144 (1974), State Department; Jan Brownlie, *African Boundaries* (Berkeley, Calif.: University of California Press, 1979), pp. 489–514.
4. See William Hance, *The Geography of Modern Africa* (New York: Columbia University Press, 1964), pp. 33–35.
5. These dimensions are adapted from Nzongola-Ntalaja, "The Continuing Struggle for National Liberation in Zaire," XVII *Journal of Modern African Studies* 4:595–614 (1979).
6. There is some good literature on Mobutu's rule. See Jean Rymenam, "Comment le regime Mobutu a sapé ses propres fondements," *Monde*

Diplomatique 278:8–9 (May 1977); Jules Chome, *L'Ascension de Mobutu* (Brussels: Editions Complexes, 1975); J-Ph. Peemans, "The Social and Economic Development of Zaire Since Independence," *African Affairs* 74:148–79 (April 1975); Mpinga-Kasenda, *L'Administration publique du Zaire* (Paris: Pedone, 1973); S. Vieux, *L'Administration zairoise* (Paris: Berger-Levrault, 1974); J. C. Willame, *Patrimonialism and Political Change in the Congo* (Stanford, Calif.: Stanford University Press, 1972); J. Vanderlinden, ed., *Du Congo au Zaire 1960–1980* (Brussels: CRISP, 1982); V. S. Naipaul, "A New King for the Congo," *New York Review of Books* 22:11 (26 June 1975); Michael G. Schatzberg, *Politics and Class in Zaire* (New York: Africana, 1980) and *The Dialectics of Oppression in Zaire* (Bloomington: Indiana University Press, 1988); and Crawford Young, "Zaire: The Unending Crisis," DVII *Foreign Affairs* 1:169–84 (fall 1978). On pre-Mobutu Zaire, the basic work is Crawford Young, *Politics in the Congo* (Princeton, N.J.: Princeton University Press, 1965). See also Elise Forbes Pachter, *Our Man in Kinshasha* (forthcoming), as well as testimony in *Hearings on Economic and Military Assistance to Zaire*, Africa Subcommittee, House Committee on Foreign Affairs, 5, March 1979.

7. See particularly David Gould and M. Mushi, "Les multirationalities et l'administration du developpement: l'écologie du processus decisionnel au Shaba," *Canadian Journal of Political Science* (June 1977); David Gould and J-G. Katuala, "Decision-Making and Administrative Reform in Local Zairois Administration," African Studies Association meeting in San Francisco, 1975; David Gould, "Local Administration in Zaire and Underdevelopment," XV *Journal of Modern African Studies* 3:349–378 (1977).

8. On the background of 1966–67, see *Les dossiers du CRISP: Congo 1966* (Brussels: Centre de la recherche et d'information socio-politique, 1967), p. 345, and "Congo: End of the Mercenaries," *Africa Confidential*, 27 July 1967, p. 8; Young, *Politics in the Congo*, 458; Williams, *Patrimonialism . . .* , pp. 146–48.

9. *Jeune Afrique* 908:17 (31 May 1978); Nzongola-Ntalaja, "The US, Zaire and Angola," in René Lemarchand, ed., *American Policy in Southern Africa* (Washington, D.C.: University Press of America, 1978), pp. 145–170, especially p. 162; *The New York Times*, 24 May 1978; René Lefort, "La grande impuissance des opposants," *Le Monde Diplomatique* 278:9 f. (May 1977).

10. John Marcum, *The Angolan Revolution* (Cambridge, Mass.: MIT, 1978), vol. II, p. 259; *Manchester Guardian*, 15 October 1975. Crawford Young places the FAZ entry into Angola in September, independent of the MPLA-FLNC alliance. Klinghofer (note 14), p. 107, dates FAZ entry in February and July.

11. For a comprehensive analysis of the years of crisis preceding Shaba, 1973–77, see Crawford Young, "The Portuguese Coup and Zaire's

Southern African Policy," in John Seiler, ed., *Southern Africa Since the Portuguese Coup* (Boulder, Colo.: Westview, 1980). A good critical survey of the problem is found in Guy Gran, ed., *Zaire: The Political Economics of Under-Development* (New York: Praeger, 1979).

12. Reported in *The New York Times*, 8 October 1977.

13. See Marcum, *The Angolan Revolution*, vols. I and II; Gerald Bender, "Kissinger in Angola; Anatomy of a Failure," in Lemarchand, ed., *American Policy*; Marcum, Bender, Douglas Wheeler et al., Senate Committee on Foreign Relations, Subcommittee on African Affairs, *U.S. Policy Toward Southern Africa* (Washington, D.C.: GPO, 1976), René Pelissier, *La Colonie du Minotaure* (Paris: Pelissier, 1978); and excellent chapters by Douglas Wheeler and Maurice Halperin in John Seiler, ed., *Southern Africa Since the Portuguese Coup* (Boulder, Colo.: Westview, 1980).

14. In addition to the preceding, see Nathaniel Davis, "The Angola Decision of 1975: A Personal Memoir," DVII *Foreign Affairs* 1:110–125 (fall 1978); John Stockwell, *In Search of Enemies* (New York: Norton, 1978); Arthur Jay Klinghofer, "The Soviet Union and Angola," in Robert Donaldson, ed., *The Soviet Union and the Third World* (Boulder, Colo.: Westview, 1981); Arthur Jay Klinghofer, "Soviet Policy Toward Africa: Impact of the Angolan War," in Raymond Duncan, ed., *Soviet Policy in the Third World* (New York: Pergamon, 1980). This chapter does not deal with the activities of the Front for the Liberation of the Enclave of Cabinda (FLEC), where the Cuban troops effectively prevented a Zairean takeover.

15. On political space see Clement Henry Moore, *Politics in North Africa* (Boston: Little Brown, 1970), Chaps. 1 and 2; special issue on intervention, XXII *Journal of International Affairs* 2 (1968); Edward Soja, *Political Organization of Space* (Washington, D.C.: 1971).

16. As in the other areas, there is a historical parallel. In southern Africa it is the nineteenth-century struggle between Germany and England to join their colonial territories in an east-west or north-south direction, respectively. England won. See Parker Moon, *Imperialism and World Politics* (New York: Macmillan, 1926), pp. 120, 167.

17. Jorge's speech is found in *UNGA* 32/PV 31.69 of 12 October 1977; see also Prime Minister P. L. Lopo do Nascimento, *UNGA*/S10PV10/ 31 May 1978 and Ambassador E. de Figueiredo, *UNGA*/S10/PV23/ 8 June 1978.

18. Kabeyawa Mukeba, *UNGA*/S10/PV21,23/7 and 8 June 1978. For an analysis of Zairean foreign policy during the period before Shaba, see Crawford Young, "The Portuguese Coup and Zaire's Southern African Policy," in John Seiler, ed., *Southern Africa Since the Portuguese Coup* (Boulder, Colo.: Westview, 1980).

19. Kabeyawa Mukeba, *UNGA* 32/PV33.309–318/13 October 1977. See *The New York Times*, 20 May 1978, and J-C. Pomonti, "Les tribula-

tions d'un journaliste en Afrique," *Le Monde*, 16 December 1979; see also Richard Betts, "Why Intelligence Failures Are Inevitable," XXXI *World Politics* 1:61–89 (1978).

20. Nguza offered himself as this alternative in 1981, when he went into exile, but his earlier involvement with the regime undermined his credibility. See his testimony to the House of Representatives, Africa Subcommittee, 15 September 1981.

21. UNITA positions are published in the United States in the newsletter *Kwacha*, beginning in July 1980, by Florence Tate and Associates, 118 Thirteenth Street, N.E., Washington, D.C. 20002. See also *London Times*, 7 July 1980; XXXV *AFL-CIO Free Trade* Union News 10:1–16 (October 1980) for other sources on UNITA. For further discussion of the South African factor in the Cuban presence, see the following chapter on Namibia. However Dominquez had indicated that it was the MPLA government's demonstrably incomplete control over its political space in the Neto Aloes revolt and Shaba I in 1977 that reversed a Cuban decision to reduce the number of troops in Angola: Jorge Dominquez' testimony in *U.S. Interests in Africa*, Hearings Before the House of Representatives, 18 October 1979, p. 71.

22. For sound elements of a further discussion, see Gabriel Marcella and Daniel S. Papp, "The Soviet-Cuban Relationship: Symbiotic or Parasitic?" in Raymond Duncan, ed., *The Soviet Union in the Third World* (Boulder, Colo.: Westview, 1981); Cole Blasier and Carmelo Mesa-Lago, eds., *Cuba in the World* (Pittsburgh, Pa.: University of Pittsburgh Press, 1979); Maurice Halperin, "The Cuban Role in Southern Africa," in John Seiler, ed., *Southern Africa Since the Portuguese Coup* (Boulder, Colo.: Westview, 1980); Jorge Dominquez, "Cuban Foreign Policy," LVIII *Foreign Affairs* 1:83–108 (1978).

23. See *Marchés Tropicaux*, 12 May 1978.

24. Marcum, *The Angolan Revolution*, vol. II, p. 269.

25. R. W. Johnson, *How Long Will South Africa Survive?* (London: Macmillan, 1978), p. 284 f.; *Africa Research Bulletin*, March 1977; Galen Hull, "Zaire in the World System," in Gran, ed., *Zaire . . .* , p. 272.

26. *Jeune Afrique* 857 (10 June 1977) claimed that Mbumba moved because Neto threatened to disarm his troops, the plan for invasion being set for some time but quickly put into operation. Nothing confirms that explanation. The two towns north of the railroad were Kapanga, taken on 8 March and Sandoa, taken on 11 March. For a thorough study of Shaba I and the FLNC, see "Contribution à l'étude des mouvements d'opposition au Zaire: Le FLNC," *Cahiers du CEDAF*, no. 6 (1980). For a good treatment, see Oye Ogunbadejo, "Conflict in Africa: A Case Study of the Shaba Crisis, 1977," CXXXI *World Affairs* 3:219–234 (winter 1979). The account of the battle can be followed reasonably well in *The New York Times* or *Le Monde*.

27. The front-line states (Angola, Botswana, Mozambique, Tanzania, and Zambia) had already moved their mid-April meeting from Dar es Salaam to Luanda in sign of support for Angola against Zaire (*West Africa*, 25 April 1977). Mobutu had informed the OAU, as well as the UN Security Council, of the violation of Zairean territory but had requested no action, thus avoiding a debate about the nature of the attack.

28. See Young, "Zaire: The Unending Crisis," pp. 174, 178 f.; Gran, *Zaire: The Political Economics . . .* , pp. 64, 103ff.; Mobutu Sese Seko, *Discours prononcés le 1ᵉʳ juillet 1977 et le 28 novembre 1977 à NSele.* (Kinshasa: Bureau du President-Foundateur, 1977).

29. Nguza's death sentence was commuted, and he was amnestied in July 1978, reappointed foreign minister in March 1979 and prime minister in August 1980. He fled to Brussels and resigned in April 1981. See *Jeune Afrique* 1061:17 f. (6 May 1981).

30. Tad Szulc, *Penthouse*, May 1978; *Manchester Guardian*, 6 March 1978; *Tanzania Daily News*, 11 August 1977; *The New York Times*, 29 April 1978; *Le Monde*, 7 August 1977; Allen F. Roberts, "The Ransom of Ill-Starred Zaire," in Gran, ed., *Zaire . . .* , Chap. 11. Ironically, after Zaire canceled its contract in 1979, OTRAG moved its operations to Libya in May 1980; *Aviation Week and Space Technology*, 2 December 1980; *Jeune Afrique* 1040:34 f. (10 December 1980); Stanley Cohn, "What's Going Up in Zaire?" IX *Munger Africana Library Notes* 49 (1978–79).

31. See Angolan Defense Ministry Communique, Radio Luanda, 31 January 1978; Cyrus Vance, *Hard Choices* (New York: Simon & Schuster, 1983), p. 89.

32. Secretary Vance had hoped for greater "leverage in Angola" through recognition of the MPLA government; Vance, *Hard Choices*, p. 71.

33. *The New York Times*, 22 March, 13 April 1977.

34. Drafts dated November 1977 and 20 December 1977.

35. For a thorough study of Shaba II, see Jean-Claude Williams, "La seconde guerre du Shaba," XVI *Geneve-Afrique* 1:10–26 (1978).

36. *The New York Times*, 16 June 1978.

37. For an FLNC statement of intent, see *The New York Times*, 24 May 1978; *Afrique-Asie* 162 (21 May 1978).

38. *Washington Post*, 29 February 1976; Radio Kinshasa, 28 February 1976; Lopo do Nascimento interview, *Le Nouvel Observateur*, 1 March 1976.

39. *West Africa*, 24 January 1977. Zaire was a cosponsor of Angola's application for UN membership. Cf. *West Africa*, 24 February 1977; *Le Monde*, 26 February 1977.

40. *African Research Bulletin*, April 1977; *Manchester Guardian*, 28 April 1977.

41. *Financial Times, London*, 26 January 1978.

42. See good articles by Flora Lewis, 1 and 7 June 1978. *The New York Times*; for the aftermath, see *The New York Times*, 11 November 1978.

43. See Tom Wicker, *The New York Times*, 30 June 1978; Graham Hovey, *The New York Times*, 10 July 1978. I *Africa Index* 4:2, 5:1, 9:1. The trip was followed by a visit by Assistant Secretary of State for African Affairs Richard Moose in November (*The New York Times*, 17 November 1978).

44. *Jeune Afrique*, 927:35 (11 October 1978), 933:94 (22 November 1978); 947:18 (28 February 1979); Lannon Walker, in III *African Index* 9:31 (26 May 1980).

45. *Africa Contemporary Record* 1979–80 (New York: Holmes and Meier, 1981), pp. 450, 678; UNHCR, *Report on Assistance Activities in 1981–82* (UN Document A/AC. 96/606/26 August 1982, pp. 117, 144, 155; *Financial Times, London*, 16 January 1979; *The New York Times*, 14 August 1979; *Gecamines Annual Report, 1980*, p. 32, for figures on expatriate employees, which dropped from 1,232 in 1977 to 663 in 1978, 733 in 1979, and 999 in 1980.

46. For a discussion of the issue, see *Jeune Afrique* 908:20–22 (31 May 1978); 909:29–31 (7 June 1978); 911:55 f. (21 June 1978); 907:20–24 (24 May 1978); *The New York Times*, 24 May 1978; 7, 8 June 1978.

47. *The New York Times*, 14 August 1979.

48. A Shaba III was discussed in the beginning of 1980, supposedly to be carried out for Zairean refugees in Zambia, including members of the Lunda tribe who had joined Joshua Nkomo's ZAPU, or in Congo. There were reports of a border incident with FLNC followers on the Zambian frontier in March 1982. Mobutu claims to have met FLNC leaders in January 1980 to defuse remaining problems. See *Le Monde*, 6 November 1979, 14 February 1980. On Angolan policy toward Zaire after President Neto's death, see *Jeune Afrique* 994:37 (23 January 1980); for Zairean policy after Shaba, see Thomas Callaghy, "Zaire in Southern Africa," in Callaghy, ed., *Southern Africa in the 1980s* (New York: Praeger, 1984), and *Jeune Afrique* 1259:26 (26 February 1985).

49. *The New York Times*, 11, 12 October; 9 December 1980.

50. *Le Monde*, 27 January–12 February 1980.

51. *Jeune Afrique* 1118:24–27, 9 June 1982.

5
Conflict in the South

A long high wall around the house in the end will bring war.
Ovambo proverb

The door is open, the ball is in your court.
Contact Group saying

Africa is at the end of its struggle for collective independence from European colonization and at the beginning of its struggle for individual equality against apartheid.[1] The two struggles are basically quite different—as is not usually recognized—but the process of the struggle in both cases involves an underlying similarity. Forces of change obtain agreement for change from the current ruler only when they can promise the incumbent a future as agreeable as the status quo or when they can make the present more painful than the predicted future. The tactics are those of carrot and stick, often involving a deadline, a specific moment when the stick will be invoked and things will change for the worse if there is no agreement to change them for the better. There is no other way. But more importantly, those who do not have the sticks to make the present unpleasant must resort to carrots; if they cannot beat the enemy into agreement, they must win that agreement with assurances—in terms that are all the more difficult to make convincing because of the existing enmity—that change will not be unpleasant. Again, there is no other way.

Conflicts of the first type, over decolonization, end when the parties work out an agreement to pass power from the former rulers to the inhabitants of the territory. The dynamics of such a process are classic: in exchange for an agreement to leave now rather than later and, therefore, save lives and avoid conflict, the colonial ruler receives some consideration in the disposition of its present holdings and perhaps of future access as well. The earlier the agreement during the liberation struggle, the more consideration the colonial ruler is likely to receive. The longer the struggle, the more radical— and less "considerate"—the new government is likely to be.[2] Conflicts of the second type, over sociopolitical equality, end by definition only when the sides themselves disappear.

The Namibian setting is a complicated combination of the two.[3] The fact that the colonial ruler is next door rather than across the seas means that independence has implications for the relations of power within the region and that the considerations of decolonization are likely to involve not only economic matters, but security as well, and even have internal ramifications for the colonizers themselves. The price that a contiguous colonizer wants for an agreement is higher than that available to a colonizer farther away whose security interests are not as directly affected by the outcome. Furthermore, decolonization is inevitably part of domestic politics for the contiguous colonizer, much more than for the distant one. On the other hand, the aims and interests of the party seeking national liberation are no more limited in one type of colonization than in the other. The interest of those seeking liberation in accepting restrictions on independence, sovereignty, security or economic freedom, however, lies only in the relatively momentary consideration of shortening the struggle and saving lives and property; if after independence the liberationist is condemned by contiguity to live under the shadow of the former colonizer, this position is likely to be resented and resisted mightily. Turkey and Greece, Britain and Ireland, Egypt and Sudan, and, in prospect, Ethiopia and its Eritrean and Ogaden provinces are all cases in point. Conflicts over contiguous colonialism are, therefore, likely to be more difficult to resolve and more difficult to keep resolved over the long run as the conditions of any initial agreement are repeatedly called into question by conflicting aims in application.

Namibia has spent forty years in search of its final status.[4] The conflict began in 1946, when an attempt by South Africa to annex the territory provoked an international reaction within the United Nations, followed by the organization of the first forms of a nationalist protest within the territory itself. The General Assembly and Security Council continued pressure while pursuing contacts with South Africa until 1973, when the members of the UN lost hope and instead began to work directly toward implementing a declaration of independence. The conflict took on a new form after the fall of the Portuguese cordon sanitaire and the independence of Angola in 1975, when South Africa adopted the UN goal of independence for Namibia but combined it with apartheid and South African dominance. Before South Africa could reach its goal on this track by the 1978 deadline, the five Western members of the UN Security Council launched a farsighted initiative designed to open a second track leading to an independence acceptable both to the world community and to South Africa. Again South Africa changed its course and in June 1977 canceled its project for confederal independence, agreeing instead to install an interim administration and to hold one-man-one-vote elections under UN and South African supervision for a constituent assembly. Two years of further effort brought near agreement on several occasions but no final settlement on the final details of the elections.

At least the South Africans' movement along the first track was delayed, and independence was not yet unilaterally declared. The problem with the Western initiative, laudable and skillful though it was, was that it contained neither carrots nor sticks. With no sanctions—against either side—for failure to agree, it was unable to take control of the deadline out of South African hands. The crisis in the conflict was of South Africa's making, in the form of a threatened deadline for independence on its own terms, and that crisis was avoided, or postponed, rather than solved.

Then in 1981 came a new American administration with a clientele sympathetic to South Africa and a self-assigned challenge that it solve the Namibian problem so that it could get on with the business of better relations in the region. Its corrective to the previous policy was to apply carrots—constitutional guarantees and a more complicated electoral system, improved relations with South Africa immediately, and a linkage between the withdrawal of South African troops from Namibia and a withdrawal of Cuban troops from Angola, and finally regional disengagements to create trust. But the outcome of the process still hung on the stick rather than on the carrot and, specifically, on the ability of the Reagan administration to convince both sides that the improved status quo could not last and that now was the time to come to terms in order to get the best deal, in a situation where the two sides' evaluations of a good deal tended to be the reverse of each other's and where the mediator had no stick of its own except withdrawal from the process. Only when there was a compelling reason to see that time as short or, in its absence, a willingness by the mediators to shorten it by using some sort of sanctions to impose a deadline, could the conflict be resolved through agreement. A sudden doubling of Cuban troops on the Namibian border coupled with a desire to leave, and the impending end of the Reagan administration seemed to fill these conditions in 1988. The moment was ripe and twelve years of negotiations finally ended in an agreement.

Background

"Namibia" comes from the Khoisan word given to the large coastal desert of Southwest Africa, *!namib*, meaning "enclosure." Perhaps as appropriately, without the ! (click), the word means "mirage," another term of the desert. The country is desert and steppe land, poor on the surface and rich underground. It holds about 1.1 million people, including over 100,000 whites and 65,000 coloureds of various types, with one of the lowest population densities in Africa at one person per square kilometer. There are twice as many cattle and 3.3 times as many sheep as there are people, the karakul sheep industry being the country's one major agricultural activity.[5] The Atlantic coast, washed by the cold waters of the Benguela current, was also rich in fish. Both the land and the waters have been depopulated by overgrazing and overfishing in recent years. Underground, however, is one of the world's largest sources of diamonds and uranium plus copper and other metal ores. A mountain chain runs down the center of the country, with the Namib Desert on one side along the coast and the Kalahari Desert on the other into Botswana. Population is located in the central highlands and in the north along the Angolan border. In the north lives the largest ethnic group, the 600,000 Ovambo; the other large Bantu groups are the 70,000 Hereros, in the center around Windhoek, the 70,000 Kavangos to the northeast, and the 40,000 Caprivians in the Caprivi Strip to the northeast. Khoisan-speaking groups are the 40,000 Damaras along the northcentral coast, the 45,000 Namas in the southwest, and the 35,000 Bushmen between the Hereros and the Kavangos along the Botswana border.

Each of the ethnic groups has its own social and political organization. Official political structures are generally organized under a chief collaborating with colonial authorities, as is the usual arrangement in colonial countries. Indigenous social structures have either been used as the basis for a nationalist political organization competing with the official tribal structures or, when the social as well as political structure is under control of the official chief, nationalist leaders seek to bypass it in the name of a higher, Namibian nationalism. Thus, ethnic and territorial national consciousness is cultivated at the same time by both nationalist (Namibian) and colonialist (South African and collaborationist) sources.

The growth of nationalism followed both these directions and provides examples in the standard patterns of nationalist development. In the 1950s, the South West Africa Student Body (SWASB) and the South West Africa Progressive Association (SWAPA) were formed among the small category of modern intellectuals, leading to the South West African National Union (SWANU); and the Herero Council and the Ovamboland People's Congress and then Organization (OPO) were formed among their separate ethnic groups.[6] SWANU allied with the Damara Tribal Executive and other groups to form the Namibian National Front (NNF); it rejected homeland status and condemned South African control but refused to turn to militant violence and so it lost the support of the OAU from its very beginning. The Herero Council under Chief Clemens Kapuuo also resisted resettlement on a homeland, but took part in South African constitutional negotiations; during these negotiations in 1977, a Herero Association for the Preservation of the Tjamuha-Maherero Royal House was established to contest Chief Kapuuo's credentials. The OPO, founded by Herman Toivo ja Toivo, was broadened into the South West African Peoples Organization (SWAPO) in 1960, and in 1967, when Toivo was moved from house arrest in Ovamboland to jail in Robben Island, Sam Nujoma became its leader. It organized a major strike among Ovambo workers in 1971 and a boycott of Ovamboland elections in 1973 and was joined by other organizations from the Nama, Damara, Caprivian, Coloured (Rehoboth), and Herero ethnic groups through the 1970s. However, it has also been split into factions—an internal and largely Ovambo SWAPO, an external SWAPO including the Peoples Liberation Army of Namibia (PLAN) and the missions abroad, and Democratic SWAPO (SWAPO-D) founded in 1978, when Andreas Shipanga, a colleague of Toivo and rival of Nujoma, was released from Zambian prison.[7]

The territory, occupied by Germany at the time of the Congress of Berlin, had been given to South Africa in 1920 as a League of Nations "class C" mandate after its capture from Germany in World War I; a "class C" mandate is administered as an integral part of the governing state (League Covenant art. 22.6). In the beginning of the century, Germany had led a genocidal campaign against the Hereros and Namas, killing off three-quarters of them, and had encouraged settler colonization; in the interwar period, South Africa also sought to increase the white population on reserved land in the highlands. The white population was given a government and legislative assembly in 1925, under the higher authority of South Africa. After World War II and especially since the 1948 National party victory in South

Africa, the governing state tried to incorporate the territory as its fifth province under the pretext that the mandate had lapsed with the League of Nations. In 1951 the white inhabitants of South West Africa were given representation in the South African parliament, and in 1955 native affairs were put under the direct administration of the Bantu Administration Department. The introduction of the apartheid system at that time was complemented a decade later by the Odendaal Commission of Enquiry Report, which provided for the creation of separate homelands, generally in the desert areas, for the ten native ethnic groups. Seven "native nations" were established or were in the process of being set up by 1977. At the same time, the South West Africa Affairs Act of 1969 removed many legislative subjects from the jurisdiction of the South-West African (white) legislative assembly, reducing it to the level of the four provincial councils of the Republic of South Africa and moving further toward de facto annexation of the territory. Annexation for the whites and apartheid for the black African groups were the marks of the system rapidly being put into place.

During this entire period South Africa was under pressure from outside and inside the territory to proceed with decolonization. The removal of the protective buffers of Angola and Mozambique in 1974 had a profound effect on South African thinking as did the failure of the United States to pursue a strong policy in Angola and the ability of the South African Defense Force to keep the Cubans in Angola at bay.[8] A buffer state under South African control, similar to the buffer state under Ian Smith's control in Rhodesia, was deemed necessary to provide the necessary protection. In 1975, after thirty years of trying to incorporate South West Africa, South Africa reversed its policies and prepared to grant the territory independence in its own image, giving up integration into South Africa for whites in order to maintain apartheid in Namibia for blacks. On 1 September, it organized a constituent conference at the Turnhalle in Windhoek, composed of representatives of eleven ethnic groups or, where established, homeland governments. Nonwhite political parties (for example, SWAPO) were excluded from participation. The conference issued a declaration of intent in August 1976 in order to meet a UN deadline and then terminated its work on 19 March 1977 after adopting a South West Africa Charter. Its proposal provided for independence by the end of 1978 with a confederal system of autonomous homelands. No national or even universal local elections were planned; each ethnic group would be consulted as and if its leadership wished. A referendum among the whites approved the proposal two months after the end of the conference. After the conference, the tribal representatives and white parties involved formed a Democratic Turnhalle Alliance (DTA) under the chair of the National party secretary Dirk Mudge and the presidency of Chief Kapuuo in order to bring self-government on the Turnhalle plan. The goal of South Africa was to create a sovereign territory in its image that would be sympathetic to and dependent on it. It was a major policy reversal, but too late to be effective.

South Africa made further concessions in principle at the same time in response to the first American mediatory demarche in the conflict, initiated by Secretary of State Henry Kissinger.[9] In discussions in September 1976, South Africa agreed to a seven-point program that foreshadowed the Zimbabwean settlement: a Geneva conference of various internal and external parties would first negotiate a constitution, postindependence relations with South Africa, elections, and any other issue a party wished to introduce; the UN would be present but only as an observer, and South Africa would accept the results; independence would occur by the end of 1978. SWAPO rejected the program, insisting on a conference with South Africa and the UN, based on Resolution 385. Although it is scarcely likely that this approach would have been any more rapid or successful than the demarche subsequently pursued, it did contain some elements—constitution, non-UN venue—that might have circumvented later problems. Its greatest weakness, however, was that it came too early in a ripening process to succeed—it was a necessary but insufficient step. In February, as the new administration came to Washington, South Africa refused to confirm its previous agreement to the seven-point program.

A particularly troublesome aspect of the colonial heritage concerns Walvis Bay, a coastal enclave about 100 kilometers square that contains the only important port along the entire Namibian coast and the major ocean terminus of Namibia's dorsal rail line.[10] The British occupied Walvis Bay as a trading post in 1878 before the Germans took over the hinterland, and it was then administered as part of the South African colony and from 1910 until 1922 as part of the Union of South Africa. The sovereignty of South Africa over Walvis Bay was recognized when it was specifically excluded from the mandate by the League of Nations in 1920. Because it is the commercial outlet for South West Africa and is a territorial anomaly as part of South Africa 1,300 kilometers away by rail, however, it was joined administratively to South West Africa in 1922. Nevertheless its importance to the British and lately to the South Africans has been as a control over the territory when the hinterland is in different hands from the port. As a result, South Africa returned the enclave to its status of half a century before as a part of Cape Province on 31 August 1977 and declared the new status nonnegotiable. South Africa was also concerned about the fishing and offshore oil rights that came with possession of the coastal enclave (and with a series of twelve islands on down the coast that may be involved as well). But, above all, Walvis Bay is important as an ultimate hedge against the future—for control or for bargaining.

To South Africa, the conflict has not been over a country as much as over a boundary—not as a simple borderline but as a determination of whether the southern African battleline will be on the Orange or on the Cunene and Cubango rivers, along southern and northern Namibia respectively, and whether the territory between the two will be a boundary-in-depth (buffer state) or will fall to one side or the other. Objectively, although South African spokespersons have not necessarily seen it this way at all times, South African interest lies not so much in preserving its political control over the territory as in denying it to unfriendly control and in protecting its economic interests. The nul possession or neutralization formula could, therefore, apply, assuming that the other side saw it that way, too. South Africa's initial policy reversal in 1975 and its subsequent concessions under mediation seemingly made the resolution of the conflict easier and possible. When it turned out to be as difficult as ever, frustrated participants and observers alike could only suspect bad faith and double-talk. To the contrary, South Africa felt that it had advanced so far in meeting the other parties' terms that it should be afforded some consideration on details.

The other side's position, however, is not symmetrical. Although it is likely that other groups would gain some popular support in a free election, the UNGA and the African states have equated SWAPO with Namibia.[11] SWAPO's interests are dual: sovereignty and control, the one against South Africa, the other against South Africa and rival Namibian organizations. Nujoma's self-proclaimed—if woolly—Marxism and his Fanonistic belief in the need for violent conquest of independence are not designed to convince South Africa of his neutrality or make it easy for him to fill a role that South Africa would consider acceptable. Thus, agreement on independence merely shifted the conflict to the equally difficult question over the form and outcome of the transfer of power.

But there is even more to the conflict. In decolonization confrontations, it is the colonizer who has given way, and colonizers can do
so—in terms of those basic philosophical concerns that underlie all
politics—because their existence is not at stake whereas that of the
emerging, colonized entity is. On SWAPO's side, this is true in
Namibia as well. Namibian nationalists are seeking to create a new
entity and give it control over its own affairs, humanity's highest
political goal. But unlike the case of the distant colonizer, South
Africa, too, sees the conflict over Namibia as a struggle for itself. Not
only does South Africa see South West Africa as part of its federal
union, the fifth province whose final incorporation remained all but
legally accomplished, but it also sees the area as a testing ground for
its own future by both friend and enemy. Observers have felt that the
government, particularly in its somewhat *verligte* (enlightened) form
under P. W. Botha, was trying out various ways of removing legal
apartheid and integrating national (ethnic) political activity in Namibia before applying them to South Africa. Blacks have watched
efforts to give decisive political expression to other blacks under
South African rule, evaluating government reaction and seeing how
close to home the dominoes could fall. White South Africans have
feared that the outside world—the West, the UN, the Communists, in
ascending order of devilishness—in turning South West Africa into
Namibia, was carrying out experiments that presaged the larger
operations of turning South African into Azania. Legal and social
innovators have examined the territory of Namibia as a model for the
province of Natal.

This philosophical engagement has its reflection on the level of
practical politics. Many South Africans, including South African
politicians, had roots or ties in South West Africa, and the National
party of South Africa was in South West Africa as well, infighting
and all. Whereas issues elsewhere involved many other elements than
simply the ethnic government question, Namibia was a battleground
in the war over apartheid in its essence. As Botha was neither strong
nor foresighted in his party leadership, however good his intentions
or clever his politics may have been, he could not push his Namibian
policies too far out in front of his party lest he lose his leadership to
the *verkrampte* (conservative) faction—and, after 1981, separate
party—of the Transvaal politician Dr. A. P. Treurnicht. Because
Namibia was a philosophical and political issue of self-determination
for South Africa, it was characterized by open options and indecision, not by clear choices and easy concessions.

Conflict

The conflict over the southern African battleline pits a regional power against various diffuse elements that become stronger only as they are farther away. South Africa is the incontestable power in the subregion, and all the states on its border are militarily weak, generally underdeveloped, and economically dependent on South Africa. They can provide sanctuary and support to guerrilla activities and can cooperate to reduce their dependency in trade, technology, and infrastructure. In time, Angola and Mozambique, Zimbabwe, and then behind them Zaire all have the potential and even the head start to becoming successfully developing countries and subregional powers, but they do not have the weight to impose their will on South Africa. They can and do, however, organize with other African states and then with the Third World majority to bring pressure on South Africa in world forums. They can also borrow power from the developed countries, which can place their resources of persuasion and coercion at the disposal of the black African states.

The two models for the place at which black and white African regimes meet are the battleline and the buffer. The image of the wave of liberation sweeping across the continent since the late 1950s suggests that more radical regimes are likely to appear at the leading edge of that wave as it crashes against the white bastions of the south, with calmer conditions obtaining behind the battle line as the older independent countries settle down to the job of development. The regimes in Angola, Mozambique, and Zimbabwe can be called radical because of the leftward evolution of their own long struggle against colonial rulers and of the support they attracted from the Communist states while the West sat by, unaware that radicalism is abetted by trying to slow down history rather than by keeping pace with it. The front-line states of the 1970s—Angola, Mozambique, Tanzania, Zambia, and Botswana—gave active support to the national liberation movements operating southward even though the latter two states were scarcely radical in other policies. In a subsequent evolution, a radical Namibia and a radical Zimbabwe could reinforce Mozambique and pull along Botswana to provide a troublesome array of neighbors against South Africa. Their newly won independence would give inspiration to incipient national liberation movements in South Africa, who would see brothers in less developed countries running their own affairs. Even if the new front-line states' offensive capabilities were meager, they could at least provide sanctuary, supplies, and training for guerrillas.

Nonetheless, states that have gone through a long struggle for national liberation generally seek an equally long period of national reconstruction to replenish their depleted resources and drained energies, and the front-line states are no exception. This element suggests that other models than the battleline might be more appropriate.

The other model is that of a buffer zone made of border states protecting South Africa from direct incursions and held in their neutrality both by their own security concerns against foreign (specifically, Communist) subversion and by the mutual benefits of the South African coprosperity sphere. In this view, radicalism is not on the front lines but in the distant command posts, and it attenuates on contact with the opponent. The wave of liberation is spent by the time it finally reaches the south, and South Africa can buy time with space. This view also sees a subregionalization of African relations into a constellation of cooperation around a power center, with cooperative economic relations based on labor migration, market domination, transportation networks, and technical services. South Africa's considerable economic penetration of Namibia, Botswana, Mozambique, Zimbabwe, Malawai, and even into the Copper Belt of Zambia and Zaire provide a basis for this view of a regional security system. The model also has contradictory elements of its own, however, for the idea of a buffer zone undermines the need for security and protection on the part of the buffer states.

Battleline has long been the African model; and buffer, the South African. Nonetheless, the two models are more distinct in theory than in practice as the cited examples show. Mozambique is both radical and dependent on South Africa, and Zimbabwe is likely to continue to be the same; Botswana is both moderate and dependent. Furthermore, South Africa turned to its own version of battle line throughout most of the 1980s when buffer proved elusive and inadequate. Constellation and confrontation coexist, pursued by the same parties on both sides of the frontline. Newly independent states are tied economically to South Africa but pursue the national liberation struggle on behalf of their neighbors—Zimbabwe and Namibia in the late 1970s, Namibia and South Africa in the 1980s. South Africa presses its cooperation and economic penetration of states to the north while also maintaining military pressure on them. In the process, constellation undermines confrontation as economic and technological dependency remains despite African states' efforts at delinkage. But confrontation also destroys constellation, rendering its political aspects impossible; too weak to confront effectively, the front-line states are too competitive among themselves to coalesce on

South Africa. It is on the ambiguity of these two elements that much of the problem of the Namibian conflict and its resolution have hung.

Important as it may be, international structure is not the only key to understanding the conflict, for the conflict is not just about power relations with the dominant subregional state of South Africa. It is also about power relations within the social system of apartheid in that state itself. Unfortunately, concern with the righteousness of cause and the ultimate goal of broad social and political change in the southern part of the continent often clashes with the need to deal with South Africa in more immediate confrontations, as, for example, in Namibia. It is difficult to deal with and to change South Africa at the same time, and the behaviors dictated by the two goals often get in the way of each other. It is certain that South Africa is likely to be more responsive to means of pressure against its policy in Namibia if it could be made to feel that such pressure is directed against that policy alone and not against the very nature and existence of South Africa itself. It is equally certain that such pressure is likely to be more popular and gain greater support in the rest of the world if it is seen as part of the onslaught against the white regime's very nature and existence. Conflict can focus on an issue between parties or on the very existence of one party, but conflict resolution involves recognition of the legitimacy and interests of the parties involved. It becomes hard to help South Africa find a solution to the parties' mutual interest or to help South Africa solve a mutual problem—two ways in which conflict resolution has been characterized—if the notion of legitimate interests itself is in conflict. Such recognition is not a defense of South African internal politics, for the resolution of one conflict to mutual satisfaction does not mean that other conflicts cannot be pursued subsequently. The argument is tactical, not strategic, and it should be possible to keep the two separate.

Even so, the conflict among legitimate interests is not easy to bridge, for it exists on a number of levels. It is a conflict over decolonization and, specifically, over the means or degree or results of decolonization. Whether the independence of Namibia should be accomplished by ethnic group consultations or by free elections or by guerrilla war, whether independence is compatible with dependence on South Africa or impossible unless total and complete, whether independence is conceivable with a SWAPO government or with a DTA (Democratic Turnhalle Alliance) government—these are all questions on which important interests conflict.

American interests in the Namibian conflict are both principled and political. The primary matter of principle is the termination of a colony of racial domination and its replacement by self-government based on the rights and interests of individuals. Other issues of principle include respect for the process of decolonization as established by the United Nations bodies, especially as it concerns a mandated territory, and also respect for the interests of sovereign state members of the UN, whatever their internal system of government.

American national interests in the conflict are, above all, political, concerned with maintaining a smooth, peaceful, and stable transition from colonial rule to self-government. Specifically in South West Africa, this means avoiding war and the search for outside allies it would bring, which would, in turn, draw the Soviet Union into an active role in the conflict and, even worse, place the United States before the choice of allying with South Africa or finding a wobbly middle course needing complicated justification. To the extent that interests are related to economics, the United States has an interest in keeping the area open to American trade and investment. American investments have not been particularly dissuaded by the UN resolutions of the 1970s barring exploitation of Namibian minerals[12] or the domestic campaigns against investment in South Africa, but they are small, only rising from $2 to $15 million through the 1970s or one-half of 1 percent of the U.S. total African investment, essentially by Anglo-American deBeers, American Metal Climax, and Newmont Mining. The size of American economic interests in Namibia is not great enough to dictate a particular outcome.

Few would argue, since the South African policy changes of the mid-1970s, that it is more in American interest to perpetuate South African sovereignty over Namibia against international norms and pressure.[13] After 1975 the narrower question has been whether an "internal solution" of independence only in name and in continued close relation with the Republic of South Africa, rejected by the world community, is acceptable or whether UN-recognized independence, probably exercised by a Marxist SWAPO government, is compatible with American concerns. But even if the criterion of interest is the ability of American investments to remain and operate on the spot, the longer-range conclusion can only be that the longer Namibian nationalism, legitimized by UN support, is resisted, the more radical and, therefore, hostile to American interests and investments the government is likely to be. American policy has, therefore, been to work for a smooth and early transition.

Other Western states reached the same conclusion on the basis of their own, often diffuse, interests.[14] Britain has the greatest interest in

South Africa and in Namibia, to the point where its economy—and the economy of the sterling area—is tied to that of the rand area. Britain buys about half of its uranium from Namibia. On another level, Britain is torn between its ethnic ties to its former colony and its political vulnerability to pressure from the new Commonwealth states of Africa. France is in a different position, at a lower degree of involvement. It has some investment in Namibia in a crucial sector, notably its participation with Britain and South Africa in Rössing Uranium, the only uranium company in Namibia. But it is also vulnerable to pressure from its African allies, who do not favor South African rule over Namibia in any form even if they believe in dialogue with South Africa and who are unable to oppose other Africans' pressure to press their former metropole. Germany, too, has mining and mineral processing investments, but is also subject to pressure from the metropolitan relatives of the large German-speaking population in Namibia left over from the days of the German colonization and those newly arrived after World War II, many of whom have kept their German citizenship. Canada has the least direct interest in the territory, for there are no important channels of pressure in either policy direction, and Canada's mineral investments are small. All of these countries—who were the Western members of the Security Council in 1977—saw their interest in a policy that would avoid a domestic and international race war in South and South West Africa and would assure a smooth and peaceful transfer of power to an independent government and that also in the short run—where policy is made—would avoid their having to make a decision under African pressure about sanctions on South Africa.

The Soviet position south of the battleline has been freer of constraints with no interests to lose or defend and everything to gain. Russia's only immediate interest in the area is in not foreclosing later opportunities. Russia arms and slightly trains SWAPO. But it does not appear to have any deep hold on the SWAPO leadership either through ideological conditioning as in the Angolan MPLA or through military training as in Somalia. Russia, of course, has no investments in Namibia. Yet an eventual policy geared to controlling natural resources or to military assault on South Africa as the southern bastion of racial industrial proletarian exploitation would find Namibia a useful base from which to operate. The Soviet leadership probably did not believe that a negotiated solution was possible or that an independence mediated by the West and accepted by South Africa could be real. But as long as the front-line states accept such mediation and do not seek greater Russian intensification of the struggle from their territory, there is little Russia can do about it. From the Soviet point of view, unless there is an old and firm ideological base—again, as in the MPLA—a national liberation movement is a less stable and sure object of attention than a sovereign state: Gratitude evaporates so rapidly in international politics that help to a national liberation movement never assures much more than initially friendly relations upon independence. As a result, it might be surmised, the Soviet Union has been more tolerant of attempts at conflict resolution and less willing to pay the costs of keeping conflict alive than might have been expected otherwise, its objections presently giving way, under Gorbachev, to active support.[15]

The conflict has been pursued most actively outside the region, where South Africa is weakest. The UN institutions have been the forum of the broadest attack because they are the successors to the source of the colonial authority—the League of Nations mandate that South Africa exercised over the territory. Thrice the International Court of Justice was called on.[16] In 1950, it gave an advisory opinion that the mandate was still in operation under the United Nations; in 1966 after six years of litigation it refused to rule against South Africa in a case brought by Ethiopia and Liberia over its performance of the mandate; and in 1971 it ruled that, subsequent to the withdrawal of the mandate by the General Assembly in 1966, the continued presence of South Africa in the territory was illegal and its acts invalid, as the Security Council had declared in 1970. But South Africa refused to recognize its decisions.

During this same period, the General Assembly and the secretary general tried to negotiate some sort of transition to independence, first through the establishment of a trusteeship and then directly, but without avail. Ever since its first resolution in 1946, the General Assembly has sought to block annexation and to restore accountability under the mandate. Seeing South Africa moving in the other direction, toward integration of South West Africa into its own political and social system, the General Assembly terminated the mandate in 1966 and proceeded to work toward direct transition to independence.[17] The decision was taken through the leadership of U.S. Ambassador Arthur Goldberg, working with the African members. The year after this action, at a special session, the General Assembly established a council and a commissioner for Namibia to administer the territory.[18] But when the UN sought to apply its decisions on the ground, it found that the commissioner was unable to gain access to Namibia, and after a last round of attempts to establish UN authority by the secretary general in consultation with Argentina, Somalia, and Yugoslavia on the Security Council in 1972–1973,[19] the Security Council decided to discontinue contacts with South Africa. In 1973 the General Assembly recognized SWAPO as the sole and authentic representative of the Namibian people and granted it permanent observer status in 1976,[20] two moves of desperation that were to cause great difficulties when mediation began. The same year, the Security Council passed its most detailed procedural resolution (385) calling for one-man-one-vote (that is, nonethnic) elections under UN supervision and control. Until the late 1970s, UN action was totally ineffective because it contained only goals and condemnations. Their implementation was dependent on South Africa alone, and their enforcement was impossible because of Western unwillingness to support measures that would make noncompliance costly for South Africa.

In fact, the conflict has not imposed a heavy cost on South Africa, and whatever cost there has been has neither been any significant increment to South Africa's pariah status in general, nor has it been significant in comparison with the cost of the conflict to the African side. Organized violence began in August 1966, when SWAPO, after a period of political organization, turned to guerrilla warfare and developed military bases in Angola, Botswana, and Zambia for the Peoples Liberation Army of Namibia (PLAN).[21] Guerrilla warfare remained weak until early 1975, when safer sanctuary in newly independent Angola enabled it to intensify. Reliable casualty or even encounter figures are difficult to obtain, but incidents every month or so indicate the level of guerrilla activity in the mid-1970s. By 1979, encounters had increased to the average of one a day, causing South Africa to extend martial law over the northern half of Namibia in May. Casualties were highest of any year in 1980—nearly 100 South Africans and over 1,500 SWAPO. By 1982, the war was estimated to cost South Africa half a billion dollars a year but only 77 deaths out of a total outlay for all activities in Namibia of $1.25 billion;[22] as host and sanctuary for SWAPO, Angola suffered losses twenty times higher than this figure and spent half a billion dollars for annual rental of the Cuban army alone, not counting the cost of its own military operations and losses. South Africa has claimed some 300 PLAN members killed in its summer raid into Angola each of the first four years of the 1980s.

Conflict has gradually intensified, but not to the level of any of the other cases studied here nor of Zimbabwe during its struggle for independence. Until 1988, it is hard to see real escalations—crossing of thresholds or changes in salience—and the gradualness of "intensification" seems more accurate; in timing, intensifications have frequently corresponded with UN General Assembly sessions. The main types of SWAPO operations include the laying of mines, sabotage of civilian and military installations, impressment of school children into SWAPO service in Angola, and systematic assassination of tribal authorities (including Chief Kapuuo in March 1978), as well as occasional battles with South African forces when they intercept SWAPO units. Late in the 1970s, SWAPO training in Angola and Zambia was taken over from the Cubans by East Germans, benefiting from one of Namibia's second languages, and SWAPO military capabilities improved. Until 1987, the Cubans have stayed out of the way of South African raids except for one encounter in January 1982; in August 1981 a Russian officer was killed and another captured in a South African raid on SWAPO in Angola. In early 1980, SWAPO began to attack South African forces. In April 1982 a 100-person SWAPO unit operated for a month in the Tsumeb mining and farming area deep behind the South African defense perimeter, leaving 59 SWAPO guerrillas, 7 civilians, and 11 South African soldiers dead before the raid was brought under control and also considerable doubts about the effectiveness of South Africa's raids across the border, and in February 1983, some 800 SWAPO troops infiltrated into Namibia from Angola, with 130 killed in battle the first week.[23]

SWAPO's strategy has been a long-range one, designed to use the conflict to build its strength rather than to force a decisive contest as yet with South Africa. In seeking to punish collaboration and win over recruits in Namibia, SWAPO gave up short-term showdowns by avoiding military targets against which it was less effective. Rather, it works for independence in the long run by maintaining international moral and domestic guerrilla pressure on South Africa, building support and strength until more direct confrontations can be planned and presumably won. SWAPO rides on this track, benefiting from as much as contributing to it, but the movement must struggle to keep itself active enough to provide a credible referent for UN demands and to live up to its UN legitimization. The UNGA approach contains a blanket condemnation of South Africa and exclusive endorsement of SWAPO, but it does keep a door continually open for even a partial acceptance of its proposals. Negotiations for such acceptance constitute the second track to independence, for in the short run UN and SWAPO pressure is designed to bring about South African agreement on conditions of departure, not to do the more difficult job of driving out South Africa militarily.

South Africa's first-track strategy is to take over the UN goal of independence and approach it in its own way, going through the procedures of constitution making and elections with those groups that would accept its sponsorship, combating those (external SWAPO) that would not, and putting off any final decision—such as an independence vote—until its groups were in a strong enough position to win. To do this, it deployed some 60,000 troops throughout the vast and sparsely inhabited territory by 1979, with all the problems of effectiveness inherent in any counterinsurgency operation; two years later the figure was 80,000. South Africa's main emphases in standard counterinsurgency operations were the clearing of a no-man's-land along the Angolan border at the end of 1976 (matched by a similar measure on the Angolan side) and increasingly frequent and deep raids into neighboring countries—in early May 1978 into Angola at Cassinga; in August 1978 into Zambia; in March and October 1979, in June–August 1981, and in June–August 1982 into Angola again, each at crucial times in the negotiations. In 1981, these incursions reached a level and length equal to the invasion of 1975–76 during the Angolan civil war. Yet the deeper they went, the more they spread the war without reducing SWAPO attacks against authorities and collaborators in Namibia.[24] Then, at the end of 1983, South Africa began efforts to turn the political-military stalemate further to its advantage by negotiating a mutual removal of foreign forces—Cuban, SWAPO, South African—from Southern Angola, culminating in the disengagement agreement of mid-February 1984. This development reduced the cost of the conflict for all parties without actually solving it—management without resolution that left out a major participant in the conflict: SWAPO. The South African Defense Force has also undertaken a civic action program since 1975 and has also built up a 24,000-man South West African Territorial Force of tribal militias that it plans to leave in place when it leaves.[25]

A second track to a negotiated solution has thus never been a preferred course and has been considered only as external pressures have made such consideration unavoidable. Namibia has long evolved in the shadow of Rhodesia-Zimbabwe. As long as the interracial option provided by the Smith-Muzorewa government had a chance of recognition abroad, South Africa's first-track strategy had a precedent. The campaign and then the election of a conservative government in England in 1979 seemed to improve that chance, and a search for a second track would have been actually harmful to that precedent's chances. But after the Lancaster House agreement of December 1979, which replaced Smith-Muzorewa with a transitional

British authority; after the February 1980 elections in Zimbabwe, where Muzorewa was roundly defeated by the most radical of the three Zimbabwe party groups, led by Robert Mugabe; and then after the bitter internecine and interethnic war in Zimbabwe, which began in 1982 against Joshua Nkomo's ZAPU (Zimbabwe African Peoples Union) and Ndebele followers, South Africa's worst fears were confirmed. But the internal solution for Namibia was weakened—even though it was thereby made most necessary in South African eyes.

South Africa could set up its own "independent" state—it had all but done so by mid-1980—but that would be no solution if no one recognized it. SWAPO, on the other hand, had much recognition but none of South Africa's strength. It could be defeated but not eradicated. In the long run, it would either attract enough Soviet support, with African permission, to trigger a real military confrontation coupled with a rising level of internal South African dissension, or it would continue its harassment from inside and outside Namibia and the UN until some intermediate solution were devised. The conflict ripened for resolution through the end of the 1970s and continued ripening in the 1980s—all as a result of events external to it. The American elections of 1980 and 1984 changed but did not arrest that process. Indeed, a curious aspect of the conflict is that it has kept on getting riper, unlike the Horn or the Sahara with their distinct ups and downs, but the ultimate judgment of whether ripe enough has depended on external events—particularly foreign elections that promise reprieve—and not on the conflict itself.

Conflict Resolution

Namibia is close to a pure case of mediated negotiation. Despite its desultory war of national liberation, only in the 1980s did it begin to approach the characteristics of full hostilities found in the Sahara, Zimbabwe, the Horn, or the Shabas. Indeed, the bloody conflict against which the parties are negotiating is in the future. As a representative from Canada, one of the Western Five, once said, "We are in this to avoid a bloodbath in southern Africa." It was this somewhat distant danger that moved the United States, Britain, Canada, West Germany, and France, soon after the inauguration of the Carter administration in early 1977, to undertake a preemptive mediation. This makes the Namibian case quite different from others where conflict paced resolution.

The more specific element in the timing of the initiative had to do with the calendar of the South African first-track strategy and the threat of fait accompli that it carried. The Turnhalle conference issued its preliminary report in August 1976 in order to meet the Security Council deadline in Resolution 385 for an answer to its goal of independence. In the report, June 1977 was set as the target date for the installation of the Turnhalle constitution.[26] OAU members of the UN indicated that they would push for sanctions if South Africa continued to flout the will of the UN, and the West would be faced with the dilemma that it wanted most to avoid. The sudden need to do something, even with the new administration barely in place, does not remove credit from the remarkable preemptive demarche of the West, a rare case of preventive problem solving.

Once South Africa had made its first policy reversal and embarked on the Turnhalle solution, it admitted that friendliness to South Africa was an insufficient, if necessary, characteristic of a Namibian solution and that some international legitimacy—at least to an extent that could be combined with friendliness—was part of the desired outcome. Thus, South Africa and the UN created the limits of the ensuing negotiations. When the UN declared that Turnhalle was by definition unacceptable because of the white settler dominance of the process and the apartheid in its outcome, the way was indicated for a second track that would combine the aspects of South African friendliness and legitimacy. The mediators' priorities were the reverse of South Africa's: legitimacy first plus just enough friendliness to South Africa to ensure South African agreement. Because SWAPO refused to accept substantive guarantees of friendliness, the mediators sought to focus instead on procedure in the hopes that fairness of choice—through elections—could be somehow made acceptable to South Africa as a substitute for friendliness of results. Understood in this way, the effort was obviously a long shot.

The Western Five thus sought to reconcile the two sides' first tracks seen as two opposing processes—illegitimate Turnhalle elections versus legitimate SWAPO war—into a formula for legitimate elections on a one-man-one-vote model under paired South African and UN auspices. That formula was soon satisfactory to both sides and represents a major South African and a much smaller SWAPO concession: South Africa ran the sure risk of giving up power, and SWAPO ran the lesser risk of sharing power. The mediators then proceeded to grapple with the details of electoral auspices to satisfy both sides, a more difficult job than finding the initial formula.

During the negotiations, both sides followed their two-track strategies. South Africa's first track was strong in its feasibility whereas SWAPO's was strong only in its legitimacy. It has been this imbalance that has framed the negotiations. South Africa continued to negotiate with the Western Five in order to create conditions for a "UN election" as favorable to it as a "South African election." Under such conditions the first would be preferable because it would have international legitimacy as well as a friendly outcome. At the same time, South Africa proceeded with its own plan, which is preferable in the absence of a reduced "UN election." However, these preferences are not fixed items; they change as outside events change the chances of their successful implementation, through shifts in British and American domestic politics; in the evolution of other spots in the cordon sanitaire such as Zimbabwe, Mozambique, and Angola, and in the vagaries of South African economics and politics.

On the other hand, SWAPO continued to negotiate with the Western Five in order to create conditions for a "UN election" that are as favorable to it as a guerrilla victory. Under such conditions the election would be preferable because of its assurance, speed, and lower cost. At the same time, it proceeded with its guerrilla struggle, which is preferable in the absence of a guaranteed "UN election" victory. As with South Africa, too, these preferences were not fixed items for SWAPO but varied with events that modify their chances of success.

The relations among these two double tracks are important to an understanding of the two parties' strengths and strategies and, ultimately, of their raitonality. The hard or first track in each case serves both as an alternative and insurance to the negotiated solution and, therefore, as a threat against it that strengthens the bargaining hand. The hard track provides the "security point" for the negotiators, the reference point below which the negotiated solution becomes unattractive and unacceptable. Negotiators, therefore, may try to improve the attractiveness of the negotiated solution—which is difficult to do when attractiveness to the two parties is measured in opposite terms—or they may try to weaken and lower that security point, making the negotiated solution appear more attractive in comparison. Thus, the Western Five continually threatened South Africa that they would drop their veto on UN economic sanctions if it continued with the Turnhalle option, and South Africa repeatedly made its counterinsurgency strikes against SWAPO bases in front-line states. However, at the same time, like any bargaining chips, alternative strategies may turn into preferred strategies in their own right. In fact, they can only be effective as bargaining alternatives if they are real alternatives, courses the party is perfectly willing to follow.

As long as the imbalance between the ends and the means of SWAPO and South Africa continued, progress was difficult. But the authority vacuum in the war zone pulled in the northern neighbor of Namibia as well as its southern colonizer, opposing one sovereign state to another. After 1980, intensifying means left SWAPO further and further behind and placed Angola and South Africa in a direct dialogue over the withdrawal of military forces from the region, allowing a balanced formula for an agreement.

Finally, the rationality of the parties' strategies depends on the way in which positions and outcomes are evaluated. On the one hand, the parties can be seen as presenting positions that have an intrinsic defensibility and importance, with any whittling down of those positions representing an attack on their integrity. This is a commonsense interpretation: Diplomats are unlikely to pose inflated demands and sham conditions, particularly after the negotiations have left the general area of agreed goals and justifications and focus in on details. On the other hand, parties can be seen to be bargaining toward estimated outcomes, seen either as midpoints or as other compromise positions, or to be searching for general formulas governing a final agreement. This is also a commonsense interpretation to the extent that diplomats or any other bargainers ask for more than they may expect to get and that in the end it is process, not justice, that determines outcomes. In this view, initial positions and demands have to be evaluated, not as intrinsic policy statements but as starters whose meaning lies in where they head rather than in where they stand. Wisdom suggests that there is a bit of both in any negotiating exchange, but in that case—as in much else in negotiation—the ambiguity gives both strength and confusion to the way the process is pursued.

The mediated negotiations have gone through eight phases in twelve years. The *first* began on 7 April 1977 with the entry of the Western Five into the negotiation process and ended with the formulation of a package presented to both sides in early February 1978.[27] The Contact Group started by sounding out both sides and the gradually identifying and specifying of the package's elements, supported by Western pressure on South Africa and front-line pressure on SWAPO.[28] Each party was briefed after discussion with the others. The two parties responded on some occasions with hardened positions and on others with concessions or modified counterproposals until the autumn of 1977 and early 1978, when both sides broke and took to the field in an intensification—but hardly an escalation—of the conflict.

The Western Five sought to shape the UN one-man-one-vote election plan as contained in United Nations Security Council (UNSC) resolution 385 (1976) into a form acceptable to South Africa without losing its acceptability to the UN majority or SWAPO. The UN resolution called for free elections under UN supervision and control for the whole of Namibia as one political entity, adequate time to establish the supervising machinery, withdrawal of the South African administration and South African military forces, release of political prisoners and return of exiles, and end of racial discrimination—without spelling out further details. The Western Five put forward no position themselves until January 1978, and when they did, it was not as a basis for negotiating but as a practical means for implementing 385.

Its first track blocked, South Africa made its second major policy reversal. At the end of April 1977, Prime Minister Vorster agreed to abandon the Turnhalle project for "ethnic democracy" and instead to install an interim administrative authority in Namibia and to consider UN or Western observation of elections for a constituent assembly in which SWAPO could participate. In early June, movement on these positions continued:[29] South Africa agreed to one-man-one-vote elections but under its own auspices, then to an international observer mission of jurists under the UN secretary general, then to the release of political dissidents selected out of criminal prisoners by an international panel of jurists if the front-line states would also release SWAPO dissidents whom they held, then to the appointment of a UN staff working with the South African administrator general, and finally to the gradual withdrawal of troops on the administrator's appointment, to be completed by independence unless the troops were requested to stay. In each case, modified acceptance or related counterproposals were advanced, moving the South African position away from exclusive South African supervision of the transition and toward a paired UN and South African presence.[30] These counterproposals were then rejected by SWAPO at the OAU meeting in Libreville in July 1977.

SWAPO's initial position foresaw continued warfare until South Africa agreed to direct talks under UN auspices, accompanied by the release of all political prisoners, and leading to the withdrawal of South African Defense Forces and the holding of one-man-one-vote elections under UN supervision.[31] This position was reiterated in detail through the UN Conference on Southern Africa in Maputo in May and the OAU meeting of July,[32] after which SWAPO made its first small change in position. By accepting the presence of UN peacekeeping forces along the northern Namibian border in order to seal the border against its own guerrilla infiltration, SWAPO accepted the predominance of UN presence over SWAPO presence during the transition. It also agreed to allow junior South African civil servants to remain until the elections. In December, under pressure from the front-line states, SWAPO accepted a gradual South African military withdrawal until it reached a level of 1,500–3,000, equal to that of the UN forces.

Nonetheless, the process of extracting concessions from South Africa toward the acceptance of a new formula continued. In August, South Africa accepted a UN monitoring staff and representative and a possible restriction of South African troops to designated areas.[33] By October, its position had moved to acceptance of a large contingent of UN military observers independent of the South African Defense Forces and a gradual withdrawal of those forces if SWAPO accepted a cease-fire, acceptance of a visit by the UN commissioner for Namibia, Finnish Ambassador Martti Ahtisaari, as personal representative of the UN secretary general, and permission for SWAPO to hold public meetings.[34] At the same time, South Africa installed its new administrator general, Judge Marthinus Steyn, and put port facilities under naval control in Walvis Bay on 1 September.[35] Both tracks were operating—the negotiating process and the process of positioning for unilateral action—without any decision as to which was to be the final strategy.

In reaction, SWAPO reiterated its total demands, and the pressure on South Africa tightened another turn. UN members threatened measures against South Africa; South Africa responded that condemnation would lead it to break off talks and destroy the second track; the General Assembly then passed a long resolution including an arms embargo, but without sanctions or enforcement.[36] At the end of the year, South Africa, under Western pressure, moved a bit more, agreeing to military withdrawals down to 4,000–5,000 men, UN monitoring of the force reductions, military confinement to bases in the north, and UN military forces within the UN contingent. After the conflict intensification that accompanied the UN General Assembly session and the call for a special General Assembly session in April 1978 on Namibia, South Africa added the parallel demand for an equal monitoring of SWAPO guerrillas.

The pattern of maneuvering down to the submission of the package proposal in February 1978 thus generally began with Western and UN pressure that produced both South African concessions on the negotiating track and, under the cover of those concessions, faits accomplis on the unilateral track. South Africa's general policy was to keep its first track up-to-date with its second, so that it could always shift from one to the other without having to go back and update its possibilities for unilateral action (as a policy and/or as a threat). South Africa's acts on both tracks produced, in turn, reaffirmations of SWAPO's unchanging position. Changes in SWAPO's position, however, were caused by a general consolidation of its support in a diplomatic forum (such as OAU or UN) plus front-line pressure, particularly from Angola, its primary sanctuary. SWAPO concessions were then generally followed at a distance by further South African concessions, and the process moved on.

An apparently zero-sum situation—as territorial questions tend to be—obtains in regard to Walvis Bay, the port enclave that has been administered by both South Africa and South West Africa on past occasions. South Africa refused to give up the territory during the negotiations, in part because Walvis Bay was the last card it had with which to buy SWAPO (or independent Namibian) concessions and in part because it was a position from which to monitor and control Namibian actions after independence—again the two-track strategy. SWAPO, backed by the UN, has demanded the full return of Walvis Bay. Throughout the negotiations, there has been no movement on this position; eventually, there was agreement to postpone the issue. South Africa did agree not to increase its military strength in Walvis Bay during the transitional period and, more significantly, to allow Namibians in the enclave to vote in the UN elections.

Phase two covered discussions on the Western Five's package, from February to July 1978.[37] The "final" package, as submitted to the extended list of parties in South Africa, SWAPO, other Namibian political organizations, the front-line states, Nigeria and the OAU presidents' states—and discussed in proximity talks in mid-February in New York—embodied the formula of a paired UN and South African presence preparing one-man-one-vote elections.[38] South African troops were to be reduced to 1,500 over a period of 3 months and were to be confined to 2 camps (Oshivello and Grootfontein) in the north, the UN presence (United Nations Transition Assistance Group—UNTAG) would take the form of a peacekeeping force somewhat larger than the South African force plus a civilian group to help administer during the transition, political prisoners of both sides would be released, South African white and tribal paramilitary forces would be dissolved, and discriminatory legislation would be repealed.

In response, South Africa appeared to be more concerned about the detailed implementation of the paired UN-South Africa formula than about the formula itself whereas SWAPO continued to press for another formula, that of South African subordination to the UN during the transition. SWAPO, in addition to its reservation on Walvis Bay, wanted the 1,500 South African troops to be stationed in the south (Karasburg) out of the way, the South African police force disarmed, and the UN special representative generally placed "in a superior authority" to South Africans in Namibia.[39] South Africa was less clear in its challenge to the paired formula; it asked to reexamine the relation between its administrator general and the UN special representative and wanted 3,000 of its own troops and only enough UN troops to maintain order and supervise elections.

At the end of March 1978, the Western Five submitted new "final" proposals close to those of the previous month[40] and in April made further "clarifications" to South Africa:[41] Walvis Bay was to be resolved only after independence: South African troops could remain in Namibia if so requested by the newly elected assembly; but the phased reduction of South African forces would be accomplished within three months of a "complete cessation of hostilities"; SWAPO guerrillas and South African forces alike would be confined to bases; South African police would continue to maintain law and order, bearing only small arms; and a joint South African and UN administration would prepare free constituent assembly elections under UN supervision, with the assistance of UNTAG. South Africa accepted at the end of April, and SWAPO rejected the package.[42]

The American mediator, Donald McHenry, has estimated that agreement by both parties was attainable within a week. Previously, South African concessions—to a package that was closer to initial UN than South African positions—predictably had led to a temporary reaffirmation of SWAPO positions and a SWAPO hard line of a diplomatic forum—as provided by the special General Assembly session on Namibia in late April and early May 1978—was then to be expected, followed by concessions urged on it by its front-line supporters once its general support had been consolidated. Of course, certain elements of the package—such as Walvis Bay—were still incompatible with SWAPO's announced positions, but negotiation is the process of changing positions. At the same time, concessions have been generally associated—before and after—with intensification of the conflict as parties reasserted their will to fight if necessary (first track) along with their will to compose (second track), seeking to assure themselves the best position on the ground in the face of an impending agreement. A combination of these explanations might suggest that early May was the wrong time for South Africa to launch a military intensification—let alone escalation—but that an intensified conflict might have been expected earlier, before the General Assembly session. Yet, in reality, the only effect of intensification was to delay but not disrupt progress toward agreement, and this was consistent with the strategic evaluations of both parties, each of whom felt that time was on its side.

On 8 May 1978, the day that further discussions on the package were to have begun between the Western Five and SWAPO, South Africa made a deep attack into Angola against SWAPO bases in Cassinga, 250 kilometers north of the border and just south of the Namibe (Moçamedes) defense line along the fifteenth parallel.[43] SWAPO broke off talks, but it continued to make concessions, such as acceptance of the principle of confinement for its own forces as well as South Africa's. Early in June, the front-line states, meeting in Luanda, accepted the package; on 11 June SWAPO resumed talks; two weeks later, McHenry in Angola won agreement to press SWAPO to accept the package; and in mid-July SWAPO accepted.[44] The accepted package provided for repeal of remaining discriminatory legislation, release of both sides' political prisoners and return of exiles, cease-fire, confinement of SWAPO and South African forces to their bases, gradual withdrawal of South African forces except for the 1,500 in two northern bases, demobilization of paramilitary forces, installation of a UN peacekeeping force, and joint supervision of the transition and elections by the UN special representative and the South African administrator general; Walvis Bay was reserved for negotiation after independence. Following the OAU, a special meeting of the Security Council endorsed the plan.[45]

The *third phase*, in which the two parties' agreement fell apart, began as soon as the agreement was registered in July, and continued to stalemate in September. Four interpretations can be given for the cause of the breakdown.[46] The phase may be interpreted as approach-avoidance tactics by South Africa on its second track in order to give time for the first track to develop. When SWAPO agreed despite the Cassinga raid, South Africa was surprised and withdrew its own agreement to a plan that it never did expect to see implemented. It may also be interpreted as "normal" breakdown of negotiations when they move from principles to details and the parties discover that implementation of the agreed formula leaves them with details that are unacceptable but were not foreseen in the earlier phase. It can be interpreted as a failure of two crucial items in the negotiation process: deadline and effective pressure on the parties' security position (their outcomes without an agreement). The only deadline in the negotiations, the independence target date at the end of 1978, favored the unilateral track rather than the negotiated one, and the pressure from the West in the form of threatened sanctions became less credible the closer it came to a test. Finally, the breakdown may be seen as a reaction—particularly on the part of South Africa—to changing internal and external conditions that appeared to improve either the chances or the desirability of first-track policies.

In the real world, causes usually fall under the category of "all of the above" rather than under a single judgment. It is the theme of these case studies, however, that best explanations are frequently found in the process of conflict resolution rather than in decisions outside that process, and therefore decisions are better understood as being based on such elements as suspicion over details, absence of deadline, and changing estimates about the alternatives than as steps in the purposive pursuit of a single policy.

No sooner had the package been tied up than it began to fall apart.[47] One of the Western mediators has said that negotiators always try to get back on the next round the items that they gave up on the last, an apt characterization of the process of bargaining over details. However, that process also has its reactive component affecting the general acceptance of the agreement. Even before the Security Council meeting of July 1978, SWAPO—which had never yet clearly stated its unequivocal acceptance of the package—began to demand a firmer commitment on Walvis Bay, a single base for South African troops, and the withdrawal of troops from Walvis Bay (not a new demand). South Africa indicated the second demand was possible, rejected the rest, and then at the end of July provisionally withdrew its acceptance of the package, announced only four days earlier;[48] at the same time, it nonetheless agreed to the visit of UN Special Representative Ahtisaari the next day. SWAPO retorted that there would be no cease-fire until the South African troops were confined to their base, the discriminatory legislation was repealed, and the prisoners released;[49] South Africa maintained that implementation of the plan depended on an initial cease-fire, and within two weeks the guerrilla war had intensified again. South Africa then increased its demands, threatening to augment its troops and not to begin withdrawals until after 3 months of "visible peace" and rejecting the figure of 5,000 for the UN force. It also proceeded with its own voter registration for the election and independence by the end of the year, points that caused problems in the discussions between Ahtissari and Steyn.[50]

Into this deteriorating situation, as guerrilla attacks and retaliatory raids intensified, entered UN Secretary General Kurt Waldheim with his own proposal, submitted in response to the Security Council request for an implementation plan.[51] The proposal assigned a figure of 7,500 to the UNTAG force required to perform the assigned functions, included a separate 360-man police force, and noted that elections could not be held until 7 months after the acceptance of the report, hence after the end of 1978. The UNTAG figure is an interesting case of the means and pitfalls of determining details. When the parties could not agree on a figure for the force, they shifted their referent and agreed on a function, leaving the secretary general to translate the function into a figure. This was done on a technical basis, comparing the South African forces required to do the same task and computing in a leave-and-replacement rate. But the figure so determined fell outside the figure earlier rejected by South Africa, and South Africa rejected it again at the end of August.[52] It also questioned the functions, looking for a monitoring rather than a peacekeeping force; challenged the addition of a police force not in the April package; and insisted on an initial cease-fire and independence by the end of the year.[53]

SWAPO accepted Waldheim's report a week later under pressure from Nigeria and Angola, calling for a formal and binding agreement to be signed with South Africa.[54] SWAPO also called for a cease-fire and, under Zambian and Angolan pressure, suspended operations until near the end of the year. South Africa rejected the SWAPO proposal the same day, reiterated its objections to the Waldheim report, and two weeks later canceled its agreement to the whole April proposal.[55] On the same day 20 September, the Vorster government resigned in a scandal and P. W. Botha was chosen prime minister. The negotiations were at a stalemate.

It may well be that the entire South African negotiating exercise was a delaying tactic until the first track could be set up, and it is probably true, from observers' accounts, that South Africa was surprised by SWAPO's acceptance. However, it is rare and, therefore, unlikely in the real world of diplomacy that South Africa be able to carry off participation in the negotiation as an extended Machiavellian hoax, and South Africa's surprise is surprising, given the closeness of the package to the UN-SWAPO positions. SWAPO, after all, was giving up a means—guerrilla warfare—for a reasonable chance of maintaining its end—coming to power. South Africa, on the other hand, was allowed to keep its means in altered form—elections—but was in great danger of losing its end—a friendly Namibia.

What is more likely, but less frequently noted, is that South Africa came to the end of acceptable concessions as it gradually worked out the implementation of the package and, in the process, discovered that the apparently acceptable formula translated itself into unacceptable details. Western mediators have complained that South Africa simply rejected, never arguing their point, a behavior fully compatible with the notion that the last details changed their view of the whole picture: The camel with the broken back does not argue about the last straw; he complains of the whole load even though it was bearable up to the last moment. In addition, South Africa appears to have feared that there would be still more straws and that the Western mediators would continue to produce a package that was even closer to SWAPO's position than to South Africa's.

Yet South Africa made no final decision. Without closing the door on the second track and while reaffirming its adherence to the April package in its earlier form, it proceeded with preparations for its own one-man-one-vote elections without SWAPO. The move was consistent with South Africa's two-track approach; under the cover of an on-and-off negotiation, it brought along its first track, not to the point of precluding the second, but at least to the point of keeping the option alive and up-to-date as a viable alternative and, therefore, as a reinforcement of its own bargaining position.

The *fourth phase* ran from the September stalemate through the end of 1978; despite its appearance of continuing negotiations over details within the same formula of a paired transition, it marked the collapse of the demarche through the mediators' inability to bring the parties to a decision. After the rejection of the report, South Africa announced a delay in its elections until December.[56] The Security Council accepted the secretary general's report in its basic Resolution 435 and gave South Africa twenty-five days to change its policy. At the same time, Waldheim softened some of his details, indicating that fewer than 7,500 people could be required and that the elections would be held no later than April 1979. However, the leader of the Turnhalle parties (DTA) also began making more frequent pronouncements, indicating that they would not participate in the negotiations before the elections; after the elections, there would be greater strength in the first track, legitimized by Namibians' votes.

While SWAPO sat unmoving, the Western mediators discussed carrots and sticks at the highest level during the twenty-five-day grace period and thereafter, once it had passed without triggering a deadline. In mid-October the Western foreign ministers (or, in the French case, his deputy) visited Pretoria and caved in. Although the

National Security Council (NSC) meeting on 6 October had decided that "the time had come for direct pressure" and had authorized Secretary Vance to carry a handwritten letter from President Carter offering to receive the new Prime Minister Botha in Washington, to seek SWAPO's agreement to elections in the spring and to reduce the UN force to 3,500 plus 1,500 support personnel—all if Botha would reverse the South Africa rejection of 20 September—no such agreement was forthcoming.[57] In case of rejection, the NSC had decided to support sanctions ("but only after we assessed the results of the Pretoria talks"), and the Contact Group meeting in New York had narrowed them down to secondary, specific measures such as restrictions on South African airplanes' landing rights and on South African access to Western export financing. Botha apparently let the five ministers leave the meeting without an agreement, then reopened negotiations with Secretary Vance while saying good-bye. As a result, the final American-South African communiqué agreed to continue talks between UN Special Representative Ahtisaari, South Africa, and the new representatives chosen in the elections that Botha was resolved to hold in December. South Africa had gone to the diplomatic brink and had won; it had not been deterred from its own first-track plans, and in exchange it had agreed to let the UN continue to talk to it. In addition to the joint communiqué, separate statements by the two parties spelled out lesser areas of disagreement.

The reasons for the Western collapse are clearly stated by the participants.[58] Canadian Foreign Minister Donald Jamieson indicated that the compromise statement was agreed to by the West in order to avoid having to impose sanctions, and indeed the communiqué was used in the Security Council debate in November to head off an African resolution threatening sanctions if the December vote were held. Secretary Vance has written of the ministers' strategy going into the meeting: "It was essential that we convince the new South African government to continue working toward an acceptable settlement. The alternative was a bitter confrontation with Pretoria, collapse of the negotiations, and intensification of the guerrilla war." In the event, South Africa agreed to postpone agreement by talking, and confrontation and intensification ensued. When alternatives are viewed in the way presented, when sanctions of any kind are feared more by those who would apply them than by the target, it is clear that deadlines are in the hands of the latter, and the mediator has neither leverage nor determination.

When, at the end of November, the president and the secretary of state met Foreign Minister R. F. Botha and warned that further disregard of Resolution 435 would lead to greater pressure for sanctions, the threat had lost its credibility.[59] The administration had shifted to a policy described as "more of the carrot, less of the stick" at a time when the evolution of the negotiations demanded the reverse. To be sure, it was an unlikely time to expect capitulation from South Africa because a new premier was being asked to reverse his predecessor's policy under foreign pressure at the end of his third week in office. Yet a Western decision to back words with action could have set the stage for mutual deescalation if the West had viewed the alternatives differently. In substance, the October compromise reaffirmed the paired transition formula: The UN police force would monitor the internal security arrangements of the South African police force; consultation between the two administrators would determine the size of UNTAG, the date of entry of UN troops, and the date of UN-sponsored elections. SWAPO, the front-line states, and the UN African group rejected the compromise, but with no more force than a verbal condemnation of South Africa for holding its December elections.[60] In the event, the UN deadline passed unobserved, without any screw-tightening measures, showing South Africa that no sanctions, no deadlines, and no worse alternatives were included in the UN and Western mediation. These lessons of October 1978 were such a heavy burden on the process that no mediator was able to overcome them for ten years.

It was to the South African first track that attention turned, as the unilateral option became a subject of bargaining that strengthened South Africa's position. Initially, the Western Five proposed considering the December election as merely a preliminary to the later UN-supervised vote, but in the end they refused to consider the election at all, for it went outside the package formula, and Waldheim indicated he would not deal with the newly elected officials. South Africa refused to cancel its election plans, and Botha's talks with Carter and Waldheim produced no specific agreements on the unresolved points.[61] The elections in early December saw 80.2 percent participation out of 95 percent registration of 443,441 eligible voters comprising all people over 18 born in Namibia or living there since 1974 although the percentages drop to 72 percent and 59 percent if a demographically more accurate figure of 550,000 eligible voters is used.[62] The Turnhalle coalition (DTA), whose hard-line stands flanked South Africa on the right, won 82 percent of the vote in relatively free voting; but SWAPO-D, NNF, and internal SWAPO boycotted; and external SWAPO declared that armed struggle was the only way. With its first track in place, South Africa agreed to

UN-supervised elections if held before the end of September 1979[63] and accompanied its concession with increased demands for monitoring SWAPO bases in Zambia and Angola as well as Namibia; renegotiation of the size of UNTAG; and reservation of police, administrative, and legislative functions for the South African side of the paired transition.

The *fifth phase* ran from the end of 1978 to January 1981. The images and policies of the new Botha government hardened through the process of further maneuvering on details until finally the second track was shelved for all practical purposes by South Africa, at least until the implications of the successive British, Zimbabwean, German, and American elections became clear. In such a situation, the logical role for SWAPO would be to hold to the package, which was essentially in its favor. Instead, because SWAPO imitated South Africa's behavior and returned to its own unilateral position, the negotiated track was abandoned as a preferred position by both sides, and SWAPO's intransigence provided justification for South Africa's maneuvering. SWAPO continued to make equivocal statements and even, during Ahtisaari's second visit in mid-January 1979, raised its demands for a new formula whereby the UN authority would be fully superordinate to the South African role during the transition (Ahtisaari over Steyn, South African police disarmed and under UN supervision, all South African troops withdrawn) and proclaimed its adherence to its first track—guerrilla warfare to the end—if it did not win the elections. Not until later in 1979 were the front-line states able to get SWAPO back to the package.

During this period, a number of issues of detail continued to raise further questions, both during Ahtisaari's visit and in Waldheim's subsequent report issued on 26 February. The 7,500-person figure for UNTAG was accepted by South Africa; the year-end deadline was replaced by South Africa's deadline of September 1979, with a cease-fire proposed by Waldheim for March 15.[64] The Zambian government denied that it held SWAPO dissidents "in Zambian jails" to release in exchange for South African release of SWAPO prisoners and detainees; the composition of the UNTAG force was accepted by South Africa even though it contained none of the South African nominees; the South African demand in December that SWAPO bases in neighboring countries be monitored by the UN was accepted by Zambia and Botswana but not until early 1979 by Angola although it was not clear whether this demand had been accepted by the Western Five or whether the UN had the means to do the monitoring. South Africa's demand in April that SWAPO be confined to bases in Namibia now appeared to be guaranteeing SWAPO internal bases where it had none previously. In all points but the last, South Africa found itself making the concessions, and this perception began to color its view of the entire mediating process and of the impartiality of the Western Five.[65]

South Africa's charges of "serious deviations" from the April proposal appear unfounded, but its discovery that the resolution of specific details was not in its favor was not irrational. In early March 1979, South Africa rejected the cease-fire date and attacked SWAPO bases in Angola.[66] The military action was to be expected in view of a possible cease-fire because parties are likely to maneuver to the best positions just before hostilities are suspended. The rejection of the subsequent cease-fire, however, had no other justification than South Africa's general and crystallizing view of the process. A new meeting of the Western Five foreign ministers with the South African foreign minister and the DTA parties and with Waldheim and SWAPO at the UN in mid-March did not change this view.[67]

Instead, the details under discussion in the South African view began to form the basis of a single judgment: UNTAG, already too large, was not large enough to keep SWAPO from spreading once the cease-fire, the South African troop withdrawal, and the elections took place; and neither the UN nor the Western Five were committed to the political action necessary to keep SWAPO from taking advantage of the situation. Although repeating that it "was not closing the door" on any UN-supervised elections or on further talks, South Africa began searching about for a broader context for its first track.[68] Faced with the annual spring UN session on Namibia at the end of May 1979, South Africa early in the month decided to turn the newly elected constituent assembly into a Namibian legislature (but not to empower it to declare independence),[69] withdrew its demand for and agreement to any SWAPO bases within Namibia (but not its rejection of SWAPO's participation as a political party),[70] declared that prospects of returning to the April package were "slim" (but not purporting to "close any doors"),[71] and then in August appointed Professor Gerrit Viljoen, head of the Broederbond, as successor to Steyn (but continued to dismantle racial discrimination by legislation).[72] In speeches in April and November 1979, Botha spelled out an explicit concept for a boundary-in-depth or buffer zone by calling for a "constellation of states" that would provide security and economic well-being through close ties with South Africa and protect African states in the southern hemisphere from economic decay and Communist penetration.[73]

A shift in mediators occurred in late 1979 as the UN Secretariat took over much of the Western Five's activities after one last American attempt. In mid-July McHenry returned to Luanda and worked out a new proposal on the basis of concessions by President Neto of Angola. Neto's proposals included a demilitarized zone (DMZ) of 50 kilometers on each side of the Angolan-Namibian border to prevent attacks by and against SWAPO, Angolan supervision of camps in Angola for SWAPO forces unwilling to participate in the elections, and a UN presence in Angola to ensure compliance with (but not monitor) the agreement.[74] Presentation of the new proposal to South Africa in mid-August produced no immediate acceptance, only measures to reinforce the autonomy of Namibia on the first track.

After the opening of the UN General Assembly session in the fall, the UN secretary general's office entered the mediation efforts by assigning the undersecretary for special political affairs, Brian Urquhart, to reinforce the efforts of the Western Five. In mid-November 1979, Urquhart convened a special meeting in Geneva to discuss the new proposal.[75] In addition to the five front-line states, the five Western states, and SWAPO, South Africa finally also agreed to attend but brought along representatives of the DTA, SWAPO-D, the NNF, a hard-line white party (Aktur), and three lesser parties, all of whom demanded equality with external SWAPO in the discussions. After the prolonged proximity discussions, South Africa left to study the proposals, having marked a further point for its modified first track by having the other parties recognized in preparation for a solution. Three weeks later, in early December, it accepted the idea of a demilitarized zone, but with six new details to be included as well.[76] No solution could take place on any track, however, until the outcome of the Zimbabwe negotiations, elections, and transfer of powers had occurred and been evaluated by the parties. The Namibian situation, therefore, stopped in both its tracks until mid-1980.

The Zimbabwe elections, with the defeat of the internal settlement parties and the overwhelming victory of Mugabe's ZANU, had serious effects on South African thinking about Namibia. On one hand, the South Africans alone were surprised at the result, and it gave them pause in their confidence about the results of a similar election in Namibia. On the other hand, the South African government felt that, in Zimbabwe as in Namibia, the internal solution was still the best bet and could be brought to fruition if only done right, with military support and plenty of time. The error in Zimbabwe was seen not in the construction of an internal black-white conservative coalition, but in the way the coalition was supported. The emphasis sought at Geneva was, therefore, continued, and a major thrust of South African policy became to use every opportunity to obtain UN recognition and legitimacy for the internal parties, notably DTA and NNF. At the same time, settlement lost any urgency it may have had.

Nonetheless, progress continued to be made in nailing down details. Urquhart continued to work on South African technical reservations about the transition arrangements and in June reached agreement that the demilitarized zone would contain twenty South African monitoring bases on the Namibian side and seven bases manned by Zambian and Angolan troops on their side of the border. At the same time, as was its custom, South Africa took important steps to reinforce its first track. In mid-June it began a major three-week offensive against SWAPO bases within Angola, producing the highest casualties of the war on both sides.[77] Surprised by the resistance and heavy armaments it met, it nonetheless dealt a heavy military blow to the guerrillas. The day the offensive began, South Africa authorized the transfer of authority over most governmental matters except foreign and financial affairs to a new SWA/Namibian executive council comprising Mudge and other DTA members of the elected assembly. These moves kept the first track abreast of developments on the second, a matter of greater importance for South Africa than a firm outcome on either track.

Other components joined in making this conclusion. An item that had been mentioned from the beginning by South Africa but never pressed as the major obstacle took on new importance: the impartiality of the UN as the administrator of the elections. With the UN General Assembly declaring SWAPO to be the sole legitimate representative of the Namibian people, UN agencies giving aid to SWAPO, and the UN secretary general making statements more appealing to the majority of his constituency than to South Africa on this issue and forgetting that it exercised an expired authority over the territory, South Africa found a logical complaint. The impartiality argument was useful to the general strategy of delaying progress on track two because it could be pressed endlessly and, therefore, gain time, and it would strengthen the internal parties, who would benefit from impartiality. In the midst of a desultory exchange of letters with Waldheim throughout much of 1980, South African Foreign Minister Botha at the end of August raised impartiality to a major issue and a precondition to the transition process.[78]

At the end of 1980, the negotiations took a further step that appeared to head toward agreement, but in fact only bought time to strengthen the internal parties. This occurred in the midst of the

American election campaign and the victory of a candidate judged to be more understanding of the South African position, another external event that convinced South Africa of the urgency of delay. In late October, the South Africans received Urquhart (a full month later than the date proposed by Waldheim for the meeting) and agreed to a cease-fire in March 1981 and the election of a constituent assembly some six months later, but on condition that there be a face-to-face meeting of South African, internal party, and SWAPO representatives in January.[79] The idea of such a meeting, outside the framework of the Western Five's mediation effort but conceivably complimentary to it, was raised in a secret meeting between South Africans and Angolans in Paris in April but refused in October by other front-line states worried about South Africa's intent.[80] Ostensibly, the face-to-face meeting would be to complete details of the transition and build trust, but SWAPO and some Africans felt that South Africa would turn it into a further delay by making it a constitutional conference, like the Lancaster House exercise, preceding the cease-fire and elections.

The fears were correct—for the wrong reasons. It was not a constitutional drafting session that South Africa sought, but more time to strengthen the DTA and to benefit from the Reagan administration's declared sympathies. Rather than guarantees, it was the equally elastic issue of impartiality that was imposed as the theme of the meeting, along with elaborate attempts to assert the autonomy and equality of the internal parties and the new SWA/Namibian executive. When the Pre-Implementation Meeting (PIM) convened in the second week in January 1981, Nujoma, counseled by his African supporters, calmly repeated his willingness to establish the cease-fire, but Mudge and Dannie Hough, the new administrator general, talked of recognition and impartiality and then ended the meeting, declaring that the moment to put the transition and conflict resolution into effect was not yet "opportune."[81]

The *sixth phase* began in January 1981 with the collapse of the PIM although it was in preparation six months before and ran to September 1982. With the nomination and possible election of Ronald Reagan in the United States, the South African government had seen less reason than ever to enter into a Namibian agreement, and after the American election, the process stopped completely. South Africa judged the PIM a success because it put a hold on the second track and strengthened the first; the advent of a conservative regime in Washington gave hopes for a renewed strategy of joining those two tracks together to create, with Washington's help and support, an internal solution that would have international legitimacy. But first there needed be a lengthy process of testing the new regime and going back to a nearly clean slate (or at least back to April 1978) in the negotiations.

The African reaction to the election was, of course, the reverse. SWAPO renewed its belief in the need for victory through guerrilla struggle whereas the front-line states and particularly Nigeria berated the new administration for its Pretorian proclivities. Not until the visit of Nigerian Foreign Minister Ishaya Auda to Washington in late March was there the beginning of a working understanding between Washington and Africa.[82]

In fact, the African face of the Reagan administration lived up to neither party's caricature but was instead a very clear-sighted, if delicately poised, reaction to the previous four years of Namibian negotiations. Africa was the one foreign policy area in which the new administration came to office with a specific goal and a means to attain it in mind.[83] The new assistant secretary of state for Africa, Chester Crocker, recognized some of the weaknesses of the previous demarche and believed that the orientation of the new administration would enable him to correct these failings with new mediation tactics aiming at the same goal; this would allow him to bring home a foreign policy victory that would both credit the new administration and facilitate its relations with South Africa and, incidentally, with the rest of the continent. The new tactical orientation was dictated by the previous shortcomings: Because South Africa was the occupying power in Namibia and the balking party in the negotiations, it would have to be bought off with appropriate attention to its concerns and interests. Where the previous administration dispensed neither carrots nor sticks, its successor would use carrots, assuring the South Africans a better future through a Namibian settlement, equivalent to the perception of a better future that independence for Namibia would bring the Africans. In the event, these carrots would also be consistent with the orientation of the new administration, which favored better relations with South Africa. Furthermore, just as the Carter administration had reacted to the Nixon rigidity and secrecy in foreign affairs with a freewheeling openness and pluralism, so the Reagan administration reacted to its predecessor's style with a close-to-the-chest style of secrecy in its Namibian negotiations.[84] Finally, as South Africa was continually adding new concerns and thereby delaying agreement, it would be asked for a final list of all its demands but then told that matters, once settled, could no longer be revived.

The carrots were to be three: improved relations, constitutional guarantees, and the Cuban connection, the last amounting to a new, expanded formula. First, to create a better working atmosphere and soften the hostile attitudes that the previous administration held toward South Africa, the Reagan administration would remove some of the "petty pariah" measures of ostracism as a down payment and continue to improve relations as South Africa moved toward Namibian settlement.[85] There was no question of removing the basic American antipathy to apartheid or of directly contravening the UN military sanctions; in the same speech in which President Reagan spoke of not turning our back on a friend like South Africa, he also termed apartheid "repugnant."[86] However, lesser matters of mutual importance, such as restoration of military attachés, defense-usable licenses and matériel (trucks and planes), nuclear and intelligence cooperation, could be instituted immediately, with more to come.[87] Lesser or slower measures would not have restored the necessary South African confidence in the mediator's good intentions. Yet the measures that were taken tended to inflate South Africa's confidence and exaggerate its expectations while making the United States look like an accomplice to the African side.

Second, to allay fears that the independent Namibian government might take revenge on the white or other minorities and their property, Crocker's plan was to follow the Zimbabwe (and, indeed, general African) model and write at least parts of the constitution to reassure minorities before the referendum rather than afterward. In early April, Crocker undertook a trip to twelve African countries to assess the reaction toward this change in the order of constitution and referendum stipulated in Resolution 435, and through the broadly negative reactions he found enough encouragement to pursue the idea.[88] The original idea was to have an entire constitution written by a panel of experts, but this was altered in discussions with Africans and the Contact Group to refer only to a set of principles providing protection for minorities. In November, both sides agreed to nine provisions[89] that would require a two-thirds vote of the constituent assembly for passage of the Namibian constitution, a bill of rights "consistent with the . . . Universal Declaration of Human Rights," separation of powers and an independent judiciary, and others. Although these agreements were later to come under strain, they were translated into more detailed provisions about an electoral system (the same process of unraveling that had characterized the 1978–79 negotiations), and the attention to constitutional principles was an appropriate attempt to fill in a real gap in the proceedings as well as an attempt to restore South African confidence. Nor, unlike the first carrot, did the second contain anything that directly threatened the confidence of the African parties.

Third, to meet South African concerns for security in the region and to provide a better context for neutrality of an independent Namibian government and at the same time to use the Namibia settlement to accomplish a major American policy objective in Africa, Crocker proposed to relate the South African withdrawal from Namibia to a Cuban withdrawal from Angola.[90] Although the concern was shared, the proposal was American. It was the most specific of the three carrots designed to make the future settlement more agreeable than the present conflict to South Africa. The connection was "logical," as the Crocker team never tired of pointing out, but it was a risky gamble. It was clearly outside the bounds of Resolution 435, and so no explicit and binding linkage could be established in the negotiations. It was highly susceptible to the very complexities that the American mediators ought to avoid, for either withdrawal could easily be posed by either party as a precondition to the other; indeed, all the technicalities of withdrawing up to 20,000 and 90,000 troops effectively removed any possibility of exact simultaneity and, therefore, forced consideration of phases and balances. Most seriously, it was outside of the clear power of the Americans to deliver and depended entirely on a two-handed salesmanship job that would leave one or both parties bitter if the deal were not made.

As such, it was a mighty gamble, worth the try. There were indications enough that Angola was interested in exploring a Western opening and in removing Cuban troops. The same logic that tied the two problems together argued for their solution: Once the Cubans were gone, South Africa need not worry about militarily occupying its Namibian buffer, and once the South Africans were gone, Angola had no further need for protection by the Cubans (who in fact had offered precious little direct protection against South Africa or even against UNITA, but simply served as a backup to the Angolan army in the field and a palace guard in Luanda).[91] Unfortunately for the logic, the same reasoning went on to include the need for a solution to the problem of UNITA, which occupied the southeastern quarter or third of Angola with South African support. Crocker's thoughts also involved UNITA, but it is not clear—and probably was not yet clearly worked out in his own ideas—whether there was a further UNITA connection to the Namibia settlement or whether that aspect would simply follow its own evolution.[92] Optimally, the MPLA government of Angola and UNITA would later negotiate their differences and form a national coalition, but in fact UNITA would probably not have the necessary strength to force such an agreement—despite its regional base—if South African supplies and support were cut off. More likely, a Namibia-Cuban settlement would leave UNITA high and dry, paying the cost of the larger agreement. Thus, the "UNITA seam" of the Namibia-Cuban package was open enough to keep the latter from being a self-contained whole and to promise further problems in the future.

The Crocker proposals contained one more element that was sorely lacking in the previous efforts: a sense of deadline. According to the timetable, the constitutional guarantees were to be negotiated in 1981, and the details of withdrawal, established during 1982, providing for independence in 1983. It was clearly stated from the beginning that patience would run out at the end of 1982, and if the South Africans were not willing to accept the improved package of conditions and relations offered by the Reagan administration by that time, they would have lost their chance.[93] Presumably (as it was contrary to the prevailing philosophy about treatment of South Africans to make threats explicit) this meant that positive gestures (the first carrot) would be withdrawn and that the administration would cease its efforts at helping South Africa find an internationally acceptable solution.

Unfortunately, there were flaws in the concept. The threat not to find a way out of Namibia was a threat that the South African government could easily live with, and the threat (implicit or explicit) to restore pariah status was one that Afrikaner thinking, in its heart of hearts, expected of the world anyhow (and indeed was electorally useful). Threats to reduce pressure and to do what one is expected to do anyhow are not very powerful. Yet the only other threat was one of sanctions, a threat of untested effectiveness that was already shown to be more powerful against the Carter administration than against South Africa and one that simply was not in the vocabulary of the Reagan administration. Furthermore, the South Africans appeared to have a timetable of their own—and a contingent one at that. It called for a four-year period from the 1980 American elections to renegotiate an acceptable track-two agreement while at the same time using the same period to strengthen track-one possibilities—notably, internal political organizations in Namibia. Only then, in the light of the prevailing electoral possibilities of the Reagan administration seeking a second term, would it evaluate whether it was necessary to make a decision at all between the two tracks or whether they could not—as in the past—simply be pursued parallelly into the future. When the second Reagan election came in fact, South Africa was close to a decision because the two tracks had been brought closer together. At the same time, the African states and SWAPO had no fixed deadline at all and no way of imposing one. They could, therefore, only contribute to the breakdown of the process, not force its successful conclusion, for any offers to South Africa short of capitulation would merely prove the wisdom of South Africa's strategy of holding out.[94]

As happens in life, the mediator's timetable was respected only in the beginning. The Reagan administration's phase one began under fire in early 1981 and ended in an equivocal understanding in the fall of 1982. Crocker's Senate confirmation as assistant secretary was held up until May by carping from the Republican right, notably from Senator Jesse Helms, so that the trip to Africa in April, for example, had to be undertaken as merely assistant secretary-designate. The first requirement was to reestablish coordinated working relations among the Western Five (which also contained a new French Socialist government after the French elections of April). This was accomplished in meetings in London in April, on Crocker's way home from Africa; although it did not prevent the need to use the veto in the Security Council debates on sanctions at the end of the month, it did result in the ensuing discussions in the adoption of the French proposal for a bill of rights rather than an entire constitution.[95]

In dealing with the African side, the administration was hampered by its decision to work out terms acceptable to South Africa first, in diplomatic secrecy, and then present them to SWAPO and the front-line states.[96] It was not until September 1981 that Secretary Haig could announce that South Africa was more or less back to the position it had agreed to and then abandoned in 1980 and not until November that South Africa agreed to the additional constitutional provisions, with a few reservations.[97] The African states followed, also with reservations, sending the mediators into the subsequent task of finding an acceptable electoral system. The original proposal for "fair representation" through "proportional representation or appropriate determination of constituencies or a combination of both," was translated into a proposal for "one man two votes" in which half of the constituent assembly would be elected from single-member districts and half from party lists by proportional representation. This proposal, similar to the voting system used in West Germany, was submitted to the two sides in mid-December and achieved South African agreement at the end of January 1982, but—

in a sense because of that very fact—ran into African objections.[98] It was modified to provide for one-man-one-vote counted twice, once for a single candidate and once for a nationwide party list, but the modification did nothing to overcome SWAPO fears that what was preferable for South Africa was unfavorable to SWAPO. Finally, in mid-July, agreement was obtained from both sides to use either one system or the other but leave the choice between single-member (favored by South Africa) or list voting (favored by SWAPO but acceptable to South Africa) to a decision by the South African administrator general with the agreement of the UN special representative, joint administrators of the transition.[99]

Even before phase one was over, to make up for lost time, in late May negotiations had moved on to the Reagan administration's phase two to set up details of the seven-month transition between cease-fire and elections.[100] In effect, the pre-1981 agreements on details were restored; the UN was considered "impartial" enough to supervise elections, following new statements by UN officials, agreements to suspend aid to SWAPO, and the election of Secretary General Pérez de Cuéllar to replace Waldheim; the 7,500-person UNTAG force was again accepted, and it was agreed that its position was to include troops from Yugoslavia, Panama, Bangladesh, Sudan, and perhaps Japan; SWAPO bases in neighboring countries were to be monitored by UN troops; and other small points were established. Optimism rose during the summer, South Africa declared that elections would be held in March 1983, and a cease-fire was called for 15 August.[101] By the end of July, essentially all details were in place except for the matter of the Cuban troop withdrawal.

The Cuban connection had been sitting by discreetly since the initial American soundings in April and June 1981.[102] In early February 1982, a joint Cuban-Angolan declaration announced Cuban agreement to withdraw its troops once Angola was no longer threatened by invasion; earlier on two occasions, in 1976 and 1979, Cuban troop withdrawals had begun, only to be interrupted by South African attacks on Angola.[103] After discussions in March between Special Representative General Vernon Walters and Cuban authorities in Havana, the United States decided that it was appropriate to make the connection more explicit, and the matter was pursued by Crocker with the Angolans.[104] Success on the Cuban issue, however, was possible only if the matter ran parallel—but attached—to the Namibian issue, so that the danger of preconditions that Crocker had foreseen from the beginning would be avoided. To this point, the Western Contact Group had remained aloof from the Cuban issue, leaving it to the United States alone to pursue. But in early June, following discussions by General Walters with Angolan President Eduardo dos Santos in Luanda, the Contact Group presented new proposals not only involving the postponement of a decision on the electoral system but also evoking "other long-standing problems of the region at present hindering the development of the climate of security and mutual confidence necessary for a Namibia settlement."[105] For the first time, the Western Five were divided on an aspect of the mediation, with France, Germany, and Canada opposed to the connection, and the Africans were given ambiguous signals on the solidity of the linkage. But before a response could be obtained, South Africa became quite explicit. As SWAPO and front-line states were meeting in Dar es Salaam to complete agreement on phase one, Prime Minister Botha announced at Oshivello base in Namibia that a Namibian agreement was conditional on Cuban withdrawal, although no timetable was given, and at the same time confirmed the March deadline for new elections.[106] The Angolan response was to repeat the February Cuban-Angolan declaration making a Namibian settlement (but not a settlement over UNITA) a precondition for Cuban withdrawal.[107] Public debate escalated a step higher at the end of July when Premier Castro declared that Cuban troops would not be withdrawn until South African troops had left Namibia, foreign aid to UNITA had ended, and all danger of aggression to Angola had been eliminated.[108]

Nonetheless, negotiations continued, primarily hinging on the process of gearing one withdrawal to the other without making the connection too apparent. Ideas, such as a preliminary cease-fire before the formal cease-fire, which would permit an initial Cuban withdrawal, or alternatively a withdrawal of South African forces then raiding deep into Angola, followed by a withdrawal of SWAPO and Cuban forces from the border areas of southern Angola, were advanced to test the application of the connection through space and time.[109] Angola began to discuss possibilities of staggered withdrawals. But SWAPO rejected both the connection and the mid-August cease-fire, and the deadline passed; a new cease-fire date a month later also passed as discussions slowed down. On 13 September, Botha told a National party congress that "the government is not prepared, nor will it ever be in the future, to implement any settlement plan for SWA unless prior agreement is reached in terms of which Cuban forces must be withdrawn from Angola."[110] In early October, meeting with Secretary of State Shultz, Angolan Foreign Minister Paulo Jorge reinterpreted the February Cuban-

Angolan declaration to provide for a "new program of gradual withdrawal" if there were progress on Namibian negotiations, an Angolan-South African cease-fire, a UN border force, and "considerable reduction in the threat of invasion by South African forces";[111] the promise was repeated by Angolan ambassador to Paris Luis de Almeida a week later.[112] The connection was clearly recognized but not pinned down as a clear offer. A week later, the South African Defense Minister Magnus Malan decided, "If the Cubans do not withdraw from Angola—I mean every one of them, not just a percentage—the problem can't be solved."[113] The momentum of the summer of 1982 was destroyed, as South African statements pulled away from convergence toward agreement.

Once again, as the list of unresolved issues grew shorter and the parties balked at the last points of agreement, the mediator too drew back from taking any moves that would make nonagreement costly for the parties. By the end of the year, instead of a deadline, officials were talking of merely a timetable and indicated that if agreement did not come on schedule, the Contact Group would nevertheless keep on trying. Even once the new formula of "Cuban withdrawal for South African withdrawal" were accepted, the details and schedule of those withdrawals would have to be spelled out; and then a six-to-eight month period would be required for cease-fire, elections, and independence. At the end of that period lay 1984, the American election year, when firm measures and concentrated attention could not usually be expected from Washington, and as that year approached, South Africa began to consider the idea that it might have four more years to try for a good bargain. The idea of a longer period to work with also carried with it the possibility of a more prominent role for UNITA as the fortunes of South Africa's ally in Angola rose, and the need for an agreement faded even further. All of these developments indicated that the ripening moment had again passed, with no firm conciliator's hand to stay its passing. The need to enforce its own deadline began to appear very unappealing to the Reagan administration if it was faced at all. There was no threat to break off mediation if progress were not registered in order to extract public commitments from Angola and South Africa. Deadlines are only observed if it is thought that they would be enforced if they were not observed. Yet it was becoming the characteristic of the administration in many areas—Mideast, Falkland Islands, Russian pipeline, Namibia—to speak loudly but not even consider carrying a stick.

Although the momentum of the negotiations in 1982 was creating a ripe moment, in fact neither side was internally strong enough to make an agreement. Although there seems to have been little interne-cine struggle over tactics within most front-line states or SWAPO,[114] the policy to be adopted toward Namibia and Cuban withdrawal entered into the rising divisions between MPLA *mestiços* and Afri-cans and between the administration and the army respectively be-hind them, in Angola. The *mestiços* were led by Party Secretary Lucio Lara, favoring a policy closer to the Soviet Union, and the Africans led by Planning Minister Lopo do Nascimento and includ-ing Interior Minister Lieutenant Colonel Alexandre Rodrigues Kito, favoring a rapprochement with the West; not only did their divisions hamper a decision, but it was also suggested that the *mestiços* wanted the protection from the army that a Cuban "palace guard" gave them.

But the deeper divisions over Namibian policy were felt by the South Africans, both in South Africa itself and in Namibia. In South Africa in March, just as the tightest negotiations were going on over phase one, the hard-liners of the National party were expelled and, under the leadership of Treurnicht, founded a new Conservative political party. Although it initially appeared that Botha was left for the first time with a homogeneous group of supporters and no need to placate conservatives within the party, it soon was seen that the Conservatives posed a greater threat to Nationalist leadership than originally suspected. Already in the general election of April 1981, left and right opposition had eaten into the Nationalist majority; in a 1982 by-election, six months after the foundation of the new Conser-vative party, the two right-wing opposition parties outpolled the National party candidate in a formerly safe Johannesburg district by three to two; in May 1983, in a series of bellwether by-elections, Treurnicht won handily, but a National party minister only squeaked through in his own district. Piloting a major constitutional reform through the political system, Botha was beleaguered and in no need of an external issue that could be raised against him. Indeed, South Africans recalled that the National party never did so well as in 1977, during what was called the "Carter election," when it could use American criticism to strengthen its credentials, and never so badly as in 1981, when on the best of terms with the Reagan administration.

Finally, the political conflict posed an even worse situation in Namibia itself. The two-track approach depended on a credible Namibian political force that could be kept alive to carry out an internal settlement, and the entire South African strategy up through the 1981 PIM and afterward was to gain recognition for the internal Namibian parties and give them time and opportunity to gain

strength and credibility. But by 1982, that political force was falling
apart. Already in November 1980, the governing DTA was defeated
in regional (all-white) elections by the hard-line National party of
Namibia, losing its claim to be the spokesperson for the white Namibian population. Over the following year, the DTA lost further
credibility for its inability to deliver benefits either to its white
constituency or to the black constituencies of some of its component
alliance members. In February 1982, DTA President Peter Kalangula
withdrew his Ovambo National Democratic party from the DTA
over the whites' insistence that the DTA remain an alliance of national (racial) groups rather than an integrated party. Botha made a
quick visit to Namibia as a result and urged business and political
leaders to form a new coalition against SWAPO. Groping further for
alternatives, he instructed Administrator General Dannie Hough in
September to find a new framework for a Namibian government that
would be more "effective" and "representative." But in mid-January
1983, Mudge resigned the position of chairperson of the Council of
Ministers, which he had held since the 1978 elections, citing interference by Hough in the creation of an attractive alternative to SWAPO;
in response, Hough dissolved the assembly elected in 1978 and resumed direct rule, casting about for an alternative that would keep
the first track in shape.[115] Guidelines aimed at including a broader
range of party representatives in the interim government, including
the National Party and other ethnic spokesmen, but these groups had
little in common. Yet the very heterogeneity of the ostensible coalition pointed to a new period of some years that would be required to
build up its credibility as an alternative to SWAPO. Added to the
rising reference to the Cuban withdrawal as a precondition for a
Namibian settlement and the fears of the UNITA issue waiting to
come off the shelf as a further obstacle to settlement, the domestic
political situation in Namibia was merely another indicator that
South Africa was willing to keep on negotating but had not yet felt
the need to make a decision.

The *seventh phase* began in the fall of 1982 in the full deterioration
of the southern African situation and continued into 1985 with the
establishment of security agreements—and indeed even dialogue—
across the battle line. In this phase, the Contact Group suspended its
activities, the United States was the main mediator, and the states of
southern Africa were the main participants, much to the exclusion of
SWAPO. It is an open question whether such reduction and management of conflict leads to the resolution of conflict or merely reduces
any compelling pressures for it. The year 1983 saw the militarization

of South African politics and the use of destabilization raids against neighboring countries to beat them into reasonableness.[116] South Africa supported guerrilla movements in each of its neighboring countries—the Mozambique National Resistance (MNR), Lesotho Liberation Army (LLA), and UNITA, above all—and on occasion made direct military raids across the border—in December 1982 in Lesotho, in January 1981 and May 1983 in Mozambique, and since Operation Protea in August 1981 had kept over 2,000 troops in southern Angola, expanding further operations in November 1981 and March 1982 and then launching a new massive operation in August 1982. The purpose of this destabilization policy appeared to be less the overthrow of nationalist governments than retaliation for, pressure against, and elimination of nationalist activity in South African territory by SWAPO and the African National Congress (ANC).

But destabilization was an unstable policy for South Africa, not only illegitimate in its logic but costly in its execution. Far preferable would be a complementary strategy that would engage neighboring states to do their own policing of the nationalist movements to which they gave sanctuary by bargaining the removal of South African destabilization operations against the imposition of neighboring states' control. Eventually, such a conflict management measure might create enough confidence on both sides to lead to withdrawal of all foreign forces from the area, notably South African from Namibia and Cuban and SWAPO from Angola. Initiative for the policy came from South Africa, although impetus came from interested mediators—American officials Crocker, Walters, and Deputy Assistant Secretary of State for African Affairs Frank Wisner, who had all held talks with Angolans throughout 1982 and into 1983, but even more so from Zambian President Kenneth Kaunda who met with Prime Minister Botha at the end of April 1982 on the South African-Botswana border. Angola, alone among the front-line states, welcomed the Kaunda-Botha meeting, and President dos Santos visited Lusaka in early December.

The following day, 8 December 1982, secret talks opened on Sal in the Cape Verde Islands between Angolan Interior Minister Rodrigues Kito and other Angolans and a South African delegation headed by Foreign Minister Botha and Defense Minister General Magnus Malan.[117] Discussions focused on mutual withdrawals—of the South African Defense Force to the Namibian border, and of Angolan and of Cuban forces 300 kilometers north and SWAPO forces 400 kilometers north of the border; the withdrawal would be preceded by a jointly patrolled cease-fire for two months. A second meeting at Sal at the end of the month produced a third at the end of February, at the urging of American Ambassador to Zambia Nicholas Platt.[118] But the South African delegation that met Rodrigues was at a lower level, and Prime Minister Botha had announced in advance that a large infiltration of SWAPO forces into Namibia in February had diminished prospects. American officials pursued the negotiations with Rodrigues in March in Paris and in April in Washington, but the agreement had unraveled from both ends. Despite a purge of opponents in January, the MPLA leadership was still uncertain of its course; and the South Africans, faced with uncertainty on the other side, were not ready to pursue the initiative. Although there was a feeling among American officials that an agreement on the Cuban linkage was within sight in the summer of 1983,[119] there was little in the surrounding elements of the situation that supported such an outcome.

The South Africans and their supporters, therefore, went back to the battlefield while other parties sought other arenas for both conflict and conciliation. The Security Council meeting in Namibia, initially focused on a three-step plan involving a new Geneva conference, turned instead to the secretary general and asked him to mediate a settlement.[120] Javier Pérez de Cuéllar left in mid-August for a two-week tour of the area, during which he achieved final South African agreement on the last of the seven states composing the UN force in Namibia (Yugoslavia, Panama, Bangladesh, Sudan, Malaysia, Togo, and finally Finland) and on the end of the South African challenge to UN impartiality, but made no progress in separating the Namibian issue from its Cuban linkage.

In Namibia, a new administrator general, Dr. Willie van Niekirk, was appointed in February and immediately formulated plans for elections for a new constituent assembly.[121] The plan, finally enacted in mid-July, called for an appointed council with powers only of recommendation and found little cooperation among the parties of the territory.[122] It took until mid-November to form a new alliance—the Multi-Party Conference (MPC)—of six Namibian parties (SWANU, DTA, Namibia Christian Democratic party, SWAPO-D, and the Rehoboth Liberation Front), which three other parties joined when the MPC adopted its charter in mid-April. Even then, neither the conference nor the individual parties were in any position to stand as the moderate respondent to SWAPO's challenge in an open election. The South African strategy of keeping a first track up to strength with the second had no strong local representatives to rely on. Yet a number of government investigations in late 1983 brought to light the fact that the administration of Namibia was a costly and inefficient burden on South African finances.

On the other hand, within South Africa itself, Botha's government found itself in an increasingly strong position. The turning point in its fortunes came on 3 November, when the government's constitutional reforms won support from two-thirds of the white electorate despite opposition not only from the conservatives on the right but from the liberals on the left. The reforms not only gave some self-government powers to the coloured and Asian communities, requiring sharply expanded budgetary outlays for rising expectations and expanded bureaucracy, but it also gave authoritarian powers to a white president. Thus, Botha entered 1984 both stronger to press demands and freer to make concessions.

The most crucial of the developments in the latter half of 1983, however, were the rising success of the South African supported guerrilla movements within the front-line states and the growing impunity of South Africa's own military adventures across the border. The Mozambique National Resistance (MNR) increased its operations against the government of Samora Machel, aided by the catastrophic drought in the region. Even more impressive were the advances of UNITA. In January the guerrillas moved into the northern part of Angola and in mid-September struck within 150 kilometers of Luanda. The effect of the continuing struggle was both to impose on Angola a $2 billion annual cost of waging the war plus $10 billion damages and to reduce the productive capacity of the country by an incalculable amount.[123] The increased UNITA activity, in turn, increased Angola's vulnerability to Russian and Cuban advice and dependence on Russian and Cuban military. Cuban troops apparently increased to about 25,000 in 1982,[124] and Dos Santos signed arms supplies agreements with the Soviet Union in mid-May 1983 and early January 1984.[125] Thus, by the end of the year, both South Africa and Angola had evolved in directions of both strength and weakness since their aborted encounters a year ago: Although South Africa was in military control of both Namibia and southern Angola and the government was strong from its recent internal political victories, the military effort was becoming costly at a time when the economy was down and the new constitution required important new expenditures. Although Angola was beleaguered by both South Africa's and UNITA's forces, UNITA was stretching its lines and was unable to hold the points it captured while the Angolan forces were newly strengthened by large deliveries of Soviet arms.

On 6 December, the same day as South Africa began Operation Askari, its twelfth annual campaign in Angola, Crocker met Foreign Minister Botha in Rome and urged some unilateral gesture to deescalate the fighting and begin to build confidence.[126] Ten days later, as the 2000-person South African force pursued SWAPO units into Angolan positions south of the Namibe—Lubango—Menongue defense line, Botha sent a message to the UN secretary general, proposing a thirty-day truce beginning at the end of January, with possibilities of extension to a disengagement of forces; the offer was suspect because of its timing, coincident with both the military campaign and the opening of a new Security Council debate on Angolan charges of aggression, and it was rejected unless preceded by a unilateral South African withdrawal. In early January, Angola revised its position to accept the offer if South Africa would implement Resolution 435 for Namibian independence, and SWAPO called for direct cease-fire talks with South Africa—on the subject and not "a public relations charade."[127] South Africa rejected the answers, but at the same time announced a troop withdrawal from Angola, just before the rains. South Africa also sent an official to Cape Verde to meet Angolan representatives, and Wisner did the same to urge that the disengagement not be disrupted by attacks such as the SWAPO campaign at the beginning of the year.[128]

The 2,000 troops of Operation Askari were withdrawn across the border by 25 January 1984 although some 1,000 South African troops stationed in southern Angola since 1981 still remained. Crocker carried Angola's assurances to South Africa the next day, and on 31 January, Botha announced his intention to implement a cease-fire and begin disengagement from Angola. At the same time, he reiterated his position on Namibia—that it is not and never has been part of South Africa (and indeed that it is a costly burden to South Africa), that self-determination under conditions of peace and security is a guiding principle, that the Multi-Party Conference was ready to play its role, and that the presence of Cuban troops in Angola was the last remaining obstacle to a Namibian settlement. The role of the American conciliator in bringing about the formula for Angolan disengagement, in sensing the appropriate time for it, and in providing clear communications among the parties was crucial. But at the same time the Cuban issue's hold on a Namibian settlement was reaffirmed, alongside SWAPO's hold on the disengagement agreement.

In another ring, a similar process had begun and was being carried further. South Africa and Mozambique had held talks sporadically since the end of 1982, often just before or after military encounters; American officials had also had continuing contacts with Mozambique outside of normal diplomatic channels, the latest being meetings with Wisner in early November 1983 and late January 1984, followed by a visit by Crocker to Maputo. In between, in mid-January, South Africa and Mozambique began discussions in Johannesburg on topics of mutual interest, beginning with tourism and the Cabora Bassa dam in Angola and heading toward mutual restraint of guerrilla groups—MNR and ANC—receiving support from one state against the other.[129] At the next meeting, in Maputo on 20 February, the two countries announced their intention to sign a formal security agreement. Dialogue continued at Cape Town at the beginning of March, and the nonaggression pact was signed at Nkomati on 16 March.[130] American conciliation efforts had proved effective in restoring dialogue to southern African states and a precedent for the Angolan-Namibian situation, although at the expense of the national liberation movements from both sides. By early October, South Africa had held discussions with Mozambique, spelling out further areas of functional cooperations and had brokered a further cease-fire between Mozambique and the MNR, monitored by South Africa. The functional equivalent of constellation was being put in place.

At the other end of the battleline, events moved rapidly along with the Mozambican precedent. In mid-February, with U.S. officials presiding, Foreign Minister Botha and Interior Minister Rodrigues met in Lusaka to establish a joint commission to monitor the disengagement in southern Angola.[131] Both the military and the political days of the meeting proceeded rapidly as did the first meeting of the commission nine days later in the disengagement zone. There a four-stage plan was established for withdrawal and monitoring, ending with the evacuation of South African forces from Angola by the end of March.[132] The emergency meeting at Cuvelai—a former SWAPO and Angolan headquarters—was called by South Africa because of the detected movement of a large SWAPO force across the zone. For the first time in the history of relations in the area, an incident was not seized upon as an excuse for breakdown; instead, the commission took joint measures to handle the problem (which, in the event, appeared to have come from outside the disengagement zone). The joint patrols clashed with SWAPO guerrillas on occasion in March, but the agreement held down to the last disengagement stage at Ngiva, where it got stuck on continued SWAPO activity.[133] Angola threatened to cancel the agreement if not fully implemented, but at the same time found it attractive enough to look about for other ways to anchor it through further agreements on the Mozambican model.

"We don't have a deal on Namibia. We do have a first step that could produce a climate for a deal," said an American participant in the negotiations.[134] The disengagement agreement and the corresponding agreements of South Africa with Mozambique, Swaziland in 1982, and Lesotho in 1983 were attempts to form a larger constellationlike context, create momentum and confidence, and ripen the moment for an agreement on the central Namibian issue. Thereafter, efforts focused on testing and softening the remaining stumbling block—not the Cuban linkage, but the timing relation between the South African and Cuban withdrawals from Namibia and Angola. The United States attempted to clarify the point that disengagement was a step-by-step process and not "all Cuban troops should leave before anything else happens."[135] A meeting between Castro and Dos Santos in mid-March after the cease-fire agreement with South Africa stated that the conditions for Cuban withdrawal were unilateral South African withdrawal from Angola, acceptance of Resolution 435 calling for South African withdrawal and Namibian independence, and cessation of aggression against Angola by all parties and of their aid to UNITA.[136] Prime Minister Botha, on a striking tour of Western Europe in June, repeated his theme that Namibia was a burden and his other theme that South Africa would withdraw after the 25,000 Cuban troops left Angola.[137]

The breakthrough came in October, resulting from both the pressure and the confidence created by the incomplete disengagement mediated by the United States. On 18 October, Wisner returned from Angola with the offer whose absence had caused the breakdowns of 1982 and 1983—a proposal to send home most of the Cuban troops in phased withdrawals over a few years and to concentrate those remaining in the Luanda and Cabinda areas in exchange for implementation of UN resolution 435 and the cessation of South African support for UNITA.[138] The offer, which implemented the new formula for Namibia, while denying the linkage, was the 1982 Cuban-Angolan agreement put in Nkomati form—withdrawal of Angolan protection for SWAPO in exchange for withdrawal of South African support for UNITA. At the end of the month, Crocker met Foreign Minister Botha in Cape Verde to convey the proposals, and Dos Santos explained them to the OAU meeting in Addis Ababa at the same time. In mid-November, Crocker was in Pretoria to receive South Africa's response, which moved from the formula to discussion of details.[139] For example, the original offer appeared to envisage retaining about 8,000 Cubans; the South African response found "anything from 3,000 to 4,000 upward" unacceptable; and the formal proposal made by Angola in a letter of the UN secretary general offered to remove 20,000 Cubans in three phases over three years, preceded by an initial withdrawal of 5,000 by the end of March 1985—thus presumably leaving the number finally retained at about 5,000.

At the end of 1984 the ball was in the South African court again, and the mediation had returned to heavy bargaining on both formula and details. On the first level, the Cuban-South African withdrawal linkage had been recognized and its timing relationship discussed, but now the element of UNITA was squarely brought in as a new part of the formula. Angola's definition of that element called for withdrawal of South African support (the Nkomati formula of February 1984) whereas South Africa's definition called for cease-fire, recognition, and eventually negotiations over UNITA's inclusion in the Angolan government (an extension of the Nkomti formula of October 1984). Ambiguity remained over South Africa's acceptance of the UN role in the cease-fire and the subsequent Namibian elections. The UN was basic to Angola's proposal, but, without the UN, South Africa could finally see its two tracks joined together. On the level of details, items such as troop totals, phase dates, troop and monitoring locations, and all the new specifics of the UNITA element in the agreement all provided material for further lengthy discussions. For South Africa, not *any* Namibian settlement was acceptable, even in the economic constraints of the mid-1980s, and so details were worth haggling over. Yet undeniably the Namibian problem and its larger Angolan-South African context had taken a major step toward settlement through the patience and persistence of the American mediators.

With the 3-year Angolan *Plataforma* and the 3-month South Africa response, both of November 1984, in hand, the Africa Bureau sought to entice further moves from the two parties to bridge the gap in formula and detail. When nothing was forthcoming, the United States took the next major step in the evolution of its mediatory role by preparing a middle-of-the-road proposal of its own. In mid-March 1985, Crocker was back in the region with an American compromise.[140] Angola would move the Cuban troops north of 13° (roughly; the Benguela railroad through Huamba across the middle of the country) and remove 25,000 of them within a year; Namibian independence and UNSC Resolution 435 would be set into motion, and the remaining 6–10,000 troops would be reduced to a support group around Luanda and Cabinda within two years. The reception on both sides was encouraging. Furthermore, there was an expectation that changes were about to take place within the Angolan government that would signal a pro-Western reorientation, providing that timely internal shift in one side that so often accompanies the final moves of a negotiation. Indeed, in 1984, Jorge had lost his position of foreign minister to Alfonso van Dumem Mbinda, a rising member of the new political bureau of the MPLA after the December 1985 party congress.

Unfortunately, other items rose to crowd out further progress, most of them originating from South Africa but one from the mediator itself. In mid-April, less than a month after Crocker's last visit and contrary to diplomatic warnings, Botha announced plans to establish a new internal government in Namibia. The move was another step in keeping the first track up with the second, as the mediation moved events forward along the multilateral track, and Botha argued that it was only an interim measure until an internationally-agreed government could be achieved. While the best bargaining chip is a real one, thus far South Africa had given more energy and reality to its attempts at an internal settlement than to its use in negotiations. Second, a month later, in mid-May, Angolan troops captured a South Africa commando in Cabinda preparing to blow up Gulf oil storage tanks, with likely casualties among American employees. Angola reacted by declaring the negotiations at an impasse until an "explanation" was forthcoming from South African government about the raid. Third, in July and August the two houses of Congress again debated and finally repealed the Clark Amendment which had prohibited overt and covert aid to Angola's nationalist factions, notably UNITA, and after much open and bureaucratic debate, the Reagan administration announced a program of $15 million military aid to UNITA in mid-February 1986. Already in mid-July 1985, following the first part of congressional action on the Clark Amendment, Angola declared that it was breaking off all diplomatic contact with the United States.

Negotiations were thus ended with both the adversary and the mediator. Crocker returned to Luanda at the end of November 1985 and the beginning of January 1986, but the contacts were more part of an effort to deter the United States from aiding UNITA than of negotiations with South Africa. Nonetheless, Crocker got an agreement from Angola to the current offer if South Africa would agree, which it did at the beginning of August. The ball was back in Angola's court but Angola was taking time out. While the White

House and Congress were uniting to put pressure on Angola, which had hitherto not been the recalcitrant party, South Africa's moves showed it not only eager to keep its two tracks in tandem but also to blow up the negotiatory one, in the Cabinda raid. For a third time, promising efforts and an apparently ripe moment could not bring the process to a conclusion. In addition to a disengagement agreement on Angola that deescalated the conflict without contributing to its resolution, the period saw two mediated attempts, in 1982 and 1984–85, that came close to tying the package together but faded away or broke off when agreement seemed within reach. Alongside, an attempt by a new mediator to circumvent the formula of Resolution 435 by bringing together all the Namibian political parties in Lusaka supposedly came "within a couple hours" of agreement in mid-May 1984, according to Zambian president Kaunda, the mediator.[141] In the process and despite the failure, Angola had been brought back into the negotiations with active offers, and South Africa, while breaking up the negotiations, was also searching about for ways of reducing costs and disengaging. Yet delays were both parties' priorities; only the United States was in a hurry but was unable to accelerate the process, unwilling to give substance to deadlines, and unready to nail down agreement already reached.

The year 1986 was lost. The *eighth phase* began with 1987 and continued through 1988. On the surface, the parties had left the last phase remarkably close together, yet more interested in lowering the cost and level of conflict than in resolving it. Something was needed to make the deadlock a truly hurting stalemate, with no possibility for either a decisive escalation or an economical deescalation that would leave the conflict and stalemate intact at a less burdensome level. Two events cause a dramatic turn of events at the end of 1987 and into 1988, although their decisiveness was laced with ambiguity. One was simple but the most ambiguous: the certain ending of the Reagan administration and the uncertainty of succession gave the parties a deadline and incentive, although it was not clear whether the succession pointed to approach or avoidance. In any case, when signals came from southwestern Africa, Crocker was eager to hear and test them.

The second element was more delicate in its operation and rarer in its occurrence. It was an "escalation to call," as opposed to an "escalation to raise," a deliberate move to raise the stakes and pose a further threat, strong enough to force the other party to come to terms but not large enough to actually win. As such, the escalation was enough to make the stalemate truly hurt, and indeed hurt mutually, and it also conveyed the sense of an impending catastrophe if the other side did not respond. The move was the dramatic increase in the number of Cuban troops in Angola and their sudden move to the Namibian border, poised for hot pursuit, just at the time when it was also known that Cuba was ready to withdraw its troops—and the Soviet Union was pressing it to do so—under the right terms. On the other hand, if South Africa did not respond favorably and come to terms, the danger of a larger, most costly, and even less popular conflict was tremendous. The consequences, real and implied, of the move were enough to shake the South African government's winning mentality, split its ranks, and lead a faction of it to turn the first event—the mediator's elections—into an opportunity to shape a deal.

The Lusaka Agreement never had produced a total South African withdrawal from Angola. By mid-1985 it was clear that the mutual move had broken down, and the South African Defense Force operated freely over a 35-mile-deep strip along the border and even more deeply to 16°, south of the Lubango defense line. With the beginning of the dry season in July 1987, however, military activities increased. In late July and again in early November, South African troops engaged SWAPO units in Angola and Angolan army units with them and claimed to have caused over 150 casualties each time. The Angolan army launched a major dry-season offensive from its base at Cuito Cuanavale against UNITA, and in November, South Africa admitted that some of its 6,000 troops in Angola had been fighting alongside UNITA units to repulse the attack. The Angolan surge was halted; the UNITA counterattack began at the end of the year and the battle of Cuito Cuanavale continued to March. With the launching of the UNITA and South African offensive, however, came a decision by the opposing parties to outescalate South Africa and bring to bear the necessary force to bring it to negotiations. The battle for Cuito Cuanavale was an expensive draw. There are no reliable figures, but a combination of claims can lead to an estimate of over a hundred deaths on the South African side and some 4,000 Angolans, resulting from heavy air, artillery and tank combat.[142] While both sides claimed victories of sorts as a result of their own non-defeat, it was clear that Angolans and Cubans were dug in to stay and that massive South African efforts could produce only casualties, not a change in fortunes.

More broadly, the strategy in Angola and Namibia had come increasingly to appear in South Africa as a particularly flawed case of the current regional policy, led by the military faction in South African government. Support for UNITA alone cost South Africa

$200 million per year, a cut of the same amount in the Namibian budget in 1987 reduced it in half, and military engagement in Angola brought home a higher toll of dead and wounded to South African families (even if much lower than on the other side) than ever before. The Lusaka agreement had not lowered the cost of the conflict, and the destabilization strategy which stood before it had provided cost without much benefit. In March 1988, at the end of the Cuito Cuanavale draw, the Foreign Ministry faction in South African government was able to push aside (rather than convince) the military faction and decide to look for a negotiated solution. This financial and strategic calculation, and the internal shift it occasioned, were to be the basic elements in reaching an agreement in the final round of negotiations.

To clinch that perception with urgency, however, an impending catastrophe was needed to prevent the parties from simply negotiating a less costly stalemate. In the first half of 1987, the number of Cuban troops in Angola stood at the all-time high of 35,000, up by perhaps as much as 5,000 from the figures discussed at the end of 1984. By the beginning of the 1987 dry season offensive, the number was estimated at 37,000 by U.S. officials, but reinforced by a massive Soviet arms buildup worth $1 billion in May. During the evolving standoff at Cuito Cuanavale, Angolan President Dos Santos and Castro met with Soviet officials in Moscow and agreed on the need for a larger number of more experienced troops, and within a month new Cuban troops and new senior officers began arriving in Luanda, and immediately moved to southern Angola with orders to challenge South African troops wherever they found them. Suddenly, in January 1988, Cuba announced a new total of 40,000 troops, twice the levels of the 1970s. Then in April another 6–7,000 Cuban troops arrived, most of whom were moved south for the first time, across the tacit separation line of 16° and down to within 30 kilometers of the Namibian border. Stretched along a new defense line from south of Namibe parallel to the Cunene river, then 100 kilometers north of and parallel to the border, and then northeast through Cuito Cuanavale, the new reinforcements encouraged rumors of hot pursuit. To reinforce the threat, the Cuban troops launched a surprise attack against the South Africans in southern Angola at the end of June, killing a dozen or more South Africans as well as an uncertain number of Angolans and Cubans; South Africa cried foul, forgetting that it too had made attacks during negotiations, starting with its deep raid on Cassinga a decade before. But the military influx continued, to total over 50,000 by September, edging above the

50,000 figure for South African troops across the border in Namibia. Concentrated along the new defense line, around Cuito Cuanavale, and along the Benguela railroad, the troops were prepared for a new escalation.[143] Were the war to be extended, a whole new situation would arise, bringing direct combat and casualties close to South Africa.

On the other side, there was also growing interest in coming to terms.[144] Among the Soviets, the Gorbachev era brought a desire to shorten lines and cut losses in such farflung outposts as Angola, coupled with a perception that the collapsed society run by the MPLA was really not a showcase of Marxism-Leninsim that was worth indentifying with. The Cubans displayed the same strong dissatisfaction toward their MPLA hosts, yet the South African offensive and the U.S. aid to UNITA required an equivalent response. Linkage had been admitted and denied by Cuba on a number of occasions but the 1984 joint Cuban-Angolan statement still stood, and Cuba was ready for an "escalation to call" as a final move to secure Namibian independence and go home. Even SWAPO had become tactically more accommodating; notably, it had come to accept the South African position on Walvis Bay, whose status would be determined after independence and not before, so as not to give South Africa an excuse for upsetting progress on negotiations. But SWAPO was no longer the major negotiator; the ball was in the Angolan court.

During the fall 1986 session of the UN, before these military pressures had begun to make their weight felt, Angolan Foreign Minister van Dunem told U.S. Undersecretary of State Michael Armacost that Angola wanted to reopen the diplomatic impasse. The intimation led to an initial meeting between Crocker and Kito in Brazzaville in early April, where the two sides agreed to resume talks and Angola promised to make a new offer. Promising signs were building up: van Dunem met Crocker in Washington in June and promised progress, while later in the month a captured American civilian pilot was released in Luanda to a visiting Congressional delegation. The meeting took place in mid-July in Luanda but it led only to the sharpest judgment the Americans ever issued on a round of Namibian negotiations: calling the two-day visit "a waste of time," Crocker maintained that the Angolans were still divided and were looking for a military victory over UNITA, and that the Cubans did not want to leave and so were linking withdrawal to the end of apartheid (as Castro had indeed announced to the Non-Aligned Movement in Harare in September).[145] At the same time, the U.S.

Senate, on its own track, denied most-favored-nation trade status to Angola.

With the feint failed and the dry-season offensive flagging, Dos Santos and Castro issued a reaffirmation of their flexible intentions, from Havana in early August, followed by a new offer.[146] The newness was only in the details of their proposal; coupled with the standard elements, the offer lowered the Cuban partial withdrawal time from southern Angola to two years and proposed four-party negotiations to include Cuba as well as Angola, South Africa and SWAPO to work out an acceptable time for total withdrawal. The pace sagged again, and Dos Santos and Castro reverted to their military option in their Moscow meeting in early November, further tightening the pressure on South Africa. In mid-January 1988, from Lisbon, Dos Santos again announced that he was ready to negotiate, and then proposed a meeting with the United States at which the Cubans would be present.

The tripartite meeting at the end of January produced the beginnings of a breakthrough in details but above all indications of a spirit of movement through the exchange of concrete offers. Cuba and Angola for the first time explicitly offered a complete withdrawal of Cuban troops, although as yet without a timetable and therefore as yet nothing to convey to South Africa. The United States continued to work for a withdrawal schedule short enough that South Africa would have no excuse for delays on its side—one year from the south and three years from all Angola.[147]

Before moving on to a more precise timetable, the Angolans wanted to make sure that South Africa was still in the negotiations; yet that could not be tested without a precise timetable. A U.S. mediating group went to Luanda for further information in mid-March and came back with a proposal to begin the withdrawal in 17 months and complete it in 30 months, after which Crocker met with South African Foreign Minister R. F. Botha in Geneva. While the minister publicly dismissed the proposals as "vague," South Africa at the very moment was in the midst of its own policy reevaluation.[148] Earlier in the month, it had made gestures directly to the Soviet Union on the possibility of a bilateral deal similar to the Soviet Afghan withdrawal, while at the same time other South African sources aired the notion of a renewed Lusaka arrangement, pitting Cuban withdrawals against South African withdrawals from Angola, presumably leaving the MPLA and UNITA face to face and Namibia out in the cold. None of these probes was productive. Instead, the collapse of the efforts against Cuito Cuanavale, combined with the persistence of the mediator and the signs of interest from Soviets and Angolans alike, brought the parties together to test the moment for ripeness.

Full exploratory talks among Angolan, South African, Cuban and American representatives started at the beginning of May, in London.[149] With the Angolan proposal on the table for a four-year staged withdrawal of all Cuban troops from Angola and a one-year withdrawal of all South African troops from Namibia, which would then become independent, the South Africans presented a detailed commentary but as yet no conterproposal. South Africans and Angolans met alone in Brazzaville the following week to consider bilateral issues for the South Africans to take home and study. The London meeting had been preceded by a meeting between Crocker and Soviet Deputy Foreign Minister for Africa Anatoly Adamishin, and the two met again in Lisbon a week after the Brazzaville talks, as Crocker briefed the Russian and discussed ways to keep the Angolans and Cubans flexible and participating. Adamishin has claimed that Crocker guaranteed South African implementation of Resolution 435 if the Cubans withdrew in 3 years. They met again several times during the U.S.-U.S.S.R. summit in Moscow at the end of May and gave themselves four months to produce an Angolan-Namibian settlement, with the deadline set for the tenth anniversary of Resolution 435, at the end of September. With the great power backers of the two sides coordinated, the mediator again turned back to the principals in the conflict.

The debate on details in London tested the seriousness of the parties but it also hid a wider difference on the formula itself. Was withdrawal to be simultaneous or preconditional, and what withdrawals were involved? The questions were not only basic but they also raised again the issue of preconditions which Crocker had tried to rule out from the beginning of his attention to the problem. The Angolan formula called for prior cessation of U.S. and South African support for UNITA before the matched troop withdrawals, whereas South Africa called for prior Cuban withdrawal before Namibian independence and also a national reconciliation between MPLA and UNITA.[150] The parties agreed to study the proposals and reconvene, but the next meeting was delayed by a procedural dispute over the next venue. In the meantime, at the end of June, an Angolan delegation came to Washington to counter the visit of UNITA's Savimbi and in the process of official discussions dropped the requirement for an end of U.S. support to UNITA, a point the administration had ruled out with firmness. The second four-party meeting was finally held in Cairo at the end of June.[151] While it clearly moved from diagnosis to a serious attempt to create a joint document out of the two proposals, the meeting almost broke down when the Cubans and Angolans launched into an ideological tirade against apartheid. It took the intervention of the Soviet Deputy Minister for Southern Africa to bring the negotiations back to seriousness. Angola maintained its demand for an end to South African support for UNITA, while South Africa continued to insist on national reconciliation and a true count of Cubans as a basis for withdrawals.

The third in the series on talks, on Governor's Island in New York in mid-July completed the process.[152] The parties continued to work on the joint text, each side offering points of agreement, until they had drawn up a list of 14 points. The timetable was set aside in favor of a list of "indispensable principles" for a "complete settlement." They included general principles such as cooperation (aid) for development, right to peace, right to self-determination, non-aggression, non-interference, non-use of force, and respect for territorial integrity and inviolability of frontiers, as well as recognition of roles— United States as mediator and permanent members of the Security Council as guarantors. The operational clauses were straightforward: The parties would recommend an agreed date for implementing Resolution 435, Namibia would become independent through free and fair elections, northern redeployment and staged, total withdrawal of Cuban troops, good faith negotiations, and monitoring and verification. The principles were ratified by the signatory governments a week later, accepted by SWAPO and the ANC (but not by UNITA), and publicly endorsed by Castro. Whether the principles were new or not is open to question, but it is certain that the public statement subscribed to by all parties was necessary to the process.

Negotiations then shifted to the details of the timetable.[153] Cuba had made a public statement of its plan, involving a Cuban and South African withdrawal from southern Angola 15 days after UN peacekeeping troops arrive at the Namibian border to implement Resolution 435, with 20,000 Cubans repatriated within two years thereafter and the remaining 27,000 within four years. When South Africa made its own plan public at the beginning of August—calling for withdrawals from Angola by 1 September by South Africa and by 1 June 1989 by Cuba, only then followed by implementation of Resolution 435—the Cubans and Angolans raised a hue and cry over the leak, even more than over the reversed order which put the formula into question. Nonetheless, the talks settled down in Geneva and by the end of the week, there was agreement on the initial steps of the timetable. A cease-fire and a South African withdrawal from Angola would begin immediately, on 8 August, and SWAPO and Cuban troops would remain north of a line that approximated the current defense line; and implementation of 435 in Namibia would begin on 1 November. The South African withdrawal was accomplished two days early, and the cease-fire was immediately observed, not only by the signatories but by UNITA as well, despite later statements that it would not abide by the results of negotiations to which it had not been a party. Tripartite monitoring teams were quickly established to verify the withdrawals.

The South African evacuation of Angola and the Cuban and SWAPO pullback from the border—the reaffirmation and implementation of the Lusaka agreement of 1984—would have been a comfortable, stable resting place for both sides. Nowhere did the implementation of the agreements go beyond measures already tried in earlier rounds of negotiations. What would have been necessary, on the pattern of the earlier rounds, would have been for South Africa to throw off the connection to Namibia. The meeting of late August was "suspended for consultations" on the highly disputed matter of the timetable for the Cuban withdrawal, and the next meeting at the end of September in Brazzaville also ended in failure. At the same time, South Africa revived its old tactic of raising new issues, with a knack for finding undeniably serious ones that had not yet been resolved. It demanded assurances that the estimated $600 million costs of implementing 435 could be covered from UN sources, and also called for the dismantling of 7 ANC training camps in Angola. Behind these questions and the Cuban timetable also lay the larger question of UNITA and national reconciliation.

October–November 1988 was a long moment of truth for both sides. Under the encouragement of the Soviet Union, Angola and Cuba had already decided in favor of an agreement but within certain limits. Castro was ready to withdraw his troops if that would bring independence to Namibia. Dos Santos' government was also ready for Cuban troop withdrawal, but only on the condition that the withdrawal not leave it naked before the troops of UNITA supported by South Africa. This meant that Cuban troops would have to be phased out over several years and would have to be preceded by the total evacuation of South African troops from an independent Namibia. Botha's government had also come to an acceptance of Namibian independence linked to Cuban withdrawal from Angola, but set up in such a way as to create the conditions for a friendly and manipulable Namibia and Angola. The formula of two linked and roughly simultaneous withdrawals was thus well rooted and the negotiations passed to its details, whose precise form would govern the decision of the two sides on the ultimate acceptability of the formula, and hence of the overall agreement.

The process of closure translated an effort to convert these partly contradictory interests into an agreement on details that was faithful to the principles of the comprehensive formula. South Africa had begun with a Cuban troop withdrawal deadline of 6 months, and Angola with a deadline of 48 months. The mediator had presented an imbalanced compromise of 18 months at Brazzaville at the end of August, but the discussions of September settled instead on a span closer to the middle of the two extremes of 24–30 months, but without being able to reduce it to a single figure. To get out of the impasse, the parties began to play with the elements of the withdrawal decision, notably with stages within the total period and with the geographic divisions of withdrawal within a single country. The mediator proposed a complicated mixture of these elements in New York, at the beginning of October: Of the 52,000 Cuban troops, 4,000 would be repatriated before the end of the year; the 7 month period needed for the implementation of 435 would begin on 1 January 1989 and the rest of the Cubans would be withdrawn north of the 15th parallel (the parallel of Namibe and Cuito Cuanavale) during the first 3 months of 1989 and north of the 13th parallel (the parallel of Benguela and Huambo) in the next 3 months; the Namibian elections would take place on 1 August; 36,000 Cubans would be repatriated within the following year and the last 12,000 by 1 August 1991— thus, a period of 33 months after 1 November 1988 or 31 months after 1 January 1989 or 27 months after April, depending on the starting date. The figure of 27 months for the withdrawal period was retained, since it was the split of the difference between 24 and 30 months and between 6 and 48 months.

The parties discussed the proposal at New York and then at Geneva in the middle of November, after the electoral storms had passed. 1 February was proposed as a starting date, 1 August as the deadline for the withdrawal of half the Cubans and the date of the Namibian elections, and 1 August 1990 as the deadline for two-thirds of the Cubans; all the Cubans would be north of 13° a month before the Namibian elections. Angola and Cuba accepted the proposals at the next meeting, in early December but South Africa's agreement was not forthcoming. Instead, a high level delegation from Pretoria, presided by the Foreign Minister, paid a visit to Savimbi in Kinshasa, declared in Brazzaville that the matter of the verification of the

Cuban troop withdrawals had not been resolved to its satisfaction, and left—a performance that the Angolans termed "sensationalist." In fact, the departure was calculated to reassure the hardliners in the South African government that the agreement was not being accepted lightly. But it served also to delay the starting date for the process, which had already been pushed back to 15 February and then to 15 March. Nonetheless, the South Africans were back at the next meeting in Brazzaville, in mid-December, where an agreement in principle was initialed, before being signed in New York on 22 December. The final calendar provided that after an initial departure of 3,000 Cuban troops, the 7-month timetable for the Namibian elections and the 27-month timetable for the total Cuban withdrawals would begin on 1 April; the Cubans would withdraw north of 15° by August and north of 13° by 1 November 1989, presumed date of the Namibian elections and deadline for the withdrawal of half (25,000) of the Cuban troops. A year after the beginning of the process, on 1 April 1990, two-thirds (33,000) of the Cubans would be gone; by 1 October all but 12,000 (76%) would be home; and the evacuation would be completed by the end of June 1991. Verification would be the domain of the Angola-Cuban commission, with provision for an appeal commission, as discussed in the negotiations at Geneva, specified in the December agreements, and later formalized by the UN Security Council. With all the possibilities of potholes on the road toward mutual withdrawal of foreign troops from the two countries (the agreement accorded Cuba and Angola "the right to modify or alter their obligations" if South Africa reneged on Namibia), a solution was nonetheless in place, after 12 years of negotiations.

What explains this outcome, after so much effort at apparently unripe and then recently riper moments? Crocker himself has spoken of "the right alignment of local, regional, and international events—like planets lining up for some rare astronomical happening"—and Herbert Cohen, African specialist on the National Security Council, has cited "a single word—economics. . . . Fortunately Crocker has remained persistent throughout the eight years so that he was there at a time when all the interests converged."[154] To be sure the basic element for the two parties was the economic situation in which the continuation of the unilateral, military track became too costly to be bearable. But the rising costs took their specific forms. Nearly 10% of the $4 billion in arms sent by the Soviet Union to Angola during the second half of the 1980s was lost to UNITA in the spring 1988 offensive; Angola's $4.5 billion debt to the Soviet Union had become unpayable. Similarly, after 1986 Angola could no longer pay the $1,000 per day per soldier that it owed to Cuba. At the same time, the Soviet, Cuban and Angolan side saw that the present would be long, for the 1984–85 uprising in South Africa would not be able to shake the white government in the short run. But for the South African government, costs of the status quo rose too. The loss of South Africa's air superiority and of its Mirage fighters over Angola raised the price of the war. At the same time, with the withdrawal of American banks in 1985 (the moment from which the South Africans date the onset of sanctions) and the imposition of economic sanctions by Congress the following year, indicating a loss of international economic confidence in the country, monetary reserves became increasingly scarce in South Africa after mid-1987, just as in Angola, to reach a level of only about 1½ month's imports by September 1988. For both sides, war had become too expensive, in 1987 for Angola and the following year for South Africa. The respective diplomatic shifts corresponded to these dates.

The economic situation was crystalized by the military situation, the second "planet" to fall in alignment. The Cubans' escalation to call was the big stick or forcing act of the negotiations.[155] Without being able to dislodge UNITA, it blocked the South Africans' attempt to dislodge the Cubans and Angolans, leaving the two sides in a costly, conclusive stalemate. Unable to move ahead, yet unable to remain in place either, the only path open to both sides was to pull back. But without the pullback of one side, the pullback of the other was impossible, and vice versa, and both would be condemned to maintain the costly, frustrating status quo or to try a desperate attempt to escalate their way out, an attempt the previous year had shown to be doomed in advance.

These perceptions could probably not have been arrived at without some external pressure or assistance. Cohen was right to insist on the importance of the mediator's persistence and of his presence when the other elements of the ripe moment were in alignment. The mediation was particularly adroit in that it was carried out without benefit of either negative or positive means of pressure—with neither carrots nor sticks. The sticks of sanctions, so long an anathema for the American government, were suddenly made inapplicable to the Namibian negotiations in 1986 by being wielded directly against the system of apartheid. After 1978 sanctions were shown to be unavailable on the Namibian issue, and after 1986 even the threat of sanctions was removed; thereafter it took a certain time for the effect of the sanctions to be felt. At that point, they were no longer a stick to wave but an element in the hurting economic stalemate (imposed, moreover, on the mediator by the U.S. Congress). There were no longer any carrots except the attraction of a successful offer extracted from the other side, and there were no sticks left except for the mediator's threat to withdraw from the process (which Crocker finally brandished in July 1987).

In an effort without carrots and sticks, one may well ask whether American aid to UNITA was an element useful in the mediation. The aid, particularly through the Stinger missiles, made some contribution, of indeterminable magnitude, to stopping the Angolan dry season offensive of 1987. But beyond the fact that it was voted by Congress for internal reasons, to help pass the South African sanctions by pairing them with support for "Our Freedom Fighters," this assistance did anything but facilitate the mediation. It could not be controlled or manipulated tactically, and it reinforced the most difficult matter to manage in the conflict, the Angolan national reconciliation.

Despite its necessary contribution, the American mediation was not the only external element in constituting the ripe moment. The decision of the Soviet government under Gorbachev to cut its losses in Angola provided the basis for an increasingly active role, particularly after the Cairo round of negotiations in June 1988. Although the initiative was always American, the Soviet Union supported the mediation wholeheartedly with increasing effectiveness. By the same token, the African role was more and more useful, in two senses. Against the wishes of Angola, which wanted the negotiations to take place in Europe in order to prevent South Africa's using them to gain entry into Black Africa, Egypt and then especially the Congo agreed to serve as the meeting place, thus avoiding a potential obstacle to the progress of negotiations. On the other hand, several countries—notably the Congo, Nigeria, Zaire, Gabon, Ivory Coast and Morocco—urged the two Angolan parties to a reconcilation and served as mediators in starting the discussions that were to last long after the New York agreement. Finally, as in the Western Sahara, despite the absence of the UN as a mediator, the prior existence of an apparatus for the implementaion of the Namibian transition and of a Security Council to take formal decisions, circumventing the more partisan role of the General Assembly, provided capital elements in closing the negotations. Indeed, the successful management of the conflict was the product of a ripe moment when the economic, military, political and external "planets" were properly lined up. Then, when the momentum started, with signatures provided at a number of checkpoints along the way, it was increasingly difficult for any party to derail the process.

It is the theme of this analysis that South Africa had been negotiating—keeping the second track to a solution alive—in good faith just as it had been keeping the first track current and up-to-date at the same time, but had never felt the need to make a decision as yet between the two tracks.[156] The mediators had been most effective in moving the negotiations ahead, but they had been ineffective—indeed, sometimes inattentive—to the need to force a decision. For an enduring moment, South Africa had found it preferable to keep the conflict contained but its options open rather than choosing a particular outcome.

Yet despite the fact that their unilateral solutions were not solutions at all, the parties long found stalemate preferable to a track-two bilateral solution. Under the pressure of the front-line states, SWAPO's interest in continued stalemate appeared to wane in 1980, for a continuation of conflict was costly and likely to lead to other outcomes—Soviet involvement, devastation of the country—before it led to independence. SWAPO, therefore, agreed to the proposed track-two solution but had no interest in making further concessions toward South Africa. Then, in the Reagan rounds, the mediators put the decision to agree in the hands of one of the front-line states, Angola, by raising the issue of the Cuban connection that they thought would override South Africa's preference for stalemate. But Angola, too, long preferred stalemate, particularly when the cost of South Africa raids was removed, and until late 1984 was unable to make a good offer that would remove both South Africa and the Cubans; instead, it could only negotiate a disengagement and cease-fire along the border that would make the stalemate livable and remove the pressures for something more.[157] Soviet pressure, Cuban disillusionment, inpayable costs, and a mediator produced perception that an offer of withdrawal might well bring Namibian independence and cut the link between UNITA and South Africa finally brought Angola to see that there was indeed an alternative preferable to stalemate.

South Africa's interest in stalemate is more complex, and it shows that policy choices can often be rationally based on a stronger interest in non-choice than on choosing between given alternatives. First, instead of comparing the first- and second-track solutions as offered and making a clear choice in favor of one of them, South Africa compared choice now with choice later. Once the Western Five had let the December 1978 deadline pass without enforcement,

South Africa realized that choice later was quite possible. Coinciden-
tally, the years after 1978 carried a number of events that made the
future look brighter than the present, making choice later not only
possible but preferable. These events were the growing support for an
internal solution in Rhodesia/Zimbabwe in 1979, the British elections in 1979 and the subsequent Lancaster House negotiations, the
German and then American elections in 1980, and then the chance of
favorable American elections in 1984 after the favorable mid-term
elections of 1982. Except for the American events, none of these
turned out the way South Africa wanted, but each gave it hope. Only
the 1988 elections provided an outcome where the successor would be
different and less favorable, suddenly making it urgent to get the best
deal now.

Second, South Africa's strategy does not appear to have crystallized until 1978, but when it did, it emphasized delay with a purpose,
not just as an avoidance of choice until a better moment.[158] Delay
was meant to buy time for the internal parties to weaken the external
party and to make track one acceptable. South African strategy was
not to prevail with its track-one solution, but to join the two tracks—
to enable the track-one parties to win on track two. Coupled with the
previous point that delayed choice was possible and preferable and
with the belief (that no one else shared) that time worked for them,
the South Africans have tried to hold out as long as they could,
avoiding final acceptance of track two and keeping track-one parties
alive and well. Again, only after 1985, when the last attempt at an
internal solution through the Transitional Government was put into
effect, did it become evident that no credible political force could be
created that would beat SWAPO at the polls, and that conditions
after 1987 were the best they were ever likely to be for a decent
electoral performance against a weakened SWAPO. At the same
time, it appeared that South Africa shifted its track-one option from
a political party to a paramilitary force as it emphasized the South
West African Territorial Force as its proxy after Namibian independence.

Third, within South Africa itself, Namibia was a disruptive issue at
a troubled moment. Regarded by many as South Africa's fifth province, its white politics dominated by a splintered remnant of the
National party, considered by others as a testing ground for various
parties—the West, the Soviet Union, the South African government—for campaigns and designs for change in South Africa itself,
Namibia arose as an issue just as the South African National party
was split into *verkrampte* and *verligte* factions, the former bitterly

challenging Prime Minister P. W. Botha's leadership and direction for the country.[159] One could analyze each turn in the Namibian negotiations in terms of the current phase of the party conflict after Botha succeeded Vorster as party leader and prime minister in the fall of 1978, but the general conclusion at each moment would be that stalemate, nonchoice, and reinforcement of the first track were the preferable decisions in terms of the intraparty and then interparty conflicts, all the way down to 1988 when the two Bothas made common cause against the military faction within the government and the conservative hardliners outside.

Lessons from the past process—some of them applicable to the future—have to be found primarily in the means of pressure on the parties and the relationship between the tracks.

1. The Carter mediation erred in its total hostility to South Africa but also in not providing certain substantive guarantees of outcome. South Africa was concerned about its own military security against guerrilla attacks, about minority guarantees, and about the economic security of its investments in Namibia; such items could have been covered by a declaration included in the formula. They could also have been balanced by an assurance of noninterference given by South Africa in general or to Namibia in specifics. As it was, the mediated proposal was all procedure and did not cover the real concerns of all the parties. The notion of certain guarantees—or even, for that matter, the notion of a constitution, if it had been raised earlier—was not outlandish. Nearly every African state has been born with a constitution or at least with certain guarantees and reciprocal agreements.[160] The claim that that was a characteristic of decolonization in the 1960s but not the 1980s can be countered by the fact that the removal of contiguous colonization leaves real interests to be dealt with. Because the liberators' stick is not strong enough, South Africa must be bought off with carrots, and a righteous unwillingness to provide them leaves the would-be liberators without their desired outcome. The Reagan rounds' attention to this problem closed a serious gap in the proceedings, but it did not close the bargain. Its mistake (the executive and Congress taken together) was that it played out both its carrots (improved relations with South Africa) and sticks (sanctions against apartheid) before an agreement, disarming its own mediation.

2. The Western Five made as much headway as they did in large part because they worked so closely among themselves and with African front-line states. As a result, Africans were brought into the mediation process itself, not simply courted as one of the parties, and

the allies of SWAPO were engaged in looking for a solution rather than simply pursuing a conflict. In their role, the front-line states— but particularly Angola, Mozambique, Tanzania, and Zambia—effectively exercised their dual function, speaking toughly in public and pressing imaginatively and creatively for solutions in private. SWAPO concessions and final agreement in the early Carter years were essentially the result of the front-line states' pressure. Thereafter, they played an increasingly creative role, beginning with President Neto's suggestion on a fifty-kilometer DMZ in 1979; that role continued in the years 1982–84, when Angola brought out a shadow of a plan for parallel withdrawals and then finally began to give it a detailed form, and then when the disengagement process was worked out. By this time, at least one front-line state had become an actual party to the negotiations rather than a mediator.

3. Namibia has seen conflict without escalation, and the mediations have lacked the basic ingredients of pressure for movement and deadline for success. One deadline, provided by the Zimbabwe evolution of 1979–80, worked for nondecisions in Namibia until the dust settled. The other pressures and deadlines were all South Africa's and everyone else's threat to apply pressure was a called bluff. The greatest missed opportunity was on 23 October 1978, when South Africa learned that a promise to keep the door open would call off any sanctions and when the West learned that it feared pressure more than the pressured. The other missed opportunities came in the summer of 1982 and again in the spring of 1984, when the mediators let the public announcement of a cease-fire slip through their hands. All details (except the specific electoral system) were decided, the Cuban connection was recognized by both sides without as yet hardening into a mutually negating precondition. What was missing was a self-committing announcement of a deadline, confirming the cease-fire and backed up more quiet indications of worsening conditions— such as unfavorable consideration of the impending IMF loan to South Africa and private banks' loan to Angola,[161] for example—if the deadline were not met. Because the Reagan administration was not willing to consider such pressures, it let the cease-fire and the parallelism of positions on the Cuban connection escape with impunity.

In Namibia, there has not been enough conflict for successful conflict resolution. Until the escalation of 1988, the Western Five had no first-track strategy, only a second track. They, therefore, had no alternative to consider and so no alternative with which to threaten the stalling parties. There *was* an alternative, of course: It involved such elements as massive South African sanctions, Soviet-Cuban engagement in the Namibian fighting, and polarization of the conflict: it was, therefore, a threat against the West, not against the parties it was seeking to influence. This is the worst position in which a conciliator can find itself—one in which it needs the conciliation more than the parties do. In 1986, the American Congress filled the leadership vacuum on African policy by voting sanctions against South Africa, not to aid the Namibia negotiations but to advance the war against apartheid itself, thereby depriving the mediators both of their carrot and of their threat of a stick.

The West feared sanctions more than it should have because it was unable to invent graduated, repeatable, Namibian-specific measures, which nonetheless exist.[162] It should be clear that the sanctions this chapter has been discussing are not the total economic boycott frequently proposed, nor are they directed toward changing the whole nature of the South African political system or bringing down the South African regime. Passport restrictions, denial of tax credits, air travel restrictions, among others, could be used to show intent and make nonchoice more costly. A clear distinction between Western hopes for Namibia—immediate independence for an international territory—and for South Africa—gradual evolution of an internal social problem—is a legitimate necessity in order to reassure South Africa that the two are separate and different situations. As much as a carrot, the Namibian case required a stick, which the Cubans finally provided.

Notes

1. In addition to citations, material for this chapter has been gathered from discussions with negotiators from the Western Five and the front-line states and from the UN Secretariat and also from discussions with government and private sources in South Africa. I am particularly grateful to Martti Ahtisaari, Donald McHenry, Chester Crocker, Lannon Walker, Frank Wisner, John Seiler, and Marianne Spiegel for insights and to Sara Steinmetz for her help.
2. On matters of postcolonial bargaining and relations, see Donald Rothchild, "Racial Stratification and Bargaining: The Kenya Experience," in I. William Zartman, ed., *The 50% Solution* (New York: Doubleday, 1976); William B. Quandt, *Revolution and Political Leadership: Algeria* (Cambridge, Mass.: MIT Press, 1969); I. William Zartman, "Decolonization and Dependency," LIV *Foreign Affairs* 2:325–343 (January 1976).
3. Most available studies of the structure of conflict in southern Africa antedate the Portuguese revolution. See, however, Robert I. Rotberg,

Suffer the Future: Policy Choices in Southern Africa (Cambridge, Mass.: Harvard University Press, 1980); Timothy M. Shaw, "Southern Africa from Detente to Deluge?" *1978 Yearbook of World Affairs* (London: Stevens and Sons, London Institute of World Affairs, 1978); John Seiler, ed., *Southern Africa Since the Portuguese Coup* (Boulder, Colo.: Westview, 1979); Richard Bissell and Chester Crocker, eds., *South Africa into the 1980s* (Boulder, Colo.: Westview, 1980). For those pre-1975 studies that are still relevant, see Kenneth Grundy, *Confrontation and Accommodation in Southern Africa* (Berkeley, Calif.: University of California Press, 1973); Herbert Adam, *Modernizing Racial Domination* (Berkeley, Calif.: University of California Press, 1971); Leonard Thompson and Jeffrey Butler, eds., *Change in Contemporary South Africa* (Berkeley, Calif.: University of California Press, 1975).

4. On Namibia, see Ruth First, *Southwest Africa* (Baltimore: Penguin, 1963); Solomon Slonim, *Southwest Africa and the United Nations* (Baltimore: The Johns Hopkins University Press, 1973); Roger Murray, "No Easy Path to Independence," *Africa Report*: 17–21 (May 1977); John H. Wellington, *Southwest Africa and its Human Issues* (New York: Oxford University Press, 1967); "Namibia," *Africa Contemporary Record* (New York: Holmes & Meier, annually); François Lacoste, "Le Sud-ouest africain—Namibia en 1979," *Politique Internationale* 3:251–281 (Spring 1979); UN Department of Political Affairs, *Decolonization* no. 9, revised (October 1977) #78-36819; John Dugard, ed., *The South West Africa/Namibia Dispute* (Berkeley, Calif.: University of California, 1973); International Defence and Aid Fund, *Nambia: The Facts* (London: IDAF, 1980); Gerhard K. H. Tötemeyer, *Namibia Old and New* (New York: St. Martin's, 1978); and *Southwest Africa/Namibia* (Randburg: Fokus Suid, 1977); Reginald Green et al., *Namibia: The Last Colony* (New York: Longman, 1982); Alfred Moleah, *Namibia: The Struggle for Liberation* (Wilmington, Del.: Disa Press, 1983).

5. Interesting economic assessments and projections are found in Robert I. Rotberg, ed., *Namibia: Political and Economic Prospects* (Lexington, Mass.: Heath, 1983); Reginald H. Green, "Namibia in Transition: Toward a Political Economy of Liberation," in Timothy Shaw, ed., *Alternative Futures for Africa* (Boulder, Colo.: Westview, 1981) and in Wolfgang Thomas, *Economic Development in Namibia* (Mainz: Kaiser-Grünewald, 1978); see also Chester Crocker and Penelope Hartland-Thunberg, *Namibia at the Crossroads: Economic and Political Prospects* (Washington, D.C.: Georgetown University Center for Strategic and International Studies, 1978), and the Future for Namibia series of the Catholic Institute of International Relations and the British Council of Churches (London).

6. Tribal components of the early years are well described by F. Jariretundu Kozonguizi, "South West Africa: Historical Background and Current Problems," in John Davis and James Baker, eds., *Southern Africa in Transition* (New York: Praeger, 1966), and in the works of Gerhard Tötemeyer, *Namibia Old and New* and *Southwest Africa/Namibia*, also "Uniting and Disruptive Forces in Political Organization in Namibia," in Hendrik van der Merwe and Robert Schrire, eds., *Race and Ethnicity* (Cape Town: David Philip, 1980).

7. See Robert Rotberg, *Suffer the Future*, pp. 203–14. On Nujoma, see Colleen Hendriks, "Sam Nujoma: Profile of SWAPO's Leader," XI *Munger Africana Library* (1980).

8. On the effects of the Angolan civil war, see John Seiler, "South African response to international pressure," III *International Affairs Bulletin* 1:7–14 (June 1979); John de St. Jorre, "South Africa: Up Against the World," *Foreign Policy* 28:53–85 (Fall 1977).

9. See Vance, *Hard Choices*, (New York: Simon & Schuster, 1983), p. 273; Henry A. Kissinger, address at Lusaka, 17 April 1976; R. W. Johnson, *How Long Will South Africa Survive?* (New York: Oxford University Press, 1978), pp. 256ff., 264.

10. For discussions of Walvis Bay and the islands, see *London Times*, 1 September 1978, XVIII *Africa Confidential* 19:1–3 (23 September 1977); *The New York Times*, 3 September 1977; Donald Sparks, "Walvis, Bay, Plum-pudding and Penguin Islands: Their History and Economic Importance to Namibia," paper presented to African Studies Association, 1979; The Geographer, *International Boundary Study* no. 125 (12 July 1972), State Department (which curiously does not mention the islands), nor does Ian Brownlie, *African Boundaries* (Berkeley, Calif.: University of California Press, 1979), pp. 1273–1288.

11. *UNGA/R* 153 (XXXI) of 20 December 1976.

12. UNSC/R283 of 29 July 1970; Council of Namibia decree 1 of 27 September 1974; *UNGA/R* 3295 (XXIX). See also Allan D. Cooper, *U.S. Economic Power and Political Influence in Namibia* (Boulder, Colo.: Westview, 1982). Investment figures from U.S. Interests in Africa, Subcommittee on Africa. House of Representatives, October–November 1979, p. 191. Namibia ranked about thirtieth in U.S. trade with Africa (ibid., pp. 187 f.).

13. Even William Yarborough, *Trial in Africa* (Washington, D.C.: Heritage Foundation, 1976), supports Namibian independence (p. 25). Crocker and Hartland-Thumberg, *Namibia at the Crossroads . . .*, p. 22, feel that even a Marxist Namibia would trade with the West.

14. See Commonwealth Secretariat, "The Mineral Industry of Namibia," London 1978; W. S. Berthold, "Namibia's Economic Potential and Existing Economic Ties with the Republic of South Africa," German Development Institute, Berlin, 1977; R. Murray et al., "The Role of

Foreign Firms in Namibia," Africana Publications Trust, London 1974; UN Secretariat, Activities of Foreign Economic and Other Interests in Namibia (A/AD.109/L.1160), 1977; UN Secretariat, Activities of Transnational Corporation in Southern Africa (E/C.10.26), 6 April 1977; William Raiford, *The European Role in Africa and U.S. Interests*, Congressional Reference Service report, July 1981; Rockefeller Commission on U.S. Policy Toward Southern Africa, *South Africa: Time Running Out* (Berkeley, Calif.: University of California Press, 1981), especially pp. 301–306, 420–421, 426–427; David K. Willis, *Christian Science Monitor*, 2 December 1981.

15. See *The Economist*, 13 September 1980; Daniel S. Papp, "The Soviet Union and Southern Africa," in Robert Donaldson, ed., *The Soviet Union in the Third World* (Boulder, Colo.: Westview, 1981).

16. 1950 ICJ Reports 128 at 131–144, quoted in extenso in Dugard, *The SouthWest Africa/Namibia Dispute* . . . and discussed in ibid., chap. 6; 1966 ICJ Reports 6 at 17–51, quoted in extenso in Dugard, op. cit., and discussed in ibid., chap. 8; 1971 ICJ Reports 27–58, quoted in extenso in Dugard, op. cit., and discussed in ibid., chap. 10.

17. *UNGA/R* 2145 (XXI) of 27 October 1966; see discussion in Dugard, op. cit., chap. 9, and, on the U.S. initiative, in Waldermar Nielsen, *The Great Powers and Africa* (New York: Praeger, 1969), pp. 316 f.

18. *UNGA/F* 2248 (S–V) of 19 May 1967.

19. See Dugard, op. cit., pp. 521 ff.

20. *UNGA/R* 3 III (XXVIII) of 12 December 1972 and *UNGA/R* 152 (XXXI) of 20 December 1976.

21. On the development of SWAPO guerrilla warfare, see Grundy, *Confrontation and Accommodation* . . . ; Grundy, *Guerrilla Struggle in Southern Africa* (New York: Grossman, 1971); Richard Gibson, *African Liberation Movements* (New York: Oxford University Press, 1972); Dugard, op. cit., pp. 216–224, 414–420; Deon Fouri, "South Africa: The Evolving Experience," in James Roberts, ed., *Defense Policy Formation* (Durham, N.C.: Carolina Academic Press, 1980), especially p. 103 f.; M. Morris, *Armed Conflict in Southern Africa* (Capetown: Jeremy Spence, 1974); International Defence and Aid Fund (IDAF), *Apartheid's Army in Namibia*, Fact Paper 10 on Southern Africa (London: IDAF, 1982).

22. *Washington Post*, 15 August 1982; P. W. Botha in XIII *South African International* 1:43 (July 1982); *The Economist*, 4 July 1983.

23. See chronology in *IDAF News Notes*, June 1982; *The New York Times*, 26 February 1982. On the Cuban presence, see Carmelo Mesa-Lago and June S. Balkin, eds., *Cuba in Africa* (Pittsburgh, Pa.: University of Pittsburgh Press, 1982); Pamela Falk, *Cuban Foreign Policy* (Lexington, Mass.: Lexington Books, 1983); Maurice Halpern, "Cuban Role in Southern Africa," in John Seiler, ed., *Southern Africa since the Portuguese Came*.

24. *Baltimore Sun*, 22 March 1982. The heaviest South African loses in one day, on 11 August 1982, were 15 to the claimed 341 SWAPO (and presumably other Africans); *Christian Science Monitor*, 12 August 1982. The relation between the invasion and possible agreement was missed in the Randall Robinson interview (William Rasberry, *Washington Post*, 13 September 1982).

25. Richard Dale, "The Armed Forces as an Instrument of South African Policy in Namibia," XVIII *Journal of Modern African Studies* 1:57–71 (1980) at 70; Seiler, "South African Response . . . ," at 10; IDAF, *Apartheid's Army*.

26. XVII *Africa Confidential* 1:2–5 (23 May 1977).

27. A good public review of the first phase is found in the debates of the UN General Assembly at its ninth special session, 24 April to 3 May 1978, on Namibia.

28. *The New York Times*, 18, 21 May 1977. At the same time there was also discussion within the State Department over various strategies with regard to sanctions. (*The New York Times*, 14 May 1977).

29. *London Times* 11 June 1977. Vorster's new plan was essentially the same as the Basson-Eglin proposals, made by spokesmen for the opposition United and Progressive parties in 1971–72; excerpts found in Dugard, *The Southwest Africa/Namibia Question*, pp. 534–540.

30. XVIII *Africa Confidential* 15:1–3 (22 July 1977).

31. Statement by SWAPO's observer at the UN, Ben-Theo Gurirab, *The New York Times*, 12 June 1977.

32. *The New York Times*, 22 May 1977. Texts are found in UN Department of Political Affairs, *Decolonization* No. 8 (July 1977).

33. BBC interview with Prime Minister P. W. Botha, 15 August 1977.

34. *The New York Times*, 6 October 1977.

35. Steyn immediately invited Nujoma to Windhoek under safe conduct to discuss the holding of elections, but SWAPO rejected the invitation; *London Times*, 9 September 1977.

36. *UNGA/R* 39/9/D of 4 November 1977.

37. A good public review of the second phase is found in the debates of the UN General Assembly at its ninth special session, 24 April to 3 May 1978, on Namibia.

38. The South African troop figures were the last stumbling block. South Africa long held out for a maximum 80 percent reduction in forces to 4,000 for law and order purposes, but the Western Five insisted on 1,500: *Economist*, 17 December 1977; *The New York Times*, 11, 12, 13 February 1978.

39. *The New York Times*, 2 April 1978.

40. UNSC Document S/12636 of 10 April 1978, reprinted in IDAF, *Namibia*, pp. 74–78. See *The New York Times*, 31 March, 1 April 1978.

41. *The New York Times*, 26 April 1978; *South Africa Digest*, 21 and 28 April 1978.

42. *The New York Times*, 28 April 1978. On the following McHenry estimate, see *The New York Times*, 30 April 1978; *Keesing's*, 23 February 1979, p. 29461.
43. *The New York Times*, 9 May 1978; Nujoma speech to the UNGA, 28 May 1978, reproduced in *Namibia Bulletin* 1/78:19–24 (May 1978).
44. Three good articles were by Kathleen Teltsch, *The New York Times*, 13 July, and John Burns, *The New York Times*, 8 and 14 July 1978.
45. *UNSC*/PV2082 (27 July 1978).
46. On approach-avoidance, see Lloyd Jensen, "Approach-Avoidance Bargaining on Arms Control," in I. William Zartman, ed., *The 50% Solution* (New York: Doubleday, 1975). On breakdown from formula to detail, see I. William Zartman and Maureen Berman, *The Practical Negotiator* (New Haven, Conn.: Yale University Press, 1983), pp. 135–138, 146–149.
47. Kathleen Teltsch, *The New York Times*, 5 August 1978.
48. The Western Five enraged South Africa by voting in favor of UNSC/R 432 (1978) in favor of the future return of Walvis Bay to Namibia; the West, however, had thought that it could avoid offending South Africa while supporting the front-line states and SWAPO by insisting that the Walvis Bay Resolution be separate from the General Resolution UNSC/R 431 (1978) on Namibia. The procedural distinction did not work (*The New York Times*, 18 and 25 July 1978; *London Times*, 1 August 1978).
49. *London Times*, 2 August 1978.
50. *London Times*, 12, 14, 17, 20, 22 August 1978.
51. UN S/12827. The report is summarizd in XV *UN Chronicle* 8:51–55 (August 1978) and reprinted in IDAF, *Namibia*, pp. 79–86.
52. *London Times*, 31 August 1978.
53. *London Times*, 6 and 9 September 1978.
54. UN S/12841; see also XV *UN Chronicle* 8:9–11 (August 1978).
55. UN S/12936; see also XV *UN Chronicle* 8:4–9 (August 1978); "South African Response to the UN Secretary General's Report on the Implementation of the UN Proposal" and André Pisani, "Analysis," South African Institute of International Affairs (October 1978); *London Times*, 21 September 1978.
56. *London Times*, 27 September 1978.
57. The following account is taken primarily from Jim Hoagland, *Washington Post*, 20 October 1978, and Cyrus Vance, *Hard Choices*, pp. 308–311, quotes from p. 308; see also Hoagland, *Washington Post*, 24 October 1978, and 6, 15, 18, and 19 October 1978.
58. *Washington Post*, 20 October 1978; Vance, *Hard Choices*, p. 309. On 10 November, Carter did sign legislation restricting Export-Import Bank financing for South African trade.
59. *The New York Times*, 1, 3 December 1978; Vance, op. cit., pp. 310–311. Yet in reflecting on the 1977 change in the South African position, Vance sees the probable cause as the Western threat that it "would no

longer present sanctions unless they began seriously negotiating," p. 275. Deon Geldenhuys, in his excellent book *The Diplomacy of Isolation* (New York: St. Martins, 1984), pp. 212, 223, affirms that South Africa fully expected sanctions to be applied in 1978 and that fear of sanctions had its effect on South African bargaining behavior.

60. *The New York Times*, 14 November 1978.
61. *The New York Times*, 3 and 4 December 1978; *Washington Post*, 1 December 1978.
62. See Gerhardt Tötemeyer, "Uniting and Disruptive Forces in Political Organizations in Namibia," p. 179.
63. UN S/12983 of 22 December 1978.
64. *The New York Times*, 27 February 1979.
65. It is a thesis of the excellent analysis by Marianne Spiegel that failure in the fifth phase was largely due to delays and hesitations in the American response to South African demands, which could have been answered successfully to clinch an agreement during this period: Marianne Spiegel, "Western Mediation in Namibia, 1977–84," in Saadia Touval and I. William Zartman, eds., *The Man in the Middle: International Mediation in Theory and Practice* (Boulder, Colo.: Westview, 1984).
66. *The New York Times*, 7 and 15 March 1979.
67. *The New York Times*, 13, 19, 21 and 23 March 1979; *Washington Post*, 21 March 1979.
68. *The New York Times*, 15 May 1979.
69. *The New York Times*, 9 May, 14 August 1979.
70. *The New York Times*, 7 May 1979.
71. *The New York Times*, 15 May 1979.
72. *The New York Times*, 2 April 1979. For a sensitive and unvarnished appreciation of the extent of formal versus informal elimination of apartheid in Namibia, see Joseph Lelyveld, *The New York Times*, 31 December 1980.
73. See *Le Monde*, 24 November and 20 December 1979, and a particularly good article by Gerard Chaliand, 20 November 1979; D. Venter, "South Africa as an African Power," VIII South African Institute of International Affairs *Newsletter* (1976), pp. 7–12. See also Rockefeller Commission, *Time Running Out*, pp. 293–294.
74. *The New York Times*, 11 August 1979.
75. *Le Monde*, 8, 14, 15 and 18 November 1979.
76. *Le Monde*, 7 December 1979.
77. *Le Monde*, 28 June and 3, 4 July 1980.
78. Interview with Derek Auret; John Seiler, "Namibian Negotiations: Hiatus or Collapse?" *The Seiler Report* 3:1–4 (August 1980); *The New York Times*, 4 September 1980.
79. *The New York Times*, 22 September, 24 November 1980. For Urquhart's views on mediation, see Brian Urquhart, "Ralph Bunche and Peace-Keeping," V *UNITAR News* 1:3–7 (1973).

80. *The New York Times*, 2 October 1980.
81. *The New York Times*, 7, 8, 9 January 1981. See analyses by André du Pisani, "Namibia—On Brinkmanship," VIII *Politikon* 1:1–10 (June 1981); "Namibia—The Search for Alternatives," XII *South Africa International* 1:292–302 (July 1981); and "Namibia: From Incorporation to Controlled Change," 1 *Journal of Contemporary African Studies* 2:281–306 (April 1982).
82. *The Washington Post*, 29 March 1981.
83. See Chester Crocker, "South Africa: Strategy for Change," IX *Foreign Affairs* 2:323–351 (Winter 1980).
84. The newness of the team, wishing to protect itself against unwelcome criticism, also contributed to the secrecy. Material in this section will be documented with public sources where available, but it also comes from interviews during the period with the Africa Bureau of the State Department.
85. To capture the spirit of the differences, Ambassador McHenry summarized his administration's view toward South Africa by saying, "We did make it clear to them that there could be no improvement in our relations unless there was progress on three issues: Rhodesia, now Zimbabwe, Namibia, and apartheid," I *TransAfrica Forum Issue Brief* 1:1 (February 1982). Sensing that the remaining two issues got in each other's way, the Crocker team focused on Namibia alone (although to buy Namibian agreement, they also focused on Angola, and again the two issues got in each other's way).
86. *Washington Post*, 29 March 1981. The fullest statement on apartheid came from Under Secretary of State Lawrence Eagleburger in 1983; *The New York Times*, 24 June 1983. See also *CSIS Africa Notes* 12 July 1983.
87. *Washington Post*, 29 March 1981; Elizabeth Schmidt, "Marching to Pretoria: Reagan's South Africa Policy, II *TransAfrica Forum* 2:3–16 (Fall 1983). For the subsequent lesser items, on defense-usable products, see *Washington Post*, 27 February and 16 March 1982; on nuclear cooperation, see *New Republic*, 18 November 1981; Ronald Walters, "United States and South Africa: Nuclear Collaboration," II *TransAfrica Forum* 2:17–30 (Fall 1983); on metallurgical equipment, see *Washington Post*, 16 September 1982; on computers, see NARMIC, *Automating Apartheid* (Philadelphia: American Friends Service Committee, 1982). On problems caused by South African misperception of the "new spirit," in regard to military intelligence officers, see *The New York Times*, 16 March 1981.
88. *The New York Times*, 13, 24 April 1981. See State Department Memorandum of Conversation, 15 and 16 April 1981, reprinted in I *TransAfrica News Report* 10 (August 1981); *The New York Times*, 1 and 19 April 1981.

89. *The New York Times*, 20 November 1981; 1 *TransAfrica Issue Brief* 1 (February 1982). It is not known what the form or the contents of South Africa's "final list" were although some items were probably constitutional guarantees, UNGA recognition of SWAPO, UNTAG members and uniforms, SWAPO bases, and Cuban forces south of the "red line" in Angola (*Economist*, 26 September 1981). See Michael Sinclair, "Namibian Constitutional Proposals," XII *South Africa International* 4:508–516 (April 1982).

90. See the discussion in the State Department Memorandum of Conversation, 15 and 16 April 1981, in TransAfrica . . . ; answers to Senator Helms, *The New York Times*, 1 May 1981; *Washington Star*, 15 May 1981: Under Secretary Clark's visit to South Africa in June 1981; *The New York Times*, 15 July 1982. Note that Cuban removal was not on the "list" noted in *Economist*, 26 September 1981.

91. South African military contact with Cuban troops in January 1982 was the first since mid-1975 (*Washington Post*, 6 January 1982).

92. In a "Voice of America" interview with I. William Zartman and Helen Kitchen, on 23 June 1982, Chester Crocker indicated that "we feel very strongly that it's not the US role to attempt, to pretend to mediate between Angolan parties." Nor was UNITA on the *Economist* "list," nor did Jonas Savimibi receive very preferential treament in his often postponed visit to the United States in mid-1981. Crocker was more positive toward UNITA, "a significant and legitimate factor in Angolan politics," in his speech of 29 August 1981.

93. See "Voice of America" interview, 23 June 1982; Crocker Talking Paper for Haig, 14 May 1981, reprinted in I *TransAfrica News Report* 10 (August 1981); Roger Manning, *New Republic*, 18 November 1981; Crocker speech, 1 September 1981.

94. For a discussion of this effect, see I. William Zartman and Maureen Berman, *The Practical Negotiator* (New Haven, Conn.: Yale University Press, 1982), p. 195 f.

95. The modification also had German and Canadian parentage; AF/S Memorandum to Crocker, 13 May 1981, reprinted in I *TransAfrica News Report* 10 (August 1981); *Washington Post*, 8 July 1981.

96. The problem surfaced frequently, particularly in 1981, but was overcome by more balance thereafter. See criticisms in *The New York Times*, 14 and 28 April 1981; *Washington Post*, 1 September 1981. It also lay at the basis of the slow Angolan contacts criticized by Dr. Gerald Bender, *The New York Times*, 8 January 1982.

97. See the exchange of memoranda reprinted in I *TransAfrica Issue Brief* I (February 1982). South Africa had reservations over nondiscrimination in private organizations (*Washington Post*, 18 December 1981); whereas the front-line states had reservations over the three-branched government and regional elections (*Washington Post*, 21 November 1981).

98. See Anthony Lewis, *The New York Times*, 12 April 1982; *Washington Post*, 19 November 1981, 26 January 1982.

99. The UN secretary general was notified of the phase one agreement on 12 July 1982 (*The New York Times*, 14 July 1982; *Washington Post*, 7 and 12 July 1982; *Washington Times*, 16 June 1982). The remaining point to be decided was the type of proportional representation system to be used.

100. *The New York Times*, 22 May 1982.

101. *The New York Times*, 1 August 1982.

102. *The New York Times*, 3 June 1982; *London Times*, 4 June 1982. In his last-minute and first meeting with Jorge, Haig did not raise the Cuban connection and said afterward that the Cubans were "not on the agenda" in Namibia (*Washington Post*, 4 November 1981; Gerald Bender, *The New York Times*, 8 January 1982). For the substance of the January talks, see *Afrique-Asia* 258:7-10 (1 February 1982).

103. *The New York Times*, 1 July 1982; *Christian Science Monitor*, 7 October 1982.

104. *The New York Times*, 3 June 1982; *London Times*, 4 June 1982.

105. *The New York Times*, 1 and 5 July 1982; *Washington Post*, 3 June 1982. This was why the German member of the Contact Group announced that phase two was completed and independence expected momentarily (*The New York Times*, 1 August 1982). French Foreign Minister Cheysson said that for France and others "the linkage is not acceptable" (*The New York Times*, 13 October 1982).

106. *The New York Times*, 18 June 1982; *London Times*, 18 June 1982. March elections were called for by U.S. Ambassador Herman Nickels on 1 June and the DTA leader Dirk Mudge on 4 June 1982 (*Washington Post*, 4 June 1982).

107. *Financial Times*, 9 July 1982.

108. *Washington Post*, 28 July 1982.

109. *The New York Times*, 10 and 26 August 1982.

110. Text in *South Africa Digest*, 17 September 1982.

111. *Washington Post*, 6 October 1982; *Christian Science Monitor*, 7 October 1982.

112. Le Monde, 16 October 1982; *Jeune Afrique* 1138:36 f. (27 October 1982).

113. *The New York Times*, 28 October 1982.

114. In March 1984, South Africa released Toivo ja Toivo from sixteen years on Robben Island in the hopes of creating leadership rivalries, but he immediately rejoined and supported SWAPO (*Washington Post*, 2, 3 March 1984). For a South African expectation see André du Pisani, "Toivo: Man of the People," X *South Africa Foundation News* 4:1–4 (April 1984).

115. *Washington Post*, 11 January 1983; *The New York Times*, 19,

23 January 1983; *Financial Times*, 12 January 1983; *Christian Science Monitor*, 20 January 1983.

116. Botha ordered the military strategy prepared at the beginning of 1980. See *The Economist*, 18 June 1983; Kenneth Grundy, *The Rise of the South African Security Establishment* (Johannesburg: South African Institute of International Affairs, 1983). The similarity with Israeli policy at the same time and the permissive Western reaction toward it were not lost on South Africa; see Colin Legum, "Southern Africa," *Africa Contemporary Record 1982–1983* (New York: Africana, 1984), pp. A5–A6. For an account of the Angolan incursions, see Willem Steenkamp, *Borderstrike* (London: Butterworths, 1983).

117. John de St. Jorre, *Washington Post*, 9, 13 December 1982, 17 February 1983; *The New York Times*, 28 January 1983, 3, 26 February 1983; *Baltimore Sun*, 28 January, 3 February 1983; *Africa Contemporary Record 1982–83*, p. A32.

118. Allister Sparks, *Washington Post*, 24 February 1983; *The New York Times*, 26, 28 February 1983.

119. Wary enough not to crow prematurely, they raised little hope through the press; for a rare reflection of optimism, see *The Baltimore Sun*, 11 June 1983.

120. *Christian Science Monitor*, 19 May 1983; *The New York Times*, 1 June, 26 August, 1 September 1983.

121. *The New York Times*, 3 March 1983; *Washington Post*, 16 April 1983.

122. Allister Sparks, *Washington Post*, 23 July 1983; *The New York Times*, 31 July 1983. On the financial reports, see *The New York Times*, 11 September 1983; *Washington Post*, 17 September 1983.

123. See Barry Streek, *Baltimore Sun*, 22 September 1983; Charles Frankel, *Washington Post*, 7 October 1983; Leslie Gelb, *The New York Times*, 3 February 1983. There may be some doubt about the accuracy of the $2 billion figure (the same amount as the Gulf oil revenues to Angola) as the cost of the Soviet and Cuban troops; a lower cost basis could put the figure as low as $65 million per year.

124. There are no accurate figures on the number of Cuban troops in Angola, and there is considerable doubt about the increment of 10,000 new troops leaked by the CIA to the press on 9 December 1982. However, there does seem to be agreement that the total number is around 25,000 and that around the end of 1983 Cuban troops being withdrawn from Ethiopia were sent to Angola (with no numbers known): *Africa Contemporary Record 1982–1983*, p. A28; *Christian Science Monitor*, 7 December 1983; *Baltimore Sun*, 10 March 1984.

125. *Washington Post*, 17 May 1983; *The New York Times*, 13 January 1984. The U.S.S.R. warned South Africa that it would take such measures after the success of Operation Askari at the end of 1983 (*Washington Post*, 5 January 1984). Angola began a major offensive

against UNITA soon after (*The New York Times*, 23 January 1984). The argument on the ripening moment is well presented by Allister Sparks, *Washington Post*, 7 February 1984.

126. *The New York Times*, 30 December 1983, 26 January 1984; Charles Frankel, *Washington Post*, 5 March 1984.

127. Allister Sparks, *Washington Post*, 12, 20 January 1984; *The New York Times*, 20 January 1984. Direct talks held on 25 July in Cape Verde without effect (*Washington Post*, 26 July 1984; *The New York Times*, 27 July 1984).

128. *Washington Post*, 25, 26 January, 5 March 1984; *The New York Times*, 25 January 1984. For a statement by Wisner, see his speech in Munich on 3 November 1983, reprinted in XIV *South Africa International* 5:466–473 (January 1984).

129. *Washington Post*, 10 November 1983; 25, 26 January 1984; *The New York Times*, 20 January 1984.

130. *Washington Post*, 21 February, 3 March 1984; *The New York Times*, 21 February, 17 March 1984. Prime Minister Botha specifically referred to Nkomati as a foundation for constellation (*South African Digest*, 16 March 1984, pp. 5, 17).

131. *Los Angeles Times*, 18 February 1984; *The New York Times*, 19 February 1984. The United States had a diplomatic, confidence-producing headquarters role in the commission, but it suffered casualties, nonetheless (*Los Angeles Times*, 18 Feburary 1984; *The New York Times*, 16 April 1984).

132. *Washington Post*, 25 January, 29 February 1984; *The New York Times*, 7 March 1984.

133. *Washington Post*, 3 April 1984; *Christian Science Monitor*, 19 June 1984; *The New York Times*, 18 June 1984.

134. *The New York Times*, 19 February 1984.

135. *Washington Post*, 10 February 1984.

136. *Washington Post*, 20 March 1984. Conditions to be applied "flexibly," according to President Dos Santos (*Le Monde*, 13 September 1984).

137. *Washington Post*, 9 June 1984.

138. *Washington Post*, 15 October, 11 November 1984. A crucial turn also came on 22 October when Foreign Minister Jorge was sacked for opposition to the new Angolan offer (*Washington Post*, 23 October 1984). See also interview with President Dos Santos, *Washington Post*, 14 October 1984.

139. *Washington Post*, 2, 3, 12, 17, 21, 23 November 1984.

140. *Christian Science Monitor*, 27 November 1984; *Washington Post*, 23, 27 March, 6 April, 14 June 1985.

141. *Washington Post*, 16 May 1984.

142. Unlike 1980, the African deaths were Angolans, not SWAPO. South Africa claimed 800 SWAPO deaths in 1987; *Washington Post*, 2 November 1987. Also *The New York Times*, 20 April 1988.

143. On the military escalation, see *Jeune Afrique* 1432:42–44 (15 June 1988); *Baltimore Sun*, 22 January 1988; *Washington Post*, 1 May 1987, 9 January, 12 May 1988; *The New York Times*, 16 December 1987, 29 May, 30 June, 6 July 1988.

144. See *Baltimore Sun*, 1 May 1988; *Jeune Afrique* 1432:42–44 (15 June 1988), 1427:34 f. (11 May 1988); *The New York Times*, 6 June 1988.

145. *Washington Post*, 23 July 1988; *Christian Science Monitor*, 20 July 1988.

146. *The New York Times*, 9 August 1987; *Washington Post*, 11 August 1987, 10 January, 12 March 1988.

147. *Washington Post*, 2 February 1988; *The New York Times*, 30 January 1988.

148. *The New York Times*, 15 March 1988; *Washington Post*, 7, 15 March 1988.

149. *Christian Science Monitor*, 9 May 1988; *Washington Post*, 14 May, 26 June, 30 September 1988.

150. *The New York Times*, 23 June 1988; *Jeune Afrique*, 1436:46 f. (13 July 1988).

151. *The New York Times*, 7 June 1988; *Washington Post*, 27 June 1988; *Jeune Afrique*, 1435:36 (6 June 1988).

152. *Washington Post*, 3 August 1988; Department of State, Selected Document 31, 20 July 1988.

153. *Washington Post*, 15 July, 3, 4, 5, 6, 9 August, 1 September 1988; *The New York Times*, 1 September 1988.

154. Cited in David Ottoway, "The Peace Process," *Washington Post*, 22 December 1988; see also Christopher Wren, "The Crocker Formula," *The New York Times*, 17 December 1988; text of the agreement is given in *The New York Times*, 23 December 1988. On the fall 1988 negotiations, see *Washington Post*, 30 October, 3, 4, 5, 6, 20 December 1988; *The New York Times*, 3, 4, 5, 12, 13, 20 December 1988; *Jeune Afrique*, 1458:27 f. (14 December 1988), 1459:38–47 (21 December 1988).

155. On forcing or precipitating acts, see Harold Saunders, "Reconstituting the Arab-Israeli Peace Process," in William B. Quandt, ed., *The Middle East Ten Years After Camp David* (Washington, D.C.: Brookings, 1988), esp. p. 437 f.

156. Geldenhuys, *The Diplomacy of Isolation*, pp. 225 f., 229, also interprets the problem as one of South Africa's avoidance of a decision on either track as long as it was not required to do so.

157. So has it been for a long time, the question of timing aside. Among the many references that can be cited—including Angolan and Cuban ones—is the statement of Assistant Secretary of State Moose before the House African Subcommittee on 30 September 1980: "We continue to work to create, conditions such as a Namibia settlement that would promote the early withdrawal of South African troops from Namibia and Cuban combat troops from Angola."

Ripe for Resolution

158. An excellent analysis of South African thinking is found in Allister Sparks, "Why SA Is Stalling in SWA," *Rand Daily Mail*, 20 September 1980, although the "Lifeboat" thesis, that South Africa is preparing to set a DTA government afloat as an independent state that can then negotiate with SWAPO without compromising Botha's government, is not accepted here. See also Geldenhuys, *The Diplomacy of Isolation*, and Sparks on changes in *Washington Post*, February 1984.

159. The military, like the party, had its splits. Some military recognized that the South African border with Namibia, a sparsely populated desert, is far better for defense than the Namibian border with Angola, moderately populated bush country. At the beginning of July 1980, General Jannie Geldenhuys, commander of SADF in Namibia, was summarily reassigned to Pretoria, reportedly for favoring acceptance of the UN elections and accommodation with SWAPO (Sparks, *Rand Daily Mail*, 20 September 1980; Seiler, "Namibian Negotiations . . .").

160. For example, the Evian Accords on Algeria, see I. William Zartman, "Les relations entre la France et l'Algérie," XIV *Revue française de Science politique* 6:1087–1113 (1964).

161. See Jonathan Powell, *Baltimore Sun*, 5 August 1982; *Financial Times*, 20 July 1982.

162. The subject has been discussed, however inconclusively: *The New York Times*, 13 May 1977; Andrew Young, *Washington Post*, 28 July 1980; Indar Rikhye, "Negotiating the End of Conflicts," New York: International Peace Academy, 1978; Tony Roenderman, "Sanctions: A Reappraisal," *Briefing Paper 27*, South African Foundation, August 1980; Senator Dick Clark, "U.S. Corporate Interests in South Africa," Subcommittee on African Affairs, U.S. Senate, January 1978, pp. 180 f.; Elisabeth Landis, "Namibia: The Beginning of Disengagement," II *Studies in Race and Nation* 1:17–34 (1970); "South Africa and Economic Sanctions," VII *South Africa Foundation News* 2:2–3 (February 1981); Robin Renwick, *Economic Sanctions* (Cambridge, Mass.: Harvard University Center for International Affairs, 1981); David Willers and S. Begg, eds., *South Africa and Sanctions: Genesis and Prospects* (Johannesburg: South Africa Institute of International Affairs, 1979); P. Wallensteen and M. Nincie, eds., *Dilemmas of Economic Coercion: Sanctions in World Politics* (New York: Praeger, 1983). For a theoretical justification of sticks as well as carrots in the South African case, see Marc Levy, "Mediation of Prisoner's Dilemma Conflicts under Conditions of Uncertainty: Namibia," XXX *Journal of Conflict Resolution* 2 (December 1985).

6
Conflict Resolution in Africa

Never treat crises when they're cold, only when they're hot.
Henry Kissinger

Peace is a process—a way of solving problems.
John F. Kennedy

Conflict in Africa becomes more than just historically or politically interesting when it is examined for some general lessons about crisis management and conflict resolution. The cases can tell a good deal. They indicate that there is frequently a greater American interest in conflict resolution than in seeing one side win; that conflict resolution is made possible by a "ripe moment," defined in terms of escalation that can best be understood in the context of policy alternatives or "tracks"; and that the mediator needs both to find a formula that meets the parties' demands and also to manipulate the conflict—verbally or materially—in order to mediate effectively. These and other lessons from the African cases, which will be examined further on, give rise to policy implications with fairly broad relevance.

The policy implications are directly applicable to the United States—that is, an outside great power with important although not necessarily predominant political and economic interests in the crisis area—but they are also relevant to other external powers such as European states. Of course, policy discussions must also necessarily take into account the perspectives of African states, for it is their interests that cause the conflict, and they are also often the primary mediators. Any outside power trying to reduce conflict and help the parties channel their energies into more useful activities must not only look to its own interests but must also act in accord with the dynamics of the parties. By the same token, this discussion is framed specifically in terms of Africa, but it need not be so. The same problems and the same methods are relevant for much of the Third World, specifically the Mideast and Asia, and also for Latin America, where the United States in the future is condemned to play a role of conflict resolution.[1] However, because the starting point for this analysis is an understanding of African conflict in African terms, the ensuing discussions will remain explicitly in Africa, with broader applications left implicit.

Comparisons

Two cases of active conflict resolution have been examined, each with instructive failures.

In Shaba, after the second crisis, the United States and its allies pressed Zaire into an agreement just at the moment when the other African state in the conflict, Angola, was also beginning to see the moment as ripe for resolution. Both the mediators and one of the conflicting parties—Angola—saw the danger of escalating crises and the futility of pursuing the previously first-choice policy of conflict. The mediators had the means to convince Zaire of the need for a negotiated settlement because they held the financial and political remedies Zaire needed to get back on its feet again. Confidence was built between the two African states through their common interest in controlling the leftover liberation movements and in seeing one another's liberation movements controlled.

A year and a crisis earlier all this could probably have been accomplished, with only slightly more effort, had the American government been able to treat Angola's MPLA regime as a serious negotiating partner rather than dismiss it as a Soviet puppet. All the elements that contributed to resolution in 1978 were present in 1977 except for the Angolan perception of the ripening moment, and even on this point there were internal differences of interpretation in Luanda. A Western demarche in favor of reconciliation, reinforcing existing African efforts, might have brought an earlier solution.

In Namibia, the Western Five working through the front-line states got SWAPO to move toward an agreement; working directly on South Africa, they also got Pretoria to change its position three times and to abandon its first track of a unilateral solution, at least in its original form (annexation) and second variant (the Turnhalle formula). But once South Africa made major concessions and accepted at new formula based on the UN plan, which was quite close to the demands of SWAPO, the Western Five could not elicit those last concessions on detail. This seems to have been either because South

Africa had not made the basic agreement in good faith or, as is more likely, because South Africa never felt really compelled to make any decision on a final choice betweeen either of the two tracks—unilateral or multilateral—toward Namibian independence, both of which it carefully kept alive.

The mediation process destroyed rather than built confidence in the neutrality and fairness of the procedures as well as in the acceptability of the outcome. Even more serious, no pressure was applied by the mediators on South Africa to match that which the front-line states were able to place on SWAPO alongside their assurance of support. South Africa alone set the deadlines. The mediators had no credible sanctions to force cooperation or to block unilateral solutions. The mediation thus led South Africa to conclude that its modified first-track solution was not only the preferable option, but that it stood a good chance of succeeding.

When the mediation was revived under a new administration in 1981, the new strategy was to overcome this weakness by providing South Africa with a preferable second track through a new formula. The UN plan for South African withdrawal from Namibia was to be linked to a plan (to be negotiated) for Cuban withdrawal from Angola. But in the process, Angolan agreement to the new formula was lost, and so South Africa again could avoid the need to decide. Furthermore, in Namibia itself the chances of any party friendly to South Africa winning any significant part of the vote withered away, and for several years the South African government—like the Angolan—was in such a delicate political position internally that it could take no chances on a risky decision, no matter how statesmanlike. Only after four years did Angola come up with an offer that South Africa could not refuse, and then only by further expanding the formula to include UNITA and the chance of renewed bargaining on details all over again. It took a massive escalation on the part of the Cubans to make South Africa take this offer seriously, and then not until four years later, in 1988.

Zimbabwe provides an interesting comparison.[2] The course of the American and Anglo-American initiatives from 1976 to 1979, with all their laudable efforts and their practical shortcomings, paralleled the developments in Namibia. Britain and America utilized some of the important components of good mediation, notably their display of persistence and patience and their use of allies. But although the front-line states helped bring the Patriotic Front of ZAPU and ZANU toward agreement, the mediators had no leverage over the various governments of Ian Smith, no control over a deadline, no ability to demonstrate the catastrophe lying in wait at the end of the chosen course, and no ability to block the first track of either party.

Four new elements appeared in 1979 that gave the mediator the ability to overcome the previous shortcomings. First, elections brought in a new Conservative British government willing to recognize the internal solution in Zimbabwe-Rhodesia, thereby reassuring the Smith-Muzorewa government enough to bring it to agreement. Second, on the other side, the continual raids on the Patriotic Front bases had taken a heavy enough toll so that the national liberation movement saw a fair agreement now as preferable to a delayed military victory in the long run. Third, and by reason of the first two points, British Foreign Secretary Lord Carrington was able to impose deadlines on the actual mediation process and hold to them. Finally, Lord Carrington chose to negotiate the prize—the constitutional framework for the new state—before negotiating the way to get there, thus putting the horse before the cart where it belonged. (In contrast, the Namibian mediation never even provided a horse in its first five rounds.)

Again, as to the Namibian/South African negotiations, no trust was created between the parties through the suspicion-ridden process; but there was trust in the fairness of the procedural solution, in the acceptability of the substantive constitutional framework, and in the equitable outcome of the elections, which each party expected to win. Britain could give assurances to the side that was stronger in the short run and put pressures on the side that would be stronger in the costly longer run. In Namibia, the Western Five lacked this flexibility because they were acting under the explicit constraints of United Nations resolutions and the implicit constraints of United Nations politics.

Two other conflicts erupted into crisis in the 1970s and moved toward resolution in the 1980s after having previously undergone some immediately successful but ultimately ephemeral efforts at conflict management applied by fellow African states in the 1960s.

The first and striking lesson of the Saharan and Ethiopia/Somali conflicts is that whereas conflict management can be fruitfully purchased with a promise of conflict resolution, construing an agreement to agree as the final agreement leads to reintensified conflict and crisis when raised hopes are dashed. In the Horn of Africa, the potential great power mediators were by the 1970s in intense competition to destroy one another's power base. Mediation either unilaterally or cooperatively was impossible. Russia and Cuba tried, but never touched the basic conflict. Podgorny and Castro had no formula for its resolution; like all good Marxists, they could not understand the national question. Somali expectations were raised high by the earlier promises of Haile Selassie and then by the collapse of his government—just at the time when any Ethiopian government was least likely or even able to be flexible. At the same time, neither the United States nor indeed other Western or moderate Arab states were willing to give Somalia enough help to hold on to its conquests and make Ethiopia negotiate, for much help was needed and the cause was generally perceived as illegitimate.

In sum, the moment was manifestly unripe for resolution. Instead, continuing Somali guerrilla activity eventually produced an escalation as Ethiopia invaded Somalia. The consolidation of the Ethiopian regime may gradually favor resolution, but the United States is in a poor position to produce it. Only the ally of the country making the concessions would be able to buy an agreement, and the Soviet Union has too much to gain from continuing conflict to put such pressure on Ethiopia—if indeed it has any such leverage. However, the United States was in a good position to start the process by helping to consolidate the reconciliation between Somalia and Kenya, as a model for Somalia and Ethiopia.

In the Sahara, the situation is more promising, for the conflict is neither impossible to resolve, as in the Horn, nor patently unripe, as it may have been in the past. Throughout 1978, before and after the Mauritanian coup, and around the 1979 and 1980 OAU Summits, balanced stalemates, at various levels, favored conciliation. In each case, the United States had means of pressure that France and the African and Arab states could have reinforced. Instead, individual Arab and African states undertook mediation with no encouragement or support from outside powers. The missing ingredient was either the mutual hurting stalemate or the credible deadline. These could have been created by United States' threats to recognize either the Madrid partition or the Polisario, but unfortunately, the United States never considered the problem to be that serious. Washington could also have used restraint on arms supplies to Morocco as an inducement for Algeria or Morocco to talk. Instead, it was the threat of international recognition of the SADR that brought Morocco to offer to agree to a political solution by referendum. However, as time went on, both the Algerians and the Polisario seemed more interested in increasing that threat than in the referendum, and the crisis worsened. As more time went on and the stalemate hardened until only catastrophe could provide the exit, and as external needs required the states' attention and cooperation, an external mediator (Saudi Arabia) and a technical assistant (the UN Secretariat) were able to provide the formula and details of a solution.

These cases, then, provide histories of opportunities missed or fumbled (in the Western Sahara and Somalia) as well as examples of the way "political engineering" can work to create better outcomes (as in Zaire and Namibia). They clearly show—perhaps so unmistakably that the conclusion should be a commonplace—how much better off the mediator and the parties to the conflict are with an agreement than without one and how an unresolved problem only gets worse rather than fades away. In Shaba, both parties are in a more favorable situation after the reconciliation, as they themselves recognize, because the political threat to the Zairean and Angolan governments is reduced (even if not eliminated, for reasons generally outside the accord). Both parties can turn more attention to domestic development and reform. For its own part, the United States gained increased leverage for reforms in Zaire and much improved relations with Angola as a result of the reconciliation though both benefits were relative. The parties that paid the price of the reconciliation were the leftover national liberation movements.

In Zimbabwe, things are better for all sides—with qualifications, of course. Although some white settlers have been losing confidence, their earlier lack of realism made this inevitable to some extent. The outcome of the mediation was the best they could have gotten even if not the best conceivable in their own terms. The Patriotic Front has collapsed, but half of it, ZANU, has triumphed. Mugabe's stand on global relations during the crucial early years of independence has been nearly all that the United States might want, and as far as the United States is concerned at least, the negotiated settlement and elected government are preferable to a contested internal solution and a continuation of the Soviet-supported guerrilla campaign. The parties who paid the price of this agreement were the African partners of the internal solution—who played their role in history and were then passed by—as well as followers of the defeated nationalist leader, Joshua Nkomo.

Despite the current stalemate in Angola, the Namibian mediation has averted several undesirable first-track outcomes that direct pressure and verbal condemnation alone, without concomitant efforts to find an acceptable alternative, could never have done. Even if South Africa were to pursue its modified first track, it has so changed the original formula that the outcome is far preferable to the original version. Yet a solution itself still goes abegging. So long as that remains true, the dangers of explosion and Soviet penetration—and of the pernicious effects of continued conflict for Namibians—are still present. Free and fair elections will show who bears the cost of agreement; until then, the costs of nonagreement are borne by the victims of the continuing conflict.

In the Horn, the results of nonagreement are far more immediately destructive. The plight of the million and a half refugees from drought and terror is catastrophic beyond imagination, one of the poisonous by-products of political leaders' disputes borne by their suffering people. The calamitous drought that triggered the Ethiopian revolution was small by comparison. The border problem remains where it was in 1961, but history never allows exact replays; the bitterness and hatred and the deep feelings of deception and cruelty make the situation even worse than it was thirty years ago, because traditional animosities have now been continued by modern events. It is hard to judge whether the United States is better off with Somalia as its new associate. Pluses include the base at Berbera, Somalia's membership in the Arab League, and its support for the Mideast peace process; but these are offset by its irredentist cause, unpopular in Africa, and its basic poverty. What is certain is that the ongoing conflict in Ogaden and Eritrea provides an excuse for the continued Russian—if not Cuban—military presence, obstructs the opening up of Ethiopia to more active Western diplomacy, and subjects the people of the Horn to misery. Perpetuation of the conflict seems to benefit no one except the Soviets although, even for them, the conflict has become an economic drain.

In the Sahara, the only party that benefits from continuing conflict is the leadership of the Polisario. The desert people themselves are not better off in confinement to refugee camps. Morocco and Algeria have walked themselves out on a limb on the issue, and Libya lost its chance at the OAU presidency because of it. National budgets and national energies are sapped in Morocco and in Mauritania—and to some extent in Algeria. Restraint on the part of the United States has brought it no benefit in its relations with either Morocco or Algeria. Mediation may not satisfy the parties, but worried neutrality or careful verbal tilting is even worse. Although the Soviet Union has not appeared directly, its position in the conflict is not as uncomfortable as America's, and prolongation of the conflict could open the way to greater Russian penetration of the region and bipolarization.

Other conflicts in the 1970s did not provide as clear opportunities for mediation, and some were clearly impossible situations that were rightly avoided. Uganda was a rare case, where only violence could remove a violent regime, leaving its legacy to plague Idi Amin's successors. In Chad, until Libya intervened, the United States had neither interest nor leverage, and even France and Nigeria, which did, have failed. Once Libya intervened direcly to fill the vacuum, the United States and France urged the Africans collectively to provide their own peacekeeping force. In the event, if it did not keep the peace, the OAU Inter-African Force at least provided the conditions for a resolution of the Chadian conflict by the Chadians themselves. When Libya again intervened, France undertook a patient and delicate job of supporting the Chadian government and mediating the conflict. However, other conflicts are likely to arise in the 1990s to embroil African states and raise dangers of bipolarization unless they are managed and headed toward resolution in time.

One likely type of conflict results from a power vacuum on which outside forces press—for example, where succession problems combine with external intervention as they may in coming areas of tension like Uganda, Sierra Leone, Guinea, Mauritania, Tunisia, Zambia, and Sudan. Another type involves conflicts stemming from refugee pressures, not only in the Horn and in the Sahara, but also in Sudan, around Lake Chad, and along the new southern African battle line. A third category concerns pressure on ministates and enclaves, smaller power vacuums such as Djibouti, Cabinda, Swaziland, Lesotho and the Bantustans in South Africa, Walvis Bay, and the Spanish Mediterranean enclaves on the Moroccan coast. Finally, political conflicts arising from the need to share scarce resources will be an increasingly prominent type of conflict in the 1990s and beyond. Already Egypt and Ethiopia have opened a still symbolic conflict over the Nile waters (and indirectly over Sudan) between them.[3] Tunisia has squabbled with Libya and Algeria over undersea and undersand oil, and Nigeria, Equatorial Guinea, and Cameroon have also disputed offshore oil, as have Senegal and its two Guinean neighbors. The river boundaries and courses of southern Africa and the oil deposits and offshore resources of the continent, particularly when disputed by neighbors of different ideological tendencies, can turn into conflicts that require management and resolution.

It would not be very fruitful to make a balance sheet of costs and benefits in such likely but hypothetical cases. The list of potential conflicts alone suggests that conflict is dysfunctional, and equitable settlement is in American as well as African interest in such cases. The United States has no direct interest in these conflicts except the humanitarian one of avoiding death and economic ruin for the people of the area and the political one of avoiding Soviet and Cuban intervention on one side or the other. It is, moreover, unrealistic to call for U.S. mediation as a blanket policy. External powers such as the United States cannot spend all their time trying to resolve conflicts or have conflict management as their only policy; indeed, constant efforts may be self-defeating. Successful mediation depends on the course of conflict and the ripeness of the moment, to which the analysis now must turn.

Patterns

There was no lack of early warnings over Shaba I or Shaba II or over the Ogaden or Saharan wars or certainly over the Namibian conflict. What *was* absent was a sense of threshold or timing, an ability to determine whether a trigger event was a buildup to a larger crisis or merely a brief flare-up of hostilities. Also lacking was a sense of profile or evolution of events that could alert interested parties to the moment to move and the moment to wait.[4] The most important lesson to be drawn from the study of current African crises is that conflict resolution depends, above all, on the identification of the ripe moment in differing patterns of conflict and escalation.

Three distinct patterns of conflict appear very clearly in current African crises: the consummated crisis, the escalating crisis, and the grinding crisis. Each has very different implications for management and resolution. Opportunities for conflict management may be present even before hostilities or a crisis break out, but the conflict may not be at a level of demonstrable seriousness sufficient to warrant great power mediation. Mediation by African states can often be useful in such cases. Furthermore, it may be necessary to let the crisis blow up and then mediate disengagement. The parties can then show their own constituents that they have made the effort that justifies their acquiescence in the status quo or that confirms a relationship of power equality. This assumes, however, that the crisis will blow up without hurting anyone very badly—which is not always the case.

1. *Consummated crisis.* The consummated crisis has been the normal pattern of African crises: a sudden flare-up of military hostilities, in the extreme case resulting in an invasion, followed by defeat of the invaders and return to the status quo. Usually, the crisis runs until curent military stocks are depleted and then comes to a halt (frequently without much loss of territory) before any replenishment can occur. Conflict management consists in preventing replenishment and then providing the good offices necessary to arange a cease-fire and allow the participants to disengage with their honor intact. The more extreme the case—that is, the greater the penetration into

one territory and the greater the magnitude of the contending forces—the more difficult it is to negotiate a cease-fire ending the crisis and to enter into a settlement of the basic conflict beyond the crisis.

The extreme case of the pattern is the Ogaden War, which ran somewhat beyond current military stocks on the Somali side and well beyond current stocks on the Ethiopian side. A cease-fire occurred in the Ogaden in 1978, but it was never formally established, nor was the basis of the conflict ever touched. The cease-fire was soon broken. On the other hand, both crisis management (cease-fire) and conflict management (attenuation of other symptoms of the conflict) had been effected in the earlier Ogaden conflict of 1964.

Cease-fire ended the 1963 Moroccan-Algerian war, followed nine years later by an actual border treaty (conflict resolution), but a new crisis renewed the conflict. The status quo has frequently been formally recognized by the contending parties in other, lesser disputes, for example, the Ugandan-Tanzanian war of 1978, the Somali-Kenyan skirmishes of 1963–67, the Libyan-Egyptian crisis of 1978, and the Nigerian-Cameroonian crisis of 1981.

During the crisis the parties got bogged down either along the invasion front or in the return to the status quo. In the former case, conflict resolution is more likely to be based on change of the status quo. If Somalia had taken and held a portion of the Ogaden militarily and the parties had gotten stuck on the new battle line, they would have been more likely to address the issues underlying the conflict.

2. *Escalating crises.* Escalating crises are defined by a series of successive hostile outbreaks that follow each other closely at regular intervals and with increasing intensity. Such crises force themselves on the attention of the international community and impose questions about "the next time." Like the consummated crisis, they often return to the status quo at the end of the flare-up, but they do leave their mark. The difference between a single crisis and a series is, of course, only distinguishable after the second outbreak of hostilities. Once that has occurred, however, it radically changes the climate for conflict management and resolution. The escalation creates a series of peaks, which allows observers to "plot" the third crisis and motivates them to prevent it. Escalation also bestows a sibylline quality to the efforts of conflict resolution, for the terms of the reconciliation after the second round are usually worse for both parties than they could have been after the first, though better than they are likely to be after the third.

The Middle East wars are the prime example of escalating crises (well beyond two in number), but the eloquent case in Africa is the series of Shaba crises. There the second round led to reconciliation because it was more destructive than the first, because the parties had the resources (or the absence of controls) to have another go at it again in a more intense way the following year, because a third round would have had to be even worse, and because the return to the status quo showed that the outbursts were in themselves ineffective. The status quo held a powerful logic of its own. On the other hand, the Ogaden war of 1977 was the second peak of an escalating crisis, following the first of 1964, but the peaks were too far apart to be effective in motivating conflict resolution. The first round of the conflict had been forgotten, and indeed it had occurred under different administrations in both Somalia and Ethiopia. The Somali return to military engagement in 1980, provoking an Ethiopian response and thus threatening a third peak, did, however, bring the American government to consider putting the Ogaden on the political agenda. Similarly, the two Saharan wars (in 1963 and since 1975) were too far apart to be remembered as a series although the interlude was filled with alarums and excursions.

3. *Grinding crisis.* The variety of crisis known as the grinding crisis begins with a flare-up of hostilities that attracts international attention. But the crisis does not then return to the status quo ante; rather, it moves into stalemate on the basis of a different relationship between forces in which a new and unstable status quo is created. In such cases in Africa, one (or both) of the participants is often a leftover national liberation movement or runaway client seeking independent legitimacy and recognition. The stalemate allows it to attract attention and gradually assume legitimacy, often by accumulating the various accoutrements of recognition characteristic of current international relations—diplomatic recognition as a national liberation movement, observer status at the OAU or the UN, diplomatic recognition as a government in exile, state status—and the elements of political and military support that accompany such recognition. Usually, recognition is a goal of higher priority to the movement than victory in the crisis, in part because recognition is the precondition to any success. Recognition and legitimization permit negotiation; once they have been attained, conflict resolution can come into play to regularize the new status quo. The intervening step of recognition or legitimization is what makes conflict resolution so difficult—and drawn out—in a grinding crisis. Yet a positive out-

come to this step is not inevitable: At least one of the parties seeks to return the conflict to its bilateral interstate form and oblige the other state to recognize its patronage over the national liberation movement and reassert its control. Often the conflict is more manageable in its bilateral interstate form than in its trilateral form with the national liberation movement, but the battle over form takes a long time.

The Sahara issue, Chad, Namibia, and Zimbabwe exemplify this pattern. In all these cases, *both* sides have sought legitimization in the conflict as part of the new status quo: the Moroccans as well as the Polisario, the GUNT (Transitional Government) of Goukouni Weddei as well as the FAN (Northern Armed Forces) of Hissene Habre, the DTA/MPC as much as SWAPO, the Rhodesian government as well as the Patriotic Front. In the last two instances, it may be the internal organizations—DTA/MPC and the Smith-Muzorewa government—rather than the externals that benefited most from legitimization through stalemate. Once legitimacy as a participant (not as the sole winner) has been established, conflict resolution has a chance. The point is important for third-party mediators, who are sometimes so busy working on the legitimization of one participant that they forget the other—which then ends up too weak, relatively, to negotiate, but too strong to be destroyed.

The pattern as a whole, however, is typical of African crises, which tend to bog down in stalemate because the participants lack the necessary capability to escalate and because the crises are at too low a level to attract the attention of conciliators. Where more powerful parties might commit the resources required to provide a decisive turn to the conflict, African states and insurgent forces do well just to hang on. Those cases that are characteristic of this pattern are the ones that have no deadline, no decisive pressures to come to terms, and no resolution.

Dimensions

Within these crisis patterns, three dimensions determine the suitability of the moment for conflict resolution. One is the vertical dimension of *intensity*, often referred to as *escalation*; the second, the horizontal dimension of *alternatives*, often discussed here as *policy tracks*; and the third, the *power relations*.

Decisions to escalate and de-escalate and to choose among alternative strategies are turning points that define the possibilities of conflict resolution. In Shaba, there were two FLNC decisions to escalate the conflict with Zaire, in early 1977 and early 1978; their implementation in March and May, respectively, immediately triggered two Zairean decisions to counterescalate with foreign assistance, and the unsuccessful counterattack in 1978 finally prepared the way for a mutual decision by Zaire and Angola in June of that year to reconcile differences over the heads of the national liberation movements. In the Horn, a Somali decision to prepare guerrilla warfare in early 1975 was followed by a decision to commit regular army units to the attack in mid-1977; it was met by the counterescalating Ethiopian decisions to invite foreign assistance in November and to counterattack in February 1978, then to stop at the border in March, and then to go on in 1982. This time the successful counterattacks led neither side to a decision to reconcile. In the Sahara, the Moroccan-Mauritanian decision to appeal to the World Court in 1974 was followed by the Moroccan decision to escalate the conflict with Spain through a civilian invasion in October 1975 and then to de-escalate by settling out of court and off the battlefield in November. Polisario countered by deciding to oppose the subsequent military takeover of the area, but was defeated. This defeat led to a decision in mid-1976 to focus on Mauritania and then to the decision in July 1978 to concentrate on Morocco through attacks on both sides of its pre-1975 borders. Morocco then changed its military strategy, and Polisario decided to turn to the political battlefield and to Libyan support. The Moroccan tactical decisions of 1980 brought much of the territory under its control, but the Polisario decision to push for an OAU membership made the king decide to accept a referendum, but too late. Stalemate finally brought on Algerian decision, imposed on the Polisario, to seek (and grant) a political solution rather than maintain the deadlock.

In Namibia, the South African decision to elaborate confederal independence in 1975 was followed by the decision to prepare unitary independence in 1977, taken under Western pressure, and then implemented as an electoral decision in December 1978, again without decisive outcome or effective counteraction. Subsequent South African decisions to destabilize after 1980 and to disengage in 1984 and 1988 led to many probes and a split among decisionmakers on both the Angolan and South African sides. What makes for ripeness in these patterns of escalation?

1. The point when conflict is ripe for resolution is associated with two different sorts of intensity—called here *plateaus* and the *precipice*—which produce different sorts of pressure—called respectively *deadlocks* and *deadlines*. A plateau and its deadlock begin when one

side is unable to achieve its aims, to resolve the problem, or to win the conflict by itself, and they are completed when the other side arrives at a similar perception. Each party must begin to feel uncomfortable in the costly dead-end into which it has gotten itself. A plateau must be perceived by both not as a momentary resting ground, but as a hurting stalemate, a flat, unpleasant terrain stretching into the future, providing no later possibilities for decisive escalation or for graceful escape.

Conflict resolution plays on perceptions of an intolerable situation: Things "can't go on like this." Without this perception, the conciliator must persuade the parties that escalation to break out of deadlock is impossible. Indeed, the conciliator may even be required to *make* it impossible, if necessary. Thus, deadlock cannot be seen merely as a temporary stalemate, to be easily resolved in one's favor by a little effort or even by a big offensive or a gamble or foreign assistance. Rather, each party must recognize its opponent's strength and its own inability to overcome it.

For the conciliator, this means emphasizing the dangers of deadlock as each party comes to recognize the other's strength. Each party's unilateral policy option (the action that it can take alone without negotiation) must be seen as a more expensive and less likely way of achieving a possible, acceptable outcome than the policy of negotiation. A plateau is thus as much a matter of perception as of reality for the parties and as much a subject of persuasion as of timing for the conciliator. Successful conciliation produces a shift from a winning mentality to a conciliating mentality on the part of both sides. This shift is obviously a delicate matter. It occurred in Angola and Zaire after Shaba II, and it may have occurred temporarily with Algeria and Morocco in 1978, 1983, and 1988; with SWAPO and South Africa during 1978, again in 1980, 1982, and again in 1984 and 1988; and in Ethiopia and Somalia between 1986 and 1988.

A *precipice* is, of course, the conceptual opposite of a plateau. It represents a realization by both sides that matters will swiftly get worse if they have not gotten better in ways that negotiation seeks to define. Here a catastrophe threatens the mutual checks the parties impose on each other. A precipice can be an impending catastrophe, as the term implies, or one that has been encountered narrowly and just missed. But it can also be a catastrophe that has just occurred or one into which the parties are already sinking deeper and deeper. Kennedy and Khrushchev negotiated the Cuban missile crisis under the first conditions; Sadat and Meir negotiated the Sinai disengagements under the second; Neto and Mobutu negotiated Shaba II under the third; and Nkomo, Mugabe, and Smith negotiated the Zimbabwe settlement under the fourth.

In Africa, as elsewhere, conflict resolution—when it comes—comes most frequently after a crisis has just occurred, with losses on both sides, that has left the basic conflict unresolved. The tragedy of the Capulets and the Montagues is the dominant setting of conflicts that need resolution. Yet these conditions also pose problems for mediation.

First, they leave a memory of bitterness that hampers conflict resolution. A stalemated crisis that has involved the army alone is likely to be shrugged off as a case of casualties for those whose business it is to inflict and to bear them. But a recent tragedy with innocent victims carries bitterness along with its shock. Through their deaths, the Europeans and South Africans in Shaba contributed a shock effect that hurried resolution, but victims in other attacks in the Sahara, Namibia, and the Horn only made relations worse.

Second, a catastrophe come and gone sets no deadline. Conflict resolution depends on a sense of urgency; without a deadline for agreement, parties become accustomed to living with a receding sense of shock. When a deadline is set, the impending, rather than the recent, catastrophe is clearly a much more effective anchor. When conflict resolution follows the close call or the catastrophe, there is often a need for mediators to create a subsequent, artificial deadline. Like Secretary Kissinger and President Carter in the Middle East, Lord Carrington at Lancaster House made his own deadlines in the absence of those naturally imposed by events—and enforced them with a threat to withdraw from the conciliation process.

2. The second dimension of conflict resolution concerns policy tracks or alternatives. The conciliator's task is to deflect the parties from competing attempts to impose unilateral solutions (first tracks) and into a joint search for a bilateral solution (second track).

The mediator's challenge is to present to the conflicting parties an alternative that incorporates some of the goals of their first tracks while eliminating or reconciling their more conflictual elements. Two separate actions are involved: First tracks must be blocked, and a second track must be found and sold to the two parties. Conflict resolution, therefore, depends as much on rendering the conflict option unattractive as on conveying an attractive option of management and resolution. These are, of course, related; the attractiveness of the second is a function of the unattractiveness of the first.

First tracks can be blocked or rendered unattractive at several points in their course: in the beginning, in progress, and at the moment of final choice. Initially, the parties can be persuaded that their chances of effectively pursuing the conflict are slim. This strategy is obviously preferable to later blocking, for it reduces costs in lives and property, but because no one can be sure the first track might not have been productive if the mediators had not meddled in the conflict, it is difficult to achieve. South Africa's Turnhalle was a first track that was deflected toward the second before it got very far because it looked likely to fail even before it began. Conflict can also be stymied either through loss of momentum or when one party blocks the other or is even blocked by the mediator. Zimbabwe is an African example of the latter two possibilities during 1979. Such a situation is difficult although if it brings a solution favorable to the probable eventual winner while saving something for the other party, as in Zimbabwe, it still is advantageous.

Finally, first tracks that have reached an unsatisfactory dead-end can be used to spur conflict resolution. The repeated inability of the FLNC to achieve its aims and of Zaire to prevent FLNC attacks contributed to a search for a second-track alternative. But the ineffectiveness of the first tracks had to be shown, rather than argued in prospect, for predictions of failure were not convincing.

Mediators' efforts to switch the parties from first- to second-track strategies are complicated by some strong contrary tendencies. Growing attachment to first-track strategies despite any inherent attractiveness of alternatives can take three forms: the bargaining chip, the sidetrack, and the overcommitment. Bargaining chips are unilateral policy options that are invented in order to enhance a party's bargaining position, but that sometimes take on a life and attractiveness of their own. Produced to threaten the other side, their threat value depends on their viability; but their very viability may set them up as rivals to the second tracks they were designed to reinforce. South Africa's internal election plan, if it was intended as a threat alone, is an example of a tactic that was kept alive and up-to-date until it finally displaced the other track. The UN General Assembly's recognition of SWAPO as sole and legitimate spokespersons and South Africa's nonnegotiable position on Walvis Bay are further examples. The Polisario may have started out as an Algerian first track that subsequently became so important an investment that the Algerians could not abandon it. Changing Zairean and Angolan attitudes toward the FLNA and FLNC, on the other hand, show that bargaining chips can be dropped if the outcome is worth it.

Sidetracks occur when a party reacts to counterthreats against its own position and loses sight of its goals, thereby confusing means for ends. Parties can become so involved in secondary escalations that they are unable to respond to attempts at conflict resolution though they are also unable to pursue a successful first-track strategy. King Hassan's refusal to attend meetings with President BenJedid on pretexts afforded by various Polisario attacks and Boumedienne's refusal to continue talks with Morocco because of differences over the Egyptian peace initiative are examples of sidetracked strategy that was not purposely oriented either toward winning unilaterally or reaching agreement multilaterally.

Overcommitments occur when a party is so procedurally or emotionally attached to track one that it cannot switch to the other track no matter how attractive the potential reconciliation and no matter what substantive bridging of differences might have been accomplished. Parties usually make one last attempt at improving their position on the ground before making the final negotiated agreement. This must not be mistaken (sidetracked) by the other party as bad faith, and it must not become so successful as to deter the first party from following through with an agreement. South Africa's deep raids in 1978, 1980, and 1982 and SWAPO's in 1983 and 1984 illustrate all these dangers. Parties also usually make—or are ready for—one last attempt at reconciliation before implementing a first track already prepared, but sometimes such attempts are too late for the party itself to be able to uncouple from first-track commitments, particularly in regard to parts of its home establishment. Sadat could not enter into mediation attempts in the summer of 1973, and Mengistu could not answer calls for negotiations by the Eritrean guerrillas in the summer of 1978 or with the Somali guerrillas in late 1977, just before each country's big offensives. Both would have lost credit in the eyes of their military had they decided to talk at that point. The moment was ripe for war, not for resolution.

Finally, there are dangers of commitment for the mediator as well. It has been asserted here—perhaps controversially—that the mediator may actually have to be engaged in the conflict to the extent of blocking one party's attempts at a unilateral solution that is unstable or otherwise undesirable in order for a multilateral solution to be found. Yet the mediator must not become overcommitted to one side in perception or in reality. The danger is often present, and most successful mediators skirt it rather than avoiding it completely. In the Arab-Israeli mediations of the 1970s and in Lebanon in 1982–83, the United States acted effectively even though it was closely involved— and closely perceived as being involved—with Israel's war effort. In Zimbabwe, the Anglo-American mediators were perceived by each party as being too sympathetic to the other, and that same perception has slowed down Namibian talks throughout their course. Yet the United States and its Western associates mediated a reconciliation after Shaba despite their close ties with Zaire and their strained relations with Angola. The United States made a major error in the early 1980s by not coupling its reactivated arms supply role for Morocco with audible insistence on a political solution. It thereby contributed to the perceived "bipolarization" of the conflict and made it more difficult to mediate. The mediator sometimes cannot avoid a blocking role with regard to a party's first track, but that role must be coupled with equally strenuous efforts to open up a mutually attractive second track at the same time.

3. Thus far, the discussion has assumed a symmetry in the parties' positions, with no consideration of the fact that two parties are likely to travel down their first tracks at different rates with different ups and downs. Obviously, the mediator is out of a job when one party's first track becomes decisive in the conflict. But before that point, there may still be enough asymmetry between the two parties' positions that one of them may entertain hopes of unilaterally deciding the outcome. Because the parties may not be of equal strength or position in the conflict, the proper moment for mediation occurs when the upper hand starts slipping and the underdog starts rising.

Decolonization provided classical cases of this effect, with the conciliator playing a facilitating role. When the former ruling power felt its time had come and wanted to come to terms before it lost everything and when the nationalist movement felt its strength growing and wanted to win early and cheaply rather than face a protracted struggle (and possibly the replacement of current leaders by more radical rivals), then the moment was ripe for a conciliator to step in. These elements constitute a nutshell description of what happened in Zimbabwe and at least a major ingredient in the parties' motivations in Namibia as well. The slipping trends were not clear enough in the Horn or in the Sahara to provide an obviously ripe moment.

In sum, the success of mediation is tied to the perception and creation of a ripe moment in the conflict—either when the parties are locked in a mutual, hurting stalemate marked by a recent or impending catastrophe; when unilateral solutions are blocked and joint solutions become conceivable; or when the "ups" and "downs" start to shift their relative power positions. Parties can come to perceive these moments themselves, to be sure, but they frequently need the help of a conciliator. Once the moment has come, parties and mediator can turn to the more creative, meticulous, trial-and-error job of finding an acceptable way out of the conflict.

Conceptually, the moment stands out, but in reality it is buried in the rubble of events. Even when clearly defined, it may be recognized only after it has passed, but by the same token, it cannot be recognized at all if not clearly defined. Once would-be conciliators sense its approach, they then have the difficult task of bringing the parties to recognize that the time has come. Diplomats often complain that their leverage is so limited in the absolute and also in relation to the parties' expectations, and this is, of course, very true. Mediators are not magicians, pulling solutions out of hats. They are patient, persistent, dogged workers, gradually pressing to change perceptions and behaviors. Their leverage comes primarily from their ability to construct a perception of a better outcome for both parties than the one at the end of the plateau or the first track, not from any dominant relationship that allows them to pull strings on puppets. The United States did not have the leverage that was sometimes expected over Hassan II or Ian Smith or P. W. Botha or Haile Selassie or Siad Barre or Mobutu. But in some cases it kept on trying and eventually, with some help from its friends, brought Mobutu, Smith, and others to a solution.

Like any metaphor, the idea of the ripe moment should not be taken too literally. Moments, when ripe, do not fall into one's hands; they have to be taken with skill. Furthermore, in an imperfect world, moments are rarely totally ripe, or, no matter how ripe they are, there are usually counterindications and communications problems that can make them most unready for treatment if mishandled. Indeed, across enough time, there is an evolution composed of a few somewhat ripe moments that, if well handled, can serve to move the conflict toward a solution and that are separated by distinctly unpromising periods that may even worsen or set back the conflict. Failures and near misses at the riper times, including inconclusive crises, can shape the terms of reference for a solution. Thus, for the conciliating power, it is a question not only of correctly identifying the right times to move but also of moving the times with skill.

Methods of Conflict Management and Resolution

Only time resolves conflicts, but time needs some help. Yet if conflict resolution is rare, its frustrations should not dissuade conciliators from seeking conflict management instead by inhibiting the pursuit of conflict and creating a momentum that parties can follow to gradual coexistence and toward resolution. Unlike conflict, with its diverse patterns, conciliation follows essentially one pattern, in which both the substantive shape of an agreeable solution and its procedural complement of the ripe moment are present. What does vary considerably is the degree of management and resolution that can be accomplished, given the type and pattern of the conflict.

Trust between the parties has been cited by diplomats as the defining element for the moment of ripeness. But that confuses cause and effect. If trust were required, mediation would not be necessary. What is actually indispensable, however, is trust in the conciliator, who then builds trust between the parties by becoming a channel between them. Indeed, it is the initial absence of trust between the parties that makes the conciliator's role necessary. But trust should also be strengthened during the resolution process. The parties must be brought to understand better the motives and interests that impel each other and to see the necessity of curtailing and adjusting their own. They must also be brought to convince each other of their good faith, credibility, and reliability. Otherwise, the conflict will move into crisis again the moment the conciliator turns his back or the moment a new interstate incident arises.

On the other hand, internal strength of the parties is rarely given the importance it deserves in analyses of conciliation. Parties need to be domestically strong to make foreign concessions. When internally weak, divided, or beleaguered, parties will not—or will not be able to—make the compromises that could be used against them by their threatening opposition. Obviously, strength must be divided into arenas, such as domestic and foreign, for if a party were strong enough in its external position, it would not have to make compromises. But its internal strength is another matter. The cases here are nearly unanimous in supporting this important element, which often overrides other dimensions in the definition of the ripe moment. Only when Mobutu had been rescued from attack and had shown his standing among his supporters was he able to negotiate, and only after Neto had overcome the revolt of Nito Alves did he join as well. Only when Chadli BenJedid had accomplished his domestic consolidation of power could he meet Hassan II. Hassan could only make his original concession at Nairobi in 1981 after he had overcome his domestic riots (which almost disrupted the king's trip to Nairobi, with foreseeably fatal results for the conflict), and he met BenJedid as his domestic control was being consolidated in the elections of the summer of 1983. Botha and Dos Santos never felt strong enough at home until 1984 to make the concessions necessary for an agreement, and one might surmise that Mengistu and Siad Barre were not secure enough even by then. Unfortunately, of course, domestic strength is only a necessary but not a sufficient condition for conciliation, and it alone does not guarantee a ripe moment.

The conciliator's job runs through four phases: *contacts*, *deadlock*, *proposal*, and *implementation*. The phases are not sequential, but rather mutually reinforcing, cumulative, and even circular: The first phase continues even after the second begins, and both continue through the third and then the fourth.

Effective preemptive action requires a diplomatic presence. American sources of information and diplomatic leverage were badly hampered in two of the four cases previously discussed by the absence of an ambassador for extended periods: In Ethiopia for two years there was no chief of mission, and in Angola there never has been an embassy. In the latter case, if sending an ambassador with a full-size mission would be too much of a statement, a liaison officer (as was used in Chad and in Rhodesia) would be an effective intermediate measure and would convey a useful message as well. The notion that American recognition is a good that should be withheld until the recipient demonstrates suitable behavior makes the United States an international licensing agency rather than a state trying to act effectively.

Proscriptions against dealings with national liberation movements and the notion that official diplomats can talk only to recognized state representatives come from a bygone notion that meeting is recognizing and recognizing is approving. These are compounded by the special problems noted earlier about the legitimizing of national liberation movements—especially when they are enemies of U.S. allies. Although ways of getting around this problem are tricky and only semieffective, the inhibition against Western diplomats' contacting Polisario representatives (not to speak of the downright embarrassing proscription against contacts with the Palestine Liberation Organization) is a senseless barrier against necessary information gathering.

Effective preemptive action requires a sense of ideological disinterest and forward commitment. Nostalgia for a friendly but dead emperor, antipathy to a Marxist but incumbent regime, righteous condemnation of revolutionaries and terrorists' sympathizers are all luxuries of true belief that obscure the real goal of policy. Policy makers are too frequently pressed by public interest groups to establish a foreign policy position through condemnation rather than through effective action. In a world of Marxists and monarchs, terrorists and colonialists, it may be hard to recognize "our own kind" and painful to have to deal with brutish and ruthless rulers. In some cases, such as Namibia, American negotiators have been remarkably deft in dealing with all kinds of parties, but in other caes the insistence on "reform first and conflict resolution afterward" makes the fleeting ripe moment hard to grasp.

Conflict resolution is best carried out in concert. If a number of conciliators are available to the parties themselves and if a number of friends of the conflicting parties can coordinate their good offices and pressure, the chances of success are improved. When agreement on a proposal is being arranged, it is best to start with allies of the principals, as was done in Namibia and Zimbabwe. By the same token, it is important that a conciliator bring its own allies along in the effort; an attempt to resolve conflict by a Great Power (like the United States) when a secondary power with close African ties (such as Britain or France) is sitting it out or quietly undermining the effort is a handicapped race. Indeed, the European ally at times is best suited to lead the mediation; and the United States, best suited to support (as in Chad), provided that mediation does take place. The resolution of conflict in Africa demands extremely close coordination with both African states and European powers. One might even include the Soviet Union where relevant although the U.S.S.R. has never operated very effectively in such a collaborative role. (Indeed, the Soviet Union has rarely mediated effectively to reduce conflict, even when operating alone, and has only sought to benefit from others' efforts.)

In the second stage of conciliation, the conciliator must use his soundings of the parties to convince them that *deadlock* potentially lies at the end of their first tracks and that catastrophe impends or would be required to break that deadlock. Then, this perception must be reinforced with a *deadline* or moment when things will become worse if something is not done about them. Deadlines work best if they are independent of the conciliator, but they may need recalling, reinforcing, and even sanctioning in order to be made to hold. Boxed in, the parties should begin looking about for some help out of their problem—including a conciliator with some good ideas.

Southern Africa, in the Shaban and Zimbabwean conciliations, provides the best examples of this felt need, although the pair of combatants in the Saharan crisis, more than those in the Horn of Africa, eventually felt the need for a conciliator when they felt boxed in by their problem. The conflict that is closest to building its own box is the Eritrean one, where—unique among African disputes—the Soviet Union is best placed to offer good offices because of its ideological affinities for both sides.

Reinforcing the attractions of compromise may require using both carrots and sticks. Inducements may include economic and military aid, arms sales, supportive policy statements, and other instruments of diplomacy. Whereas positive inducements tend to be costly and habit-forming when they succeed, they also tend to create a more agreeable relationship and to be additionally useful as a basis for negative sanctions at another time. Negative inducements, too, can only be used sparingly by a conciliator. They most frequently take the form of contingent withdrawal of benefits, or threats, but may also be framed as warnings, or authoritative indications of unpleasant consequences outside the control of the parties (as, for example, in the comments of Secretary Kissinger during the Mideast shuttles).

Beyond this, however, the reinforcement of conflict is often required to force recognition of the deadlock and the deadline. This may mean reinforcing a faltering party, as France tried to do with Mauritania in 1977 (albeit unsuccessfully) or as the West did twice with Zaire. A Morocco or Somalia with its back to the wall will never get an Algeria or an Ethiopia to recognize its grievance, but will still be strong enough to cause trouble for friends and neighbors alike. As already noted, military aid to one side does not prevent the donor from also being an effective conciliator, especially if the aid is used to bring concessions from the aided party.

In fact, the relationships with both sides of a well-placed conciliator can provide a ready supply of carrots and sticks, making the conciliator a distant balance-holder. By shifting weight from one party to the other in the conflict, a conciliator can reinforce deadlock and enforce deadline, particularly if it is able to reduce support for a client that is on top but not firmly enough to be able to win. The Kissinger-Sadat strategy in the Middle East is the best example, but the Shaba negotiations are also a case in point.

The many real limitations must be acknowledged, however. Two cannot play the game lest a shifting of weight become a *renversement des alliances*, as in the Horn. Moreover, if the conciliator's own ally is not on top, shifting weight may merely serve to weaken one side without buying concessions from the other, as in American policy toward Morocco during the early years of the Saharan dispute.

The stage of the *proposal* comes when the parties have been convinced they need a way out, although sometimes a proposal is needed even earlier to bring out the insufficiencies of the first track.

The characteristic of the successful second track is a formula that frames the nature of the solution, either defining the terms of trade or establishing a principle to be applied to both parties. The formula must appear relatively just and satisfactory to both parties, must therefore cover major issues of the conflict (although not necessarily all of them), and must include important demands from both sides (not necessarily all of them)—enough to ensure compliance with the agreement. The formula in Shaba was the mutual restraint of hostile movements and the mutual return of refugees; the formula in Namibia was one-man-one-vote elections under paired UN-South African auspices, augmented in the Reagan round to cover also South African withdrawal in exchange for Cuban withdrawal. A number of formulas available in the Sahara and the Horn of Africa have been discussed, but none of them has been the right one at the right moment although a Moroccan north and a Polisario south associated with Mauritania is the most prominent formula for the Sahara.

Principles—such as self-determination, the inviolability of frontiers, or noninterference in internal affairs—are important legitimizers for political solutions and should be used as such, but should not dictate the choice of the solution. Principles are no guide to a choice among themselves; indeed, the cause of conflict can usually be traced to the parties' self-interested adherence to *conflicting* principles. It is better to seek a balanced distribution of power than to apply a pure principle. A Saharan outcome that merely states that a specific referendum is the only correct translation of self-determination but that does not handle the problems of Algero-Moroccan relations or the nature of the Mauritanian entity is no solution. An agreement to one-man-one-vote in Namibia that does not deal with problems of structural relations in southern Africa would be ephemeral. An outcome in the Horn of Africa that merely reaffirms the sanctity of inherited boundaries perpetuates the conflict.

Conflict resolution requires an outcome that has something for everyone. Parties cannot be expected to give up their claims without receiving compensation. Somalia cannot be expected to settle its problems with Ethiopia merely in return for a pat on the head from the world community. Resolution of the Saharan crisis cannot be accomplished without giving something to Morocco, something to Algeria, and, unless it is destroyed (which seems very unlikely), something to the Polisario as well. Simple as this idea may be, it seems to be difficult for Americans in particular to remember in the heat of conflict, in part because policy-makers are pressed to view conflicts in zero-sum terms as a matter of right and principle and in part because adversary proceedings and debating contests are so much a part of the American way of doing things.

In some cases, it will be possible to work directly toward a solution and, in others, only to get agreement on a first step that points the conflict in a more manageable direction. The conciliator should have an idea of a feasible and conceivable outcome and work toward it. Without some notion of a goal, process can lose its direction. Nonetheless, the goal should not be held to against all contrary movement and evidence from the discussion, but should be viewed flexibly. It should not be imposed on the parties but should be made to grow out of contacts with them.

Projecting a solution ahead of time permits separation of the conflict into those aspects that can be included in the settlement and those that must be left to the healing effects of time. (This distinction may also separate out knotty issues that can be resolved after the general settlement, such as Walvis Bay in Namibia or the composition of the army in Zimbabwe, from those susceptible of immediate settlement.) Management of the immediate crisis is more acceptable to the parties when they see possibilities for the resolution of the deeper conflict as well. At this point the conciliator cannot be expected to chaperon the parties until all their disputes are resolved, but can be expected to include provisions whereby the parties are headed toward working out an agreement on their own, perhaps with the pressures or monitoring of the OAU. For management is not enough, and the idea that managed conflicts can be forgotten even though the basic conflict is not touched is a dangerous illusion. More often than not, they break out again, with renewed violence, in a worse form, at a worse time, easily ignited by a new incident, posing the problem of both management and resolution all over again.

Projecting a solution also permits consideration of the best relations between procedural and substantive elements. Although procedural solutions such as referenda or adjudication are no substitute for substantive solutions, they may be the best available. They are neutral in appearance, for the conciliator is not opting for one type of outcome but merely for one way in which an outcome can be reached, substituting a peaceful for a violent means of conducting conflict. Procedural solutions have a further advantage of setting up new patterns and routines that can help the parties through the early phase of weakly institutionalized relations.

But the limitations of procedural solutions are considerable. They are accepted by both sides because each thinks it will win, and after the results are in, disappointment can be violent. The only exception is those situations where a procedural solution effectively removes one of the parties, as in Zimbabwe; but even there the losers of the election were only removed from formal power. Where the parties remain to challenge the procedural results, procedural solutions are shaky. Wherever possible, referenda should be used to ratify, not to establish, terms of agreement.

Agreement in the formula stage should be signed and publicly agreed to before the search for implementing details begins to tear at the agreement. This may be a pious wish, and in the case where it could have been helpful—Namibia—it was hard enough to get even a tentative agreement (that later fell apart), let alone a signed one. In the Sahara, there was both general and specific agreement among the parties at a number of points, which still did not prevent a total collapse of understanding, but more explicit and public statements— by Algeria, for example, of its commitments—would have prevented backtracking. Nonetheless, an agreement in stages can be helpful in building assurance. (If the agreement on a general level is accompanied by some gesture of de-escalation—exchange of prisoners, regrouping, amnesties, end of hostile propaganda—momentum can be increased.)

Finally, the *implementation* stage requires another expenditure of vigilance and perhaps pressure from the conciliator. If secrecy is useful during the diplomatic discussion, publicity is necessary during the implementation to enhance commitment and keep the process honest. Public statements, monitoring, and witnessing are all helpful instruments to ensure implementation. Like solemn and public marriage celebrations, conflict resolutions should be given the maximum ceremonial attention to assist their future observance.

Implementation goes on and on. To be fully effective, conflict resolution must contain means for handling future incidents that will certainly challenge the present conciliation. Therefore, part of the agreement should include machinery for dealing with foreseeable problems, either through an affirmation of normal procedures or through a provision of exceptional mechanisms. The Shaba agreements provided for means of handling refugee repatriation; the Zimbabwe and proposed Namibia agreements provided for normal state machinery with some special provisions to govern relations among the parties in their new independent situation. Unless some provisions are made for future eventualities as well as for past grievances, the conciliation will soon fall apart under new attacks.

Policy

America needs—and Africa deserves—a policy that recognizes the importance of Africa to the United States within the context of its global obligations. Elements of such a policy include recognition of opportunities for trade and investment that are rapidly growing in the continent, identification of important states with realistic policies who deserve economic support and assistance, and a limited arms transfer policy that is prepared to meet only legitimate, basic defense needs. But none of these is adequate by itself, and none is complete without an active policy focused on the resolution of interstate conflict.

The United States has a broad range of concerns in Africa, including business investments and trade, access to raw materials, support for political equality and racial justice, avoidance of global conflict and domination by hostile foreign powers, and encouragement of African political systems capable of developing citizen participation and solving national problems. American interest lies in a stable African development process that may in many instances prevent instability and conflict from overcoming the frail possibilities of progress and from embroiling outside powers. Particularly at a time when many African countries are facing catastrophic conditions of underdevelopment and difficulties in achieving growth in a depressed world economy, the mitigation of conflict that may obstruct domestic development is crucial.

Opting for a policy of crisis management means that the United States must be willing to play an active role, seeking solutions, applying pressure, and enforcing deadlines—rather than simply exhibiting an endless supply of patience and inaction. Obviously, this is not a policy for every little crisis or for every deep-seated conflict. But it is a policy that recognizes that Africa can no longer be cordoned off and left to its own squabbles. On the contrary, African disputes are now long and deep enough so that even if America is not initially involved, it will very likely find itself drawn in later at a higher and less manageable level of conflict. Greater involvement early on, therefore, means less danger of involvement on the wrong terms—and perhaps with global implications—later.

The policy debate usually breaks down at this point into so-called globalist and Africanist perspectives. The first assumes that Africa is unimportant in and of itself and becomes of interest to the United States only when the bipolar strategic balance is affected. The other assumes that African affairs have causes and values of their own and can only be understood and participated in on the level of African interests. The discussion becomes a debate solely when argued in its extremes, for, in fact, each side's appreciation is correct if it drops the "only"—its exclusive claim to wisdom.

As this brief summary suggests, a policy of positive and active attention can be justified both from an Africanist and a globalist perspective. If American policy is to find its justification in terms of American interests, the globalist perspective provides the best rationale for a positive, active policy whereas the Africanist perspective provides the best understanding of the terrain to which policy is directed. It is helpful to deal with objections to conflict resolution, as raised by one school or the other in order to understand more fully how such a policy would work.[5]

First, it is sometimes argued that conflict resolution in Africa is up to the Africans because it falls within the mandate of the Organization for African Unity. Indeed, as is not often recognized, mediation within the OAU has been quite successful in resolving low-level squabbles, particularly those involving personal disputes among African leaders. In more serious disputes, African mediation was more effective in the first decade of the OAU, when the first round of conflict management in the Sahara and the Horn was carried out, than during the second. Its effectiveness has depended, above all, on treating a problem before it draws in outside allies, parties either African or extra-African. Once that happens, a conflict becomes much more difficult for African states to handle.

OAU mediations have generally been carried out by one or more heads of state, friends but usually not neighbors of the disputing parties, who provide good offices between the disputants. But in the 1970s and early 1980s, this role has been limited, primarily for two reasons: On the one hand, disputes escalated too rapidly toward external alliance to be manageable, and, on the other, the organization was progressively paralyzed by a series of crises in which action was blocked—Congo (Zaire), Biafra, Rwanda, Burundi, Uganda, Sudan, Angola, Chad—because they were defined as "internal affairs." As a result, the OAU members were unable to decide on the organization's proper role and the way to pursue it. In other conflicts, those relating to southern Africa, the OAU is itself a party, albeit a weak one, and consequently able neither to win nor to resolve the conflict.[6]

In the crises of the 1970s and 1980s, many African states acting collectively within or outside the OAU have played a variety of roles, but they have been most effective when working with an interested outside conciliator (though in none of these cases did the African states lose their own goals, interests, and autonomy). In the Shaba and in the southern African cases of Zimbabwe and Namibia, African states collaborated effectively with Western efforts to manage the conflict by pressing the parties to negotiate. Nigeria and the front-line states made a sovereign contribution to a common effort that ended in success in two of the three cases. Moreover, in Shaba, a number of African states contributed to an inter-African force and thus helped reduce the chances of recurrence.

In the unsuccessful cases in the northeastern and northwestern corners of the continent, the situation was different: Not only was there no external mediation effort, but the African groups of Wise-men sent by the OAU lacked the leverage that outside powers might have been able to apply. In both cases, resolution of the basic conflict was subordinated to the OAU norm, affirming the legitimacy of colonially inherited boundaries and units. (On the other hand, no OAU norms prevent states from coming to a peaceful agreement among themselves for the solution of outstanding—even territorial—problems.) In sum, African efforts at conflict resolution are not an alternative to American (or other Western) efforts, but rather a necessary concomitant.

Second, it might be objected that to proffer good offices is risky. Because a mediated solution involves total satisfaction for neither party, the conciliator may well end up with more enemies than it had at the start. What good will it do America to meddle in the quarrels of faraway Africans?

Despite all the rhetoric about nonalignment and decolonization, both Africa and the West consider their worlds to be related. Non-alignment would not need to be proclaimed in Africa if it were not contesting a different perception just as there would be no Western talk of "losing Africa" if some notion—no matter how mistaken—of "having it" did not persist. There is no doubt that the dominant foreign presence in Africa is Western, that African states were born of Western values, and that the dependency doctrines correspond to certain aspects of reality. If there is some perceived responsibility, there should be a role for the West that minimizes the temptations of other outside powers. What kind of societies and relations can the West encourage in its sphere of influence? Conflict resolution is part of the answer.

Compared with other types of intervention, conflict resolution is likely to be the "safest" course. In a choice between winning and conciliating, the first would be tempting if it were that clear and simple. But the choice is not clear because the identification of a great power with only one side in an African dispute is usually not direct and unambiguous and is not simple because even a "winning" intervention becomes less decisive when it provides the excuse for counterintervention by another great power.

One of the dangers of Third World relations for a great power is too close an attachment to an erratic and unreliable client whose real interests and capabilities prevent it from ever (in the working future) being an ally. To be sure, some states have been associated with the West in recent conflicts—formerly Ethiopia in the Horn, Morocco in the Sahara, Zaire in Shaba. But African allies are uncertain, as the events of the Horn show. Great power division of Africa, which would permit writing off one of the states in an African conflict, is not in the American interest, as the Saharan case shows. Even when one state is closely tied to the West, both influence and independence vis-à-vis the African state can be gained only through a certain distance between the two parties, as Zaire shows.

Thus, supporting one party's drive to victory may assure some benefits if it works, but at the high cost of serious involvement in the conflict and of incurring the animosity of the other side. The policy of friendly assistance to both sides in overcoming their mutual problem may not succeed either, but even in failure it can foster good relations with both sides while at the same time leaving the great power in a position of independence vis-à-vis the parties. The role of a conciliator is a more benign and less domineering role for a great power than that of direct intervention, but with greater influence on outcomes than that of total abstention.

The strongest argument for a policy of crisis resolution is the avoidance of outcomes that would necessitate future involvement in a worse crisis at times not of our choosing. The Western Sahara or the Ogaden or the location of the battleline/buffer in southern Africa may be of no direct concern to the United States (although the same cannot be said of Shaba), but as open sores they are attractions to rival powers, they obstruct cooperative policy actions, and they overload the capabilities of the international system. The Horn of Africa provides compelling evidence, for it was the territorial dispute, not merely an ideological affinity, that made both Somalia and Ethiopia invite the Soviets in. The Sahara and Shaba are just as eloquent: Unresolved in the first round (1963 in the Sahara, 1977 in Shaba), the conflict returned with increased ferocity in the second round to do real damage to Western interests.

Therefore, if conflicts can be portrayed as burdens on the parties, creating troubled waters in which outside powers can fish, conflict resolution can be seen as beneficial to all. In a policy of conflict resolution, the problem—and not one of the parties—is the "opponent." If conflict resolution can be undertaken and presented as an evenhanded, positive-sum exercise, helping parties out of conflicts that they could not win and into a more constructive relation from which they will benefit, its costs to the conciliator can be minimized.

Third, some would say that conflict is sometimes useful, and African states should be left to thrash out their internal and external problems. Left-of-center critics cite Shaba and even the Sahara as conflicts that could have served to change conservative governments in Zaire and Morocco if they had not been held within limits by outside powers, and blame mediation for selling out SWAPO and forcing the Cubans out of Angola. Right-of-center critics cite the Ogaden as a conflict that might have served to topple a repressive leftist government in Ethiopia if a great power had not intervened to support it, and they blame mediation for selling out UNITA and keeping the MPLA in power in Angola.

All governments have their unpopular aspects, and Third World governments are especially vulnerable to charges of not providing for their citizens' welfare, given their small resources and their necessarily unequal distribution of the attributes of modernization over a long transition period. Occasionally, a clearly exceptional and extreme case appears, where the conflict is directly linked to domestic opposition against a widely and demonstrably unpopular regime. Nonintervention of any kind is the best policy stance for an external power in such a case—the best example being Uganda in its troubles with Tanzania.

In less flagrant cases, an international conflict is a slow, indirect, and uncertain way of remedying domestic grievances; and conflict resolution could be the vehicle for great powers to press for domestic reforms at the same time that they manage the crisis. Critics of Mobutu's regime object that the weak impact of Western pressures for reform makes Zaire an example of the very inadequacy of the argument, but comparison of the alternatives, with probabilities as well as payoffs taken into account, suggests that reconciliation and a measure of reform were the most reasonable goals for the West. Furthermore, conflict in Africa, particularly in its interstate form, tends to be chronically indecisive. Left to themselves, African conflicts tend to fall back to the status quo after each crisis, intensified by the outburst but no closer to a solution. Such conflict is wasteful, not functional.

It might be objected from a purely globalist point of view that the preceding reasoning is all wrong to justify policy in terms of African costs and benefits. Instead, a proper policy in American interest should either be—in the logic of the cold war—to counter the Soviets where they appear (and not move above a benign level of inattention otherwise) or—in the logic of detente—to extend the rules for East-West competition to Third World areas outside immediate spheres of influence, such as Africa. To argue the latter first, the moment for renewed and even extended detente may perhaps return in the late 1980s, but did not exist before. The hard-line approach to Africa became ascendent in the U.S.S.R. in the early 1970s after a confrontation between two policy schools there, and it has Angola and Ethiopia on its list of "successes" precisely because it overthrew previous East-West conventions favorable to the West. It is being reversed by Gorbachev's regime. New conventions of detente, were they to come, would likely take the form of a superpower understanding either to let Africa pursue its disputes undisturbed or to share in monitoring African conflicts, jointly or on behalf of each power's respective clients. Of the two, the latter is more likely. It would not be in U.S. interests either to stand passively by in the face of runaway African conflict, even if Russia did the same, or to encourage a more active Soviet role in Africa, where it has few deep-rooted interests to defend.

The other globalist policy, of fighting the cold war directly in Africa and confronting the Soviets wherever they may be (not wasting efforts on conflicts that do not involve our adversary), might seem at first appropriate. But it is clearly a policy of too much too late. The effort required is more than the United States will expend, as Angola shows, and even when extra-African leverage is taken into consideration, it is neither likely to be employed, in the final analysis, nor likely to be effective, as Ethiopia shows. Involving the African allies of the conflicting parties is a more effective way of blocking Soviet disruption in the mediation process than directly challenging Russia, either directly or through linkage with global issues. A policy of conflict resolution to eliminate the targets of opportunity that invite Soviet intervention has already shown its advantages in Zimbabwe and aims at the same purpose in Namibia. In Zimbabwe and Namibia, the conciliators brought other African states into their effort, and the national liberation movements were not left alone with the U.S.S.R.

To date, U.S. willingness to conciliate seems to have been impaired by a sense of incapacity. In part, this may result from the trauma of Vietnam. In part, it reflects on observation of reality: American diplomats in the Zimbabwe conflict frequently complained that Africans seemed to believe the United States could produce an agreement from Smith or Vorster at will, when the means for achieving an immediate impact were, in fact, quite limited. Yet the United States was involved nonetheless, impelled by the magnitude of the problem and the possibility—eventually actualized—of an opportunity to be helpful. In Shaba, the chances of leverage over the wily Mobutu and, a fortiori, over Neto, could only appear slim, and yet mediation was tried and worked. The prospects of leverage in Namibia, when conciliation was tried, and the Sahara, where it was not, are no less in comparison.

In part, therefore, the sense of incapacity comes from an underestimation of means, a lack of confidence, an unwillingness to engage. It is an easy matter to show the limits of American power and responsibility in any African conflict, and the opposing case is unprovable until tried. With prudence arguing against attempts at conflict resolution, a cautious, passive policy is adopted—not because the outcome is likely to be more favorable, but because in that way the United States apparently will not be "involved."

Instead, the United States could take measures to balance the conflicting parties' power, so as to reinforce a stalemate and at the same time indicate the potential ill consequences of pursuing the conflict. Providing air defense equipment to Zambia and Mozambique (not arming the guerrillas); holding South Africa to its commitments to a mutually accepted deadline with selective Namibia-specific sanctions (not a comprehensive economic boycott); providing already contracted arms to Morocco under the 1960 agreement interpreted as it was meant to be at the time (not necessarily providing Sahara-only armaments); recalling the exceptional character of the Ogaden and Saharan boundaries as declared before the OAU in 1963 (not endorsing the actual Somali or Moroccan claims)—all are elements that could insert some flexibility into thinking about outcomes and could equalize the parties within a stalemate. Each of these actions deserves further debate, but, taken together, they provide a greater range of possibilities than were perceived at the time. The range can be extended if a much closer coordination is achieved with states more deeply involved in Africa and holding a similar view, including Britain and France, but, above all, including leading African states.

With greater firmness and conviction, however, more favorable outcomes can be obtained. Worst-case predictions should be viewed as incentives to avoid mistakes, not as reasons for hedging. Too frequently there is a halfhearted attempt in the right direction, whose subsequent failure is cited as proof that a more concerted effort would not have worked.

The time may come and should be prepared for when Africa can undertake the major share of its own conflict resolution. Until then, it should be aided in accomplishing its purposes. Like any good aid program, Western and U.S. conciliation should, above all, provide interim help and on-the-job training to Africans associated in any efforts at conflict resolution. Africa's life history as a regional system of international relations is so short that it is quite unreasonable to expect smooth operations immediately. The colonial experience provided negative and positive training in some political functions. It is in both American and African interests to provide assistance in regional peacekeeping and peacemaking functions now.

Notes

1. This extension is pursued by the author and others in Alexander George, ed., *Managing U.S.-Soviet Rivalry: Problems of Crisis Prevention* (Boulder, Colo.: Westview, 1983); Jeffrey Z. Rubin, ed., *The Dynamics of Third Party Intervention: Kissinger in the Middle East* (New York: Praeger, 1981); and Saadia Touval and I. William Zartman, eds., *The Man in the Middle: The Theory and Practice of International Mediation* (Boulder, Colo.: Westview, 1984).
2. Zimbabwe is analyzed by Stephen Low in Touval and Zartman, eds., *The Man in the Middle*; by Jeffrey Davidow, *A Peace in Southern Africa* (Boulder, Colo.: Westview, 1984); and by Robert Jaster, *The Rocky Road to Lancaster House* (New York: Oxford University Press, 1985).
3. See John Waterburg, *Hydropolitics of the Nile Valley* (Syracuse, NY: Syracuse University Press, 1979).
4. The construction of a fine-screened conflict profile remains elusive. An effort was made in this study to make a chart of casualties and of events-data, but reliable data are unavailable. Arms data are interesting but are not sensitive to short-run changes. For further discussion, see I. William Zartman, "Profiles of Conflict: A Methodological Note," in J. David Singer and Richard Stoll, *Quantitative Indicators in World Politics* (New York: Praeger, 1984).
5. This treatment has not dealt much with the constraining role of Congress in foreign policy and the need to run executive actions through an often idiosyncratic congressional gauntlet either in its general argument or in the specific cases studied. This element is important, to be sure, but is simply not the primary focus of the discussion. However, to the extent that the congressional role is based on informed arguments in a broad policy debate, the following treatment of these themes should be relevant.
6. For an evaluation of the OAU, see I. William Zartman and Yassin El-Ayouty, eds., *The OAU After 20 Years* (New York: Praeger, 1984).

Index

Ovamboland People's Organization (OPO), 174

Pan-African Freedom Movement in East, Central, and South Africa (PAFMECAS), 120
Peace, preservation since World War II, 3
Peoples Liberation Army of Namibia (PLAN), 174, 185
Peres, Shimon, 64
Perez de Cuellar, Javier, 66–67, 70, 218
  as Sahara conflict mediator, 71
  as Waldheim's replacement in UN, 212
Plan Cobra 77, 149
Platt, Nicholas, 218
Podgorny, Nikolai, 101, 258–259
Policy
  alternatives or tracks, 255, 266, 269–272
  first tracks, 269–270
  overcommitments, 271–272
  second tracks, 270, 278
  sidetracks, 270–271
  zero-sum approach to, 109–111, 194, 279
Polisario, 9, 14, 33–34, 259
  Algeria's efforts on behalf of, 44–46
  attack of Mseid by, 62
  camps of, 38, 39
  cease-fire with Mauritania and, 38
  compensation for, 278
  conditions for cease-fire, 56
  conflict escalation decisions of, 267
  conflict with Morocco and, 20, 35, 68
  diplomatic victory of, 57–58
  "encircle and attack" strategy of, 41
  end of military success of, 42–43
  independence of, 35
  leadership of, 261
  Libyan arms to, 64
  military activity of, 65–66
  in ould Daddah overthrow, 52–53
  request for separate peace by, 52
  in Saharan conflict stalemate, 48–49
  seeking legitimization of, 61–62
  shift to Algeria, 34–35
  state of, 28
  strategy in Saharan conflict, 36–37
  victory for, 30
Polisario-Mauritania agreement, 77*n*
Polisario-SADR leadership, 35
Political alliances, external, 16
Political Bureau of the Popular Movement of the Revolution (MPR), 150
Political engineering, 260
Political space, wars over, 13

Pompidou, Georges, 90
Portugal, entry into European Common Market, 65
Portuguese decolonization, 7, 33
Power struggles
  decolonization, 12–13
  losers in, 13
Power vacuums, 72–73
  conflict with, 262
Preemptive action, 275–276
Pre-Implementation Meeting (PIM), 206
Principles, 278
Procedural solutions, 279–280
Proposal, 277–280
Provisional Government of the Algerian Republic (GPRA), 31

Qaddafi, Muammar, 25, 38
  meeting of with BenJedid, 63–64
  refusal of OAU presidency to, 62

Rabat border convention, 50–51
Radical African states, 179–180
Rapid Deployment Force in the Middle East, 59
Reagan, Ronald
  election of, 207
  nomination of, 206
Reagan administration
  African policy of, 207–208
  conflict management policy of, 8
  in Namibian independence, 172–173
  South African policy of, 172–173, 206, 207–208, 210–212, 237, 239
  succession of, 225
  UNITA aid and, 224
Reality-legality struggle, 13–14
Refugee pressures, 262
Renversement des alliances, 277
Resources, scarce, 262
Revisionist power, 11
Revolutionary Peoples Movement (MPR), 138
Rhodesia/Zimbabwe government, 187–188
  internal solution of, 238, 258
Riad summit, 52
Rift Valley, 83, 86
Ripe moment, 10, 255
  factors of, 267–273
  identification of, 263
  recognition of, 273
  trust and, 274
Roberto, Holden, 140, 160